Indispensable Reading

Books by Wm. Roger Louis

Ruanda-Urundi, 1884–1919 (1963)
Germany's Lost Colonies, 1914–1919 (1967)
(with Jean Stengers) *E. D. Morel's History of the Congo Reform Movement* (1968)
British Strategy in the Far East, 1919–1939 (1971)
Imperialism at Bay, 1941–1945 (1977)
The British Empire in the Middle East, 1945–1951 (1984)
Leo Amery and the British Empire (1992)
Ends of British Imperialism: The Scramble for Empire, Suez, and Decolonization (2006)

Edited volumes

(with Prosser Gifford) *Britain and Germany in Africa: Imperial Rivalry and Colonial Rule* (1967)
(with Prosser Gifford) *France and Britain in Africa: Imperial Rivalry and Colonial Rule* (1971)
(with Prosser Gifford) *The Transfer of Power in Africa: Decolonization, 1940–1960* (1982)
(with Prosser Gifford) *Decolonization and African Independence: The Transfers of Power, 1960–1980* (1988)
National Security and International Trusteeship in the Pacific (1972)
The Origins of the Second World War: A. J. P. Taylor and His Critics (1972)
Imperialism: The Robinson and Gallagher Controversy (1976)
(with William S. Livingston) *Australia, New Zealand, and the Pacific Islands since the First World War* (1979)
(with Hedley Bull) *The "Special Relationship": Anglo-American Relations since 1945* (1986)
(with Robert W. Stookey) *The End of the Palestine Mandate* (1986)
(with James A. Bill) *Musaddiq, Iranian Nationalism, and Oil* (1988)
(with Roger Owen) *Suez 1956: The Crisis and Its Consequences* (1989)
(with Robert A. Fernea) *The Iraqi Revolution of 1958: The Old Social Classes Revisited* (1991)
(with Robert Blake) *Churchill: A Major New Assessment of His Life in Peace and War* (1993)
(with Roger Owen) *A Revolutionary Year: The Middle East in 1958* (2002)
(with Avi Shlaim) *The 1967 Arab-Israeli War: Origins and Consequences* (2012)
(with Ronald Hyam) *British Documents on the End of Empire: The Conservative Government and the End of Empire, 1957–1964* (2 parts, 2000)
(with S. R. Ashton) *British Documents on the End of Empire: East of Suez and the Commonwealth, 1964–1971* (3 parts, 2004)

Adventures with Britannia Series, Editor

Adventures with Britannia (1995)
Yet More Adventures (2005)
Resurgent Adventures (2011)
Effervescent Adventures (2017)

More Adventures (1998)
Penultimate Adventures (2007)
Irrepressible Adventures (2013)
Burnt Orange Britannia (2005)

Still More Adventures (2003)
Ultimate Adventures (2009)
Resplendent Adventures (2015)

Oxford History of the British Empire, Editor-in-Chief

The Oxford History of the British Empire (5 vols., 1998–99)
Oxford History of the British Empire Companion Series (15 vols., 2004–)
The History of Oxford University Press, vol. 3, 1896–1970 (2013)
(with Michael Howard) *The Oxford History of the Twentieth Century* (1998)

Reinterpreting History Series, General Editor

Reinterpreting History: How Historical Assessments Change over Time (AHA National History Center and Oxford University Press series, 2001–13)

Festschrift

Robert D. King and Robin Kilson, eds., *The Statecraft of British Imperialism: Essays in Honour of Wm. Roger Louis* (1999)

Indispensable Reading

1,001 Books

From The Arabian Nights *to Zola*

Wm. Roger Louis

I.B. TAURIS

London · New York

Published in 2018 by I. B. Tauris & Co Ltd
6 Salem Road, London W2 4BU,
a division of Bloomsbury Publishing
In the United States of America and Canada, distributed by
Bloomsbury USA
1385 Broadway, Fifth Floor, New York NY 10018
www.ibtauris.com

First printing

The paper used in this publication meets the minimum requirements of
American National Standard for Information Sciences—
Permanence of Paper for Printed Library Materials

ISBN 978-1-78831-533-3

Library of Congress Control Number: 2018960341

Print production by Studio AZUL, Inc., Austin, Texas

Contents

Introduction

The phrase "1,001 indispensable books" raises the immediate question, indispensable for whom? The answer is: for myself alone, though I hope the list and its comments will be of interest to the general reader and especially to students.

The project had its origins in revising a list of recommended books for students in the College of Liberal Arts at the University of Texas at Austin. More precisely, a committee of senior faculty members proposed 150 books for students to read or at least be aware of before they graduate. The idea of reading 150 books might seem more like a long-term plan than a realistic goal for one's undergraduate years, but the list has proved to be useful and perhaps a source of inspiration. In the present collection of 1,001, the committee's 150 are singled out by illustrations. The remaining 851 are my own "indispensable" recommendations. I am well aware that this particular word runs the risk of intellectual arrogance. Yet I hope a redeeming virtue is that some readers will find the list entertaining, even useful. At least it will give them the chance to draw up a list of books they never intend to read.

I have benefited from the advice of many friends and colleagues, but three in particular encouraged me to think that this undertaking might be worth the effort. I have tried to achieve a standard of assessment measuring up to the quality of the advice given by Ferdinand Mount, the former editor of the *Times Literary Supplement*; Keith Thomas, Honorary Fellow of All Souls College, Oxford; and Felipe Fernández-Armesto of the University of Notre Dame.

The criteria for selecting the books are straightforward. I have chosen works I believe to be readable and distinctive, or because I find them to be important and influential, perhaps a classic, perhaps a recent book that advances a new interpretation. Since I am an historian, the choice might be because it is historically reliable, for example, Garrett Mattingly's *Defeat of the Spanish Armada*, in which he explains that British sailors at the time believed that the "winds of God" ultimately prevented an invasion of England.

In other words, this is a quirky list. It makes no claim to overall balance. I am certain that anyone else, especially from a different culture, would come up with an entirely different collection of titles. If my late friend Sarvepalli Gopal had drawn up something comparable, it would have reflected an Indian cultural background; but there would be, I believe, considerable overlap even if we disagreed, for example, on Gandhi and the penultimate Viceroy of India, General Archibald Wavell—who once wrote a caricature titled "Jabber-Weeks," which contains the lines "Beware the Gandhiji, my son, / The satyagraha, the bogy fast." Gopal did not like Wavell or the caricature.

One reader of the manuscript asked, I believe in jest, why no book on transvestites among the solders of the Charge of the Light Brigade? If there were such a book, it would be included, I hope, if I believed it to be significant and informative. The closest I have come to such an eccentric entry is probably Ahmed Saadawi's *Frankenstein in Baghdad*, a novel about the catastrophic consequences of the American occupation of Iraq. I mention it for another reason. It is a recent publication, and only a few new books made it onto the list. For those few, there are particular reasons. In Saadawi's case, because it has significance in contemporary affairs and, moreover, is highly amusing, at times hilarious. Saadawi won the 2014 International Prize for Arabic Fiction.

The section on art, architecture, and music is short and unsatisfactory. But I faced the problem of whether to expand in those directions or to keep an overall focus mainly on literature, history, and politics. To reemphasize the characteristic of a quirky or idiosyncratic list, this time with a point on cooking, *How to Cook a Wolf* by Mary Fisher, and another on addiction, *Pour Me* by A. A. Gill, the entries are merely those that I have found significant in my own experience.

Finally, one of the glories of reading is that it not only prevents boredom but also can be useful in combatting it. For example, a small book can be furtively read during a boring lecture. But what about the question of boring books? How does one actually judge that a book is boring? Perhaps a novel has a predictable ending? Perhaps a technical book is clogged with too much detail? I have found that a book may be important but boring. In that case, I try reading a few passages out loud, which concentrates the mind and helps one discover, perhaps, an implicit argument. But ultimately, a boring book is a boring book. It can be cast aside while looking for something worthwhile. Thus, the reader might find the present list useful if only because it could bring to mind, for example, Jacques Barzun, who in *From Dawn to Decadence* distills from a lifetime of writing and teaching his thoughts about the "Great Books" and lesser books on many subjects that he taught at Columbia.

The curious reader may wish to know a little of my background and interests. My title is Kerr Professor of English History and Culture at the University of Texas, where I am the founder of the British Studies program, now in its forty-third year. I am an Honorary Fellow of St. Antony's College, Oxford, and a Past President of the American Historical Association. But present and past job descriptions are probably meaningless without some idea of my background. Here is thus a brief autobiography, for the purpose of explaining how someone from Oklahoma acquired an interest in reading that eventually led to the present list.

I grew up in Oklahoma City, where my earliest memories include my father reading Robert Louis Stevenson's *A Child's Garden of Verses* to me. At an early age, I was the beneficiary—as were countless others—of a local Carnegie Library. I recall as some of my first books (probably all in simplified versions) *Treasure Island*, *Robinson Crusoe*, and *The Three Musketeers*. In retrospect, it is clear that I received an excellent public education. In junior high school, I read George Eliot's *Mill on the Floss*; and in high school, my English teacher insisted that her students memorize lines from Chaucer and Shakespeare. (Recently at the Library of Congress, I heard Colin Powell remark that his achieving the rank of four-star general could be attributed in part to having memorized passages from Chaucer in his school years.) In high school, I was mainly interested in music (I played French horn) and sports (I was on the swim team). Nevertheless, I remember reading *War and Peace* and *The Brothers Karamazov*.

At the University of Oklahoma, I studied in the honors program, "Letters," which required an ancient language—mine was Latin, my knowledge of which now seems to have vanished—and a modern one, for which I chose French. The other parts of the Letters program were history, literature, and philosophy. I gained the most from English courses, which introduced me to Milton, Dickens, and Conrad. I am sure that my reading at this stage did not differ from that of others throughout the country who were taking similar courses. But I did have the advantage of a year abroad.

In 1955–56, I spent a semester in Freiburg and a semester in Paris. In retrospect, I am certain that the main reward was the gaining of a little fluency in German and French, but in Freiburg I tried to read Heidegger, or as Sarah Bakewell puts it in her excellent book *At the Existentialist Café*, "to Heideggerize" on things I knew little about. I was more interested in the question of how such a prominent philosopher could have been a Nazi. I had better luck with the work of the historian Gerhard Ritter, who had been involved in the 1944 plot against Hitler. By a stroke of luck, I managed to catch some of his last lectures, and eventually I could manage in German his *Friedrich der Grosse*, in which, again, I was as much interested in recent history as in the eighteenth century—in this case, how the Nazis glorified the Prussian autocrat as a great German leader who prefigured Hitler. German students in the mid-1950s were usually reluctant to talk about the Hitler era, but I discovered that they could be lured into conversation about the Nazis by a discussion of Frederick the Great.

In Paris, it was life in the cafés more than the courses that mattered, reading Sartre, Beauvoir, and Camus, though I probably found Henry Miller more engaging. American students in Paris often yielded to the temptation to hang out mainly with other Americans (Nancy Maginnes, now Mrs. Henry Kissinger, was one of my companions); but I managed to find a couple of French friends, both of whom had read much more widely than I. With literary grace, one wrote graffiti on the *pissoirs*, protesting the war in Algeria; the other, who had served in the army in Algeria, believed that torture was the only way to force the Algerians to end the conflict. (As far as I know, the two never met.) One of the best books I read at the time was by the anthropologist Germaine Tillion, *Algérie* (translated as *Algeria: The Realities*). But the best, or at least most indelible, moment was when by chance I was in Cairo on July 26, 1956, when Nasser nationalized the Suez Canal Company.

From Oklahoma, I went to Harvard as a Woodrow Wilson Fellow in the joint degree program for economics and government. I eventually shifted to history, but I gained immensely from learning a little about Joseph Schumpeter and "creative destruction," and especially his views on the irrationality of war and imperialism: war for the sake of war, empire for the sake of empire. Though I found a home in history, the best course I took at Harvard was given by the sociologist Barrington Moore, the author of *Social Origins of Dictatorship and Democracy*. At the height of the Cold War in the late 1950s, it was extraordinary to find a scholar interested in teaching his students the fundamentals of Marxism as well as making comprehensible the writings of Herbert Marcuse.

The seminar I most profited from at Harvard was conducted by Ernest May, at that time writing *Imperial Democracy*, his book on the Spanish-American War and the emergence of the United States as a world power. I prospered not only in the reading. In May's course, every draft paper was circulated to all seminar members, who made suggestions, sometimes exceedingly critical. The drafts were then returned to the author, who perfected the final copy. I have used this method of teaching and writing in my own seminar courses, undergraduate as well as graduate. It does, however, require a warning to the students that mutual criticism can be a rough-and-tumble affair. One student burst into tears when she saw the critical comments by her peers. But she eventually became an excellent editor herself, in the process acquiring a much tougher skin.

From Harvard, I went to Oxford on a Marshall Scholarship. My supervisor was A. J. P. Taylor, who had a reputation for academic ferocity and clear writing. I found him actually to be gentle and encouraging. He set an example with his unforgettable style, characterized by staccato sentences. We became friends, and I followed the vicissitudes of his career, from ostracism by fellow historians in 1962—after writing *The Origins of the Second World War*—to his triumph with *English History* three years later. In supporting a research trip to Africa for me, he wrote—he showed me the comment—that I would produce sound work "if he is not massacred."

In Oxford, I was a student at St. Antony's College, where the strong point has always been area studies. I eventually found a home at the Middle East Centre and profited especially from working with Albert Hourani, whose substantial work at the time was *Arabic Thought in the Liberal Age, 1798–1939*, an analysis of the roots of Arab nationalism, Islamic reform, and the turn toward Islamic radicalism. It was not always easy to grasp his essential outlook, which was that the Arabs had a unified and self-sufficient society that had maintained its equilibrium for a millennium until the unprovoked intrusion by the French and British. Of all my past friends, I was closest to Albert Hourani. I keep a photograph of him on my desk.

One of the principal benefits of studying at Oxford in the early 1960s was the seminar given by Margery Perham, the author of *Lugard*, a two-volume biography of one of the last British proconsuls. She introduced students to the mystique of the British District Officer, who had no equivalent in American public life. District Officers were not without foibles or deficiencies in character, as "Miss Perham" (as she was always called) would comment while pointing out, for example, their dilemmas in suppressing the Mau Mau rebellion.

At Oxford, the subject of the British Empire's history was transformed by John (Jack) Gallagher, who was one of my examiners. He encouraged me to make imperial history my principal field of study. I later worked closely with his friend Ronald Robinson, who with Gallagher wrote *Africa and the Victorians*. I subsequently edited a book entitled *The Robinson and Gallagher Controversy*, which turns on the question of the occupation of Egypt in 1882 and the argument that the concept of collaboration is the key to understanding British rule, in India as well as Africa and other parts of the world. I wrote a new introduction to *Africa and the Victorians* for the 2015 edition.

From Oxford, I went to Yale, where I taught for eight years, 1962–70. I am certain that my reading was widely enhanced after the chairman of the History Department, Edmund (Ed) Morgan (*The Puritan Dilemma*), allowed me to teach one-semester courses on India and the Middle East—on the quite accurate supposition that the best way to learn a subject is to teach it. The historians at Yale at the time included—to give only a few examples—Robin Winks, the author of *The Blacks in Canada* (1971); Harry Benda, *The Crescent and the Rising Sun: Indonesian Islam under the Japanese Occupation* (1958); C. Vann Woodward, *The Strange Career of Jim Crow* (1955); John Blum, *The Republican Roosevelt* (1954); Jack Hexter, famous for his distinction between lumpers and splitters; and a little later, Jonathan Spence, the authority on China and a fellow President of the American Historical Association. I have listed a few of their books merely to point out how much one can learn simply by reading the works of one's colleagues.

From 1970, I have taught at the University of Texas at Austin for forty-eight years. In 1975, I organized, with the political scientist William S. Livingston, a faculty seminar called British Studies. The title is a little misleading because it encompasses the British in all parts of the world: China and India, Iran and Kenya, the Falklands and Jamaica. The seminar has met on Friday during each semester, never canceling a session (the University of Texas once closed down because of an ice storm, but British Studies met as usual). The seminar was made possible by Harry Ransom, former President of the University of Texas and founder of the Humanities Research Center. He welcomed the opportunity to provide visitors with a chance to speak about their research in the center's recently acquired collections of books and manuscripts. The lectures have thus had a predominantly literary dimension, though we have tried to keep it in balance with historical and political topics.

Our guest at the first session, in the fall semester of 1975, was invited by a stalwart of the seminar, the classicist Peter Green. Paul Scott spoke on his major work, *The Raj Quartet*. He arrived drunk, providing an unforgettable beginning to the seminar.

We were fortunate to have as one of the speakers Oliver Franks, who had been the British ambassador in post–World War II Washington. He set us straight on the "Special Relationship," which was not so special then or later, despite Churchill's melodramatic use of the phrase during World War II to secure wartime assistance. Franks explained:

> The special relationship was not a mystique of the shared inheritance of the English-speaking peoples. It arose out of common aims and mutual need of each other; it was rooted in strong habits of working together on which there was superimposed the sentiments of mutual trust.

On an entirely different point, he caused uproarious laughter. He explained that in 1948 a radio station asked several ambassadors in Washington what they most wished for Christmas. The Soviet ambassador proclaimed that he wanted freedom for all people enslaved by imperialism. The French ambassador said he would like to see peace throughout the world. Franks misunderstood the question. What would he like most for Christmas? Well, he said, "It's very kind of you to ask. I'd quite like a box of crystallized fruit."

Some of the early lectures combined personalities with a social history of postwar England. Michael Holroyd explained how the legacy of Lytton Strachey and the Bloomsbury writers extended to post-1945 intellectuals. But at times, he continued, it was difficult to concentrate on literary work because of the weather. "We are in the midst of a coal crisis," one author noted in February 1947. "I had my bath, turned on the electric kettle, filled my hot water bottle and then went into the sitting room where, wrapped in two rugs and with the hot water bottle at my feet, I settled down to breakfast in an icy atmosphere." Another lecturer commenting on the winter of 1947 described a meeting at the Foreign Office between Ernest Bevin, a key figure in the Labour government, and a Zionist delegation. The lights went out in the middle of a discussion. Not to worry, Bevin said, "we have the Israe*lites* here."

I will spare the reader the details of the 1,091 Friday afternoon seminar sessions, but I will mention a few high points (in passing, I am struck by the coincidence of the two numbers, 1,001 and 1,091). C. P. Snow reflected on his book *The Two Cultures*, explaining that he did not regard the gap between the humanities and the sciences as unbridgeable, though I think he would now be more pessimistic. Iris Murdoch talked about her book on Sartre—the first work on him to be published in English—and the themes in her novels, evil and good, sex, and the significance of an "inner life." Robert Blake discussed the difficulties of writing his biography of Disraeli, in which he came to appreciate a subtle and devious mind much more complicated than Gladstone's. Raymond Carr spoke on the Spanish Civil War, Sarvepalli Gopal on Nehru's *Discovery of India*, and Noel Annan on intellectuals between the wars. Penelope Lively anticipated intellectual trends on the question of English versus British identities. Simply to convey a little of the biographical range of the talks: Peter Stansky spoke on George Orwell, Hilary Spurling on Anthony Powell, Philip Ziegler on Mountbatten, Akira Iriye on Douglas MacArthur, and Kenneth O. Morgan on Keir Hardy.

The British Studies program publishes the *Britannia* volumes, consisting of some of the weekly lectures: *Adventures with Britannia* (1995); *More Adventures* (1998); *Still More Adventures* (2003); *Yet More Adventures* (2005); *Penultimate Adventures* (2007); and *Ultimate Adventures* (2009). At that point, we had to reinvent the series: *Resurgent Adventures* (2011); *Irrepressible Adventures* (2013); *Resplendent Adventures* (2015); and *Effervescent Adventures* (2017).

To come full circle to the reason for the annotated list of 1,001 books: part of the explanation is that I agree with the English politician Richard Crossman that the definition of paradise is a good seminar. And I am glad to say that for close to half a century, every Friday afternoon has been devoted to a discussion of ideas and books.

In the 1990s, I became the Editor-in-Chief of the *Oxford History of the British Empire*, published in five volumes (1998–99). With my fellow editors, we recruited authors from Asia and Africa as well as Britain, a plan that displeased one of the principal historians of the empire, Lord (Max) Beloff. We excluded from our roster of some 125 authors anyone already in retirement. Beloff may have piqued at being left out, but in any event he protested against our organizational purpose. In his view, the British Empire was a *British* institution and should be dealt with from a *British* perspective—whereas I tried to include authors from India and elsewhere who would represent the colonized as well as the colonizers. Beloff seemed further to believe that an American Editor-in-Chief would, consciously or unconsciously, possess a bias. Max (he and I were friends despite disagreements) published letters in newspapers in London that were reproduced as far away as Australia. Oxford University Press held firm, and the consensus went against Max. Before his death, he wrote a review of volume I, in which he virtually apologized. He gave the series a lot of publicity that otherwise it would have entirely lacked.

In the decade after the turn of the century, I was drawn, slightly unwillingly, into becoming one of the editors of *The History of Oxford University Press*. I say unwillingly because I presumed, as indeed proved to be the case, that it would be a distraction from my work on the Middle East. But I agreed. In the four-volume project, which ranges from the seventeenth century to the beginning of the twentieth-first, I took on the volume covering the years 1896–1970. This was the critical era in which the Press expanded worldwide on the principle of delegation of responsibility: each branch, whether in India, South Africa, or Malaya, would manage its own affairs, usually in a system of regional responsibility. The arrangement was the opposite of the one used by Cambridge University Press, in which each of the branches reported directly to Cambridge. I encountered many surprises, not least that it was Bible sales in America during the Depression that saved OUP New York from bankruptcy.

The most unexpected episode was my experience with the "J," or Juvenile, Department of the Press. At one point, the redoubtable Mabel George, a creative genius of children's literature, was asked by a committee of inquiry why a university press should publish books for young readers. In a withering response, she pointed out that children's literature was the basis for all further reading. At another time, she wrote to one of her artists about a scathing critique of his art. "Take no notice," she told him, "We are the Oxford University Press."

I'll not write further about the present decade other than to mention two points. At present I am completing a book on the end of the British Empire in the Middle East. It occurred to me that it would enrich my interpretation if I were able to read Arabic. Learning proper Arabic remains a vain hope, but in the summer of 2014 I received a certificate for surviving an intensive Arabic course in Oman.

The other point is that in 2016 I was invited to give the Weizmann Memorial Lecture in Israel. I was asked to speak on an emotionally controversial subject: Ernest Bevin, already mentioned as the Foreign Secretary in the British Labour Government of 1945, had attempted to block the creation of the State of Israel or at least to keep it as small as possible. To that generation of Israelis, he occupied a place in Jewish demonology only a slot or so below Hitler. Tempers cooled over time. I found my audience friendly and engaging, and while in Jerusalem I found a few recently published Israeli books that were new to me. On my return, an Israeli sitting next to me on the flight to London said that he had something interesting to show me: on his computer I saw that Donald Trump had been elected President of the United States. My immediate inclination was to return to Jerusalem and spend the next four years at the American Colony Hotel, an idea that, for better or worse, was vetoed by my wife Dagmar—above all because we would miss the Friday-afternoon seminar sessions dedicated to books and ideas.

My first and most solemn acknowledgment is to a dead friend, Miguel González-Gerth, the Mexican poet with whom I shared an office for four decades. I owe to our daily discussions my familiarity with Mexican, Spanish, and Latin American literature, and for that matter European poetry and other writing from around the world. For those still alive as this volume goes to press, I have benefited from help ranging from the cheerful, daily encouragement of my wife to the substantial and invaluable assistance of my assistant, Holly McCarthy. Others have helped me in various ways, and I hope they will forgive me for merely mentioning them without rank or station in life—with two exceptions: I am indebted to General Lord Ramsbotham for a humane as well as military perspective; and to the Very Reverend Dr. John Drury for guidance on books on the human spirit. I am grateful to James Banner, Andrew and Jaana Blane, John Darwin, Prosser Gifford, Joseph Epstein, Robert Hardgrave, Brian Harrison, Joanne and Martin Hitchcock, Michael Howard, Warren Ilchman, Boisfeuillet and Barbara Jones, Donald Lamm,

Annes McCann-Baker, David McIntyre, Al Martinich, Karl and Shereen Meyer, Adam Roberts, Karl Schmitt, Alan and Helga Spencer, Bernard Wasserstein, and, as always, Philip Ziegler.

   Without the help and encouragement of Dean Randy Diehl, this book would never have been written. I am notably grateful to Christine Nicholls for an attentive reading of the manuscript in unsparing detail. I need to thank Simon Green for his extraordinarily voluminous suggestions as well comments on the books and poetry read by generations of Fellows at All Souls College. At my other Oxford home, St. Antony's, as usual I am indebted to Avi Shlaim. Above all, I must thank my friend Kip Keller, who has worked so closely with me that I feel that the book is as much his as mine.

Indispensable Reading
1,001 Books from *The Arabian Nights* to Zola

Note: Authors of 150 highly recommended titles are in boldface. The original publication date of each title is followed in most cases by the suggested paperback edition.

History
United States

Allison, Graham *Destined for War: Can America and China Escape Thucydides's Trap?* (Houghton Mifflin, 2017). Allison quotes Thucydides's succinct explanation of the cause of the Peloponnesian War—"It was the rise of Athens and the fear that this instilled in Sparta that made war inevitable"—as a template for the collision course that China and the United States seem to be on. The Chinese are "shell-shocked" at how quickly and to what extent their world has changed. They imagine themselves an "unstoppable" force approaching an "immovable America." One of the principal virtues of the book is Allison's extended and imaginative historical reflection, for example, on the Anglo-German naval rivalry before World War I, and the motivation for Japan's attack on Pearl Harbor.

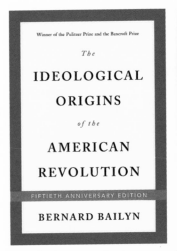

Bailyn, Bernard, *The Ideological Origins of the American Revolution* (1967; Belknap, 1992). Bailyn traces the republican ideas of the revolutionary generation to those of England's radicals, which had little significance in England but were compelling to American colonists. The Americans believed the British intended to establish a tyrannical state that would curtail the colonists' historic rights as Englishmen. On the other hand, they did not want to remake the social order but to repair what they believed to be a broken and unjust system of government. Gordon S. Wood's *The Radicalism of the American Revolution* (1991) argues that the revolution marked a complete rejection of British feudal traditions, political patronage, and ideas of nobility and commoners, making it "the most radical and most far-reaching event in American history."

Beard, Charles A., and Mary R. Beard, *The Rise of American Civilization*, 2 vols. (1927). Charles Beard was one of the most influential scholars of American politics and history. His controversial thesis that the framers of the Constitution were motivated by economic self-interest rather than abstract philosophical principles continues to be debated. *The Rise of American Civilization* blends an overarching theme of economic class conflict with political and cultural history to give a full account of the country's development up to 1920. The historian Thomas Bender described it as "the most powerful synthesis of American history in the twentieth century." Richard Hofstadter, in *The Progressive Historians: Turner, Beard, Parrington* (1968), discusses Beard and two other prominent interpreters of American history whose views were shaped by political battles of the Progressive era.

Boorstin, Daniel, *The Americans: The National Experience* (1965; Vintage, 1967). The second volume in Boorstin's *Americans* trilogy covers the period from the Revolution to the Civil War. Boorstin's writing is crisp and memorable, with an overarching theme of a search for community. In this period, Americans responded to cultural changes marked by practical triumphs. Inventors and entrepreneurs infused daily life with a creative spirit. American history was exceptional, modified by settlers' confrontations as they migrated, especially westward. Problems of class and social conflict would be resolved as America became more unified. In *The Americans*, as in his other voluminous writings, Boorstin maintains that mankind's greatest achievement is the book. For those who enjoy reading footnotes, the ones here are riveting.

Bowen, Catherine Drinker, *Miracle at Philadelphia: The Story of the Constitutional Convention, May–September 1787* (1966; Back Bay, foreword by Warren E. Burger, 1986). The singular reputation of Bowen's book rests on her command of the personalities of the fifty-five delegates from eleven of the original thirteen colonies who met for four months and wrangled over all aspects of the U.S. Constitution. Bowen allows them to speak for themselves, for example, in the debates over representation in the Senate and the House of Representatives. George Washington described the final document as a "miracle" in a letter. In view of the uneven and rocky path taken on the way to concord, the Constitution was certainly less than supernatural; but at the time the word seemed justified.

Branch, Taylor, *Parting the Waters: America in the King Years, 1954–63* (1988; Simon & Schuster, 1989). In the first volume of a monumental trilogy about the civil rights era, Branch traces the nascent movement for black equality through the Eisenhower and Kennedy years. Two figures dominate events: Martin Luther King Jr., who gained national attention at age twenty-six during the Montgomery bus boycott, and FBI director J. Edgar Hoover, who worked tirelessly to thwart King's efforts. It was during this period that the Republican Party devised its southern strategy—convince working-class whites to vote their race rather than their economic interests—a faux-populist policy still in effect. The other books in the trilogy, *Pillar of Fire* (1998) and *At Canaan's Edge* (2006), follow King and the movement through 1968.

Brown, Dee, *Bury My Heart at Wounded Knee: An Indian History of the American West* (1970; Holt, 2007). In a work that takes on one of the most controversial subjects in American history, Brown challenges the traditional perception of Indian chiefs and tribes during the conquest of the West. The main thrust is the destruction of the Indian peoples, whose numbers were reduced 90 percent. He firmly and fairly describes the massacres, battles, and broken treaties as the U.S. Army forced tribes onto ever-smaller reservations, and describes the reactions of chiefs such as Sitting Bull, Crazy Horse, and Geronimo. Ending with the massacre at Wounded Knee, South Dakota, in 1890, he relates with precise continuity the Indian side of the story while also presenting the outlook of the U.S. Army and the white settlers.

DeVoto, Bernard, ed., *The Journals of Lewis and Clark* (1953; Mariner, 1997). After the Louisiana Purchase of 1803, President Thomas Jefferson commissioned Captain Meriwether Lewis and William Clark to lead an expedition to trace the principal waterways from the Missouri River to the Pacific Northwest. Not least among the benefits of their detailed geographic and scientific records is the account of their encounters with Indian tribes, by no means always easy or peaceful, but facilitated by gifts, including weapons and whiskey. The editor, DeVoto, was one of the principal historians of the American West. DeVoto's *Across the Wide Missouri* (1948) is a history of the fur trade in the West; it won the Pulitzer Prize.

Evans, Harry (with Gail Buckland and Kevin Baker), *The American Century* (Knopf, 1998). Only rarely is an illustrated history also an engaging read, with a narrative matching the quality of the pictures. The text and the historic photographs, caricatures, and editorial cartoons in *The American Century* superbly capture the scale and complexities of the years 1900–2000, from Senator Albert Beveridge claiming at the turn of the century that it was the destiny of Americans to rule over the "savage and senile" peoples of the Philippines to the wars and social upheavals that filled the following decades. The book contains over 900 black-and-white photographs, many of them brought to light for the first time. The tone of the narrative is tolerant, skeptical, and dispassionate.

Genovese, Eugene D., *Roll, Jordan, Roll: The World the Slaves Made* (1974; Penguin, 1976). It may seem slightly odd that a Marxist historian of Italian ancestry who had a New York upbringing would write an outstanding book on southern slavery, but Genovese's *Roll, Jordan*—the title is taken from a Charles Wesley hymn that became a popular spiritual—is the best account of slavery as the slaves perceived it. He writes of strong, stable, proud black families that "developed their own values as a force for community cohesion and survival." One of the peaks of the book is the description of "black mammies," who helped create a distinctive cuisine. Writing to support the idea that "black is beautiful," Genovese paints a subtle, complex picture of slave life.

Gordon-Reed, Annette, *The Hemingses of Monticello: An American Family* (2008; Norton, 2009). Gordon-Reed in 2009 won the Pulitzer Prize for her book about four generations of a slave family owned by Thomas Jefferson. Jefferson observed a strict silence about "Black Sal" Hemings, who was sixteen when she became pregnant with Jefferson's child. She then lived with him for thirty-eight years in a monogamous spousal relationship—in effect, as his concubine—until his death in 1826. She bore Jefferson seven children, and the book deals also with their descendants, two of whom fought in the American Civil War. In the afterword, Gordon-Reed comments on the DNA evidence confirming the Jefferson-Hemings relationship.

Grant, Ulysses S., *Personal Memoirs* (1885–86). Regarded at the time as a failure as president, Grant as a military commander during the Civil War earned a reputation that stands as high as MacArthur's or Eisenhower's. His memoirs, which concentrate on the Mexican War (which he deplored) and the Civil War, are a clear account by a skilled strategist, remarkable for their honesty and heartfelt compassion. Mark Twain, who published the memoirs, called them the "best of any general's since Caesar." Edmund Wilson described its prose as "perfect in concision and clearness," and Gertrude Stein said of the book that she could not read it "without weeping." Excellent companion volumes are Ron Chernow's *Grant* (2017) and William Tecumseh Sherman's *Memoirs* (1875; Penguin, 2000), the autobiography of the other great Union general.

Halberstam, David, *The Making of a Quagmire: America and Vietnam during the Kennedy Era* (1965; Rowman & Littlefield, 2007). Halberstam tells the story of how the South Vietnamese war became an American war. He is faithful to the perspectives of the U.S. soldiers and officials in the field, and he is consistent in his affection for the hapless, bewildered Vietnamese. Step-by-step, the Americans inadvertently became trapped in the Vietnamese swamp. Individual mistakes and institutional self-deception led them into a conflict no one wanted, a major war on the Asian mainland. In *The Best and the Brightest* (1972), Halberstam focuses on foreign policy officials in the Kennedy administration, constructing a home-front mirror of *Quagmire*, one in which the mistakes and illusions are intensified.

Higham, John, *Strangers in the Land: Patterns of American Nativism, 1860–1925* (1955; Rutgers, 2002). Higham means by "nativism" nationalism and ethnic prejudice against minorities. From the late nineteenth century, public sentiment shifted from a spirit of democratic egalitarianism—"keeping the gates open"—to restrictive racism. With a sense of irony, Higham describes a Bohemian woman immigrant in World War I whose sons could not be "Americanized" because they were fighting in France. He chronicles efforts to resist nativism as well as contrary moves to limit immigration by members of "lower races." Prejudice against foreigners, Jews, radicals, and Catholics grew in towns across America. By the 1920s, restrictive legislation had "closed the gates" to "hordes of the racially inferior." This is a seminal work with a consistent moral vision.

Howe, Daniel Walker, *What Has God Wrought: The Transformation of America, 1815–1848* (2007; Oxford, 2009). Winner of the Pulitzer Prize, Howe traces developments in transportation and communications that played a vital part in American expansion. The telegraph, railroads, and newspapers facilitated the exchange of information and liberated American society from the "tyranny of distance." He deals especially with the way in which advances in technology contributed to religious revivalist movements and American attitudes toward slavery, Indians, and the rights of women. Especially critical of Andrew Jackson as a racist, he believes that John

Quincy Adams and other advocates of public education and economic integration played a vital part in the changing patterns of American life in the first half of the nineteenth century.

Jefferson, Thomas, *The Life and Selected Writings of Thomas Jefferson* (Modern Library, ed. Adrienne Koch and William Peden, 1998). Jefferson was an architect, scientist, inventor, naturalist, educator, and public servant long before he became president, in 1801. This collection of writings includes the original and revised versions of the Declaration of Independence, his inaugural addresses, and autobiographical accounts. In many ways, Jefferson was enigmatic. Richard B. Bernstein's *Thomas Jefferson* (2003) is a reliable and readable guide to a complicated life, including Jefferson's relationship with his slave Sally Hemings. No polemist, Bernstein assesses Jefferson's achievements as well as his weaknesses—above all, Jefferson as a man of his time and place.

Limerick, Patricia Nelson, *The Legacy of Conquest: The Unbroken Past of the American West* (1988; Norton, 2008). In a work dedicated to correcting the "triumphal" interpretation of Frederick Jackson Turner, Limerick argues that the frontier was primarily a place of conquest, a point of convergence for Mormons, Hispanics, white settlers, and Indians. She examines the work of traders, trappers, miners, farmers, and oilmen, and above all the government-supported railroads, timber and agricultural interests, and ranchers. Ultimately, the drive for conquest made an imprint on the West similar to slavery's on the South. In *The Fatal Environment: The Myth of the Frontier in the Age of Industrialization, 1800–1890* (1985), Richard Slotkin argues that the subjugation of the Indians helped in America's rise to wealth.

Miller, Perry, *The New England Mind: The Seventeenth Century* (1939; Belknap, 1983). Immersing himself in seventeenth-century thought, Miller saw in Puritan theology a method of depicting reality as well as a coherent intellectual perception of the human condition. He established, as had no author previously, unsuspected elements of humanism in the Calvinist tradition. He did not describe the Puritans as dour or stereotypically forbidding, but rather as a complex people finding joy in their religion and upholding the idea of the "covenant"—a code of society expressed in consent and mutual responsibilities. Miller possessed rare gifts of insight and imagination, which he combined with formidable intellectual energy to write one of the lasting interpretations of American Puritanism.

Morgan, Edmund, *The Puritan Dilemma* (1958; Pearson, 3rd. ed., 2006). Morgan writes of the hardships of the seventeenth-century Puritans in the Massachusetts Bay Colony. He explains the tension between individual freedom and the demands of authority by examining the life of John Winthrop, who once preached that the colonists' new community would be "a city upon a hill," setting an example of communal unity and upholding their covenant with God by obeying moral law—in Morgan's summary, "doing right in a world that does wrong." Another of Morgan's major works, *American Slavery, American Freedom: The Ordeal of Colonial Virginia* (1975), describes slavery as unifying whites while oppressing enslaved blacks. Morgan wrote with extraordinary accuracy, clarity, and wit.

Noll, Mark A., *America's God: From Jonathan Edwards to Abraham Lincoln* (2002; Oxford, 2005). Tracing the genesis of American culture and religious life, Noll demonstrates that the Puritanism of Cotton Mather in the seventeenth century developed into the broad-based religious divisions surrounding the question of slavery. The dispute split some Protestant denominations into northern (antislavery) and southern (proslavery) factions. The Bible does not condemn slavery, yet in the North those holding that God called believers to occupy the "high moral ground" trusted in the necessity to abolish it. Noll's argument is that religious attitudes on both sides were derived not only from the biblical text but also from contemporary social and political perspectives. The distinction helps explain what is culture and what is religion.

Osborn, William M., *The Wild Frontier: Atrocities during the American-Indian War from Jamestown Colony to Wounded Knee* (2000; Random House, 2001). Osborn evenhandedly tells of brutal white-Native encounters from 1622 to 1890. On the Indian side, the story includes intertribal warfare, raids on white settlers, ideas about property, and the devastating effects of alcoholism. Osborn reassesses the myth of white settlers as brave and intrepid pioneers, and the view of Indians as noble, morally superior victims. It is a violent story, skillfully told in graphic detail. Fergus Bordewich, *Killing the White Man's Indian: Reinventing Indians at the End of the Twentieth Century* (1996), provides a view of Indian life and sovereignty today.

Rhodes, Richard, *The Making of the Atomic Bomb* (1986; Simon & Schuster, 2012). Human history changed irrevocably on August 6, 1945, when an atomic bomb exploded over the city of Hiroshima. In an instant, the possibility of humanity's self-extinction became undeniable. Richard Rhodes's large, masterly account starts with the discovery of nuclear fission in the late nineteenth century and continues through the detonations over Hiroshima and Japan and the start of the Cold War. It covers all the scientists, politicians, and military officers involved in the Manhattan Project, along with the historical events driving their actions. The story of nuclear weapons did not stop there, of course, and Rhodes followed up on the creation of thermonuclear explosives in *Dark Sun: The Making of the Hydrogen Bomb* (1995).

Ricks, Thomas E., *Fiasco: The American Military Adventure in Iraq, 2003 to 2005* (2006; Penguin, 2007). Ricks describes the march of folly from the initial decision to attack Iraq in 2003 to the insurgency in 2006. Iraq was invaded because of 9-11; but there was no connection between 9-11 and Iraq. Despite the unrestrained optimism of the Bush administration regarding the anticipated course of the war, serious problems arose almost immediately. Key officials often did not anticipate the consequences of their actions. Anthony Shadid's *Night Draws Near: Iraq's People in the Shadow of America's War* (2005) provides a wide range of Iraqis' perspectives on the invasion and occupation of their country.

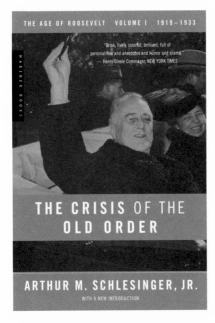

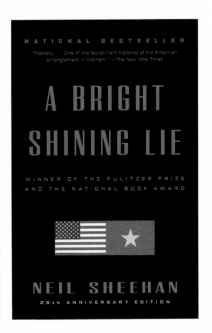

Schlesinger, Arthur M., Jr., *The Age of Roosevelt*, vol. 1, *The Crisis of the Old Order, 1919–1933* (1957; Mariner, 2003). Schlesinger was one of the preeminent historians of his time, and this book has stood the test of time as a fundamental work on FDR. Clear, colorful, and compelling, it catches the spirit of the age, jazz in the 1920s as well as the stock market crash, and brings alive personalities: FDR and his critics—who called him "a traitor to his class"—political opponents, Cabinet members, and leading figures of the time. As Henry Steele Commager pointed out in the New York Times, the most surprising detail to emerge is FDR's "profoundly conservative character"—the "greatest conservative since Hamilton." For the life of the historian, see Richard Aldous, *Schlesinger: The Imperial Historian* (2017).

Sheehan, Neil, *A Bright Shining Lie: John Paul Vann and America in Vietnam* (1998; Vintage, 1989). Vann was a lieutenant colonel who became known for telling the press about his misgivings early in the war. Discharged from the army, he returned to Vietnam to lead pacification efforts. The *New York Times* perhaps best summed up the significance of the book by describing it as capturing the Vietnam War "in the sheer Homeric scale of its passion and folly." Other incisive accounts of the war are Michael Herr's *Dispatches* (1977), firsthand reporting from 1967–69 that captures the madness of Vietnam with compassion and precision, and in Philip Caputo's *A Rumor of War* (1977), a combat memoir by a Marine who arrived in Da Nang in 1965 and left sixteen harrowing months later.

Sledge, Eugene B., *With the Old Breed: At Peleliu and Okinawa* (1981; Oxford, intro. Paul Fussell, 1990). An account of the brutality, stench, and misery in battles in the South Pacific by a Marine who was an expert in firing light mortars. Peleliu and Okinawa were two of the fiercest encoun-

8

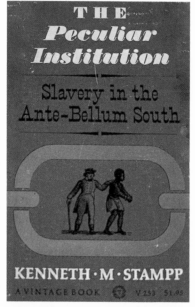

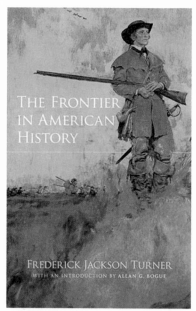

ters of World War II. Sledge kept in his pocket a small New Testament, in which he took notes on the intense fighting and the "nightmare of flashes, explosions, and snapping bullets"—and also the camaraderie of his fellow Marines. His description of the gradual dehumanization of troops on the front lines gives a sense of the horrendous toll of combat. The historian John Keegan described Sledge's account as "one of the most arresting documents in war literature."

Stampp, Kenneth M., *The Peculiar Institution: Slavery in the Ante-Bellum South* (1956; Vintage, 1989). This compelling study was the first major historical work on American slavery to base its research and conclusions on the notion of racial equality. In particular, Stampp sought to counter the notion that slavery was essentially a benign system of economic organization. It remains the starting point for any study of slavery in America. Stampp's *The Era of Reconstruction, 1865–1877* (1965) challenges the interpretation of Reconstruction as mired in corruption and incompetence, arguing, to the contrary, that the aim of civil and political equality foundered on the unremitting resistance put up by embedded, institutional racism. Stampp studied under the historian William B. Heseltine, famous for comparing intellectual history to "nailing jelly to the wall."

Tansill, Charles C., *Back Door to War: The Roosevelt Foreign Policy, 1933–1941* (1952; Praeger, 1975). Tansill was an American historian who held strong pro-German, anti-British views that represented a strain of isolationist thought in the 1930s. He never relinquished the belief that Roosevelt deliberately provoked Japan to attack the United States as a way to enter the war against Germany through the "back door." Most historians reject Tansill's view that there was a conspiracy by Roosevelt to bring the public into a war it did not wish to fight; but the controversy continues to be relevant in American political debate. In public life, Tansill supported segregation and eugenics, deplorable but significant aspects of American life in the 1930s and even later.

Tocqueville, Alexis de, *Democracy in America* (1835–40; Penguin Classics, trans. Gerald E. Bevan, intro. Isaac Kramnick, 2003). Tocqueville, a young aristocratic French lawyer, came to the United States in 1831 to study its penal systems. His visit resulted in a masterpiece of political observation and an analysis of social equality and its effects on religion, literature, the family, and intellectual life. He contrasts the strengths and weaknesses of American democracy—individualism and the "tyranny of the majority," for example—with those of the French aristocracy, exploring as well the contributions of American women to the strength of the country. Tocqueville's *The Ancien Régime and the Revolution* (1856; Penguin, 2008) is an early and historiographically useful history of the French Revolution.

Turner, Frederick Jackson, "The Significance of the Frontier in American History" (1893; included in Turner, *The Frontier in American History*, 1921; Yale, 1999). Three years after the U.S. Census Bureau announced the closing of the American frontier, Turner argued, in an interpretation that caught the public imagination, that the frontier had been the primary shaper of the American character. At the juncture between civilization and the wilderness, desert, and Indian lands, the self-reliance and ingenuity of explorers, trappers, and traders explained American development. Turner did not emphasize the darker side of western expansion, but his frontier theory became the dominant interpretation of American history. Significantly, perhaps, Turner refused to speculate on how the closing of the frontier would affect the American character.

Webb, Walter Prescott, *The Great Plains: A Study in Institutions and Environment* (1931; Nebraska, 1981). Webb describes the area of the Great Plains as stretching from Canada to Mexico and from the Rocky Mountains to the 98th meridian, which runs from Texas to the Dakotas. In the nineteenth century, much of the land was arid and without trees. Settlers often encountered hostile Plains Indians, but eventually survived and prospered, in Webb's famous phrase, by use of "the revolver, barbed wire, and the windmill." Over time, the railroads brought plank timber for houses (previously built mainly from sod), and the use of irrigation increased crop production. But water remained—and remains—a critical concern. Webb's knowledge of the environment gives the book lasting significance.

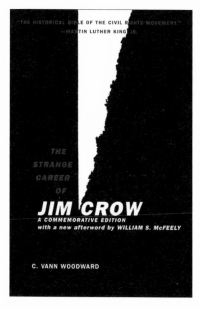 

Woodward, C. Vann, *The Strange Career of Jim Crow* (1955; Oxford, afterword by William S. McFeely, 2002). A seminal work for understanding the history of race in America. Woodward elucidates the origins and historical development of segregation, the system known as Jim Crow. Contrary to popular notions, racial segregation varied considerably from state to state, from city to city, and even more so locally. Woodward's skill at clarifying the complexity of these arrangements led Martin Luther King Jr. to describe the book as the "Bible of the Civil Rights movement." Woodward's *Origins of the New South, 1877–1913* (1951) is a study of the post-Reconstruction South that emphasizes the role of economic dislocation in shaping the region.

Zinn, Howard, *A People's History of the United States* (1980; Harper, rev. ed., 2005). In a work that has sold over two million copies, Zinn presents a radical view of American history. The overarching theme is the exploitation of the majority by an elite minority, particularly "corporate robber barons and war makers." Indians, blacks, women, factory workers, and immigrant laborers appear as rebels or victims. Criticized for the book's lack of balance, Zinn once commented, "It's not an unbiased account; so what?" His aim is to challenge national pieties and platitudes, and to encourage critical reflection about received wisdom. Few books have been so academically condemned and yet exerted such influence in popular culture. A forthright, sympathetic biography of the historian is Martin Duberman, *Howard Zinn: A Life on the Left* (2012).

History
Britain

Arnstein, Walter L. *The Bradlaugh Case: Atheism, Sex, and Politics among the Late Victorians* (1965; Missouri, 1983). Charles Bradlaugh was a mid-Victorian atheist and political activist who was not allowed to take his seat in the House of Commons because he would not swear a religious oath. He supported the birth control movement (with Annie Besant), the Fenians' nationalist activities in Ireland, French republicanism, a short-lived republican movement in England, and "native rights" in India. A champion of individual liberties, he was one of the best orators in England, often causing widespread outrage, especially on the issue of atheism. For modern work on the theme of atheism, see Richard Dawkins, *The God Delusion* (2006), and Christopher Hitchens, *God is Not Great: How Religion Spoils Everything* (2007).

Bede (St. Bede the Venerable), *Ecclesiastical History of the English People* (731; Penguin, trans. Leo Sherley-Price, 1991). Bede has traditionally been regarded as the "Father of English History." His history begins with Julius Caesar's invasion in 55 BC and ends by explaining how the Anglo-Saxons brought Christianity to England, giving an account of bishops and monks in relation to the early monarchy. Part of his purpose is to instruct readers by his spiritual example and by stories of miracles. His interpretations are mostly allegorical, but he uses critical judgment to rationalize discrepancies in symbolic meaning in the biblical text and to assess the accuracy of his sources. Not all readers will find it a compelling narrative, but it remains one of the most famous works of English history.

Carlyle, Thomas, *On Heroes, Hero-Worship, and the Heroic in History* (1841; Yale, ed. David R. Sorensen and Brent E. Kinser, 2013). Carlyle was widely known as a crotchety and argumentative public figure. In *On Heroes,* his God-inspired, resolute exemplars have the energy and character to lead in perilous times. Nietzsche developed Carlyle's heroes into amoral supermen, and Göring read passages of Carlyle to Hitler. Carlyle's concluding words perhaps best sum up his overall view: "The Great Man was always as lightning out of Heaven; the rest of men waited for him like fuel, and then they too would flame." The long-lasting, complicated relationship between Carlyle and his wife is given full treatment in Rosemary Ashton, *Thomas and Jane Carlyle: Portrait of a Marriage* (2002).

Colley, Linda, *Britons: Forging the Nation, 1707–1837* (1992; Yale, 2009). In thematically tracing the origins of British identity from the Act of Union to the beginning of the Victorian era, Colley studies cultural and social issues to understand how and why the British came to have common qualities and beliefs. How did the British think of themselves, and what were the reasons for their unity? Among the opposing factors contributing to British identity, she emphasizes Protestantism versus Catholicism in Europe; sea power rather than a massive standing army; and the historic rivalry with France. She unsentimentally raises the question of how long British identity will endure—a matter of particular importance in light of Brexit. A virtue of the book is its use of paintings and political cartoons as visual evidence.

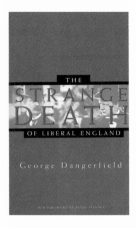

Dangerfield, George, *The Strange Death of Liberal England* (1935; Stanford, foreword by Peter Stansky, 1997). In this lucid, humorous, and humane book, Dangerfield holds that only the outbreak of European war in August 1914 prevented civil war in Britain over the Irish question. Despite war or the threat of war, the English were determined to remain calm. With unforgettable descriptive detail on such things as British Army mutineers and suffragettes, it has achieved a virtual cult status—above all because of its stylistic brilliance. Dangerfield's *The Damnable Question: A Study in Anglo-Irish Relations* (1976) covers mainly the tumultuous years 1912–22, with a particular focus on the Easter Rebellion of 1916, which he describes as a "bitter, exact and decisive gloss" on Britain's disastrous colonial policy in Ireland.

Gallagher, John, *The Decline, Revival, and Fall of the British Empire* (1982, ed. Anil Seal; Cambridge, 2004). In Gallagher's interpretation, the underlying dynamic of British Empire was a system of power characterized by constant change. It had multiple methods of expansion and a global range. At any one time, there was continual interplay of colonial, domestic, and international influences. Until 1947, India was its nerve center and the base of its economic and military power. Even after Indian independence, the empire's fate was by no means certain decline. In the late 1940s and early 1950s, British colonies and dependencies experienced an increase in English, Scottish and Irish immigrants, and in London a new sense of pride and confidence could be felt. The British Empire revived before it fell.

Hammond, J. L., *Gladstone and the Irish Nation* (1938). Hammond's father admired Prime Minister William Gladstone almost as if he were the fourth person of the Trinity; and Hammond as a child was confused about the distinction between God and the "Grand Old Man." With passion, exactitude, and fairness, he tells the story of Gladstone campaigning for Home Rule—the movement to secure internal autonomy for Ireland. Gladstone saw Britain not as a single nation, but as a partnership of four nations. Ireland was the point of breakdown. He regarded Britain's relations with Ireland as "the one and only conspicuous failure of the political genius of our race." The historian Michael Howard considers Hammond's work one of the great books in British history.

Hill, Christopher, *The World Turned Upside Down: Radical Ideas during the English Revolution* (1972; Penguin, 1991). Hill, the then-dominant figure in the study of seventeenth-century England, here accounts for the triumph of the Protestant ethic; his detailed, coherent work catches the spirit of the times while explaining how England became transformed into a great economic and imperial power. Perhaps surprisingly, the radical ideas that flourished in an era of tumultuous change benefited the few at the expense of the many as the social and emotional impulses that gave rise to the Diggers, the Levellers, and others resulted in disappointed hopes and unintended consequences. In *God's Englishman: Oliver Cromwell and the English Revolution* (1970), Hill paints a complex, nuanced portrait of a central figure in English history.

Hobson, John A., *Imperialism: A Study* (1902; Cosimo, 2005). The work of a famous journalist written against the background of the Boer War, *Imperialism* asks simple but always useful questions: Who is making a profit from this war? The munitions manufacturers? The book's influence was substantial, not least on Lenin, who repeatedly referred to Hobson. Hobson saw his own work as a "heresy" because it took into account "psychological interconnections" of social context usually ignored by economists at the time but eventually vindicated by historians. According to the historian William L. Langer, all the most divergent theories of imperialism can be traced to this "best book yet written on the subject." Peter Cain and Anthony Hopkins, *British Imperialism, 1688–2015* (3rd ed., 2016), is a monumental work in the tradition of Hobson.

Howard, Michael, *The Continental Commitment: The Dilemma of British Defence Policy in the Era of the Two World Wars* (1974; Penguin 1989). In a fundamental assessment of British military and naval strategy in the interwar era, Howard argues that far from being a naval and political advantage, worldwide colonial possessions were a liability: "The Empire brought Britain no strengths in her dealings with Germany." Army units that had proved effective in quashing colonial revolts were no match against German Panzers. The Royal Navy was deployed worldwide, since it could no longer depend on Japan to patrol the eastern seas as an ally. British strength was dissipated rather than concentrated. When war again broke out, the question was how to commit land forces to help European allies.

Hyde, Edward, 1st Earl of Clarendon, *The History of the Rebellion* (1702–4, 7 vols.; Oxford, ed. and intro. Paul Seaward, 1992). Clarendon wrote the first detailed history of the English Civil War (1642–51), in which he played a key part. This abridged version gives an account of the clash between the Roundheads (Puritans so named because they wore short hair) and the Cavaliers (adherents of Charles I). Clarendon relates frankly the inadequacies of Royalist decisions, the rise of Oliver Cromwell, and the eventual restoration of the monarchy. His own views are reflected especially in his denigrating accounts of Royalist compromises over the Anglican Church to win the support of the Presbyterian Scots, thus destroying the cause for which he believed the Royalists should have been fighting.

Kedourie, Elie, *The Chatham House Version, and Other Middle Eastern Studies* (1970; Ivan Dee, 2004). "Chatham House" refers to the Royal Institute of International Affairs, where discussion usually justified British withdrawal from the Middle East. Kedourie, however, believed that the abandonment of empire led to lawlessness and oppression. The scuttle, he emphasized, was due to British loss of nerve and left millions of people at the mercy of brutal local dictators. Kedourie's *In the Anglo-Arab Labyrinth: The McMahon-Husayn Correspondence and Its Interpretations, 1914–1939* (1976) argues that the true intentions of Britain in 1916 regarding an independent Arab state in Palestine were indiscernible; the British then invented the "myth" of a pledge to the Arabs in order to limit French and Zionist claims to the area.

Langford, Paul, *A Polite and Commercial People: England, 1727–1783* (1989; Oxford, 1994). Characterizing Georgian England as exuberant and confident, Langford explains that the book emphasizes "the changes which occurred in an age not usually associated with change." England was transformed by the spread of commerce and trade, by improvements to roads and canals, by the growth of the professions, and by the more general transition from an agricultural to an industrial society. Politeness and manners both regulated social interactions and conferred influence and power; and they illuminated the relationship between property and social class—a theme that makes politeness central to an understanding of the era. This is a witty and entertaining book with a readable style that catches the spirit of a vivacious society.

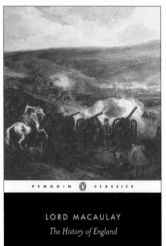

Macaulay, Thomas Babington, *The History of England from the Accession of James II*, 5 vols. (1849–61; abridged ed., Penguin, intro. Hugh Trevor-Roper, 1979). Dividing the world into the civilized and the barbaric, Macaulay held that England had reached the highest point of civilization. With ringing prose, he extolled British traditions and a forward-looking culture. He was wedded to the idea of continual progress, a concept that later became known as the Whig interpretation of history—Macaulay himself was more sophisticated than the term might imply. By drawing on novels and other writings to catch the spirit of the times, he left no doubt of his belief that England was better governed and more humane than other countries. A masterpiece of historical writing.

Maitland, Frederic William, *Domesday Book and Beyond: Three Essays in the Early History of England* (1897; Norton, 1966). In 1086, King William I ordered a survey of much of England and parts of Wales in order to compile a census for purposes of taxation and military service. The survey's coverage of geographic and demographic detail remained unmatched until the nineteenth century. Maitland, regarded as the father of English legal history, had peerless authority paired with a fluent, caustic, persuasive style. David Roffe's *Domesday: The Inquest and the Book* (2000) radically revises the standard thesis represented by Maitland's work. Maitland's masterpiece is *The Constitutional History of England* (1908), five lectures spanning roughly the period 1300–1900 in which he traces the growth and transformation of English constitutional law.

Marcus, Steven, *The Other Victorians: A Study of Sexuality and Pornography in Mid-Nineteenth-Century England* (1966; Transaction, 2008). Marcus's theme is the flourishing dark side of the Victorian virtues of ethical conduct and self-control. To some degree, he makes all Victorians seem sexually compulsive, the men having persistent fears of genital inadequacy, castration, and impotence, along with widespread social panic that masturbation might lead to insanity. The motives of pornographic writers derived from the prospect of bodily decay and suffering, particularly from syphilis. Pornography thrived in the "prosperous underworld" of mid-Victorian England, where escape into sexual fantasy brought with it a momentary sense that men were "always and infinitely potent, and all women fecundate with lust." Pornography created excitement, a diversion from reality, and a perpetuation of Victorian hypocrisy.

Mattingly, Garrett, *The Defeat of the Spanish Armada* (1959; Penguin, 1985). Against the background of Protestants and Catholics fighting for the soul of Europe, in 1588 the Spanish Armada, or fleet, of some three hundred ships set out to invade England. Spain was the great European power of the age. Victory would mean the incorporation of England into the Spanish Empire. The two fleets, roughly equal in size, engaged each other in the first naval battle to be fought mainly with heavy guns. The superior nautical and cannon technology of the British, as well as the "winds of God," played a decisive part in the Spanish defeat. One critic described the book as "written in purple prose but a royal purple, which reads like historical fiction."

McFarlane, K. B., *The Nobility of Later Medieval England* (1973; Oxford, 1980). McFarlane was a medieval historian who spent his career at Magdalen College, Oxford, where he had the reputation of being a melancholy and cantankerous man, difficult to approach but holding true and lasting friendships. He published little, but this posthumous work made an influential contribution to scholarship by revising the concept of "bastard feudalism," the late-medieval practice of satisfying feudal obligations with payments rather than service. The old consensus saw this intrusion of money as leading to "greed and civil strife," but McFarlane pointed out that different kinds of patronage could promote binding and positive ties, especially for the Crown and the landed nobility.

Namier, Lewis, *The Structure of Politics at the Accession of George III* (1929; Palgrave 1978). In this detailed, scrupulous, epoch-making account, Namier discovered the true workings of the eighteenth-century political system in Britain. He showed that the king was not a tyrant presiding over a corrupt regime, and that members of the House of Commons rationalized their actions in order to cloak deeper purposes. The companion volume is *England in the Age of the American Revolution* (1930), which examines Parliament under the leadership of the Duke of Newcastle in the early years of George III's reign. Namier's best short, readable work is *1848: Revolution of the Intellectuals* (1946), which details how the political upheavals of that year, intended as liberating, instead ushered in an era of nationalism.

O'Shaughnessy, Andrew Jackson, *The Men Who Lost America: British Leadership, the American Revolution, and the Fate of the Empire* (2013; Yale, 2014). One of this book's virtues is the retelling of the revolution from a British perspective—the side of the story virtually unknown in America. It will interest anyone curious about the political aims of the military campaigns. Instead of the military buffoons and arrogant political leaders often portrayed in American accounts, the British were usually competent and sometimes brilliant. But they faced problems in conducting an effective transatlantic war, not least concurrent conflicts in the West Indies. George III, Lord North, and military commanders, including General Burgoyne, achieved victories throughout the colonies—yet met with ultimate defeat, dramatically and accurately told by O'Shaughnessy.

Perham, Margery, *The Colonial Reckoning: The End of Imperial Rule in Africa in the Light of British Experience* (1962; revised ed., Collins, 1963). The "indomitable Margery," as she was known in Oxford, traveled extensively in Africa. By the time of World War II, she was widely regarded as a reformer as well as an acknowledged authority on colonial rule. After the fall of Singapore in 1942, she stated that the British Empire would have to be rebuilt on the basis of racial equality. She assessed the consequences of the social revolution brought about by British rule, and she held district officers accountable for humane administration, incorruptibility, and diligence in dispensing equal and fair-minded justice. In the *Colonial Reckoning* she candidly assesses Britain's record as a colonial power.

Robinson, Ronald, and John Gallagher, *Africa and the Victorians: The Official Mind of British Imperialism* (1961; Tauris, intro, Wm. Roger Louis, 2016). Robinson and Gallagher relate the history of late nineteenth-century British expansion from the occupation of Egypt in 1882 to the Boer War in 1899. They put forward an insistent argument: "The occupation of Egypt sparked the Scramble for Africa." The Egyptian nationalist who led the resistance against the British invasion was Arabi Pasha, who, the authors suggest, prefigured Gamal Abdel Nasser. The authors sum up the theme of Britain's consolidation of its territories in western, eastern and southern Africa in one word: *collaboration*—a controversial concept that plunged historians into memorable and analytically significant debate about whether *resistance* might be the better term.

Seeley, J. R., *The Expansion of England* (1883; Cambridge, 2011). Seeley is famous for the remark that the British seemed "to have conquered and peopled half the world in a fit of absence of mind," but without facing a fundamental contradiction: how could they reconcile the despotism of their rule in India with the liberties enjoyed by the colonies of white settlers? In fact, he believed that long-term possession of India might not be in Britain's best interest, since "Greater Britain" (the term he preferred to "British Empire") to him meant above all overseas colonies as an extension of England. The British Empire was an empire of kith and kin in which India formed a perplexing and alien part. The book remained in print, symbolically enough, until the fiasco of the Suez crisis in 1956.

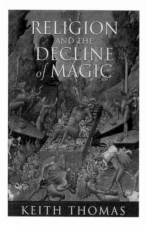

Thomas, Keith, *Religion and the Decline of Magic: Studies in Popular Beliefs in Sixteenth- and Seventeenth-Century England* (1971; Penguin, 2003). Combining history and anthropology, Thomas studies supernatural belief in the preindustrial society of early modern England. Despite the Reformation, advances in science, and the dwindling of superstition in religious practices, trust in magic continued to flourish not only among the common people but also among the learned and sophisticated. Kings had astrologers to guide them. The politically astute manipulated popular reliance on prophecies and miracles. In response to pain, distress, natural disasters, even anxiety, people at all social levels turned to magic when conventional help failed. As this learned yet witty book suggests, they continue to use magical equivalents today.

Thompson, E. P., *The Making of the English Working Class* (1963; Vintage, 1966). Few books of the past half century have had as much influence on the writing of history as this seminal work, which aims to understand the beliefs and ambitions of those "not on the winning side" in the British class system. Thompson sets out to rescue the experience of the working class from "enormous condescension," arguing that the power of historical Marxism helps generally explain working-class movements, especially from the sympathetic vantage point of the political Left. The dissident impulse against the "arrogance of the powerful" characterizes *English Working Class.* It continues to be revered as a canonical work of social history. For a useful assessment of Thompson, see Perry Anderson, *Arguments within English Marxism* (1980).

Thornton, A. P., *The Imperial Idea and Its Enemies: A Study in British Power* (1959; Macmillan, 1985). Thornton, for much of his life, believed no one could deny that the British were the champions of liberty and good government. They hoped to make their colonies profitable, but believed also that there could be a harmony of interests, or "collaboration," between rulers and ruled. He eventually concluded that in the tropical colonies, this proposition was "fundamentally bogus." The only honest principle—unthinkable to many—was "to abolish collaboration, and the dependent Empire with it." Yet Thornton, an exiled Scot teaching in Canada, lamented that Britain without its empire would be purposeless. *For the File on Empire: Essays and Reviews* (1968) is a useful collection of Thornton's diverse writings.

Trevelyan, G. M., *The English Revolution, 1688–1689* (1938; Oxford, 1965). In the first half of the twentieth century, it was a common British assumption that Trevelyan, great-nephew of Lord Macaulay, was the most widely read historian in England. In this concise account of the English Revolution, he argues that the overthrow of James II in 1688 led to parliamentary government, the rule of law, and religious tolerance. That stability allowed the British to achieve global maritime supremacy and imperial expansion. In this and other works, Trevelyan assumes an inevitable progression toward ever-greater British liberty and enlightenment. The historian J. H. Plumb described Trevelyan as "the poet of English history." The best biography of the historian is David Cannadine, *G. M. Trevelyan: A Life in History* (1993).

Woodham-Smith, Cecil, *The Reason Why: The Story of the Fatal Charge of the Light Brigade* (1953; Penguin, 1991). "Theirs not to reason why, / Theirs but to do and die: / Into the valley of Death / Rode the six hundred." Tennyson wrote these lines shortly after the event in 1854 to immortalize the valor of the cavalry bravely carrying out orders. Woodham-Smith explains the disastrous reasons. In this classic work, she focuses on the incorrigible personalities of Lords Lucan and Cardigan, who tried to cover up one of the most egregious blunders in military history. Criticism of military leadership later became an especially bitter issue during World War I. Recommended also: the film adaptation of Joan Littlewood's satirical musical *Oh! What a Lovely War* (1969), directed by Richard Attenborough.

Young, G. M., *Victorian England: Portrait of an Age* (1936; Oxford, 1977, annotated by George Kitson Clark). In assessing Victorian England (1837–1901), Young aimed to answer the question: why did England not have a revolution in the nineteenth century? His method was to explain "not what happened but what people felt about it when it was happening." Those people included leading figures in government, the military, society, and the arts. Young had a gift for trenchant observations, for example, that "gas-lighting of the streets was hardly an improvement as much as a revolution in public security," and that diplomatic history amounted to "what one clerk said to another clerk." This short book—in fact, a long essay—has been described by Simon Schama as "an immortal classic."

History
World History

Belloc, Hilaire, *The Crusades: The World's Debate* (1937; TAN, 1992). Belloc was one of the most prolific Catholic writers of the early twentieth century. Much of his work has not stood the test of time, including perhaps his most famous book, *The Path to Rome* (1902), but *The Crusades* endures because of his vigorous argument that the Crusades were necessary and that Muslims were still intent on destroying the West. Yet his lasting fame probably rests with *Cautionary Tales for Children* (1907; Houghton Mifflin, 2002), admonitory verses—wonderfully illustrated by Edward Gorey—that include "Matilda, who told lies and was burned to death"; "Jim, who ran away from his nurse and was eaten by a lion"; and "Rebecca, who slammed doors for fun and perished miserably."

McNeill, William H., *The Rise of the West: A History of the Human Community* (1963; Chicago, rev. ed., 1992). One of McNeill's purposes was to challenge Arnold J. Toynbee's theory that civilizations grow and then decline, as if unaffected by external influences. McNeill holds that civilizations affect one another through the intermingling of ideas and techniques, without one necessarily exerting a dominant influence over others. The driving force in historical change is cultural diffusion; the West has played a decisive part in this process during the last five hundred years. Hugh Trevor-Roper, who had played a prominent part in criticizing Toynbee's theories, called *The Rise of the West* "the most stimulating and fascinating book that has ever set out to recount and explain the whole history of mankind."

Phillips, Jonathan, *The Fourth Crusade and the Sack of Constantinople* (2004; Pimlico, 2005). The crusades are usually understood as a series of religious wars fought to recover the Holy Land from Muslim rule. In the Fourth Crusade (1202–4), the Europeans proved to be barbaric. On the way to Jerusalem, they turned to Constantinople, the heart of the Byzantine Empire and one of the largest cities in the world. Aflame with religious zeal, the crusaders looted the city, massacred many of its inhabitants, and attempted to burn it to the ground. The rationale: God approved of punishing the infidels—who were in fact Christians, but Orthodox rather than Catholic. This book, written with zest and scholarly accuracy, demonstrates that the crusaders spared no one in their savagery.

Spengler, Oswald, *The Decline of the West* (2 vols., 1918–22; abridged ed., Oxford, trans. Charles Francis Atkinson, 1991). Spengler wrote the first major work to treat other civilizations as entities in their own right and not as preludes to Western history. In a ponderous and apocalyptic style, he analyzes eight "high cultures" that ended as "civilizations" through inexorable stages of advancement, degeneration, cultural death, and dissolution. To Arnold Toynbee, he provided the key for the structure of his own voluminous work, *A Study of History* (1934–61). Upon publication, Spengler's book fit the mood of the German public, selling over 100,000 copies in a decade.

Toynbee, Arnold J., *A Study of History* (12 vols., 1934–1961; 2 vols., Oxford, abr. D. C. Somervell, 1987). In an immense work that took over a quarter of a century to complete, Toynbee argues that the rise and fall of some twenty-six civilizations were driven by forceful and imaginative leaders—"creative minorities"—who responded to religious, moral, and physical challenges. Civilizations disintegrated when their leaders failed to respond to such problems, often because they were trapped in militarism, nationalism, or despotism. Toynbee's critics included the eminent historians Pieter Geyl and H. R. Trevor-Roper, but he dismissed their attacks, confident in his historical interpretation and philosophy. William H. McNeill's *Arnold J. Toynbee: A Life* (1989) is an excellent account of the historian's life.

Vico, Giambattista, *New Science* (1725; Penguin, trans. David Marsh, 2000). Vico taught rhetoric in Naples, demonstrating to aspiring law students that it was necessary to understand both sides of any controversy. "Verifiable truth," the aim in the humanities and sciences as well as the law courts, could be found through reasoning and the application of common sense. By weighing arguments that seemed the most probable and had "the greatest degree of verisimilitude," he attempted to create a "science" that would explain the historical rise and fall of Oriental and Western societies. His ideas—not least his open-mindedness about the "Orient"—influenced thinkers and artists as diverse as Montesquieu, Marx, Joyce, and Said.

History
Europe

Europe
Barzun, Jacques, *From Dawn to Decadence, 1500 to the Present: 500 Years of Western Culture* (2000; Harper Perennial, 2001). For decades, Barzun taught the "Great Books" course at Columbia University with colleagues such as Lionel Trilling. His omnivorous interests are reflected in the books he wrote on, among other subjects, Darwin, Marx, Wagner, Berlioz, William James, mystery novels, race, research, and art. He is considered a founder of cultural history in the United States, and this massive, enjoyably readable account of the last half millennium of Western civilization reflects his enthusiasms and his vast knowledge. He pays special attention to literature, painting, music, and architecture, but also takes account of developments in warfare, government, and science, tracing the effects of all these on human consciousness.

Braudel, Fernand, *The Mediterranean and the Mediterranean World in the Age of Philip II* (1949; California, 2 vols., trans. Siân Reynolds, 1996). This massive socio-economic history of Mediterranean Europe, the Levant, and North Africa in the second half of the 16th century made famous the concept of the *longue durée*, an approach to history that gives precedence to slow and virtually imperceptible cultural and technological changes. Braudel belonged to the *Annales* school of thought, a type of social history that became prominent in the 1950s. It relied on the methods of the social sciences—rather than, say, Marxist class analysis—to understand long-term patterns of human development.

Cohn, Norman, *The Pursuit of the Millennium: Revolutionary Millenarians and Mystical Anarchists of the Middle Ages* (1957; Oxford, rev. ed., 1970). In Western Europe between the eleventh and sixteenth centuries, individuals and groups in different cultures and religions feared the end of the world in the wake of plague, earthquakes, and other disasters. They believed in the coming of a major social transformation that would affect all things. The flourishing of millenarianism occurred not only in revolutionary and anarchic sects but also among the rootless poor hoping to improve their conditions. Millennial thought became a feature of non-mainstream American Protestantism in the mid-nineteenth century, spawning several large denominations, and has persisted to the present day, affecting everything from national politics to popular entertainment.

Dawidowicz, Lucy S., *The War against the Jews, 1933–1945* (1975; Bantam, 1986). The author argues that Hitler's maniacal determination to kill Jews was one of the central Nazi war aims. He was resolved to eliminate Jews throughout Europe, even to the detriment of moving troops and securing supply lines. Although controversial for making that claim, the book is powerfully argued and represents a sharp and significant interpretation. Dawidowicz draws a line from Martin Luther's anti-Semitism to Hitler's and explains the Holocaust as arising from German nationalism. Above all, Dawidowicz restores agency to the Jews in the concentration camps, who had frequently been regarded as passive victims. The book was among the first to make the Holocaust comprehensible in purpose and magnitude to a general readership.

Elliott, J. H., *Empires of the Atlantic World: Britain and Spain in America, 1492–1830* (2006; Yale, 2007). Elliott compares on an epic scale the Spanish and British empires in the Americas. The Spanish colonial regime was bureaucratic and under centralized authority; by contrast, the decentralized empire of the British allowed colonists to build foundations of self-government. The overall strength of the book lies in its regional comparisons, for example, the southern areas of today's United States had more in common with Spanish settlements than with the New England colonies, and in its assessment of the cultural as well as religious dimension of Catholicism in the Spanish Empire and of the fractious Protestant sects in British America. Elliott's *Imperial Spain, 1469–1716* (rev. ed., 2002) is a full account of the rise and fall of a country that was once the master of Europe.

Guizot, François, *The History of Civilization in Europe* (1828; Penguin, intro. Larry Siedentop, 1997). As an historian, Guizot has an enduring reputation as one of the most trenchant minds of the nineteenth century. Writing in a straightforward style, he interprets the growth of the state as a process accompanied by the destruction of local autonomy and the creation of powerful bureaucracies. He demonstrates that certain features of European history are unique, for example, feudalism, centralized monarchies, and the revolutions in England and France. Guizot's history remains fundamental for an understanding of social change as a catalyst for historical development. For the relevance of the ideas of Guizot and other nineteenth-century political theorists to the European Union, see Larry Siedentop, *Democracy in Europe* (2001).

Huizinga, John, *The Autumn of the Middle Ages* (1919; Chicago, trans. Rodney J. Payton and Ulrich Mammitzsch, 1997). This translation supplants an earlier, inferior, abridged version published as *The Waning of the Middle Ages*. In a spirited study of France and the Netherlands in the fourteenth and fifteenth centuries, Huizinga interweaves the history of art and ideas. The codes of chivalry reflected a defensive response to rampant brutality and violence. Nonetheless, the conventions of love, the visions of death, and the aesthetic sentiments of medieval life culminated in pessimism and despair. By studying the psychology of artists, poets, and theologians, Huizinga establishes a prevailing mood of the darkness of medieval life. Huizinga wrote a questioning but sympathetic life-and-times biography of a towering Dutch intellectual, *Erasmus and the Age of Reformation* (1924).

Kershaw, Ian, *To Hell and Back: Europe, 1914–1949* (2015; Penguin, 2016). Beginning with the outbreak of war in 1914 and ending with Germany's division after World War II, Kershaw pursues themes of racial nationalism, territorial ambition, and the consequences of the Russian Revolution in relation to the "protracted crisis of capitalism." He emphasizes the distinctness of each national case, pointing out, for example, that Germany alone pursued a racial doctrine combined with territorial expansion. The German invasion of Soviet Russia and the genocide of Europe's Jews marked the final descent into the "pit of dire inhumanity." The book ends with the total defeat of Germany, the purging of collaborators, and continued American involvement in Europe—all absent from World War I, and all providing stability after World War II.

MacCulloch, Diarmaid, *The Reformation: A History* (2003; Penguin, 2005). The Protestant Reformation is one of the great dividing lines in European history. Before it, the continent followed one religion, Catholicism; after it, a dozen varieties of Protestantism competed with one another, and with the Church of Rome, for the people's spiritual and political allegiance. MacCulloch clearly and thoroughly covers this upheaval from its first stirrings in 1490. Principal religious and political leaders—Martin Luther, John Calvin, Charles V, Louis IV—and their ideas are discussed in detail, as are the major events of the period: the nailing of Luther's 95 Theses to a church door in Wittenberg, the Council of Trent, the Thirty Years' War. Upon the book's publication, one critic hailed it as a "masterpiece of readable scholarship."

Pirenne, Henri, *Mohammed and Charlemagne* (1937; Meridian, 2015). Pirenne was a Belgian historian famous for bravery as well his stature as a medievalist. During World War I, he became a national hero for nonviolent resistance to the German invaders, who imprisoned him. In this seminal yet controversial work, he argues, contrary to historical consensus, that Roman culture and social order survived the Germanic invasions of the fourth and fifth centuries. It was the expansion of Islam into North Africa and Iberia that ended the unity of cultures and trade in the Mediterranean. The center of Europe shifted north, giving rise to feudalism, the medieval church, and the Holy Roman Empire. Pirenne draws the provocative conclusion that without Mohammed, there would have been no Charlemagne.

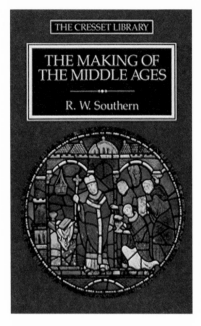

Southern, R. W., *The Making of the Middle Ages* (1953; Yale, 1992). This seminal work traces the formation and expansion of Western Europe from the 10th century to the 13th century, including the Crusaders' capture of Jerusalem in 1099 and Constantinople in 1204. The emergence of personal devotion to monastic faith prefigured the rise of individual identity in Western culture. In a broader sense, the economic strength of Europe increased, transforming its position in the world. Southern writes to a high standard, fulfilling his own slightly iconoclastic aim of portraying medieval society in such a way that self-disclosure revealed itself in the spirituality and emotionally charged prayers that "ran like fire through Europe." Southern makes comprehensible the development of intellectually inventive ideas in an authoritarian framework.

Wedgwood, C. V., *The Thirty Years War* (1938; NYRB, 2005). In May 1618, angry Protestants threw three representatives of the Holy Roman emperor out of a high palace window in Prague. That act of rebellion set off a continent-wide conflict that devastated Europe, leaving in its wake famine, disease, eight million dead, and hundreds of German states in utter ruin. What started as religious war between Catholics and Protestants became subsumed into the larger Bourbon-Habsburg rivalry pitting France against the empire. The story of this complicated, multilayered struggle is expertly told by C. V. Wedgwood in a compelling work of narrative history that remains one of the best works on the subject. The book is all the more remarkable for having been written when the author was twenty-eight.

Yates, Frances A., *The Rosicrucian Enlightenment* (1972; Routledge, 2001). Yates, an acclaimed historian of the European Renaissance, specialized in tracing the tradition of esoteric teachings in the sixteenth and seventeenth centuries. In *Rosicrucian Enlightenment*, she covers a short period just before the scientific revolution of the seventeenth century. Frederick V, Elector Palatine, and his wife, Elizabeth, the daughter of James I of England, set up court in Heidelberg, where they welcomed alchemists, magicians, Kabbalists, and Hermetists. They were responding, in part, to a pair of "Rosicrucian manifestos" that were stirring up intellectual excitement with the promise of a new understanding of man's nature. In an earlier work, *Giordano Bruno and the Hermetic Tradition* (1964), Yates describes the life and thought of a principal figure of Renaissance esotericism.

France

Bloch, Marc, *The Historian's Craft* (1949; Vintage, trans. Peter Putnam, 1964) and *Strange Defeat: A Statement of Evidence Written in 1940* (1946; Norton, trans. Gerard Hopkins, 1968). Bloch wrote two books of enduring interest. *The Historian's Craft* engagingly poses questions useful for thinking about the past. Written with a passion for history, it was unfinished at the time of his death: in 1944, Bloch was tortured and executed by the Nazis. *Strange Defeat* records his experience as a captain in the French Army at the time of the fall of France. He castigates French military leadership but attributes the defeat also to the decadence of his country's social and political traditions. Carole Fink's *Marc Bloch: A Life in History* (1991), the key biography, sums him up as "a rationalist keenly aware of the power and ubiquitousness of irrational forces."

Cobb, Richard, *Reactions to the French Revolution* (1972; Endeavour, 2016). Cobb, who had a lifelong passion for the radical phase of the revolution, conveys sympathy for the poor and marginal, those more concerned with the price of bread than politics. Cobb knew more about French archival and other sources regarding the revolution than any of his contemporaries, and he brings to life obscure people of the time: prostitutes, vagabonds, criminals, even lunatics. His work, idiosyncratic in its exuberant literary style, carries the reader to a bottom-up view of the revolution. By temperament and knowledge, he was an unsurpassed historian of the people. The autobiography of his early life, *Still Value: A Tunbridge Wells Childhood* (1984), portrays the English middle class in a state of "contented ossification."

Darnton, Robert, *The Great Cat Massacre, and Other Episodes in French Cultural History* (1984; Basic, 2009). In one of the studies gathered here, the oppressive circumstances of eighteenth-century artisans led the apprentices of a printer to rebel in what today would be regarded as a labor protest. The cats of the printer's wife were better fed than the apprentices, who were habitually exposed to cold weather and beaten. On one occasion, they rounded up the cats and subjected them to a trial for witchcraft, after which the cats were sentenced to death. The appeal of the study is the close rendering of an episode that can appear strange or opaque to present-day readers. The cultural and anthropological themes illuminate the darker yet comprehensible dimensions of the Old Regime.

Furet, François, *Interpreting the French Revolution* (1978; Cambridge, trans. Elborg Forster, 1981). Furet holds that French intellectuals as well as the public are trapped in viewing the revolution as commemorative history. The revolution is *not* the key to all aspects of modern French history. In fact there were two revolutions: one began in 1789 and ultimately represented a conflict over the meaning of egalitarian ideas; the other was the authoritarian seizure of the state that brought Napoleon to power in 1799. Furet was cosmopolitan and open to interpretations put forward by works in English, especially, for example, Alfred Cobban's *The Social Interpretation of the French Revolution* (1964), which argues that the revolution was political but with overarching social consequences.

Herold, J. Christopher, *Bonaparte in Egypt* (1962; Pen and Sword, 2005). In 1789, Napoleon Bonaparte sailed from Toulon to Alexandria with 55,000 soldiers, sailors, and civilians to capture Egypt for France. A month after landing, the French fleet was decimated by the Royal Navy under Lord Nelson at the Battle of the Nile. The Ottoman sultan then declared war on France, and tropical diseases began ravaging Napoleon's men. Despite those setbacks, for three years the scientists on the expedition traveled as far as Aswan, surveyed the Sinai Peninsula, discovered the Rosetta Stone, and launched the field of Egyptology. Herold relates these events with verve and insight. For the life of the woman who bedeviled Napoleon, see Herold's award-winning biography *Mistress to an Age: A Life of Madame de Staël* (1958).

Horne, Alistair, *A Savage War of Peace: Algeria, 1954–1962* (1977; NYRB, 2006). Algeria became an integral part of France in 1848. When a war of liberation broke out a century later, France committed more than half a million troops to its suppression. The French army resorted to torture, and the Algerian militants bombed civilian targets as well as military personnel. Over a million European Algerians, the *pied-noirs*, were driven into exile in France. Growing French revulsion at the brutality on both sides began to influence the outcome. Only rarely does such an epic subject encounter an outstanding historian. This book is Horne's masterpiece. In it he refers to the famous 1966 film *The Battle of Algiers*, a compelling companion to the book.

Lefebvre, Georges, *The Coming of the French Revolution* (*Quatre-Vingt-Neuf*, 1939; Princeton, trans. R. R. Palmer, 1979). Lefebvre was a widely acknowledged authority on the French Revolution. His major work was published in 1939; within the year, the Vichy regime had attempted to destroy all copies. Most French readers did not discover it until it was republished in 1970. The English translation (1947) was immediately proclaimed a masterpiece because of its balanced, clear, and cogent explanation of the revolution as a turning point in modern civilization. One of the book's strengths is its perspective on events from the peasants' point of view. Crane Brinton's *The Anatomy of Revolution* (1938) compares the French, English, American, and Russian revolutions.

May, Ernest R., *Strange Victory: Hitler's Conquest of France* (2000; Hill and Wang, 2001). Assessing the critical battle leading to the fall of France in May 1940, May challenges the legend of the French army's failure to take effective military action because of defeatism and degeneration into "moral rot." On the contrary, spirits were high. French armed forces were superior to the German, but suffered from a faulty network of communication, a cumbersome military bureaucracy, and fatal mistakes of judgment. The British as well as the French misinterpreted German aims: "Allied intelligence services performed abominably." There was also an element of chance, or sheer bad luck, since Hitler ordered German troops to advance despite the advice of his military commanders. A fundamentally important work on the fall of France.

Staël, Germaine de, *Considerations on the Principal Events of the French Revolution* (1818; Liberty Fund, ed. Aurelian Craiutu, 2009). This large work provides a liberal defense of constitutional monarchy and representative government, along with a vivid account of the main events and actors of the French Revolution. The ebullient and intellectually incisive author was exiled from France by Napoleon but still managed to play a vital part in his downfall. A contemporary said of her: "There are three great powers struggling against Napoleon for the soul of Europe: England, Russia, and Madame de Staël." She seemed at the time and in retrospect to epitomize the anti-Napoleon, anti-dictatorship spirit of the times. The best political study of this exceptional figure is by Biancamaria Fontana, *Germaine de Staël* (2016).

Tillion, Germaine, *Algeria: The Realities* (*L'Algérie en 1957*, 1957; Knopf, trans. Ronald Matthews, 1958). Tillion was an anthropologist who spent her formative years in Algeria. She fought in the Resistance and survived internment in Ravensbrück. *Algeria* is a short, eloquent book that makes an impassioned plea for an enduring and beneficial relationship between France and Algeria. In the year of the book's publication, Tillion met secretly, and at great personal danger, with Yacef Saâdi, the leader of the Algerian independence movement. She urged the Algerians to stop bombing in return for the cessation of torture by the French army. In view of this secret meeting, Gillo Pontecorvo's famous film, *The Battle of Algiers*, takes on an additional tragic dimension of an undepicted heroic woman attempting a peaceful solution.

Zeldin, Theodore, *France, 1848–1945* (2 vols., Oxford, 1977). In volume 1, *Ambition, Love, and Politics,* Zeldin interprets France's achievement as a nation yet also emphasizes individual experiences. He explains French emotions, enthusiasms, prejudices, and superstitions. In volume 2, *Intellect, Taste, and Anxiety,* Zeldin studies the French way of thinking and quality of life. He inquires into people's views of happiness and friendship, and their ambivalent feelings about foreigners. As the idiosyncratic topics make clear, Zeldin breaks with the forms of traditional history. His work has been received with extraordinary enthusiasm in France. According to one critic, on the basis of Zeldin's conversations, he has coaxed the French into self-revelation. Zeldin is "France's favorite Englishman": "He knows us better than we know ourselves."

Germany and Austria-Hungary

Browning, Christopher R., *The Origins of the Final Solution: The Evolution of Nazi Jewish Policy, September 1939–March 1942* (2004, with contributions by Jürgen Matthäus; Nebraska, 2007). Browning asks a central question: how did ordinary Germans become transformed psychologically into active participants in the widespread killing of Jews? He traces changing circumstances and decisions after the outbreak of war in 1939, but emphasizes the euphoria brought on by the attack on Russia in the summer of 1941, when common soldiers as well as Nazi commanders came to believe that they were invincible and that the genocide of Soviet Jews could be carried out wherever they invaded. The radical transformation of attitudes took place on battlefields as well as in Berlin.

Buller, E. Amy, *Darkness over Germany: A Warning from History* (1943; Arcadia, 2017). One of the best books in English on the Nazi youth movement. In the late 1930s, Buller held extensive conversations with Germans of different backgrounds and ranks to ask the question, how did the Nazi revolution appeal fundamentally to German youth and cause them to obey something that resembled a mystical authority? Hitler and other Nazi leaders were surprised at—and unable to explain—the enthusiasm and energy they had let loose in Germany. Buller describes a dynamic within the revolution that was fundamentally religious; Nazism and religious extremism, it turned out, had much in common. This book, written during World War II, is clear, compelling, and indispensable.

Evans, Richard J., *Death in Hamburg: Society and Politics in the Cholera Years, 1830–1910* (1987; Penguin, 2005). In 1892, in one of the most devastating urban disasters of the nineteenth century, a six-week cholera outbreak in Hamburg killed around ten thousand people—a large percentage of the working class. Evans shows how laissez-faire policies of government and business contributed to almost-yearly cholera visitations to the "free city" of Hamburg, which was not subject to regulation by the central government. Political and medical authorities, concerned more with saving money than lives, attributed the disease to "bad air," which allowed them to shrug off responsibility for counteracting it. In *The Third Reich Trilogy* (2003–8; Penguin), Evans offers a complete, monumental history of Nazi Germany.

Fischer, Fritz, *Germany's Aims in the First World War* (*Griff nach der Weltmacht*, 1961; Eng. trans., Norton, 1967). Until the early 1960s, there was consensus among historians that the European powers were more or less equally responsible for the origins of World War I. Fischer set off a major controversy by arguing, with immense archival evidence, that Germany deliberately instigated the European war in 1914, describing the German Chancellor, Bethmann-Hollweg, as the "Hitler of 1914" and drawing the conclusion that Germany was responsible for *both* world wars. Historians continue to debate his thesis that Germany's *Sonderweg* (special path) from at least 1871, with the establishment of the German state, inexorably culminated in the Third Reich.

Macartney, C. A., *The Habsburg Empire, 1790–1918* (1969; Faber & Faber, 2010). In this durable and readable book, Macartney's theme is the dynastic Austro-Hungarian Empire and the emergence of social, political, and eventually national forces arrayed against its autocracy and centralization. He begins with the death of Emperor Joseph I in 1790, which marked the turning of the tide in the struggle for control. He makes intelligible not only the old monarchy but also the peoples and provinces, and the diversity within unity that made the empire unique. Macartney was also an authority on Hungary. Macartney's *Hungary: From Ninth Century Origins to the 1956 Uprising* (1962) is a terse, meticulous, and intelligible account from the time of the nomadic Magyars to the ill-fated revolution of 1956.

Nolte, Ernst, *Three Faces of Fascism: Action Française, Italian Fascism, National Socialism* (1963; Eng. trans. Leila Vennewitz, 1965; Mentor, 1969). Nolte believed that fascism should be studied in relation to communism, arguing that Bolshevism in fact caused Nazism: the "race murder" of the Nazi death camps was a "defensive reaction" to the "class murder" of Stalin's gulags. In Nolte's judgment, the gulags were the original and greater horror. Yet in the view of his German and other critics worldwide, he denied the uniqueness of the Holocaust and diminished Germany's responsibility by relativizing it. Nolte in later years increasingly drifted into right-wing circles in Germany, but *Three Faces* remains a classic study in comparative history.

Sheehan, James J., *German History, 1770–1866* (1990; Oxford, 1993). The authoritative and standard work, Sheehan's *German History* deals with popular culture and economic diversity as part of his argument, which separates the reality of Bismarck's Germany from the national myth of emerging unity. In the 1860s there were 300 German sovereign, economically unintegrated states. In 1866, Prussia won what seemed to be a German civil war, yet the outcome was uncertain, and Bismarck's victory contingent. There was little popular national feeling. Sheehan wages a relentless assault on the traditional interpretation of unification and national identity. The book fundamentally helps readers understand the particular historical circumstances that allowed Bismarck to prevail, though his triumph seemed far less certain at the time than in retrospect.

Stern, Fritz, *Blood and Iron: Bismarck, Bleichröder, and the Building of the German Empire* (1977; Vintage, 1979). This parallel biography of Bismarck and his banker, Gerson von Bleichröder, analyzes in clear, detailed language the intersection of finance and politics. The head of the Rothschild bank in Berlin, Bleichröder—the richest Jew in a land of vicious anti-Semitism—helped finance Bismarck's railway projects as well as his military campaigns. His use of bonds and other financial instruments, often in highly secretive ways, helps explain the political economy of Germany in the latter half of the nineteenth century. Stern's *The Politics of Cultural Despair* (1961; California, 1974) is a major study of intellectual critics making the "leap from despair to utopia," in other words, to the ideology of the Third Reich.

Stoye, John, *The Siege of Vienna: The Last Great Trial between Cross and Crescent* (2008; Pegasus, 2007). In 1529, Suleiman the Magnificent laid siege to Vienna, the eastern bastion of the Habsburg Empire. The defenders, waving black and gold flags, repulsed the Ottomans' advance, despite the latter's superior logistics and Tartar allies. The great siege of 1683 has acquired near-mythical status. The Ottomans again failed to capture Vienna, in part because of the highly trained infantry of the Habsburgs and the cavalry of their Polish allies. The defeat marked the end of Turkish expansion into Europe. Andrew Wheatcroft, *The Enemy at the Gate* (2010), tells the captivating story of 1683 with particular emphasis on the Turkish side.

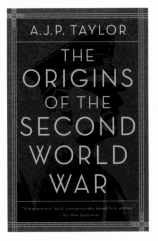

Taylor, A. J. P., *The Origins of the Second World War* (1961; Touchstone, 1996, with a preface for the American reader and the author's "Second Thoughts"). A hugely controversial work in the aftermath of publication. Breaking with conventional interpretation, Taylor presents Hitler as not exceptional but merely "an average German blown large." By shifting the responsibility from the Nazi leaders to the German people, Taylor put forward an unorthodox and unpopular view that helped to liberate the next generation of historians. Taylor's masterpiece, written with his customary vividness and authority, is *English History, 1914–1945* (1965), which thoroughly documents the upheavals in British society—women's suffrage and Irish independence among them—occurring during a period dominated by two world wars.

Trevor-Roper, Hugh, *The Last Days of Hitler* (1947; Pan Macmillan, 7th ed., 2013). In 1945 Trevor-Roper was a British intelligence officer charged with discovering the facts about Hitler's decision in May to kill himself in Berlin. His findings read like an historical detective story. Besides an account of Hitler's last ten days, he explains how the Nazis came to power and provides pen-portraits of leading German figures, including Goering, Goebbels, and Himmler as well as Eva Braun, whom Hitler married in his bunker shortly before they committed suicide. The book remains the classic work on the end of the Third Reich. *The Crisis of the Seventeenth Century: Religion, the Reformation, and Social Change* (1967) is one of Trevor-Roper's principal works in his field of undisputed authority.

Greece

Clogg, Richard, *A Concise History of Greece* (1992; Cambridge, 2002). The principal theme of this lively volume is the Greek national character, which is Mediterranean as well as European. During 400 years of Turkish occupation, Greece was isolated from the historical movements of Europe, including the Industrial Revolution, and its evolution has been marked by a close relationship with the Orthodox Church. Clogg discusses Byron giving his life in the uprising that led to the creation of the state in 1827. But he emphasizes and admires the principal figure in Greece's twentieth-century history, Eleftherios Kyriakou Venizelos, the charismatic seven-time prime minister who pursued liberal-democratic policies and helped expel the Ottoman Empire from the Balkan Peninsula. All in all, a bold and readable history of modern Greece.

Woodhouse, C. M., *The Struggle for Greece, 1941–1949* (1976; Ivan Dee, intro. Richard Clogg, 2002). In September 1942, during the German occupation of Greece, Woodhouse parachuted into the country to make contact with guerrillas and other anti-German partisans. Virtually the only member of the British military mission who could speak Greek, he helped prevent Greek communists from seizing power after the Germans' withdrawal in 1944. He describes the retreat of communist forces degenerating into a rout, and the failure of the Soviet Union to come to their aid: "Stalin let them go to their doom." Woodhouse later served in MI6 in Iran and took part in the overthrow of Mohammad Musaddiq; he eventually became a Conservative Member of Parliament for Oxford.

Ireland

Fitzpatrick, David, *Politics and Irish Life, 1913–21: Provincial Experiences of War and Revolution* (1977; Cork University Press, 1998). In tracing the everyday lives of the Irish people in the era of World War I and immediately afterward, Fitzpatrick focuses on County Clare. He traces the lives of common people in their rounds of daily farm chores. He brings to life the experiences of landlords, policemen, politicians, and priests as well as gunmen and opportunists with little concern for principles and idealism. Irish society was complex, but one theme clearly to emerge is the integrity of the revolutionary leaders fighting for independence. In a further work, *The Two Irelands, 1912–1939* (1998), Fitzpatrick studies rival paramilitary organizations against the background of collective sacrifice.

Foster, R. F., *Vivid Faces: The Revolutionary Generation in Ireland, 1890–1923* (2014; Penguin, 2015). Foster's subject is Ireland's pre–World War I generation of revolutionaries—their lives, aims, and destinies. He argues that the origins of the rebellion of Easter 1916 can be found in the radicalization of a generation as well as a specific movement to liberate Ireland from Britain. Those at the heart of the movement he describes as radical bohemians in Dublin who shaped the revolutionary goal of national, cultural, and social renewal. They fused Republican ardor, feminism, and anti-colonialism to create the "Irish Nation." Foster's other books include the two-volume biography *W. B. Yeats: A Life* (1998, 2003) and *Modern Ireland, 1600–1972* (1988), which Robert Kee describes as "magnificently authoritative and confident."

Kee, Robert, *The Green Flag* (1972; Penguin, 2001). In this robust book on Irish nationalism, Kee begins with English colonization in the sixteenth and seventeenth centuries, the confiscation of land from Irish landowners, and the creation of a Protestant identity in a Catholic country. He pays special attention to Wolfe Tone, who hoped to overthrow English rule with help from a French invasion in 1798. The story reaches a peak with the Easter Uprising of 1916 and the creation of the Irish Republic in 1924. The inimitable Patrick Leigh Fermor describes the book as "beautifully written, fair and balanced to all sides, and more than that, full of understanding and sympathy." Thomas Flanagan's *The Year of the French* (1979) is a fictionalized account of the events of 1798.

Townshend, Charles, *Easter 1916: The Irish Rebellion* (2006; Ivan Dee, 2011). This extensively researched and evenhanded history of the Easter uprising carries an emotional punch by conveying the confused and uncertain planning for the revolt and the seizure of the General Post Office in central Dublin. After six days of carnage, the rebels surrendered unconditionally, but the British commanding general ordered a firing-squad execution of sixteen of the insurgents, making them martyrs for the cause of Irish nationalism. One of Townshend's points of originality is the explanation of the "contradiction" between the goal of an "Irish Ireland" and the assumption that Ireland would form a single political unit. The Irish writer and novelist John Banville writes that Townshend's *Easter 1916* will probably be the "definitive account."

Italy

Burckhardt, Jacob, *The Civilization of the Renaissance in Italy* (1860; Eng. trans. S. G. C. Middlemore, 1878; Penguin, intro. Peter Gay, 2002). Burckhardt, a Swiss historian, dealt with the Renaissance in its entirety: history, society, art, architecture, religion, psychology, science, and education. He describes the Italian city-states of Florence, Venice, and Rome, which allowed for the flourishing of artists from Dante to Michelangelo. He celebrates the rediscovery of Greek and Latin learning and the development of humanism. From humanism arose individualism and the competition for fame, motives that still resonate overpoweringly. Burckhardt's other field of expertise was ancient Rome, and his *Age of Constantine the Great* (1853) covers attempts by the emperors from Diocletian to Constantine (A.D. 284–337) to hold together the crumbling, religiously splintered, and economically disintegrating empire.

Holmes, George, *Florence, Rome, and the Origins of the Renaissance* (1987; Oxford, 1988). Holmes's theme is the role of the Tuscan city-states, particularly Florence, as catalysts for challenges to the primacy of the medieval Church in the period 1260–1320. In building the bridge from the medieval period to the early Renaissance, cities without universities, such as Florence, experienced dynamic and original artistic and literary achievements, cultural expression resulting from popular religious sentiment, economic crisis, and political accident. For example, the book describes as "vigorous and corrupt" the era in which Dante produced his masterpiece. The story is carried forward in Holmes's *The Florentine Enlightenment, 1400–1450* (1969). Holmes edited a companion volume of sorts, the *Oxford Illustrated History of Italy* (1997), a lavishly illustrated collection of twelve essays.

Mack Smith, Denis, *Cavour and Garibaldi 1860: A Study in Political Conflict* (1954; Cambridge, 2002). The nineteenth-century movement for Italian unification, the Risorgimento, has always been clouded with romanticism, which, according to A. J. P. Taylor, Mack Smith brilliantly examines with a skeptical eye. Writing in an easily understood style of detached irony, the preeminent historian of Italy makes clear the clash of personalities and aims, Cavour possessing an inspired sense of mission in fomenting war against Austria to break the Austrian hold on the Italian north, and the more radical Garibaldi willing to use force if necessary to unify the entire peninsula. Mack Smith's *Mussolini: A Biography* (1983) pursues the theme that Mussolini turned the country into a shambles while dividing Italians among themselves.

Norwich, John Julius, *A History of Venice* (1982; Vintage, 1989). In an urbane, readable style, Norwich tells the story of Venice from its founding in the fifth century—according to tradition, by refugees fleeing Goths and Huns—to its capture by Napoleon in 1797. The city-state's improbable location, on 120 islands in a large shallow lagoon at the head of the Adriatic, provided it with protection conducive to the creation of a great maritime power. Led by a doge (a term related to *duke*), Venice served as a launching point for the Crusades, constantly battled the Ottomans, and maintained an uneasy relationship with the rest of Europe. Although strongest on political and military history, the book does not ignore the republic's role as a center of printing and international finance.

Low Countries

Humes, Samuel, *Belgium: Long United, Long Divided* (Hurst, 2014). In an interpretation of Belgian history that extends from Roman times, the theme is the unity of a linguistically divided country composed of French-speaking Walloons and the Flemish people, whose native tongue is a variant of Dutch. The historic Walloon dominance began to erode when the rise of literacy enabled the Flemish to challenge the centuries-old cultural and political sway of the Walloon propertied elite. In the Belgian Congo, most Belgians were Flemish, but governance was by Walloons. When the Flemish movement gained momentum in the post-1945 era, the Belgian polity began to fracture. The separatist crisis was cultural as well as linguistic—but "long divided yet long united" continues to characterize the country.

Israel, Jonathan, *The Dutch Republic: Its Rise, Greatness, and Fall, 1477–1806* (1995; Oxford, 1998). Though Israel deals with 350 years of Dutch history, the crucial era extends from the revolt against Spain in 1572 through the "Golden Age" of Grotius, Spinoza, and Rembrandt. The revolt was more chaotic than heroic, yet the seventeenth century became notable for Dutch domination of world trade and the development of the Dutch East India Company, which helps explain the rise of the Netherlands as a naval power and international financial center. This is a book of 1,231 pages, yet the reader wishes for more. It captivates because of the balance between general interpretation—including discoveries such as the pendulum clock—and specific detail, for example, the invention of street lamps in Amsterdam.

Kossmann, E. H., *The Low Countries, 1780–1940* (Oxford, 1978). Usually, books about the Netherlands and Belgium emphasize the differences between the two countries. Kossmann's originality lies in writing about the two as separate communities that reacted to political and intellectual challenges in almost identical ways. His emphasis is on cultural history, especially on the issue of Belgium generally preferring to use French rather than Dutch. He develops a major theme on the decline of the Netherlands in the eighteenth century and the origins of the "Flemish question" in Belgium. One of the strengths of the book is the substantial section on the Dutch East Indies in comparison with the Belgian Congo—and the contrast between Indonesian nationalism and "nationalist resistance" in the Congo.

Poland

Davies, Norman, *God's Playground: A History of Poland*, vol. 2, *1795 to the Present* (1982; Oxford, rev. ed., 2005). The best Polish history in English. "God's playground" is an allusion to a sixteenth-century poem used by Davies to indicate that the history of Poland can be viewed as a history of mankind. It places the Ukrainian, Lithuanian, German, and Jewish communities in a Polish context and brings the story down to Poland's accession to the European Union in 2004. In Davies's *The Isles* (1999), he emphasizes not "eternal England" but the cultural history of Wales, Scotland, and Ireland. A readable, iconoclastic book of 1,222 pages that reverses the Anglocentric, Whig version of English history with a jolting challenge to basic assumptions about British identity.

Portugal

Boxer, C. R., *The Portuguese Seaborne Empire, 1415–1825* (1969; Carcanet, 1991). Boxer's study remains the basic work on Portuguese exploration, military power, trade, and the creation of overseas possessions in South America, Africa, and Asia. Without neglecting the social and religious dimensions of expansion, he deals with the Portuguese who profited from the empire: their involvement in the slave trade and their impressment of local peoples to work on sugar plantations and in gold mines. Boxer's *Race Relations in the Portuguese Colonial Empire, 1415–1825* (1963) explodes the contemporary view that the Portuguese colonies had no racial barriers; Boxer demonstrates, to the contrary, that Portugal imposed an implicit and repressive color bar.

Disney, A. R., *A History of Portugal and the Portuguese Empire: From Beginnings to 1807* (2 vols., Cambridge, 2009). Portugal possessed the first global empire. Anthony Disney achieves a rare balance between metropolitan and colonial history, integrating the early history of the fifteenth-century Kingdom of Portugal with the beginnings of an empire that extended more than halfway around the world. Volume one relates the history of Portugal itself from Roman times, and the second volume deals with the overseas empire. This is a comprehensive and meticulous reinterpretation, the first in English in more than a generation. Roger Crowley's *Conquerors: How Portugal Forged the First Global Empire* (2002), provides a rambunctious, thrilling account of the Portuguese explorers as courageous and zealously religious yet also ruthless and brutal.

Romania

Hitchins, Keith, *Rumania, 1866–1947* (Oxford, 1994). Following Romania's independence in 1866, the country's political leaders sought to install modern forms of government and to shift the economy from agriculture to industry. They looked west, to Europe, rather than east to Russia for models. Their overarching aim was to unify the Romanian state and maintain its sovereignty against great-power threats. The older standard history by R. W. Seton-Watson, *A History of the Roumanians: From Roman Times to the Completion of Unity* (1934) is still useful for detail and interpretation. Seton-Watson advocated the breakup of the Austro-Hungarian Empire and the emergence of Czechoslovakia and Yugoslavia during and after World War I. After World War II, he was appointed to the new chair of Czechoslovak Studies at Oxford.

Russia

Conquest, Robert, *The Great Terror: Stalin's Purge of the Thirties* (1968; Oxford, 2007). In the first comprehensive work on this period based primarily on Russian sources, Conquest argues that the trials and executions of former Communist leaders in the purges of the 1930s were insignificant in comparison with the twenty million deaths for which Stalin was directly responsible. His estimate, widely disputed, was proved right after the opening of the Soviet archives in the early 1990s. When asked by his publishers to prepare a second edition, Conquest reportedly replied that the new version should be entitled "I Told You So, You Fucking Fools" (in fact, the suggestion came from his friend Kingsley Amis). The book remains the fundamental work on the subject. Conquest's *The Harvest of Sorrow: Soviet Collectivization and the Terror-Famine* (1986) details Stalin's deliberate starvation of millions of Ukrainian peasants in 1932–33; Anne Applebaum's

Red Famine: Stalin's War on Ukraine (2017) is based on Soviet archives and deals with the question whether the term "genocide" applies to the famine.

Pipes, Richard, *Russia under the Old Regime* (1974; 2nd ed., Penguin, 1995). Pipes's book still holds its own as one of the most important interpretations of the Russian state from the ninth century to the nineteenth. With an emphasis on cultural, religious, and economic themes, it traces the evolution of the state and its grip on the peasantry, the nobility, and the church. In the attempts to withstand the increasing absolutism of the tsarist state, intellectuals played a key part. Partly in reaction to those efforts, the government embraced legal and institutional powers that led to the creation of the Soviet Union's bureaucratic police state. A readable, comprehensive, and authoritative companion volume is Hugh Seton-Watson, *The Russian Empire, 1801–1917* (1967).

Reed, John, *Ten Days That Shook the World* (1919; Penguin Classics, intro. Vladimir Lenin and A. J. P. Taylor, 2007). Reed, educated at Harvard, was the editor of the *New York Communist*. In 1917 he found his way to Russia, where he met Trotsky and Lenin. *Ten Days* is an eyewitness account of the revolution, carefully documented yet passionately pro-Bolshevik. The U.S. diplomat George Kennan, no fan of the Soviets, praised the book for "its literary power, its penetration, its command of detail." Reed died in 1919 in Moscow, where he was given a hero's funeral and buried in the Kremlin. His story is told in the film *Reds* (1981), starring Diane Keaton, Jack Nicholson, and Warren Beatty as Reed.

Wilson, Edmund, *To the Finland Station: A Study in the Acting and Writing of History* (1940; NYRB, intro. Louis Menand, 2003). In this original and powerful work, Wilson deals sympathetically with revolutionary personalities from 1789 through the collaboration of Marx and Engels to the arrival of Lenin at the Finland railway station in St. Petersburg in 1917. The book succeeds in part because of Wilson's imaginative and exact grasp of concrete details, for example, the misfortunes of Marx and the strategic decisions of Lenin. This is a magnificent book, but Wilson's assumption about the coming of a "better world" quickly vanished. Shortly before the book was published, an agent of the Soviet secret police assassinated Leon Trotsky with an ice axe in Mexico City.

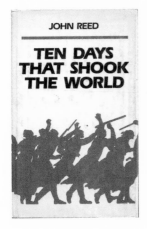

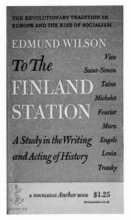

Spain

Brenan, Gerald, *The Spanish Labyrinth: An Account of the Social and Political Background of the Spanish Civil War* (1943; Cambridge, 2014). Published four years after the end of the Spanish Civil War, Brenan's book provided one of the first searching accounts of the war as it was viewed at the time, as a revolution and a counter-revolution. Brenan, who spent most of his adult life in Spain, drew on his experience with the common people as well as intellectual and political figures in Madrid. His book circulated clandestinely in Spain and provided historians there with a sense of social continuity. Jonathan Gathorne-Hardy's *Gerald Brenan: The Interior Castle* (1993) gives the sweep of Brenan's life, including his experience with the Bloomsbury group and his attempt to walk from England to China.

Carr, Raymond, *Spain, 1808–1938* (1966; Oxford, 2001). With a straightforward and subtly entertaining style, Carr surveys the intellectual, social, economic, and political course of Spanish history in the nineteenth century, carrying the story through General Franco's victory in the Civil War. The book's strength lies in its scope: its diverse subjects include rainfall and soil patterns in farming, schoolbooks and novels, ordinary solders as well as officers, and controversial constitutional issues, along with bullfights—all interspersed with anecdotes. The book's translation influenced a generation of Spanish historians, and Carr became a legendary figure in Spain. Carr served for nineteen years as Warden of St. Antony's College, Oxford, one of the periods covered in the perceptive biography of the historian by María Jesús González, *The Curiosity of the Fox* (2015).

Thomas, Hugh, *The Spanish Civil War* (1961; Modern Library, 2001). Banned in Spain during the Franco era, Thomas's book is the classic account of how Spain became an ideological battleground for anarchists, communists, monarchists, fascists, and socialists in the years 1936–39. The bombing of the town of Guernica by German aircraft, the best-known event of the war, was only one of many atrocities committed by both fascists and republicans. In Thomas's estimate, some three-quarters of a million people lost their lives. Franco emerged triumphant because of superior generalship, and he presided over a regime that lasted until 1975. A more recent account is Stanley Payne, *The Spanish Civil War* (2012), a work by one of the foremost historians of Spain and fascism.

Turkey

Lewis, Bernard, *The Emergence of Modern Turkey* (1961; 3rd ed., Oxford, 2001). Lewis's history of Turkey benefits from extensive research in Ottoman archives. He makes the broad point that much of the history of the Middle East in the twentieth century has to be understood against the background of the collapse of the Ottoman Empire. After World War I, Kemal Atatürk aimed to transform Turkey into a modern secular state, one of Lewis's major themes. In recent decades, Lewis has received criticism for not holding the Ottoman government fully accountable for the Armenian genocide; he became involved in debates with Edward Said over Orientalism; he acquired a reputation for neoconservative views; and he supported the war in Iraq. Regardless, his book on the emergence of modern Turkey remains a landmark.

Reynolds, Michael, *Shattering Empires: The Clash and Collapse of the Ottoman and Russian Empires, 1908–1918* (2011; Cambridge, 2011). Instead of dwelling on the pre-1914 Balkan wars in which the Ottomans lost their remaining territory in Europe—or on Gallipoli, or the Arab revolt—Reynolds focuses on the ancient and enduring clash between the Russian and the Ottoman Empires. Both were extinct by 1920. The contentious borders between them cut through "mixed populations" that included Christians and Muslims, Armenians and Azerbaijanis, Circassians, Georgians, and Kurds. In the imperial clashes, the victims were the peoples of the borderlands. Both empires, Reynolds concludes with significant insight, were guided by a determination to maintain the security of their borders rather than by notions of religious solidarity or nationalism.

Rogan, Eugene, *The Fall of the Ottomans: The Great War in the Middle East, 1914–1920* (2015; Basic Books, 2016). The Ottomans in 1914 made the decisive though understandable mistake of entering the war on the side of the Germans. While engaging British, French, and Russian forces, they tried to stimulate jihad in the territories of their enemies. Unlike the stalemate on the western front, the war in the Middle East moved fast and unpredictably, but in the end British forces occupied Baghdad, Jerusalem, and, finally, Damascus. Rogan makes clear that the historical evidence points to Ottoman genocide of Armenians in 1915–18. Thought the Ottomans were defeated, the war gave the Turks the experience and nationalist resolve that led to Turkish independence in 1923.

Stone, Norman, *Turkey: A Short History* (2012; Thames & Hudson, 2014). Stone is a Scot who taught in Oxford as Professor of Modern History before assuming an academic post in Turkey in 1997. He is well known for his prize-winning *The Eastern Front, 1914–1917* (1975). *Turkey* succinctly traces the country's past millennium, dwelling on Kemal Atatürk as the founder of modern Turkey. Stone joined the controversy over whether Turkey perpetrated an "Armenian genocide" in 1915. He robustly rejects the charge, arguing that the accusation is based on forged documents and circumstantial evidence and that it has never been proved in a court of law. Many Armenians died during a process of deportation, but according to Stone, the Ottoman government never intended to exterminate them.

Zürcher, Eric J., *Turkey: A Modern History* (1993; Tauris, 2004). Probably the best up-to-date survey of nineteenth- and twentieth-century Turkish history. It pursues dual themes of the modernization of state and society, and the integration of the Turkish economic system into the global economy. Beginning with the Ottoman Empire in the era of the French Revolution, Zürcher argues that the ruling elite in the nineteenth century failed to respond effectively to European intrusions, and that after 1908 the "Young Turks" succeeded in constructing a sense of Turkish identity. With an original assessment of Kemal Atatürk, he sets the context for the radical refashioning and secularizing of Turkish society. The last part of the book deals with the role of Islam in a secular state and other pressing matters, including Kurdish separatism.

Yugoslavia

Deakin, William, *The Embattled Mountain* (1971; Faber, 2011). During World War II, Deakin parachuted into German-occupied Montenegro to aid the outnumbered, encircled Yugoslav partisans and to make contact with Tito. The operation resulted in strengthening the position of Tito as a national leader and eventually the independence of Yugoslavia vis-à-vis the Soviet Union. Deakin's account of breaking out of the enemy ring became a classic account of anti-Axis resistance. The author's other major work is *The Brutal Friendship: Mussolini, Hitler, and the Fall of Italian Fascism* (2011), which relates the Italians' repudiation of Mussolini in 1943, his reappearance as Hitler's puppet in the north of Italy, and the macabre end: Mussolini's swollen corpse hanging upside down in a Milan square.

West, Rebecca, *Black Lamb and Grey Falcon* (1940; Penguin Classics, intro. Christopher Hitchens, 2007). To Rebecca West, Yugoslavia before World War II represented the vortex of European politics as well as a country under the threat of Nazi occupation. She describes above all the tensions among ethnic groups and the precarious sense of Yugoslav identity. William Shawn of the *New Yorker* described West's writing as "dazzling." West's *The Meaning of Treason* (1949) is another major work that has stood the test of time. This account of the British treason trials after World War II—including the trial of John Amery, the son of the former Secretary of State for India, Leopold Amery—explains the complicated motives for betrayal and reflects on the relationship between loyalty and treachery.

History
Africa, the Middle East, Asia

Africa

Buell, Raymond Leslie, *The Native Problem in Africa* (2 vols., 1928; Cass, 1965). Buell was a Harvard political scientist who in the 1920s traveled extensively in colonial Africa, collecting information and interviewing the "natives" as well as officials in Belgian, French, and British Africa. His purpose was to examine problems that arose from the impact on "primitive people" of the Western colonial system, and to gauge subsequent tensions between colonial rulers and African subjects. There is an undercurrent of hostility toward white settlers as well as an assessment of African protest movements. At the time, Reginald Coupland of Oxford judged the work to be candid and fair. The two volumes are an unparalleled survey, indispensable for an understanding of the interwar period in Africa.

Gluckman, Max, *Custom and Conflict in Africa* (1955; Barnes & Noble, 1999). Gluckman was a South African–born anthropologist whose research in the 1930s and 1940s concentrated on the Lozi of Barotseland, in present-day Zambia. Trained also in the law, he emphasized "case studies," then a novelty, in which he investigated collective social response to tribal rules and assumptions in the context of stability and change. *Custom and Conflict* focuses in part on inequality and aggression, which reflects Gluckman's anticolonial activism and his emphasis on the "cultural contradictions" of labor migration, urbanization, and racism. His work at the time and subsequently took on broad significance by inquiring into the relations between the Afrikaners and the English in South Africa.

Iliffe, John, *Africans: The History of a Continent* (1995; Cambridge, 2012). Iliffe succeeds in creating a single narrative around a complex story stretching from origins of mankind to the twenty-first century. The theme of this rich and readable history is the peopling of an environmentally hostile continent. For millennia, the inhabitants of Africa have struggled against disease as well as predation and a harsh climate. Economic and social institutions helped ensure their survival. They managed to sustain themselves despite the slave trade and colonial invasions. Medical progress created unprecedented population growth, and the pace of demographic change helps explain the collapse of colonial rule and the disintegration of apartheid. But contemporary Africa still faces widespread instability, driven by rapid population growth, corrupt governance, religious fundamentalism, and chronic civil wars.

Lugard, Frederick John Dealtry, *The Dual Mandate in British Tropical Africa* (1922). Lugard was a British proconsul especially renowned for creating the protectorate of Nigeria, and for his book *The Dual Mandate.* He believed that colonial rule should preserve indigenous institutions while encouraging "natives" to manage their own affairs. The title of the book meant that the British had a *dual* responsibility, to the Africans for stable development and to the British for the exploitation of resources for the benefit of their colonial subjects as well as the British. In practice, it meant a collaborative, dual regime in which a small number of British colonial officers were able to control large African populations with minimal expense but extensive and effective influence.

Mazrui, Ali, *Nkrumah's Legacy* (Ghana Univ. Press, 2000). Kwame Nkrumah was the African nationalist who in 1957 led the Gold Coast to independence as Ghana, the first British African colony to become a sovereign nation. He was deposed in 1968 after becoming a leading advocate of Pan-Africanism. Mazrui (an historian of Africa originally from Kenya) initially wrote of him as a "Leninist Czar," but four decades later refined his thoughts in a more balanced view of Nkrumah's quest for economic freedom as well as political liberty, and of his legacy in an era of globalization. According to one assessment, Mazrui became "one of the most famous intellectuals of African descent in the twentieth century." His last post was the Walter Rodney Professorship at the University of Guyana.

Moorehead, Alan, *The White Nile* (1960; Harper Perennial, 2000). The history of European exploration in Africa in the nineteenth century to discover the sources of the Nile. The author combines geographic detail on Africa's great waterways—the Congo, the Niger, and the Zambezi as well as the Nile—with biographical descriptions of such figures as David Livingstone and Henry Morton Stanley. Usually regarded today as politically incorrect because of its description of

Africans, it relates the story as seen through the eyes of the explorers themselves. Moorehead's *African Trilogy* (*Mediterranean Front*, 1941; *A Year of Battle*, 1943; *The End in Africa*, 1943)—"hefty but unputdownable," according to Clive James—offers a firsthand account of the fighting in North Africa during the Nazi drive toward Egypt, by a war correspondent who seemingly was at every battle.

Oliver, Roland, and John Fage, *A Short History of Africa* (1962; 6th ed., Penguin, 1990). Oliver and Fage were two critical figures in the creation of African history as a separate field of study. In 1960 they founded the *Journal of African History*, and two years later they published the innovative and widely praised *Short History*. It signaled the shift toward recognizing that Africa had a history of its own apart from that of European exploration and colonization. It refuted the notorious view taken by Hugh Trevor-Roper of Oxford: "There is only the history of the Europeans in Africa. The rest is largely darkness." The book, which draws on findings from archaeology and anthropology, is still widely read as the pioneering work on African history.

Ranger, T. O., *Revolt in Southern Rhodesia, 1896–97: A Study in African Resistance* (1967; Heinemann, 1978). In the 1960s and 1970s, as the history of Africa came to be written from the perspective of the colonized, Ranger shattered impressions of an overwhelming European conquest of helpless "natives." His study of the effective 1896–97 revolt against the British occupation of what became Southern Rhodesia marked a revolutionary turn toward an Africanized history of the colonial era. For an even earlier book that gave voice to the African side of African history, see George Shepperson and Thomas Price, *Independent African: John Chilembwe and the Origins, Setting, and Significance of the Nyasaland Native Rising, 1915* (1958).

Rodney, Walter, *How Europe Underdeveloped Africa* (1972; Black Classic, 2011). In advancing Marxist theories of underdevelopment, the Guyanese historian Rodney argued that Western powers had enriched themselves in Africa at the expense of the weak. He counters explanations that attribute underdevelopment to Africans' supposed innate inferiority. The sweep of his interpretation secured a popular audience, in part because he maintained that the United States took advantage of its victory in World War II to edge out European competitors and become the dominant, exploitative world power. The originality of *Underdeveloped Africa* lies less in the book itself than its influence. Rodney was a powerful orator and Pan-Africanist who played an important part in the anti-colonial movement. He was killed by a car bomb in 1980 at age thirty-eight.

Middle East

Amanat, Abbas, *Iran: A Modern History* (Yale, 2017). Covering five centuries in 1,000 pages, this book is not for the fainthearted. It is especially strong on cultural, literary, and intellectual history, and on the part played by diverse societies in the evolution of political and clerical authority. Central to the constitutional revolution that began in 1905 was the place of Shiism in Iranian political life, which developed against a background of dynastic changes, revolutions, civil wars, foreign occupation, and the discovery of oil. Would the clergy retain its control over sharia law, or would it yield to the advance of Western political ideas? Amanat balances the competing tensions within Persian Shiism with changes in Iran's political economy and cultural traditions through to the 1979 theocratic revolution of Ayatollah Khomeini.

Antonius, George, *The Arab Awakening: The Story of the Arab National Movement* (1939; Allegro, 2015). Antonius, who was of Lebanese-Egyptian descent, held a position in the British Palestine administration—yet he was reportedly refused membership in the Jerusalem Sports Club because of the "No Natives" policy. He deals with the modern renaissance of the Arabs, tracing the origins and development of the Arab national movement from its beginnings in the nineteenth century to the post–World War I era. This humane, fair-minded book has had lasting significance because it was the first to make Arab nationalism comprehensible to a European and American readership. He emphasizes in his conclusion: *"No room can be made in Palestine for a second nation except by dislodging or exterminating the nation in possession."*

Batatu, Hanna, *The Old Social Classes and the Revolutionary Movements of Iraq: A Study of Iraq's Old Landed and Commercial Classes and of Its Communists, Ba'thists, and Free Officers* (1978; Saqi, 2004). Batatu left Palestine in 1948, received his Ph.D. from Harvard, and then spent years doing intensive research in Iraq. Through a chance friendship with the prime minister, Abd Al-Karim Qasim, he was granted permission to study secret police files up to the time of the revolution of 1958. With a method based in political sociology, he wrote this 1,284-page book, which focuses on the Iraqi Communist Party in the critical years of the revolution and its aftermath. The chronological scope ranges from the 1920s to the 1970s. It is the indispensable work on Iraqi history.

Blunt, Wilfrid Scawen, *Secret History of the English Occupation of Egypt* (1907). Blunt was a Victorian radical opposed to British expansion, especially in Egypt, which was taken militarily in 1882. Believing in the cause of "Egypt for the Egyptians," he regarded himself as a Byronic hero. Prime Minister Gladstone initially agreed with him on Egypt. Blunt spent years in the Middle East writing poetry, maintaining with his wife a stud farm for Arabian horses, and living the life of a self-confessed hedonist. He later counted among his friends the arch-imperialist Winston Churchill, the anti-imperialist Roger Casement, St. John Philby, W. B. Yeats, and Ezra Pound. Among his famous lines is the observation "The white man's burden, Lord, is the burden of his cash."

Heikal, Mohamed Hassanein, *Cutting the Lion's Tale: Suez through Egyptian Eyes* (1986; Corgi, 1988). Heikal was a leading Egyptian journalist and a close friend of Nasser. His book on the Suez crisis is a full account of the Egyptian side. Earlier he had helped write Nasser's *Philosophy of the Revolution* and articulated the concept of a pan-Arab nation extending from the Atlantic to the Gulf. An outspoken champion of Nasser's ideas, he was one of the most persuasive supporters of the development of modern Egypt. Always seen smoking a large cigar, Heikal became a symbol of the era when Egyptians believed in their country's dignity and progress. Among his other books, especially important is *The Road to Ramadan* (1975), which explains the 1973 war with Israel from an Arab perspective.

Herzl, Theodore, *The Jewish State* (1896; Dover, 1989). Herzl was a Viennese journalist who laid the foundations for a national home for the Jews. He believed that Jews would never be accepted as a minority in any European country, drawing the conclusion that they had to create a separate state beyond Europe. He assumed that the state would be secular. He was a romantic in believing that the Arabs would willingly accept Jews. But Palestine was not the only place Herzl considered. He carried on extensive conversations about the possibility of Argentina, Cyprus, or Egypt. The British colonial secretary, Joseph Chamberlain, suggested Uganda. When Herzl died at age forty-four in 1904, Uganda was still being actively discussed. Nevertheless, Herzl's book is the cornerstone of the Zionist movement in Palestine.

Hourani, Albert, *A History of the Arab Peoples* (1991; Harvard, new ed., intro. Malise Ruthven, 2010). Hourani presents the history of the Arabs from the advent of Islam to the late twentieth century, from Morocco to the eastern Arabian Peninsula. This social, economic, and political history emphasizes Arabs' response to encroachment by the West, and the sense of Arab identity that gained momentum in the twentieth century. Independent Arab states were often characterized "by a weakness in the body politic," and violence has always been close to the surface. The book remains one of the most important in its field. Hourani's *Arabic Thought in the Liberal Age, 1798–1939* (1962) traces ideas and patterns of thought about Islam and politics, particularly in Egypt and Lebanon, in the formation of twentieth-century Arab nationalism.

Ibn Battutah, *The Travels of Ibn Battutah*, ed. Tim Mackintosh-Smith (Pan Macmillan, 2003). Battutah was a fourteenth-century Moroccan justifiably known as the greatest medieval Muslim traveler—the only one to visit the lands of every Muslim ruler. He left Tangier in 1325 at age twenty-one, returning some twenty years later after journeys that encompassed North Africa, East Africa, the Middle East, India and Ceylon, Southeast Asia, China, and Moorish Spain. His account, replete with political, social, and cultural observations, is on the whole reliable. Bernard Lewis and P. M. Holt's edited volume *Historians of the Middle East* (1962) recounts how the Arabist scholar H. A. R. Gibb devoted a great deal of his career to translating Ibn Battutah and making his work more widely known.

Ibn Khaldun, *Muqaddimah* (1377; Princeton, trans. Franz Rosenthal, intro. Bruce B. Lawrence, 2004). The *Muqaddimah* is a fourteenth-century work dealing with the philosophy of history, Islamic theology, and the natural sciences. Ibn Khaldun's knowledge embraced what would now be described as sociological principles applied to the state in relation to both religion and society. His encyclopedic work is indispensable for students and scholars of Islam, ancient history, and medieval history. The introduction by the historian of religion Bruce B. Lawrence is an invaluable guide to this seminal work. For an appraisal of Ibn Khaldun as an Arab intellectual and a "creature of his time" rather than a "modern man" (as he is often depicted), see Robert Irwin, *Ibn Khaldun: An Intellectual Biography* (2018).

Khalidi, Walid, *From Haven to Conquest: Readings in Zionism and the Palestine Problem until 1948* (1971; 3rd. ed., Institute for Palestine Studies, 2005). An essential reference work, this indispensable collection of documents presents the complexities of the clash between Zionism and

Palestinian nationalism in a clear and comprehensible style. It establishes diverse viewpoints and brings Khalidi's learning into focus in the celebrated introductory chapter. It reveals the depths of the passions that keep the Arab-Israeli conflict alive, above all in its detailed demographic and military statistics. Albert Hourani commented that Khalidi's introduction to the book "is the best description and explanation known to me of the way in which the indigenous inhabitants of the country were gradually and inexorably dispossessed."

Kyle, Keith, *Suez* (1991; republished as *Suez: Britain's End of Empire in the Middle East*, Tauris, 2011). The seminal work on the Suez crisis of 1956, which started with the Nasser's nationalization of the Suez Canal Company and led to the invasion of Egypt by Britain, France, and Israel. It ended with the United States forcing an ignominious withdrawal of British troops from the Canal Zone. Kyle was the first to draw on a wealth of documents proving the "collusion" of the British, French, and Israeli leaders. The Suez crisis eventually came to represent the end of Britain's status a world power and remains to the present a divisive and controversial subject in Britain. The book remains fundamental.

Nasser, Gamal Abdel, *Philosophy of the Revolution* (1955; Economica, intro. John S. Badeau, 1959). In an account of the Egyptian Revolution of 1952, Nasser looks to the future and appeals to Arabs throughout the region for unity based on their common history, religion, and culture. The success of the revolution would serve as the cornerstone of pan-Arab supremacy in the Middle East. Nasser emerges as a mastermind who overthrew the old regime and captured the imagination and loyalty of the Egyptian people. To those in Britain and the United States, however, he gradually was perceived as a threat to Western interests in the Middle East, especially oil. His *Philosophy* helps explain how he was able to speak freely about ways that British or American intelligence agencies might try to assassinate him.

Seale, Patrick, *The Struggle for Arab Independence* (Cambridge, 2017). This learned yet clearly written book thematically develops the shaping of the modern Middle East by violent turmoil in the decades after World War II. Especially valuable for its use of Arabic sources, it explains the abortive struggle for Arab unity through the lives of the Arab leaders most directly involved, particularly Ridd el-Soth, a pan-Arab statesman and the first prime minister of Lebanon. According to Seale: "Ridd's enemy throughout his life was western colonialism and especially French colonialism." For the post-war Middle East, this is an essential book, reflecting Seale's experience as a writer for the London *Observer*. Seale's *Philby: The Long Road to Moscow* (1973) is a treatment of the British spy more sympathetic than most other accounts.

Shlaim, Avi, *The Iron Wall: Israel and the Arab World* (2000; Norton, 2014). The "iron wall" is an idea seared into the Israeli psyche by Ze'ev Jabotinsky, who in 1923 proclaimed that the Jews had always to be prepared to defend an emergent Jewish state against all enemies. But it was a concept, not a political or geographic boundary or an actual wall. It was widely misunderstood. Shlaim argues that Jabotinsky believed that peaceful coexistence with the Arab states was possible. The turning point came in 1967 when Israel expanded into what became known as the occupied territories and blocked the development of a possible Palestinian state. For this critical juncture, see Wm. Roger Louis and Avi Shlaim, eds., *The 1967 Arab-Israeli War: Origins and Consequences* (2012).

China

Bickers, Robert, *Out of China: How the Chinese Ended the Era of Western Domination* (Penguin, 2017). From the mid-nineteenth century until the Communist Party came to power in 1949, China was invaded, looted, and humiliated by foreign powers, including Britain, Japan, and the United States. The symbolic moment occurred in May 1949, when the British Shanghai Club—renowned, perhaps erroneously, for having a sign on its door that said "No Dogs or Chinks"—was requisitioned and its liquor impounded. China continues to view the present and future through the lens of the past. In Bickers' own summation, "History matters in modern China and the past is unfinished business."

Fairbank, John King, *The United States and China* (1948; 4th ed., Harvard, 1983). This distillation of knowledge by the foremost American scholar of China stands virtually alone as an overall history of China and China's relations with the United States. It was read by Chinese as well as American officials in preparation for President Nixon's visit in 1972. In the late 1940s, Fairbank predicted the victory of Mao Tse-tung and was subsequently accused by Joseph McCarthy of being soft on communism. Ironically, in the 1960s he was regarded as a champion of American imperialism. Roderick MacFarquhar, in *The Origins of the Cultural Revolution*, vol. 3, *The Coming of the Cataclysm, 1961–1966* (1997), covers the story of Mao's rule from the devastating famine of the early 1960s to his unleashing of the Cultural Revolution.

Isaacs, Harold, *The Tragedy of the Chinese Revolution* (1938; Haymarket, 2010). Isaacs was an American Marxist journalist in China and later an anti-communist political scientist at the Massachusetts Institute of Technology. He dedicated his book to the "martyrs of the 1925–1927 revolution," the workers and peasants who, had they emerged victorious, might have prevented the corrupt regime of Chiang Kai-shek and later the oppressive communist government of Mao Tse-tung. Isaacs wrote about a typical British response to the revolution: "To have one's home turned upside down, to have to hastily lump a few belongings into a trunk or two and a suitcase and leave the rest behind to be looted or whatnot, is an unadulterated bother."

Peyrefitte, Alain, *The Immobile Empire* (1989; Vintage, trans. Jon Rothschild, 2013). In 1793, Lord Macartney arrived in Peking with a large delegation of musicians, scholars, and soldiers to establish friendly relations with China and open the country to British trade. He refused to perform the traditional kowtow before the Chinese emperor, bowing instead on one knee, as he would have before his own sovereign. The talks failed because of the British sense of superiority and the Chinese conviction that their society was perfect. In Peyrefitte's judgment, the complacent and bureaucratic nature of the Chinese regime rendered it "immobile," incapable of moving with the times. Peyrefitte earlier wrote *The Trouble with France* (1976), in which he puts forward a similar argument that something unique in the French character has blocked the country's progress.

Polo, Marco, *The Travels* (c. 1300; Penguin, trans. Nigel Cliff, 2016). Marco Polo, perhaps the most famous traveler of all time, began his voyages in 1271, when he was seventeen; they reached a climax in China. His book tells of the silks and spices as well as the beasts and bandits along the Silk Road, which connected Europe with Asia. His account brought about a revolution in perceptions about India, China, and Japan and expanded European knowledge of cartography—helping inspire Christopher Columbus and the voyages of exploration a century later. Above all, he describes the magnitude and wealth of China and the court of the Mongol emperor Kublai Khan, whose reputation achieved literary significance in Coleridge's poem of 1818 about the "stately pleasure-dome" built in Xanadu.

Schiffrin, Harold Z., *Sun Yat-sen and the Origins of the Chinese Revolution* (1968; University of California, 2010). Leading the movement to overthrow the final Chinese dynasty, Sun Yat-sen, after a life of constant struggle and frequent exile, became the first president of the emergent Chinese republic of 1911–12. Nationalists and communists both claimed him as a unifying figure in Chinese history. Chiang Kai-shek and Mao Tse-tung could agree on virtually nothing other than Sun's status as the father of modern China. In *The Japanese and Sun Yat-sen* (1954), Marius B. Jansen deals with a vital element of Sun's thought.

Snow, Edgar, *Red Star over China* (1937; Grove, intro. John K. Fairbank, 1994). Snow, an American journalist based in China, in 1938 traveled to the barren reaches of northwestern China to meet the leader of the insurgent communist movement, Mao Tse-tung. He was the first Western writer to provide information about Mao's background and his followers, known at the time as "Red Bandits." John King Fairbank, a Harvard professor of the history of China, judged the book to be reliable. It later became controversial, critics maintaining that Snow had been duped by Mao into believing that the Chinese communists were "agrarian reformers." The book remains indispensable as an account of Mao's early years, his vision of the past, and the birth of Chinese communism.

Spence, Jonathan, *The Search for Modern China* (1990; 3rd ed., Norton, 2012). Spence is the leading Western authority on China. His narrative ranges from the decline of the Ming dynasty in the sixteenth century to the Tiananmen Square massacre in 1989. The book explains, eloquently and concisely, Chinese history from a Chinese perspective—in the words of a critic, it is "refreshingly un-Eurocentred." Spence emphasizes social history, with a focus on peasants as well as intellectuals. The overall theme develops the quest for stability and the resilience of the Chinese people. Spence's *To Change China: Western Advisers in China* (1969) covers three centuries of efforts by businessmen, missionaries, soldiers, and diplomats to Westernize the Middle Kingdom. Spence provides a short biography of the shaper of modern China in *Mao Zedong* (1999).

Wright, Mary Clabaugh, *The Last Stand of Chinese Conservatism* (1957). Wright's theme is the attempt to reestablish centralized control in China during the mid-nineteenth-century decline of the Qing dynasty. She explains the nature of Chinese conservatism as the attempt to sustain a stable government in the face of rebellion, to reform the military, and to deal with foreign powers. She sums up the essence of the attempt as "radical innovation within the old order," led by intelligent and able leaders. Yet they were unable to hold their own against their Western counterparts. She lays to rest the stereotypes of Chinese stupidity, inertia, and corruption before the onslaught of the dynamic West, thus laying one of the foundations for the study of modern Chinese history.

India

Bayly, C. A., *Empire and Information: Intelligence Gathering and Social Communication in India, 1780–1870* (1996; Cambridge, 2000). The title is misleading. Bayly is concerned with "information" only in the sense of accurate British estimates of Indian politics, social movements, and intellectual currents. Despite their military superiority, the British were at a disadvantage in assessing local customs and beliefs because they relied on Indians who were attached to the Raj or, in a broader sense, belonged to the emerging class of Anglophone Indian intellectuals. The lack of reliable information and the inability to gauge local reactions help explain Britain's failure to anticipate the rebellion of 1857 and the rise of early Indian nationalism. The book makes a fundamental contribution to the art of gathering of intelligence.

Copland, Ian, *The Princes of India in the Endgame of Empire, 1917–1947* (1997; Cambridge, 2002). Before the Partition of India in 1947, 565 princely states accounted for nearly half the subcontinent's territory and one-third of its population. The state of Hyderabad was larger than Britain. The British did not conquer or annex the princely states but ruled them indirectly through treaties of alliance that granted them autonomy to varying degrees. The larger states aspired to independence. Copland explains why they failed and provides the background to their political demise and rapid absorption into India and Pakistan—with the exception of Hyderabad, which maintained its independence until a year later, when India took police action to annex it.

Guha, Ramachandra, *India after Gandhi: The History of the World's Largest Democracy* (2007; HarperCollins, 2008). Guha helps make India's history comprehensible by giving prominence to the lives and careers of prime ministers, especially Jawaharlal Nehru and Indira Gandhi. In a larger context, he pursues themes of cultural heterogeneity and poverty. Using the assassination of Mohandas Gandhi in 1948 as one of his points of departure, he relates events as they were seen at the time, often posing questions of national breakup or autocratic rule. Despite divisions of caste, class, language, and religion, India emerges as a united and democratic country. In this readable book, the details as well as the themes make a memorable impression.

Hardy, Peter, *The Muslims of British India* (1972; Cambridge, 2007). The reaction of Muslims in India to British rule was far from uniform. Social class, economic standing, and regional differences led to varied responses, including collaboration. Muslim aristocrats used British influence to consolidate their positions, even emphasizing to the British the backwardness of Muslims in general and the need for an encompassing authority. From the British perspective, the strategy was not to "divide and rule" but to "divide and balance" competing political forces that were gaining their own identities. Partition in 1947 did not merely divide Hindus from Muslims, but also Muslims from Muslims. For background and context, a useful companion is Francis Robinson, *Islam and Muslim History in South Asia* (2004).

Hibbert, Christopher, *The Great Mutiny: India, 1857* (1978; Penguin, 2000). In 1857, the Indian army rebelled, shooting British officers and massacring women and children. The British retaliated on an even greater scale, and the death and devastation shocked the public in England as much as the mutiny did. Hibbert's lurid account undermines later descriptions of the uprising as the first Indian war of independence, as well as the British view that the horrific suppression was necessary to reestablish British authority. Hibbert sums it up: "Seething racism on both sides," unrestrained ferocity by the rebels, stupidity and arrogance as well as vengeful brutality on the part of the British. According to *The Economist*, the book is "by far the best single-volume description of the mutiny yet written."

Marston, Daniel, *The Indian Army and the End of the Raj* (2014; Cambridge, 2016). At the end of World War II, the Indian Army had 2.5 million men. Marston argues that it remained a bulwark against anarchy and the impending breakdown of the civil service. One reason for its stability was the rapid promotion of Indian officers when British officers retired or were demobilized. At a peacetime strength of 450,000, it maintained esprit de corps and its effectiveness while facing the collapse of the civilian police and the spread of internal domestic violence. Given a three-month period in which to divide itself into two distinct units, Indian and Pakistani, the Indian Army to the end maintained a discipline that transcended communal differences.

Nehru, Jawaharlal, *The Discovery of India* (1946; Penguin, 2004). Nehru wrote his account of India's history while in prison during World War II. He argues that India is an historic nation with diverse philosophical traditions and an ancient heritage. Composed at the height of the struggle for independence, the book resonates with nationalist aspirations. The theme is the common culture that led to an Indian identity. Altogether Nehru spent some nine years in prison, immersing himself in poetry and playing badminton as well as drafting *The Discovery of India*. The published volume attracted worldwide attention. Albert Einstein wrote to him: "Your marvelous book . . . gives an understanding of the glorious intellectual and spiritual tradition of . . . India."

Thapar, Romila, *A History of India*, vol. 1 (1966; Penguin, 1990). Beyond doubt, Thapar is India's preeminent historian, known throughout the world for her knowledge, craftsmanship, and work in ancient history. In India, she has been at the center of controversy because of her refusal to endorse the Hindu nationalist version of Indian history, holding instead that the origins of Hinduism and the formation of the caste system should be interpreted as an evolving interplay between social and religious forces from the early history of India to the arrival of Europeans in the sixteenth century. For the modern era, see Bipan Chandra, *History of Modern India* (2009).

Japan

Bix, Herbert P., *Hirohito and the Making of Modern Japan* (2000; HarperCollins, 2001). In Japan, the emperor stood at the apex of the nation's political, social, and religious hierarchy, revered for his divine status. Bix relates how Hirohito gradually aligned himself with the ultranationalist movement while preserving his own power and sustaining his image as a reluctant, passive monarch. In fact, he played a central part in wartime operations before and after the attack on Pearl Harbor. After 1945, with the decisive help of General Douglas MacArthur, he whitewashed his wartime role and maintained his stature by helping convert Japan into a peaceful nation.

Dower, John W., *Embracing Defeat: Japan in the Wake of World War II* (1999; Norton, 2000). Dower's perspective maintains a balance between the American occupation, overseen by Douglas MacArthur, and the experience of the Japanese people. MacArthur arrogantly presided over a neocolonial military dictatorship; the Japanese rationalized their defeat in the face of widespread devastation and despair at the huge number of war dead. Yet they resiliently reshaped their identity and embraced democracy. The new constitution guaranteed women's electoral, labor, and social rights that remained the envy of American women half a century later. Dower provides a full account of the occupation, but above all it is his depiction of post-war cultural and social change in Japan that distinguishes the book.

Hall, John, *Government and Local Power in Japan, 500–1700* (1966; Princeton, 2008). Born in Kyoto in 1916, Hall was the son of Congregational missionaries. Before World War II, he taught at Kyoto's Doshisha University. He became one of the most prominent, productive, and imaginative historians of Japanese religion and culture, explaining how Japan's fundamentally "Eastern" culture gave rise to a modern world power. Becoming an expert on the period of Japanese history between 1600 and 1688, he was the first to study the voluminous records of one of the ruling families of the era. What he tried to do, according to one of his disciples, was to "de-exoticize the study of Japan." *Government and Local Power* introduced Western readers to twelve centuries of Japanese history.

Hersey, John, *Hiroshima* (1946; Penguin, 2002). *Hiroshima* relates the experiences of six survivors of the atomic blast on August 6, 1945: a German Jesuit priest, a widowed seamstress, two doctors, a minister, and a young woman who worked in a factory. The story follows them for a year as they attempt to cope with the aftermath. Hersey's account was first published in the *New Yorker*, occupying virtually all of a single issue. Albert Einstein ordered 1,000 copies to distribute personally. When published as a book a few months later, it was generally judged to be one of the finest pieces of American journalism of its time. As a contemporary account, it remains unrivaled.

Jansen, Marius, *The Making of Modern Japan* (2000; Harvard, 2002). Jansen, a leading American scholar of Japan, wrote fluently in Japanese and published some twenty books placing in broad context the history of Japan from the early seventeenth century. He was the first non-Japanese recipient of the Distinguished Cultural Merit award from the Japanese government. While emphasizing social and cultural history, *The Making of Modern Japan* gives a clear account of industrial and military leaders, not least the emperor, who responded to successive waves of outside influence in a way that strengthened a sense of what is unique to the Japanese nation. For the post-1945 era, Jansen explains the impact of the reforms imposed by Douglas MacArthur and the influence of the American occupation on writers, artists, and historians.

Nish, Ian, *Alliance in Decline: A Study in Anglo-Japanese Relations, 1908–23* (1972). In 1902, Japan and Britain forged an alliance that lasted nearly two decades. It proved to be indispensable to British survival during World War I by allowing the Royal Navy to concentrate on home waters and the Mediterranean while Japan patrolled the Pacific and Indian Oceans. Yet the British abandoned Japan in favor of the United States in the aftermath of the war, leaving a spirit of resentment that contributed, perhaps substantially, to the origins of World War II in the Pacific. Malcolm D. Kennedy, *The Estrangement of Great Britain and Japan, 1917–35* (1969), upholds the view that termination of the alliance had fatal consequences.

Reischauer, Edwin O., *Japan: The Story of A Nation* (4th ed., McGraw-Hill, 1989). Reischauer was born in Tokyo, the son of American missionaries. He wrote about Japan for the general reader as well as fellow scholars. During World War II, he advocated the retention of the Japanese emperor as the head of a post-war regime that would serve U.S. interests in Asia. In *The Story of a Nation*, he describes village life and the role of the common people as well as the ruling classes. He argues that Japanese society is dynamic, but its foundations, by contrast, change only slowly. One critic comments that the book is "mercifully free from academic mumbo-jumbo." Reischauer's autobiography is *My Life Between Japan and America* (1986).

Sansom, G. B., *The Western World and Japan: A Study in the Interaction of European and Asiatic Cultures* (1950). Sir George Sansom was the foremost Western historian of Japan, renowned for his three-volume work on Japan's history from 1334 to 1867, written mainly while he was in the British consular service in Tokyo (1904–40). He was the first foreign writer thoroughly to immerse himself in the use of Japanese primary sources. *The Western World and Japan*, decades in the making, emphasizes the impact of Western culture on the shape and character of traditional Japanese institutions. It remains a clear and readable account of how Western religious, legal, scientific, and military influences brought clashes and conflict, renewing Japanese society without changing its essence.

Pakistan
Hamid, Shahid, *Disastrous Twilight: A Personal Record of the Partition of India* (1986; Leo Cooper, foreword by Philip Ziegler, 1993). Hamid gives an account of the events leading up to the Partition of India in 1947 from a Pakistani vantage point. The book is all the more valuable because it focuses also on Field Marshal Claude Auchinleck, commander in chief of the Indian Army. Hamid in 1947 was an Indian Army officer and Auchinleck's assistant, later a general in the Pakistani army. He believed that the Indian Army—and, if necessary, British troops—could have been used to prevent the massacres in the Punjab. Hamid's painstaking account of Partition differs radically from the version usually accepted in Britain and the United States.

Jalal, Ayesha, *The Sole Spokesman: Jinnah, the Muslim League, and the Demand for Pakistan* (1985; Cambridge, 1994). The campaign for the creation of Pakistan in the early 1940s led to the Partition of India in 1947. The leader of the independence movement was Muhammed Ali Jinnah, a lawyer who, according to the dominant belief in Pakistan, underwent a religious metamorphosis to become a strict Muslim and Pakistan's iconic founder. Jalal argues that Jinnah did not want a separate state but instead equal rights and a "shield of protection" for Muslims in India. In Jalal's interpretation, the push for a Muslim state was a gigantic miscalculation. The argument that Jinnah did not in fact want an independent Pakistan challenges the premise that religion is the basis for the country's existence.

Southeast Asia

Bayly, Christopher, and Tim Harper, *Forgotten Armies: Britain's Asian Empire and the War with Japan* (2005; Penguin, 2005). After the outbreak of World War II, Japanese forces conquered most of Southeast Asia, including Singapore, which represented the greatest military loss in the history of the British Empire. Bayly and Harper demonstrate how Indian, Burmese, and Malayan nationalist movements were galvanized in response to the Japanese invasion. They emphasize the cultural and economic dimensions of the war as well as medical and linguistic developments. Above all, they make clear the reasons for the end of the myth of European superiority. The same authors' *Forgotten Wars: Freedom and Revolution in Southeast Asia* (2007) tells the story of post–World War II nationalist movements, communist insurrections, and the British response to both.

Benda, Harry Jindrich, *The Crescent and the Rising Sun: Indonesian Islam under the Japanese Occupation, 1942–1945* (1958; Foris, 1985). Benda was a Czech who, after fleeing the Nazis, wound up in a Dutch trading firm and spent much of World War II in a Japanese concentration camp in Indonesia. He saw firsthand the Japanese support for anti-Western Islamic leaders and the large part played by Islam in Indonesian political life. He acquired an historical understanding of the way the anti-Japanese movement crystallized around local Muslim leadership. Islam became a symbol of deliverance from alien rule. By the end of the war, the "rising tide of Indonesian Islam" was challenging the Western-educated political elite and becoming a significant influence on the post-war Indonesian army.

Fall, Bernard B., *Hell in a Very Small Place: The Siege of Dien Bien Phu* (1966; Da Capo, 2002). At the 1954 battle of Dien Bien Phu in Indochina, the Viet Minh guerrilla force defeated the technologically superior French Army, a catastrophe that acquired symbolic importance. Bernard Fall fought in the French resistance and then in the French Army in World War II. He subsequently spent much of his career in Indochina, predicting that the United States would fail there because of its lack of understanding of Vietnamese society. *Hell in a Very Small Place* was used at both West Point and the U.S. Naval War College as required reading. An account of Fall's life is Dorothy Fall, *Bernard Fall: Memories of a Soldier-Scholar* (2006).

Friend, Theodore, *Indonesian Destinies* (2003; Harvard, 2005). For 300 years, the Dutch ruled the vast area of the Indonesian archipelago, which encompasses the largest Muslim population in the world. Friend's work traces its history mainly from the World War II era, when the nationalist leader Sukarno collaborated with Japan against the Dutch. Friend's account is at once historical, anthropological, and sociological, with a focus on individuals. Attentive to detail at all levels of Indonesian society, he describes Indonesia moving from democracy toward an authoritarian regime that oversaw decades of political and economic instability, social unrest, corruption, and terrorism. Yet Friend treats the country's prospects sympathetically and optimistically.

Furnivall, J. S., *Colonial Policy and Practice: A Comparative Study of Burma and Netherlands India* (1948; NYU, 1956). J. S. Furnivall of the India Civil Service worked for twenty years in Burma. In 1920 he resigned to attempt to reform the "Leviathan" of British colonial rule. In *Colonial Policy and Practice*, he developed the seminal idea of a "plural society," in which people "mix but do not mingle," that is, a racially divided society driven by economic motives but capable of shared unity and development. In Burma, he worked toward a nationalist state that would reconcile its ethnic components while retaining its Buddhist identity. A fundamental work for Southeast Asia, and unique for the history of Burma. For another pioneering work on nationalism and colonial independence, see Rupert Emerson, *From Empire to Nation: The Rise to Self-Assertion of Asian and African Peoples* (1960).

Harper, T. N., *The End of Empire and the Making of Malaya* (1999; Cambridge, 2010). After the defeat of Japan in 1945, the internal struggles in Malaya involved both radical ethnic nationalism and communist insurgency. Harper emphasizes social change and the way in which the British handled rebellion. He deals above all with the demographic balance between the Chinese and the indigenous Malays. After a long and ultimately successful anti-insurgency campaign, the British found a solution that united the diverse Malayan communities in a federation. Independence in 1957 allowed the British to remain on good relations with the new state of Malaya (which in 1963 formed the basis of the new country of Malaysia), the world's largest producer of tin and rubber.

Kahin, George McTurnan, *Nationalism and Revolution in Indonesia* (1952; Cornell, 2003). Kahin founded the highly respected Modern Indonesia Program at Cornell University. His 1952 book remains the point of departure for comprehending the rise and development of Indonesian nationalism and the crisis of 1945 to 1949, when the United States brought about recognition of the new nation by threatening to deny economic assistance to the Netherlands, the archipelago's former colonial master. Kahin later became a strong critic of the war in Vietnam, calling it "the wrong war in the wrong place at the wrong time."

Slim, William, *Defeat into Victory: Battling Japan in Burma and India, 1942–1945* (1956; Folio Society, intro. Max Hastings, 2017). Of the several editions of Slim's book, this one is preferable because of the forty pages of black-and-white photographs and an incisive introduction by the military historian Max Hastings. Slim, an undemonstrative, imperturbable commander with a self-depreciating sense of humor, led the "Forgotten Army" in the reconquest of Burma in 1945. Knowing that Japanese soldiers would fight to the death, Slim outflanked them, leaving stranded units without supplies or support. The reoccupation in 1945 was no less significant for the uprising of the Burmese people against the Japanese oppressors. *Defeat into Victory* has long held the reputation as one of the best-written memoirs of World War II.

History
Ancient World

Dodds, E. R., *The Greeks and the Irrational* (1951; California, 2004). Dodds was an Irish scholar whose friends included Aldous Huxley and T. S. Eliot. He studied ancient history and philosophy at Oxford, but in 1916 he was asked to leave the university because of his support for the Easter Rising and Irish Republicanism. Nonetheless, a decade later he was appointed Regius Professor of Greek at Oxford, over the obvious choice of many, Maurice Bowra. In *The Greeks and the Irrational*, he combines classical knowledge with psychology and anthropology to challenge the view of Greek culture up to the time of Plato as a triumph of rationalism. Dodds argues, to the contrary, that the Greeks could be as irrational as the British in the twentieth century.

Gibbon, Edward, *The History of the Decline and Fall of the Roman Empire* (1776–88; Penguin Classics, abridged ed., 2001). Gibbon's thesis is that the Roman Empire failed to defend itself against the depredations of barbarian mercenaries, Roman citizens being unwilling to sustain the rigors of military life. Political and military assassinations led to unintended consequences as well as instability. Christianity, particularly its pacifism and otherworldliness, played a secondary role. Gibbon was recognized for unmatched erudition, use of primary sources, and his ability to write with verve and wit. A magisterial, monumental explication of Gibbon and the writing of his history can be found in J. G. A. Pocock, *Barbarism and Religion* (6 vols., 1999–2015), especially volume 1.

Herodotus, *The History* (c. 440 BC; Chicago, trans. David Grene, 1988). An inquiry into the antecedents of the Greco-Persian Wars. This founding work of history begins with the events precipitating the Trojan War, includes a detailed description of the building of the Great Pyramid, and vividly recounts the pivotal battles between Persia and Greece at Marathon, Thermopylae, and Salamis. Much of the research came from the author's extensive travels, which took him from Babylon to the Black Sea to the upper reaches of the Nile. Unusually for a Greek of the time, Herodotus is open-minded about barbarians (non-Greeks). He avoids giving a tragic cast to events, though still allowing for the gods' interference in human affairs. His curiosity is boundless, his style graceful, and his narrative engrossing.

Livy, *The Early History of Rome* (Penguin, trans. Aubrey de Sélincourt, 1971). A great work of literature as well as a history, Livy's book is one of the principal sources for the stories of Aeneas, Romulus and Remus (the twin founders of Rome, reared by a she-wolf), the rape of Lucretia, and other memorable tales. Of the 142 books that made up his account, around 35 survive. Numerous later historians borrowed from Livy. The ordering of his narrative suggests the standard division of Roman history into monarchy, republic, and empire.

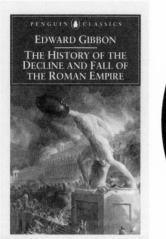

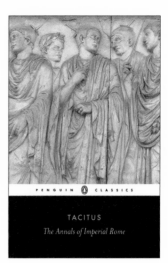

Mommsen, Theodor, *The History of Rome*, 4 vols. (1854–56, 1886; abridged ed., Dover, trans. and ed. Dero A. Saunders and John H. Collins, 2013). Chronicling the Roman Republic from its founding to the time of Julius Caesar, Mommsen's history develops the theme that older institutions grew incapable of effectively meeting new and challenging circumstances and of performing the required civic and military tasks of government, which became decayed and corrupt. The wealthy grew extravagant while the citizenry suffered misrule and financial plundering. Arnold Toynbee classified the work "among the masterpieces of Western historical literature."

Syme, Ronald, *The Roman Revolution* (1939; Oxford, rev. ed., 2002). The fall of the Roman Republic and the rise of the empire are often treated as an unfortunate development, the end of whatever influence the common people had on government, and a corresponding decline of freedom. Syme develops the theme that Augustus, the first emperor, saved Rome both from a Senate unable to govern the republic's far-flung territories and from the chaos following the assassination of Julius Caesar. By concentrating power in a faction made up of his family and favorites, he could move quickly on all fronts—military, financial, and political. Syme's appreciation of Augustus's achievements should not be taken as admiration for the man, whom he referred to as a "chill and mature terrorist."

Tacitus, *The Annals of Imperial Rome* (c. AD 116; Penguin, trans. and intro. Michael Grant, 1956). The Roman senator Tacitus is regarded as one of the great classical historians because of his accuracy, compact prose, and insight into the psychology of the Roman emperors. The *Annals*, his last work, recounts the events of 14–68, covering the reigns of Tiberius, Caligula, Claudius, and Nero. It details the wars, scandals, conspiracies, poisonings, and murders that were part of Roman politics and policy. He is fair-minded, willing to praise and criticize yet hesitant to pronounce conclusive judgment. Pessimistic about Rome's future, he believes the empire has squandered its cultural inheritance. *My First Eighty Years* (1994), the autobiography of the translator, Michael Grant, is a compelling account of life as an independent scholar.

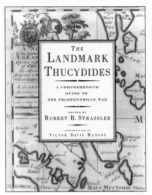

Thucydides, *History of the Peloponnesian War* (5th century B.C.; Simon & Shuster, *The Landmark Thucydides*, trans. Richard Crawley, ed. Robert B. Strassler, 1996). In this work, intended by its author to be a "possession for all time," Thucydides recounts the war between Athens and Sparta, 431–404 B.C., in which he fought. Considered essential reading for generals and statesmen from antiquity to the present, it is also a deep meditation on human nature and the forces that the author saw as driving political life, including self-interest, honor, piety, and the concern for justice. Thomas Hobbes considered the work so important that he translated it into English. Especially recommended are book 1 and the first part of book 2.

History
Miscellaneous

Antarctica and the Arctic

Peary, Robert, *The North Pole* (1910). Peary was a U.S. Navy officer who mastered the Inuits' technique of building igloos and traveling by dog sled. In 1909 he traversed some 400 miles of the Arctic, including stretches of broken and drifting ice. When he finally reached his destination, he exclaimed, "The Pole at Last." But he was challenged by a former colleague, Frederick Cook, who claimed to have reached the North Pole in 1908. There followed bitter controversy. Peary's calculations were not rigorously scientific, and later investigations discredited many of his claims. Yet no one at the time or later matched his success in inspiring American exploration in the Arctic. Frederick A. Cook, *My Attainment of the Pole* (1911), gives the other side of the dispute.

Solomon, Susan, *The Coldest March: Scott's Fatal Antarctic Expedition* (Yale, 2003), and Caroline Alexander, *The Endurance: Shackleton's Legendary Antarctic Expedition* (Bloomsbury, 1999). Robert Falcon Scott's first expedition (1901–4) to Antarctica yielded invaluable scientific information and advanced polar travel by means of mechanized sledges. His second voyage coincided with that of the Norwegian Roald Amundsen, who won the race to be the first to reach the South Pole; Scott and his crew perished in a blizzard. Shackleton acquired fame with his 1907–9 expedition, during which his team came with 100 miles of the South Pole and scaled Mount Erebus, the southernmost active volcano on Earth. A public tribute in England claimed that his exploits had disproved "the supposed degeneration of the British race." One historian of polar exploration noted in 1922: "For a joint scientific and geographical piece of organisation, give me Scott . . . If I am in the devil of a hole and want to get out of it, give me Shackleton every time."

Australia, New Zealand, Oceania

Clark, Manning, *A History of Australia* (1971; abridged ed., Melbourne, 1993). The son of an Anglo-Catholic priest of working-class origins and a pious middle-class Protestant, Clark proclaimed that his family portrayed the religion and class divisions of Australia writ large. His writing was enriched by his study at Oxford under Christopher Hill and A. J. P. Taylor. His later travels in Southeast Asia, Ireland, and the Soviet Union gave his work a broad perspective. His six-volume history (1962–87) describes Australia as a unique place for the transplanting of European civilization, and the consequences of settlement. His rambling and idiosyncratic yet coherent and honest historical method made him a national figure. The historian's peripatetic life is told in Brian Matthews, *Manning Clark: A Life* (2008).

Hancock, W. Keith, *Australia* (1930). Hancock's history of Australia develops the theme of mastering a continent, framing a polity, and forging an identity, but scarcely mentions the Aborigines (to his later chagrin). Its interpretation was enduring. He believed that Australian nationalism had to be respected as much as British patriotism. He reconciled the two vantage points by arguing that "it is not impossible for Australians . . . to be in love with two soils." His ideas of the 1930s found later expression in *Argument of Empire* (1943), published in part to explain to Americans that the British Empire represented an extensive system of freedom, as demonstrated by the national and independent status of the British Dominions.

Hughes, Robert, *The Fatal Shore: The Epic of Australia's Founding* (1986; Vintage, 1988). The brutal settlement of British convicts in the penal colony of Australia is captured by Hughes with compassion, exacting detail, and gripping prose. He deals head-on, too, with the unmatched disaster of colonization for the aboriginal peoples. For American readers, the fate of the aborigines—"savages"—will instantly recall the similar destiny of many Indian tribes. A fictionalized account of life in an Australian penal colony, where the horrors included flogging, rape, murder, and cannibalism, can be found in Marcus Clarke, *For the Term of His Natural Life* (1874). The author was an expatriate Englishman who became an Australian journalist. His newspaper assignments allowed him to write on the country's infamous prisons.

Reeves, William Pember, *The Long White Cloud: Ao-tea-roa* (1899; Merchant, 2002). *Ao-tea-roa*, the Maori name for New Zealand, means "long white cloud." Reeves was a late nineteenth-century politician, poet, and historian who worked for social reform in New Zealand, later becoming director of the London School of Economics. Factually reliable and sympathetic in its portrayal of the Maori, *Long White Cloud* was unquestionably the best book on New Zealand history for over half a century. It conveys the sense of New Zealand as a land of beauty—virtually an earthly paradise, which aroused skepticism on the part of some of reviewers. Reeves's poems such as "A Colonist in His Garden" brought him acclaim as one of the best Kiwi poets of his time.

Sinclair, Keith, *The Origins of the Maori Wars* (1957; 2nd ed., Auckland University Press, 1961). Sinclair's book was the first original interpretation of the battles in New Zealand from 1845 to 1872 between British colonists and the indigenous Maori. He argues that the conflicts were in fact wars of rebellion and conquest; 18,000 British troops finally defeated the Maori in

1860–61. He concludes that the war proved to be the prelude to the growth of a new nation that embraces two races. In *The Victorian Interpretation of Racial Conflict: The Maori, the British, and the New Zealand Wars* (1998), James Belich interprets effective Maori resistance as an innovative military system.

Canada

Bothwell, Robert, *The Penguin History of Canada* (2006; Penguin, 2007). Probably the best concise history of Canada. Bothwell emphasizes that Canada is a country with a huge North but with most of its population concentrated in the South, near the U.S. border. He deals with both physical and social problems, not least the country's underpopulation in relation to its size and resources. One of the prominent themes is how Canada has managed to avoid the kind of ethnic tensions endemic in the United States. Bothwell is good on quirky details, for example, that Canada did not acquire its own flag until 1965. Two of his other books are also worth pursuing: *Canada and the United States* (2nd ed., 1992), and *Canada and Quebec* (rev. ed., 1998).

Brebner, J. B., *North Atlantic Triangle: The Interplay of Canada, the United States, and Great Britain* (1945; McClelland & Stewart, 1966). The North Atlantic triangle is the traditional Canadian concept of the United States and Britain's relation to Canada's security and even survival. With a centuries-long historical sweep, Brebner argues that although the triangle was virtually invisible to the United States and Britain, by the mid-twentieth century it had become vital to Canada, which nonetheless resented being excluded from the inner circle of wartime decision making. J. B. Granatstein, *Canada's War: The Politics of the Mackenzie King Government, 1939–1945* (1975), is a key work on Canada in the World War II era.

Granatstein, J. L., *How Britain's Economic, Political, and Military Weakness Forced Canada into the Arms of the United States* (2nd ed., Toronto, 1989). In this concise work, Granatstein sets out to destroy the myth that Canadian politicians sold out to the United States. On the contrary: Canadian statesmen turned to the American government only after attempts to strengthen ties with the British had failed. Britain was too weak to guarantee Canada's security. British decline created a dynamic of "steady slippage to the South," moving Canada from one empire's orbit into another's. The critical point came with Britain's entry into the European Economic Community—to Canadians, a symbol of British abandonment. Granatstein's other books include a major work, *The Generals: The Canadian Army's Senior Commanders in the Second World War* (2005).

Martin, Ged, *The Durham Report and British Policy* (1972; Cambridge, 2008). In 1838, Lord Durham made the famous assessment that Canada consisted of "two nations warring within the bosom of a single state" and recommended that French and British Canada be united. Martin explains how the Durham Report marked the beginning of the British tradition of colonial self-rule, leading to the present Commonwealth of Nations: over fifty independent, self-governing countries, most of them former British colonies. Martin's *Britain and the Origins of Canadian Confederation, 1837–67* (1995) deals with the formation of the Dominion of Canada in 1867.

Winks, Robin, *The Blacks in Canada: A History* (1971; McGill-Queen's, 2000). Winks tells the story of Canada by relating the social history of black immigration and settlement. Blacks came as slaves in the early seventeenth century, as the property of Loyalists fleeing the American Revolution, as fugitives from slavery in the United States, as Maroons (involuntary exiles from Jamaica), and as immigrants from the Caribbean in the mid-twentieth century. Their experience was far from happy. They suffered under oppressive and discriminatory practices similar to those in the United States, and even the Ku Klux Klan had Canadian followers. In relation to the total Canadian population, their number is small but well represented in the Prairie Provinces, on the West Coast, and in Francophone Canada.

Mexico, Latin America, South America, the Caribbean

Bethell, Leslie, *A Cultural History of Latin America: Literature, Music, and the Visual Arts in the 19th and 20th Centuries* (1998; Cambridge, 2005). Bethell, an expert in Brazilian political, social, and cultural history, is the general editor of the twelve-volume *Cambridge History of Latin America*. The ten chapters in this book, drawn from three volumes in the series, explore specialized topics such as Latin American regional fiction, twentieth-century poetry, and indigenous culture as well as provide general overviews of music, architecture, film, and art. The volume is an authoritative survey, free from jargon, and its unifying treatment of central aspects of culture will benefit general readers as well as specialists.

Brown, Jonathan, *Cuba's Revolutionary World* (Harvard, 2017). After Fidel Castro seized power in early 1959, the Cuban Revolution seemed to have the potential to end dictatorships throughout Latin America. Its initial impact was compared with that of the French Revolution. Castro consolidated his revolutionary regime while embracing the Soviet Union as an ally. He attempted to export socialist revolution to the rest of Latin America through armed insurrection, though it often had the opposite of the intended effect. Making use of declassified CIA documents, Brown demonstrates in this rounded account how Castro paradoxically helped create regional counterrevolutions. One of the virtues of the book is that he allows Latin Americans to relate their own experiences, including the Cubans who fled to Miami and found support from the CIA.

Crow, John A., *The Epic of Latin America* (1946; 4th ed., California, 1992). Despite its age, this copious history of Latin America remains a powerful narrative. It is one of the few books that allow a reader to comprehend easily the history of Mexico, Central America, the Spanish Caribbean, and South America. Although its analysis of Latin American politics and economic development is no longer current, it presents a comprehensive account of the region's social and cultural history, including literature, art, and music, which the author experienced in decades of travel while teaching at UCLA. Present-day readers will forgive phrases such as the "stubborn individualism" of the Spanish "viceroys." It is a history that transcends the time in which it was written.

Freyre, Gilberto, *Brazil: An Interpretation* (1945; Freyre Press, 2008). Freyre was a Brazilian sociologist, anthropologist, and historian whose work defines and explains the historical development of Brazil. Despite expressing some stereotyped ideas, his writing came to offer a sophisticated explanation of Brazil's "racial democracy," moving from his previous, idealized "hymn to miscegenation" to a more critical estimate of Brazil's ongoing racial problems and a candid view of the racism expressed by colonizers and the Catholic Church. In Freyre's optimistic view of Brazil's history, sexuality, joyous and intense, is a pervading theme, along with discussions of food, clothing, religious rituals, and dance. One historian of Brazil concluded: "If you read Freyre, you will be challenged, exasperated, inspired, overwhelmed . . . But never bored."

Galeano, Eduardo, *Open Veins of Latin America: Five Centuries of the Pillage of a Continent* (1971; Monthly Review, trans. Cedric Belfrage, intro. Isabel Allende, 1997). A Uruguayan writer and poet, Galeano thematically relates the political economy of Latin America from the time of European settlement to the era of exploitation and political domination by the United States, in a way that captures the emotional memory of colonization. The book has been acclaimed for its intellectual honesty in detailing the suffering of ordinary people as foreign countries and companies extracted the region's mineral and agricultural bounty. The title refers to the veins of gold, silver, petroleum, iron, copper, and aluminum that run the length of the continent and for centuries provided immense wealth to those from elsewhere.

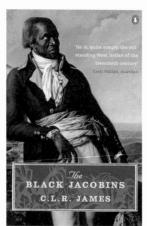

James, C. L. R., *The Black Jacobins: Toussaint L'Ouverture and the San Domingo Revolution* (1938; Vintage, 1989). Telling the story of the massive slave revolt in 1791–1804 in Saint-Domingue, as Haiti used to be called, C. L. R. James portrays Toussaint-L'Ouverture as a heroic though fatally flawed champion of independence who challenged Napoleon and inspired twentieth-century anticolonial revolutionaries. James intended *Black Jacobins* to stimulate "the coming emancipation of Africa." A Marxist from Trinidad, the prolific James wrote *The Case for West Indian Self-Government* (1933), published by Leonard and Virginia Woolf's Hogarth Press, and is famous above all for his book on cricket, *Beyond a Boundary* (1963).

Pares, Richard, *War and Trade in the West Indies, 1739–1763* (1936; Oxford, 1963). Pares deals with the balance of power in the Caribbean, first between the Spanish and the British—notably, during the War of Jenkins' Ear—and then between Britain and France, particularly during the Seven Years' War. In addition to trade policy, he analyzes plantation management and sugar markets. Pares was also editor of the *English Historical Review*, 1939–58. Toward the end of his life, he was paralyzed below the neck, but with a pole strapped to his head, bringing to mind a unicorn, he could turn the pages of *EHR* proofs. Isaiah Berlin commented: "He was the best and most admirable man I have ever known."

Paz, Octavio, *The Labyrinth of Solitude, and Other Writings* (1950; Grove, 1985). A seminal set of essays on Mexican culture and identity by a winner of the Nobel Prize in Literature. Paz takes the concept of solitude as central to an understanding of Mexico, underlying attitudes toward death, the prominence of fiestas, and the cleaving of Spanish and Native heritage. He concludes that Mexican identity is lost between indigenous Indian culture and Spanish culture, the two negating each other and leaving Mexicans behind "masks of solitude." Paz's *Collected Poems, 1957–1987* (1987) is a bilingual edition of a life's work in the literary form that established his reputation.

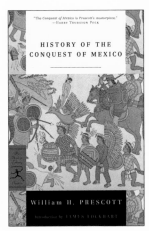 

Prescott, William H., *History of the Conquest of Mexico* (1843; Modern Library, 2001). It is rare that an historical work written in the mid-nineteenth century continues to be widely read and admired, but Prescott penned a virtually unmatched, vivid account of the Spanish subjugation of the Aztec people in the sixteenth century. Nearly blind, he nevertheless drew on original Spanish sources and firsthand Aztec recollections to portray a melancholy Montezuma vacillating between resistance and fatalistic resignation. Hugh Thomas, *Conquest: Montezuma, Cortés, and the Fall of Old Mexico* (1993), incorporates a mass of material uncovered in the 150 years since Prescott wrote and provides an original interpretation of why the highly civilized but irresolute and superstitious Montezuma did not simply crush the Spanish invaders.

Williams, Eric, *Capitalism and Slavery* (1944; North Carolina, 1994). Directly attacking the idea that moral and humanitarian motives led to the abolition of the slave trade, Williams argues that the British abandoned the sugar plantations in the West Indies for economic reasons and not for "poetic sentimentality." He holds that the profits from slavery and the slave trade contributed, perhaps decisively, to British industrialization. His radical interpretation of the preeminence of economic motives found a permanent place in the history of both slavery and the West Indies. His other significant scholarly work is *British Historians and the West Indies* (1966, intro. Allan Bullock). Williams served as prime minister of Trinidad for two decades, 1962–81, and is widely recognized by Trinidadians as the "Father of the Nation."

Military History

Clausewitz, Karl von, *On War* (1832; trans. Michael Howard and Peter Paret, Princeton, 2008). Clausewitz meant his famous aphorism "War is the continuation of politics by other means" to be understood in the context of the economy and technology of the age. He held that effective warfare depended on experience and temperament, both of which alert and knowledgeable commanders needed in order to make rapid decisions. Such expertise could help dispel the "fog of war"—Clausewitz identified the concept but did not use the phrase—that is, "the general unreliability of all information" during a battle. Lenin admired him, and Clausewitz's influence on the Red Army was tangible. He directly influenced military leaders as diverse as Dwight Eisenhower and Mao Tse-tung. Michael Howard, *Clausewitz* (2000) explains Clausewitz in the context of the Napoleonic Wars.

Grotius, Hugo, *The Rights of War and Peace* (1625; Eng. trans. A. C. Campbell, 1901; Liberty Fund, 2005). Grotius was a seventeenth-century philosopher whose work on "just and unjust wars" laid one of the foundations of international law. His principles found expression in the Treaty of Westphalia (1648), the first general peace settlement in modern history. His analysis of just causes of war included self-defense; he also addressed the just conduct of war. Grotian precedents for finding solutions to conflicts continue to have relevance in international affairs. These ideas are taken up in the fundamentally important work *Hugo Grotius and International Relations* (1990), edited by Hedley Bull, Benedict Kingsbury, and Adam Roberts.

Keegan, John, *The Face of Battle: A Study of Agincourt, Waterloo, and the Somme* (1976; Penguin, 1983). In a narrative based on the structure of the practical mechanics of battle, Keegan analyzes pivotal military encounters fought in roughly the same geographic area in three periods—medieval Europe, the Napoleonic era, and World War I. He takes especially into account the vantage point of ordinary soldiers and their commanding officers. The book has earned widespread and continued acclaim for juxtaposing the myth of battle with the reality. Keegan conveys what the experience of combat meant for the participants: the physical conditions of fighting and the emotional or psychological dimension explaining why soldiers stand and fight, and why some collapse or desert.

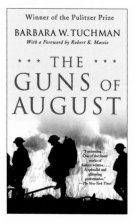

Tuchman, Barbara, *The Guns of August* (1962; Presidio, 2004). A detailed account of the first month of World War I. Tuchman describes the decisions to go to war, the devastation of Belgium, the fighting on the Eastern Front, and the initial turning point of the war: the halting of the German advance into France. Four years of trench warfare followed. President Kennedy was so impressed with the book that he had copies distributed to his principal political and military advisers, virtually ordering them to read it. Tuchman's masterpiece is *Stillwell and the American Experience in China, 1911–1945* (1971). Stillwell was the hard-driving American general in China during World War II. He referred to Chiang Kai-shek as the "peanut."

U.S. Army / Marine Corps Counterinsurgency Field Manual, The (Chicago, with forewords by General David H. Petraeus, Lt. General James F. Amos, and Lt. Colonel John A. Nagl, 2006). The rationale for this field manual can found in the assumptions of its mastermind, Petraeus, who believed it necessary to prepare for a long-term—up to fifty-year—occupation of parts of the Middle East by U.S. forces. Methods of counterinsurgency must respond to cultural and social circumstances in order to win the support of local peoples. Military personnel will assist in the building of roads, schools, and hospitals—while being prepared to shoot if necessary—and will work toward the security and prosperity of local peoples, who will see that their best interests are served by supporting American efforts.

Walzer, Michael, *Just and Unjust Wars* (1977; Basic, 2015). While protesting the war in Vietnam, Walzer began to reflect on the ethics of warfare. Though the resulting book had its origins in an antiwar movement, it is balanced and fair-minded. Walzer examines moral issues that arise before, during, and after wars are fought. When are wars justified, and what are the combatants' ethical responsibilities? He assesses the testimony of those within governments who made the decision to go to war, along with written and oral evidence from those who did the fighting. His ultimate aim is to help citizens make the necessary judgments about wars that their countries fight. *The Stanford Encyclopedia of Philosophy* describes *Just and Unjust Wars* as "the major contemporary statement of just war theory."

Naval History

Mahan, Alfred Thayer, *The Influence of Sea Power upon History, 1660–1783* (1890; Dover, 1987). Mahan was vain, pompous, and arrogant, but successful in arguing that the U.S. Navy was the principal defender of American liberty. He argued that control of the seas paved the way for Britain's emergence as the world's dominant power. The United States followed suit at the end of the 1890s, gaining control of Puerto Rico, Guam, and the Philippines, which served as coaling stations and naval bases, as well as a permanent lease on the harbor at Guantánamo Bay, Cuba. In Mahan's view, sea power, by implementing a naval blockade, could overcome the strength of any army. Historians consider Mahan's work the single most influential book on naval strategy.

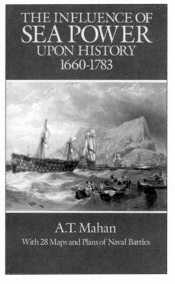

Marder, Arthur J., *From the Dreadnought to Scapa Flow*, vol. 1, *The Road to War, 1904–1914* (1961; Naval Institute Press, intro. Barry Gough, 2013). The security of the British Isles in the decade before World War I depended on sea power. Marder deals with the events leading to war, including the reluctance of the British government to increase naval spending despite the German challenge on the seas. A. J. P. Taylor wrote of Marder: "His naval history has a unique fascination. To unrivalled mastery of sources he adds a gift of simple narrative." For an earlier period of the Royal Navy, N. A. M. Rodger's *The Command of the Ocean: A Naval History of Britain, 1649–1815* (2004) is an engrossing study by one of its leading historians.

Massie, Robert K., *Dreadnought: Britain, Germany, and the Coming of the Great War* (1991; Penguin, 1992). A symbol of British naval supremacy, the *Dreadnought* was a battleship launched in 1906. Massie explains how it symbolically became a catalyst in the naval arms race between Britain and Germany. Yet the British and German fleets fought only one major engagement, at the indecisive battle at Jutland in 1916. Massie deals not only with naval armaments and battleships but also especially with personalities, including the Kaiser and Admiral Alfred von Tirpitz and, on the British side, Admiral Jackie Fisher and Winston Churchill, at the time First Lord of the Admiralty. A winner of the Pulitzer Prize, the book is distinguished for its portraits of these and other historic personalities.

Roskill, Stephen, *Naval Policy between the Wars* (2 vols., 1968, 1976; Pen & Sword, 2016). Roskill, the principal historian of the Royal Navy, wrote on the interwar era and the war period 1939–45. In the first of these volumes, he deals with Britain's main rival, the U.S. Navy, as well as the geopolitical reality of British sea power. In the second volume, he analyzes events that led to naval rearmament. In the course of his writing, he came into conflict with the other main historian of the Royal Navy, Arthur Marder. A. J. P. Taylor described it as the collision between "our historical dreadnoughts," a theme developed by Barry Gough in *Marder and Roskill: Writing and Fighting Naval History* (2010).

Historiography, Intellectual History, the History of Ideas
Annan, Noel, *Our Age: Portrait of a Generation* (1990; HarperCollins, 1991). Annan assesses significant personalities born during or after World War I. They are an improbable mix: Ludwig Wittgenstein and Margaret Thatcher, F. R. Leavis and Hugh Trevor-Roper, Evelyn Waugh and Julian Amery. The theme is the interplay of ideas across society, above all among intellectuals concerned about Britain's decline in the world. Let us praise, or pity, famous men, but who should be held accountable? *Our Age* bears comparison with other outstanding books about the spirit of an era and periodization, for example, G. M. Young's *Portrait of an Age* and George Dangerfield's *Strange Death of Liberal England*. Yet *Our Age* is unique. Christopher Hitchens described it as "an imperishable tome in the growing library of decline."

Aron, Raymond, *The Opium of the Intellectuals* (1955; Eng. trans. by Terence Kilmartin, 1957; Transaction, 2001). At once a journalist, a sociologist, and an historian, Aron inverted Marx's formulation of religion being the opium of the people to attack intellectuals and politicians drugged by Marx and the attractions of communism. He opposed the attempt to suppress the rebellion in Algeria and later criticized the self-created cult of de Gaulle. In France, he was held in public esteem in the same way as Walter Lippmann was in the United States. He thought that the greatest compliment paid to him was being called the Voltaire of the twentieth century. For his autobiography, see Aron, *Memoirs: Fifty Years of Political Reflection* (1997).

Benda, Julien, *The Treason of the Intellectuals* (*La Trahison des Clercs*, 1927; first Eng. trans. Richard Aldington, 1928; Transaction, foreword by Roger Kimball, author of *Tenured Radicals*, 1990). Benda was a French philosopher who in the 1920s denounced as moral traitors those who betrayed rationality and the intellectual values of civilized society. He was especially scathing toward writers who abandoned "truth and justice" for the cult of success or apologized for, rather than criticized, the politically powerful, and also toward scholars, on the left as well as the right, who politicized and subverted intellectual inquiry.

Berlin, Isaiah, *The Hedgehog and the Fox* (1953; Princeton, ed. Henry Hardy, intro. Michael Ignatieff, 2013). Berlin, one of the great lecturers and conversationalists of twentieth-century England, explores an idea put forward by the ancient Greek poet Archilochus: "The fox knows many things, but the hedgehog knows one big thing." Berlin uses the distinction to categorize writers, a sort of intellectual parlor game. For example, Dostoyevsky and Nietzsche are hedgehogs; Shakespeare and Goethe, foxes; Tolstoy, who gets extended treatment, is a hybrid. Henry Hardy, Berlin's longtime editor, is publishing the writer's uncollected essays, lectures, and correspondence. Berlin's *Vico and Herder* (1976) is a gripping, wide-ranging study of two prominent anti-Enlightenment thinkers. A perceptive, well-written biography of the writer is Michael Ignatieff's *Isaiah Berlin: A Life* (1998).

Butterfield, Herbert, *The Whig Interpretation of History* (1931; Norton, 1965). Butterfield believed it anachronistic to view the past through the eyes of the present, as had the nineteenth-century historians who assumed a march of progress propelled by Britain's strength and prosperity, its lead in scientific discovery, and its rule over a worldwide empire. In iconoclastic dissent, he took aim at the confident assumption of British superiority and destiny, and helped create a tradition of challenging common assumptions, taking a skeptical view of grand historical designs, and guarding against the dangers of simplistic elucidation of the present by lessons of the past. Michael Bentley, *The Life and Thought of Herbert Butterfield* (2011), presents a rounded portrait giving insight into the historian's temperament as well as an appraisal of his work.

Collingwood, R. G., *The Idea of History* (1946; Oxford, 1994). Collingwood was a philosopher and archeologist as well as an historian, and he had further interests that included the study of aesthetics and psychology. He underwent fifty sessions of psychoanalysis in order to understand the subject and its methods. He played a critical part in the rise of the history of ideas as an academic discipline, drawing on his knowledge of philosophy to argue that presuppositions are always changing. He believed in the distinctiveness of history as a form of knowledge. Historians must imagine human events, because they have already happened. By persuasively arguing that imagination plays a critical part in historical reconstruction, he became a guiding spirit in comprehending the nature and scope of history itself.

Crossman, Richard, ed., *The God That Failed* (1949; Columbia, foreword by David Engerman, 2001). Six intellectuals describe their journeys into communism, the gap between their visions of God and the reality of the communist state, and conflicts of conscience that eventually reached a breaking point. The writers are Arthur Koestler, Ignazio Silone, Richard Wright, André Gide, Louis Fischer, and Stephen Spender. For readers interested in the history of the Cold War, this book is fundamental. Crossman holds a secure place in the tradition of British radicalism; and he was the foremost British Zionist of the era. His published diaries, *Diaries of a Cabinet Minister* (1975–77) and *The Backbench Diaries of Richard Crossman* (1981), are indispensable for historians of post–World War II Britain.

Hobsbawm, Eric, and Ranger, Terence, eds. *The Invention of Tradition* (1983; Cambridge, 2012). Some traditions are created for political and other reasons and therefore lack long and intricate histories. In this subversively seminal collection of essays, Hugh Trevor-Roper argues that Scottish traditions were sometimes invented as late as the nineteenth century rather than in antiquity, and that an Englishman, Thomas Rawlinson, invented the kilt. All the essays in the collection are original and clearly written, but Terence Ranger's deserves special mention for his argument that the concept of African "tribes" did not originate in the reality of African society but was imposed by European interlopers.

Ortega y Gasset, José, *Revolt of the Masses* (1930; Eng. trans., 1932; Norton, intro. Saul Bellow, 1994). In a work regarded as a seminal study of the way that mob rule can lead to dictatorship, Ortega y Gasset expresses thoughts that have had lasting significance in the context of the Spanish Civil War, though not in the way he hoped. He holds that modern society is dominated by a complacent middle class comprising indistinguishable and mediocre individuals. Leadership, in his view, should be delegated to men who are cultivated, intellectually independent, and politically sophisticated. Intellectuals "in the service of the Republic" must uphold elite values against the mediocre and mundane. Bellow reinforces a lesson of everlasting danger: living under a "dictatorship of the commonplace."

Ranke, Leopold von, *The Theory and Practice of History* (1820–80; ed. Georg G. Iggers, Routledge, 2010). Ranke was the founder of the modern practice of writing history by the seminar method, which focuses on archival research, the use of primary sources, and the analysis of historical documents. He encouraged the writing of narrative history. Professor at the University of Berlin for fifty years, he exerted a far-reaching influence in America and Europe. Though his method was later challenged by historians such as E. H. Carr and Fernand Braudel for involving too much factual detail, his stature remains intact, and he is still widely known for his proclamation that historians should represent the past "*wie es eigentlich gewesen [ist]*"—as it actually happened.

Snow, C. P., *The Two Cultures and the Scientific Revolution* (1959; Canto, intro. Stefan Collini, 2012). Snow was both a scientist and a novelist. In 1959 he controversially argued that the intellectual world was split between the humanities and the sciences, a proposition with relevance today in view of the further fragmentation of academic disciplines. He believed that practitioners in the two disciplines knew little, if anything, about the other and that communication between them was difficult, perhaps impossible. Yet Snow believed in the vigorous exchange of ideas among scholars of all fields. The literary critic Stefan Collini argues that the passage of time has reduced the cultural divide but not removed it. Snow's skill as a novelist can be seen in the eleven-volume sequence *Strangers and Brothers* (1940–70).

Energy History

Tarbell, Ida, *The History the of Standard Oil Company* (2 vols., 1904; abridged ed., Dover, 2003). Theodore Roosevelt described Tarbell as a "muckraker," a word drawn from *Pilgrim's Progress*. Trained in what later became known as investigative journalism, she gained access to confidential documents and obscure court records to prove that John D. Rockefeller ruthlessly suppressed his oil rivals while building the Standard Oil monopoly. She doggedly interviewed oil executives, who boasted of indulging in collusion and conspiracy. She steadfastly refused to be intimidated. Her careful and respectful judgment played a critical part in the dissolution of Standard Oil by the U.S. Supreme Court in 1911 and its split into thirty-four "baby Standards."

Yergin, Daniel, *The Prize: The Epic Quest for Oil, Money, and Power* (1991; Free Press, 2008). The singular feature of this comprehensive work is the interplay of robust personalities—including John D. Rockefeller, Herbert Hoover, and the Armenian oil baron Calouste Gulbenkian—in the development of the oil and gas industry, 1859–1990. The book makes clear the technicalities of drilling, refining, transporting, and marketing petroleum. For the argument that World War I marked the point at which oil became the principal commodity for ensuring national security and promoting domestic prosperity, see Timothy Winegard, *The First Oil War* (2016). Yergin's sequel, *The Quest: Energy, Security, and the Remaking of the Modern World* (2012), covers nuclear power, renewable energy, and climate change as well as oil.

Autobiographies, Biographies, Memoirs
Britain

Bate, Walter Jackson, *John Keats* (1963; Harvard, 1979). Keats had perhaps the most concentrated career of any great poet. It lasted, in total, three and a half years (mid-1816 through 1819), and during that span, the poems for which he is best remembered were written over the course of only nine months. Keats died of tuberculosis at age twenty-five. From a poor family, he studied to be a doctor, but turned to poetry full-time after finishing his medical training. Bate punctures the caricature of Keats as a wilting flower—no one of delicate sensibilities could have endured the doctor-training regimen he pursued—and brings a scholar's attention to the intricacies of the poems. Bate wrote the similarly engrossing *Samuel Johnson* (1977), a biography fit to stand alongside Boswell's.

Beaglehole, J. C., *The Life of Captain James Cook* (1974; Stanford, 1992). Cook has the rightful reputation as the greatest explorer-seaman of all time. Beaglehole's lifework is a fluent and readable biography that carries Cook to all parts of the Pacific, including the circumnavigation of New Zealand and the first European contact with Hawaii, where in 1775 he was killed by the Hawaiians. Beaglehole's penchant for curious detail holds the reader throughout, for example, on Cook's meals of dogs and rats in Polynesia, and kangaroos, turtles, seals, and polar bears elsewhere. Whatever his foibles, Cook was unequaled among rivals then and later. He consistently displayed a rare combination of seamanship, authoritative surveying and cartographic skills, and physical courage. Beaglehole's biography does full justice to a heroic figure.

Besant, Annie, *Annie Besant: An Autobiography* (1893; Cambridge, 2011). A champion of Irish and Indian self-rule, Besant, at the height of her career, was a copious writer and powerful orator. After the death of Helena Blavatsky in 1891, she became a leading personality in the Theosophical Society and later its president. Her interests took her to India, where she immersed herself in religion and politics. In 1916, she and Lokmanya Tilak (Bal Gangadhar Tilak) launched the All India Home Rule League. She and Gandhi shared a commitment to militant nonviolent protest to achieve Indian self-rule, but disagreed on ultimate aims. She had a closer relationship with Jawaharlal Nehru, who had been tutored by a theosophist. Besant chronicles her own life in *Autobiographical Sketches*, ed. Carol MacKay (2009).

Blake, Robert, *Disraeli* (1966; Faber, 2010). In what is still the most important biography of Disraeli, Blake explains how the politician used his Jewish heritage to advantage—he described

Jews as "proto-Christians"—and how he grew from a flamboyant dandy to a parliamentary figure in a black frock coat. Blake's Disraeli is supple, imaginative, and resilient, with a love of gossip and intrigue. The book's insistent theme is his pragmatism, which helps explain his success as Prime Minister: he linked the monarchy with Asia by proclaiming Queen Victoria Empress of India; purchased shares in the Suez Canal Company; and negotiated the Turkish settlement with Bismarck in 1878, after which Disraeli returned to England to proclaim "peace with honour" and the acquisition of Cyprus.

Blunden, Edmund, *Undertones of War* (1928; Oxford, ed. John Greening, 2016). Blunden, one of the finest poets of World War I, served for nearly two years as a British Army officer in the trenches and on the battlefields of the western front. *Undertones of War* is his memoir, to which John Greening has added selected poems. Paul Fussell called the book "one of the permanent works engendered by memories of the war." Confronted with mass slaughter, Blunden became increasingly bitter toward Britain's military leadership, but nonetheless managed to keep his sense of humor. That mixture of attitudes reminded Greening of the satirical play *Oh! What a Lovely War!* (1969), by Joan Littlewood—itself a cultural landmark, later made into a film directed by Richard Attenborough.

Boswell, James, *The Life of Samuel Johnson* (1791; Penguin Classics, abridged, ed. Christopher Hibbert, 1979). An account of the life of a literary genius by a devoted disciple. Among Johnson's many talents, he was a skilled biographer, author of *Lives of the Poets*, from whom Boswell took inspiration. Besides doing research, Boswell took notes obsessively while with Johnson, leading the latter to write to a friend, "One would think the man had been hired to spy upon me." The *Life* reproduces letters, anecdotes, conversations, and opinions to give a many-sided portrait of its subject and his era. The selection of Johnson's major works published by Oxford World's Classics (2000) includes poetry, periodical essays, selections from the *Dictionary*, and the short novel *Rasselas*.

Bourke, Richard, *Empire and Revolution: The Political Life of Edmund Burke* (2015; Princeton, 2017). In perhaps a rare consensus, historians agree that Bourke "revolutionized" how Burke has been regarded. By drawing on a range of archival sources, he reconstructs Burke's major concerns as a statesman, orator, and philosopher, restoring his contemporaries' opinion view of him rather than presenting him as a partisan against progress. Bourke explains the positions that Burke took on the key questions of Ireland, America, India, and the French Revolution. David Armitage of Harvard University believes that *Empire and Revolution* "is quite simply the best book on Burke ever written: all future work on Burke must start from here." For readers disenchanted with politicians, this book serves as a reminder of the tradition of statesmanship represented by Edmund Burke.

Brittain, Vera, *Testament of Youth* (1933; Penguin, 2005). Brittain was a nurse on the western front during World War I. She lost her brother and her fiancé. Her memoir, based on her diaries, letters, and other contemporary writing, including poetry, deplores the futility of war while respecting the bravery of those who sacrificed their lives. It clearly marks out the path that led to her pacifism. She puts her own experience in a larger social and historical context, as if in an elegy for a vanished generation. Upon publication, the book represented the way in which the impact of the war continued to define a lingering but potent mood of loss and grief. Brittain was a staunch feminist and the mother of the politician Shirley Williams.

Cecil, Robert, *A Great Experiment: An Autobiography* (Oxford, 1941). Lord Robert Cecil, whose family included four prime ministers, played a critical part in committing the British government to creating the League of Nations and in drafting the covenant that in 1920 attempted to restrict recourse to war. An American official involved in the negotiations commented that Cecil was "the only man in the British Gov. who really had the League of Nations at heart." He subsequently served in Geneva as the British representative to the league, and in 1937 he received the Nobel Peace Prize as "the foremost defender of the League of Nations." At the last meeting of the league, in 1946, he proclaimed, "The League is dead. Long live the United Nations."

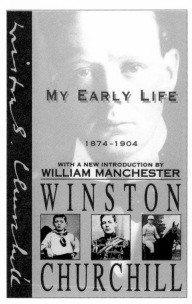 

Churchill, Winston, *My Early Life* (1930; Scribner, 1996). This memoir covers Churchill's childhood and his affection for his nanny, his education at Harrow (where he "got into my *bones* the essential structure of the ordinary British sentence"), and his escape as a prisoner during the Boer War of 1899–1902. Regarded as one of his best books, it is written with an idiosyncratic tone of comical self-mockery and reflects criticism of his contemporaries. In 1953, Churchill received the Nobel Prize for his voluminous writings defending "exalted human values," above all in his six-volume history of World War II. The landmark study separating the myth from the man is Robert Blake and Wm. Roger Louis, eds., *Churchill: A Major New Assessment of His Life in Peace and War* (1993).

Corbett, Jim, *Man-Eaters of Kumaon* (1944; Oxford, 1989). Corbett's fame rests on his hunting down man-eating tigers and leopards in India, often at the request of the government. In 1907, he shot a female Bengal tiger that had claimed over 400 human lives. In 1944, the Indian branch of the Oxford University Press persuaded him to write an account of his adventures. Corbett describes the necessary patience and skill of the hunter, the luring of leopards and tigers by imitating their calls, and the dangers of the jungle. In 1946, Hollywood made a film based on the book, portraying a hunter who wounds a tiger and is later killed by it. When Corbett saw the movie, he commented that the best actor in it was the tiger.

Gosse, Edmund, *Father and Son: A Study of Two Temperaments* (1907; Penguin, 1989). The British writer Edmund Gosse was raised by parents who belonged to the Plymouth Brethren, a branch of evangelical Christianity. His father, Philip Henry Gosse, was a gifted amateur naturalist and marine biologist, credited with inventing the word "aquarium." He strictly controlled all aspects of Edmund's life, ostensibly for the good of his soul. Edmund was forbidden to read poetry or novels, so he concentrated on scientific studies. It was only when Edmund went away to school that he discovered the wonders of English literature. He learned to circumvent his father's numerous restrictions and eventually broke with Christianity. It should be noted that Edmund's portrayal of Henry as intrusive and despotic has been credibly challenged by later writers.

Graves, Robert, *Good-Bye to All That* (1929; Penguin Classics, 2000). Graves enlisted in the Royal Welch Fusiliers to fight in the trenches of World War I. He became bitterly disillusioned with the inane, sometimes comic blunders of high-ranking British officers, and equally disenchanted with the hypocrisy of traditional values in England itself. According to the critic Paul Fussell, the book is "the best memoir of the First World War." Graves's output was prodigious. He saw himself primarily as a poet, but one of his remarkable nonfiction works is *The White Goddess: A Historical Grammar of Poetic Myth* (1948), in which he argues that true poets derive their gifts from the muse, the "Moon Goddess," whose principles have been dispossessed by male values of reason and logic.

Greenblatt, Stephen, *Will in The World: How Shakespeare Became Shakespeare* (2004; Bodley Head, 2014). Greenblatt, a Harvard professor, is the author of over a dozen books. *Will in The World* is his most popular. He allows Shakespeare to speak for himself, conveying as far as possible his background and prejudices in the era of Elizabeth I and James I. At another level, Greenblatt's aim is to make the connection between the plays and "poetic imagination" by relating Shakespeare's career in the competitive London theater world while grappling with such issues as the religious and political forces that led to public executions. This is a rich and engaging biography, perhaps comparable in its popularity and historical context to Sir Tom Stoppard's film *Shakespeare in Love* (1998).

Hardy, G. H., *A Mathematician's Apology* (1940; Canto Classics, intro. C. P. Snow, 2012). One of the twentieth century's most original and accomplished mathematicians, Hardy wrote his autobiography to make clear his collaboration with the brilliant Indian mathematician Srinivasa Ramanujan. Hardy was politically a radical, supporting Bertrand Russell in protest against

World War I, and an atheist, regarding God as his "personal enemy." The autobiography is clear and captivating, written for a general audience. The film *The Man Who Knew Infinity* (2015), starring Jeremy Irons and Dev Patel, is based on Hardy's experience with Ramanujan.

Harris, José, *William Beveridge: A Biography* (1977; Oxford, 1998). Beveridge was an economist and social reformer best known for writing the 1942 report that became the blueprint for the post–World War II British welfare state. Harris paints him as a vain and abrasive figure—yet admired by those who knew him well—with a dazzling intellect. The 1942 report described the five "Giant Evils"—"Want, Disease, Ignorance, Squalor, and Idleness"—and proposed widespread reforms to the system of social welfare. Enthusiastically received by the British public, the report provided the basis for the post-war National Health Service and expansion of National Insurance. Harris generally describes Beveridge as working toward an efficient, just, and compassionate social order, devoted to a cause that fired his moral imagination.

Holmes, Richard, *Shelley: The Pursuit* (1974; NYRB, 2003). Like his fellow romantic poet Lord Byron, Percy Bysshe Shelley was a rebel in all aspects of his life: politics, economics, and sex as well as poetry. During a short life—he drowned at age twenty-nine—Shelley wrote lyric poems that have become canonical ("Ozymandias," "To a Skylark," "Ode to the West Wind"), but he wanted to be known for his longer works and his verse dramas, such as *Prometheus Unbound*, which took on the political and social controversies of the day. This biography strips away the Victorian image of an ethereal, spiritualized Shelley to reveal a darker, crueler, more capable figure, heedless of either convention or disgrace. In this portrait, Shelley stands as a lone idealist and revolutionary.

Jenkins, Roy, *Gladstone: A Biography* (1996; Penguin, 2002). The "People's William" was a populist of towering rectitude and self-discipline. His life stretched through almost the entire nineteenth century, 1809–98, and he was prime minister four times, renowned as an unrivaled orator who often worked eighteen hours a day. He finally found his biographer in Roy Jenkins, who had insight into the workings of government because of his own experience in public office. Jenkins's Gladstone is deeply religious, self-righteous, and sometimes priggish but never hypocritical. He had a complex obsession with prostitutes and pornography, all of which is dealt with judiciously by Jenkins. "Gladstonian Liberals" today are those who believe in balanced budgets, low taxation, and government based on moral principles.

Lawrence, T. E., *Seven Pillars of Wisdom* (1922; Wordsworth Classics, intro. Angus Calder, 1997). An autobiographical account of the experiences of a British intelligence officer—known subsequently as Lawrence of Arabia—during the Arab Revolt of 1916–18 against the Ottomans. Lawrence's epic narrative tells of his adventures in hand-to-hand desert combat and blowing up Turkish bridges. Lawrence was brave, intelligent, puckish, and exceedingly complex. Although not without exaggeration and liberties of fact, *Seven Pillars* stands as one of the notable historical and literary achievements of World War I. In *A Prince of Our Disorder: The Life of T. E. Lawrence* (1976), John E. Mack, a psychiatrist, probes deeply into Lawrence's personality as a source of his actions, drawing on unpublished letters, War Office archives, and interviews with those who knew Lawrence.

Lee, Hermione, *Virginia Woolf* (1996; Vintage, 1999). With a mixture of social history and literary analysis, Lee portrays her subject not as a victim of "madness" but as a psychologically troubled woman who nonetheless managed to become one of the brilliant writers of the twentieth century. She emerges in Lee's interpretation as a feminist as well as a driven thinker and writer. She could be snobbish and racist, even anti-Semitic, despite having a Jewish husband to whom she was devoted. Not least among Lee's achievements is to rescue Leonard Woolf from the abuse he received by American feminists as a dominating figure held responsible for Virginia's illness. On the contrary: Leonard was a caring, loving husband as well as an intellectual and author in his own right.

Medawar, Peter, *Memoir of a Thinking Radish* (1986). Medawar takes his title from Pascal's "thinking reed" and Falstaff's "forked radish." He shared the Nobel Prize in Physiology in 1960 for pioneering work in tissue grafting. During World War II, a German plane crashed near his house in Oxford, and the condition of the badly burned pilot led to his interest in the field. Medawar became famous also as a scientific philosopher, adamant in his belief that science requires imagination similar to that found in poets and artists. In Oxford common rooms, he found that no subject was beyond his reach, but acknowledged that "it takes an effort to write undying prose." In *The Limits of Science* (1988), Medawar examines the nature of scientific inquiry.

Newman, John Henry, *Apologia pro Vita Sua* ("A Defence of One's Life"; 1864; Penguin, intro. Ian Ker, 1995). A prominent figure in the Church of England, Newman provoked public consternation when he announced his espousal of Roman Catholicism in 1845. Twenty years later, his actions and motives were attacked by Charles Kingsley (Regius Professor of History at Cambridge and the author of *Westward Ho!*). The *Apologia* is Newman's eloquent response, an autobiography that transcends an account of his life to explore the nature of Christianity and its place in the world in the mid-nineteenth century. The *Apologia* was important in helping break down English prejudice against Catholic priests. The standard life of the churchman is Ian Ker, *John Henry Newman: A Biography* (1990).

Pepys, Samuel, *Diary* (written 1660–69; first full publication, 11 vols., 1970–83; Modern Library, abridged ed., 2003). A ten-year account by an official in the British Admiralty of his daily life and events in London. Written in a code that went undeciphered for 150 years, the diary is famous for its candor. Pepys recounts his affairs with actresses, his money problems, and his career successes and reversals, with almost inhuman objectivity. His firsthand accounts of events such as the Great Fire of London in 1666 have been valuable to historians. His sign-off for most entries, "And so to bed," became a catchphrase. The introduction, by Robert Louis Stevenson in 1881, shows one vigorous writer's appreciation for another. The British actor Kenneth Branagh recorded an engrossing (abridged) audio version.

Pritchett, V. S., *A Cab at the Door* and *Midnight Oil* (1968, 1971; Modern Library, 1994). The title of the first part of Pritchett's autobiography refers to his impoverished family's usual method of fleeing from creditors. *Midnight Oil* traces his development as a writer: he lives in Paris, Ireland, and Spain, searching for work and for material for his short stories. The stories become so accomplished that he acquires the reputation of the "English Chekhov." In 1928 he began writing reviews for the *New Statesman*, which continued for half a century. A biographer states that they amounted to "some of the finest criticism of the age." A view of the author's life from the outside can be found in Jeremy Treglown, *V. S. Pritchett: A Working Life* (2005).

Reynolds, David, *In Command of History: Churchill Fighting and Writing the Second World War* (2004; Basic, 2007). Churchill's six-volume history of the war dominated Western interpretations for a generation. Reynolds's account of how it came to be written is scrupulous, exact, and balanced. The gist is that Churchill willfully distorted history to make the case for himself. A team of assistants drafted the chapters, but Churchill inserted phrases and flourishes of his own to give it overall coherence and a Churchillian tone. He suppressed his criticism of Eisenhower and the Allied invasion of France in 1944 while arguing for his own strategy of coming up through the Balkans. The overall effect is not to diminish Churchill's account but to help the reader better understand the course of the war.

Spear, Percival, *Master of Bengal: Clive and His India* (Thames and Hudson, 1975). In this lucid, balanced, and engaging biography of one of the architects of the British Raj, Spear describes the young Robert Clive as boisterous and aggressive yet melancholic. He arrived in Madras in 1744 as an employee of the East India Company. His military career included a punitive expedition against the Nabob of Bengal for the notorious Black Hole of Calcutta incident and the Battle of Plassey (1757), which established him as a kingmaker. Single-minded in the pursuit of private wealth, he was forced to defend himself in Parliament against charges of having illegally gained a fortune. In the House of Commons, he declared, "I stand astonished at my own moderation."

Strachey, Lytton, *Eminent Victorians* (1918). The iconoclastic, stylistically brilliant study of four Victorian "bungling hypocrites" who, in distinct ways, represented nineteenth-century England: Cardinal Manning, Florence Nightingale, Thomas Arnold, and General Charles Gordon. It marks the beginning of twentieth-century biography by rebelling against the "fat volumes" of the Victorians. Strachey's implicit attack on cherished institutions captured an immense readership, though it was frequently hostile, despite telling anecdotes and an elegant style. Perceptive readers at the time recognized the underlying theme of social criticism, all the more pointed because of a consistent interpretation of the psychology of his subjects in relation to Victorian values.

LYTTON STRACHEY
Eminent Victorians

Michael Holroyd, *Lytton Strachey: The New Biography* (1994) concludes that the problems of the 1960s were similar to those confronted by Strachey.

Wavell, Archibald, *The Viceroy's Journal* (1973; University Press, Bangladesh, ed. Penderel Moon, 1998). Wavell was a distinguished general of World War II, but in 1943 he was sacked by Churchill, who, at a loss at what to do about a further assignment, appointed him viceroy of India. Wavell served until February 1947, demonstrating a farsighted grasp of Indian affairs and trying to reach agreement on eventual Indian independence. He felt especially frustrated by "three elderly gentlemen" who held contradictory aims: Churchill (India should remain a British possession), Mohammed Ali Jinnah (proponent of an independent Muslim state), and Gandhi ("a most inveterate enemy of the British"). There is a literary quality to the journal, for example, in Wavell's allusion to the Jabberwocky: "Beware the Gandhiji, my son . . ."

Webb, Beatrice, *My Apprenticeship* (1938; Penguin, 1971). One of nine daughters of a wealthy businessman, Beatrice—as she was always known—had a precocious intellect. She developed a faith in the scientific sociology of Auguste Comte, eventually becoming an economist, social reformer, a principal member of the Fabian Society, and a founder of the London School of Economics. She worked to strengthen labor unions—the term "collective bargaining" is attributed to her. She developed a romantic relationship with the radical politician Joseph Chamberlain, with whom she shared the view that the resources of overseas colonies could help improve living conditions in England. The diary closes with her marriage to Sydney Webb in 1892; one critic described the pair as "the oddest couple since Adam and Eve."

Woolf, Leonard, *The Journey Not the Arrival Matters: An Autobiography of the Years 1939 to 1969* (1969; Harvest, 1989). An honorable and trustworthy man, Woolf recounts the details of Virginia Woolf's suicide as well as the running the Hogarth Press with her. Early in his career he was a colonial officer in Ceylon and wrote *The Village in the Jungle* (1913). He came to believe in the absurdity of one civilization imposing itself on another. Toward the end of his life, he despaired of American involvement in Vietnam. He lists as supreme virtues the qualities of tolerance, respect for intellect, love of beauty, and unremitting and efficient work. His most enduring accomplishment is his autobiography, which won him renown as one of the outstanding men of his time.

Ziegler, Philip, *Mountbatten: The Official Biography* (1985; Orion, 2001). During World War II, Mountbatten was the supreme Allied commander in Southeast Asia. He became Viceroy of India, the last one, in 1947; and from 1954 to 1959 he was First Sea Lord. In 1979 he was killed when the Irish Republican Army blew up his fishing boat. Ziegler is a gifted biographer. His account is scrupulously written with accurate detail and balanced, penetrating interpretation, especially on Mountbatten's time in India. No biography is ever definitive, but Ziegler's is probably as close as one can come. Another of Ziegler's achievements, *Diana Cooper* (1981), tells the story of a woman who was "for nine decades a symbol for all that is dashing and daring."

Autobiographies, Biographies, Memoirs
United States

Acheson, Dean, *Present at the Creation* (1986; Norton, 1987). President Truman appointed Dean Acheson secretary of state during the critical period 1949–54, when he helped forge the policy of "containing" the Soviet Union. He played a key part the creation of the North Atlantic Treaty Organization, in advising the President on firing General MacArthur, and in contemplating—and rejecting—the use of atomic weapons to support the French in Indochina. He later advised President Johnson to call an end to the war in Vietnam. His tenure as secretary of state is perhaps best summed up in his own words, "tough and energetic." Acheson was systematic, outspoken, elegant, caustically witty, and quite certain of his own intelligence. His book is indispensable for the history of the post-war era.

Adams, Henry, *The Education of Henry Adams* (1918; Library of America, ed. Leon Wieseltier, 2009). As a descendant of two U.S. presidents, Henry Adams believed that the American public needed to be guided by a moral and intelligent elite, but one tempered by realistic expectations. His autobiography emphasizes his idea of the best educational methods —simply put, reading, discussion, and reflection. Though imbued with a strain of pessimistic melancholy, his autobiography is a literary and historical landmark revealing American intellectual and political life of the late nineteenth century. In *The Political Education of Henry Adams* (1996), Brooks D. Simpson offers a revisionist account of Adams's life and failed political career, attributing the latter mainly to his abrasive personality.

Berg, A. Scott, *Max Perkins: Editor of Genius* (1978; New American Library, 2016). The fraught relationship between writer and editor hardly seems like the stuff of gripping biography. But Maxwell Perkins was the editor of F. Scott Fitzgerald, Ernest Hemingway, and Thomas Wolfe, among others, and his interactions with them can be seen as a critical part of American literary history. All of them, Wolfe in particular, acknowledged the essential contribution his editorial interventions made to their novels. Berg brings a hardworking, self-effacing member of the Yankee establishment—Perkins was the uncle of the Watergate prosecutor Archibald Cox—vividly to life. Besides superior editing, Perkins provided his authors with friendship, loans, career advice, and a constantly available audience for their conversation and confessions.

Berkman, Alexander, *Prison Memoirs of an Anarchist* (1912; NYRB, 1999). On July 23, 1892, Berkman, an anarchist and onetime lover of Emma Goldman, attempted to assassinate Henry Clay Frick, an industrialist overseeing Andrew Carnegie's steel factory in Homestead, Pennsylvania. Frick survived two bullet wounds and being stabbed; Berkman was sentenced to twenty-two years in prison (he served fourteen). While incarcerated, he went from being an arrogant young nihilist to a compassionate realist. Reading like a diary, though written after

Berkman's release, the memoir unsparingly describes pervasive corruption, brutal labor conditions, inhumane punishment, inedible food, and widespread homosexuality. Most importantly,
Berkman comes to understand the violence endemic in American society as stemming from
the country's ideals, which celebrate opportunity and self-respect while denying them to large
numbers of its citizens.

Blum, John Morton, *The Republican Roosevelt* (1954; Harvard, 1977). Theodore Roosevelt has
attracted many biographers, but Blum is exceptional in explaining Roosevelt's motivations and
especially the moral and political philosophy underlying his Square Deal, which promised to break
up large trusts, regulate railroads, ensure pure food and drugs, and, in general, provide fairness
to the American people. "TR" had a genius for governing and for getting his legislative agenda
through Congress. Forceful and energetic, he was adept in the use of power. Many books distin-
guish between TR the president and TR the more radical "Bull Moose" of later years. Blum makes
it clear that he was consistent, the same extraordinary and complex man through all phases of his
life. Blum's study makes a good companion to Edmund Morris's *Rise of Theodore Roosevelt* (1979).

Buchwald, Art, *I'll Always Have Paris: A Memoir* (1996; Ballantine, 1997). Buchwald is best
known as an American humorist who wrote a long-running column for the *Washington Post*,
but he was also known to a generation of American students in Paris in the 1950s from the
European edition of the *Herald Tribune*. When once asked by a student about learning French,
Buchwald, who had moved to Paris in 1948, replied, "Don't take it so seriously. No one can
speak French except the French." After moving from Paris to Washington, D.C., in the early
1960s, he commented that communists were in such short supply that if the nation was not
careful, "the Communist Party would be made up almost entirely of F.B.I. informers."

Chambers, Whittaker, *Witness* (1952; Modern Library, 2014). The key work on communism
in the United States. A member of the Communist Party USA, Chambers became a Soviet spy
in the 1930s. After breaking with communism, he worked as an editor at *Time*, transforming
the magazine into an oracle of spiritual and apocalyptic anticommunism. After playing a key
part in the Alger Hiss espionage trials of 1949–50, he worked with William F. Buckley at the
National Review. Arthur Schlesinger once summed him up: "He saw himself as a character out
of Dostoyevsky." Ronald Reagan credited the book with inspiring his conversion from a New
Deal Democrat to a conservative Republican. A full account of Chambers's can be found in
Sam Tanenhaus, *Whittaker Chambers: A Biography* (1997).

Dana, Richard Henry, Jr., *Two Years before the Mast* (1840; Signet, 2009). Dana was nineteen
when he abandoned Harvard for a two-year round-trip voyage on a merchant ship around Cape
Horn to the coast of California, then still a Mexican province. He endured not only the rough
life of ordinary sailors but also a mad captain, who subjected his men to sadistic floggings. On
the return journey, the ship encountered Antarctic storms, icebergs, and whales. Dana lived
"before the mast" in the quarters of common seamen, and his portrayal of the "lower classes"
is sympathetic and perceptive. In his later career as a lawyer, Dana became a champion of the
downtrodden, freed slaves as well as sailors.

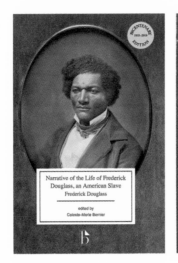 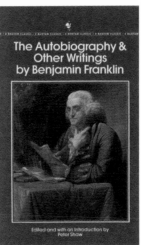

Douglass, Frederick, *Narrative of the Life of Frederick Douglass* (1845; Bedford, ed. David W. Blight, 1995). Douglass, a former slave, wrote this indictment of slavery to bring the cause of abolition to a wider audience. It develops the theme of equality of all peoples, whether black, female, Indian, or recent immigrant. Douglass believed it necessary to "reach the slaveholder's conscience through his fear of personal danger," specifically, "We must make him feel that there is death in the air about him, that . . . there is death all around him." A good guide to the complicated relationship between Douglass and the president who freed the slaves is James Oakes, *The Radical and the Republican: Frederick Douglass, Abraham Lincoln, and the Triumph of Antislavery Politics* (2008).

Eastman, Max, *Love and Revolution: My Journey through an Epoch* (Random House, 1964). The poet and literary critic Max Eastman was editor of the *Masses*, a radical magazine of the World War I era. He visited Russia in the early 1920s and found that Moscow reminded him of Greenwich Village. He later changed his mind about communism, proclaiming that the Soviet Union had led to "The End of Socialism in Russia." His political views shifted hard to the right. This memoir covers the years 1914–56, from his earliest days as a radical through his disillusionment with socialism. Besides offering a firsthand account of Russia shortly after the revolution, its pages are filled with engaging pen portraits of John Reed, Charlie Chaplin, Sigmund Freud, and David Lloyd George, among others.

Franklin, Benjamin, *Autobiography* (1791; Oxford, 2009). At age 65, Franklin presents himself as someone whose fame does not inhibit him from giving down-to-earth, practical advice. He recounts the reasons for his blunders as well as his achievements, and presents success, even perfection, as something within the reach of anyone willing to work hard enough for it. The self-taught Franklin acquired a love of books and a steadfast determination to develop his writing skills. He aimed to improve himself ethically as well as mentally and financially. His account has remained an inspiration to readers of all ages to the present. One of his persistent ideas is that it is never too late to learn. Perhaps the best short biography of Franklin is Edmund S. Morgan, *Benjamin Franklin* (2002).

Goldman, Emma, *Living My Life* (1931; Penguin, abridged ed., 2006). "Red Emma," as she was known to friends and enemies, was an American anarchist and feminist. She believed that violence could spark a revolution against capitalism—but she was not a communist. She claimed the rights for women that male anarchists claimed for men. She believed in free love and fought, along with Margaret Sanger, for access to birth control. She was lionized by the women's movement of the late twentieth century, her influence apparent in the creation of Red Emma's Bookstore Coffeehouse in Baltimore and in the popularity of her exclamation "If I can't dance, I don't want to be part of your revolution." For an account of Goldman's life from an historical perspective, see Alice Wexler, *Emma Goldman in America* (1984).

Greenstein, Fred L., *The Hidden-Hand Presidency: Eisenhower as Leader* (1982; Johns Hopkins, 1994). In 1962, at the end of his presidential term, Eisenhower was widely regarded as well intentioned but ineffective, bumbling, and inarticulate. This landmark study demonstrates that he was not only persuasive and forceful but also highly intelligent, drawing on his military career for organization and effectiveness but deliberately presenting to the public a misleading impression of a president out of his depth. Eisenhower was shrewd and sometimes cunning as well as hardworking and willing to use unconventional methods, including covert operations. Many who lived through the Eisenhower era were astonished by Greenstein's insights. Yet William Hitchcock, in perhaps the best political biography, *The Age of Eisenhower* (2018), presents the virtually opposite view of Eisenhower's leadership style.

Hook, Sydney, *Out of Step: An Unquiet Life in the 20th Century* (1987; Carroll & Graf, 1988). In this readable, humane, and candid autobiography, Hook describes how he began his scholarly career by translating the works of Lenin in 1927. He called himself a Marxist, but by the mid-1930s he was perhaps the leading American critic of Joseph Stalin. He later became a major intellectual in the Cold War and still later made scathing comments about radicals protesting the war in Vietnam. President Reagan in 1985 awarded him the Presidential Medal of Freedom. The autobiography is not without humor: when asked how he might react, after death, to discovering that God existed after all, he said he would exclaim, "God, you never gave me enough evidence!"

Kennan, George, *The Kennan Diaries* (2014). Kennan was the unchallenged American authority on Russia, its history, literature, and poetry as well as its politics. He is best known for devising the policy of "containment" toward the Soviet Union in the five years after World War II, for example in *Realities of American Foreign Policy* (1954). His diaries span his youth in Wisconsin, his lonely years as a student at Princeton, his long career in the U.S. Foreign Service, and his later years as an historian and writer on contemporary affairs. The *Diaries* convey the spirit of not only a generous, learned, and erudite man but also a pessimist of relentless gloom who despised most of his fellow Americans and believed the United States to be descending into decadent moral rot.

Malcolm X, *The Autobiography of Malcolm X*, as told to Alex Haley (1965; Penguin, 2001). While serving a prison sentence for larceny after World War II, Malcolm Little became a member of the Nation of Islam, taking the name Malcolm X. To black audiences, he brought inspiration and hope, while to others he represented race hatred as an anti-white demagogue. In keeping with the Nation of Islam's opposition to integration, Malcolm X denounced Martin Luther King as a "chump" and civil rights leaders as "stooges." He later converted to Sunni Islam and met with Gamal Abdel Nasser and Fidel Castro on his international travels. In 1965 he was assassinated by three members of the Nation of Islam.

Morris, Edmund, *The Rise of Theodore Roosevelt* (1979; Random House, 2001). The *Chicago Tribune*, famous for its criticism of Roosevelt's cousin Franklin Delano Roosevelt, proclaimed this account of TR's early life to be "one of the greatest biographies of our time." Morris captures a complex personality—naturalist, hunter, soldier, and politician—from his induction into Phi Beta Kappa at Harvard to his national fame as a Rough Rider leading the charge up San Juan Hill. Morris does not neglect the dark side of Roosevelt, for example, his reputation for violence for the sake of violence and an obsession with the "constant menace of Arab nationalism," but the overall interpretation is one of a unique figure of indomitable bravery and public spirit.

Obama, Barack, *Dreams from My Father: A Story of Race and Inheritance* (2004; Penguin, 2007). Obama was born in 1961. He writes candidly of his childhood, especially of his mother, a white American from Wichita, Kansas, and his father, a Kenyan who returned to Africa without his wife and child. His mother took him from Hawaii to Indonesia, where she remarried. The book's theme is "the fissures of race that have characterized the American experience." He discusses his sense of having a "troubled heart," "mixed blood," and a "divided soul." He describes his quest to learn more about his father as a psychological odyssey. The account ends with Obama entering the Harvard Law School in 1988. He took as a model for the book Ralph Ellison's *Invisible Man.*

Sanger, Margaret, *The Autobiography of Margaret Sanger* (1938; Dover, 2004). The radical champion of modern birth-control methods, Sanger was arrested after opening a clinic in Brooklyn in 1916. She dedicated her life to making birth control a basic human right, but later her reputation became tarnished because of her involvement in the eugenics movement, which believed, among other things, that African Americans were second-class citizens and that America's population needed to become genetically purer through forced sterilization, particularly of the poor, the incarcerated, and the "feebleminded." She nevertheless stands as a pioneer in the field of women's history. David M. Kennedy's *Birth Control in America: The Career of Margaret Sanger* (1971) is a critical but balanced account of her life.

Steel, Ronald, *Walter Lippmann and the American Century* (1980; Routledge, 1999). Lippmann wrote his newspaper column "Today and Tomorrow" from 1931 to 1967. By the end, he had spent six decades in public life, mainly as a journalist. Of the twelve presidents he had known, Theodore Roosevelt alone he found "lovable." A sympathetic and perceptive biographer, Steel paints a portrait of a towering intellectual with a cold and distant personality. Lippmann held as an axiom that America's destiny was linked with those of the European nations bordering the Atlantic. He was outspoken in objecting to U.S. attempts to be a global policeman. Lippmann's column was read throughout the country and abroad as the expression of enlightened American opinion. Steel's biography does him justice.

Stein, Gertrude, *The Autobiography of Alice B. Toklas* (1933; Penguin, 2001). The poet Gertrude Stein and her companion, Alice Toklas, lived in Paris and frequently entertained artists and writers, including Picasso and Hemingway. The first two chapters of the *Autobiography*—Stein is in fact the author—provide an account of Toklas's background, but most of the book deals with Stein. She is presented as if seen by an ordinary American woman who regards her as a literary genius. The book is written with mock simplicity, wit, and more than a tinge of arrogance. Stories of their friends—Guillaume Apollinaire, Sherwood Anderson, and Henri Matisse among them—and their fallings-out figure prominently in the narrative. The book was a commercial success, although generally disliked by the figures depicted in it.

Thoreau, Henry David, *Walden* (1854; Signet Classics, intro. W. S. Merwin, 2004). Thoreau's account of life in a cabin on Walden Pond became a touchstone of American nature writing and influenced twentieth-century environmental movements. His writings embraced transcendentalism by searching for spiritual truth and self-reliance. His major work of political thought, *Civil Disobedience* (1866), supports justifiable opposition to government. His antislavery and antiwar sentiments gave inspiration to nonviolent resistance movements, including those led by Gandhi and Martin Luther King, as well as the antiwar protests of the 1960s. For Thoreau's later influence, see Stanley Cavell, *The Senses of Walden* (1972), a perceptive work on the cultural heritage of Thoreau; and Robert M. Thorson, *The Boatman: Henry David Thoreau's River Years* (2016), for Thoreau's place as one of the first public figures concerned with environmental change.

Urquhart, Brian, *Ralph Bunche: American Odyssey* (1993; Norton, 1998). Urquhart makes a fundamental contribution to the history of the United Nations with his biography of Ralph Bunche, the grandson of a former slave. There are two overarching themes: race—Bunche was a militant critic of white Americans' racial prejudice—and the UN. He helped plan the UN in 1944–45, first at the Dumbarton Oaks Conference, in Washington, D.C., and then at the Charter Conference in San Francisco. Urquhart traces his career as the first Negro—the word Bunche always used to describe himself—to receive a Ph.D. at Harvard; his leadership in civil rights; and his Nobel Peace Prize for achieving the Israeli-Arab armistice in 1949. His achievements remain a model for working toward peace.

Utley, Robert M., *Geronimo* (2012; Yale, 2013). Geronimo was the legendary Apache warrior who fought both Mexican and American troops from the mid-nineteenth century until his final capture in 1886. A U.S. Army officer described him as one of the "most cruel of the savages" yet also "one of the brightest, most resolute, determined-looking men that I have ever encountered." Utley relates a balanced story by alternating the perspectives of Apaches and whites. He explains how Geronimo managed to remain free for decades and why he finally surrendered, eventually becoming a celebrity, meeting President Theodore Roosevelt, and performing rope tricks at Wild West shows. Utley's *Sitting Bull: The Life and Times of an American Patriot* (1993) is a biography of a spiritual and dignified figure.

Washington, Booker T., *Up From Slavery* (1901; Penguin, 1999). Born in 1856 on a plantation in Virginia, Washington at age sixteen entered the Hampton Normal and Agricultural Institute, where he trained to become a teacher. At twenty-five, he was appointed the first leader of the Tuskegee Institute, which emphasized agriculture and industry as ways "to promote the economic progress of the negro race." He did not challenge segregation, nor did he speak publicly on equality, because doing so would have jeopardized his financial support from northern white philanthropists. As a result, he was attacked by W. E. B. Du Bois and others as an "Uncle Tom." Long after his death, his papers revealed that he had secretly and financially supported the full agenda of civil and political rights for African Americans.

Williams, T. Harry, *Huey Long* (1969; Vintage, 1981). A populist and a radical, Long served as governor of Louisiana from 1928 to 1932 and as a member of the U.S. Senate from 1932 until his assassination in 1935. Often condemned as a political villain, he achieved notoriety as a quasi dictator by using political coercion and thuggery; yet he improved the lot of poor blacks as well as poor whites. In this epic work, Williams simply presents the story and lets the reader decide on the place of the Kingfish in American history. The protagonist of Robert Penn Warren's novel *All the King's Men* (1946) was inspired by Long. For a useful example of how the concept can be applied to a different time and place, see Stephen Kinzer, *All the Shah's Men* (2003).

Autobiographies, Biographies, Memoirs
Africa, Asia, Canada, Europe, Latin America, the Middle East

Africa
Hancock, W. Keith, *Smuts: The Sanguine Years, 1870–1919* (Cambridge, 1962). Jan Christiaan Smuts, an outstanding British and South African statesman and military leader, fought with the Boers against the British, served in the British War Cabinet in World War I, and later governed South Africa as prime minister. This volume carries Smuts's career through the Paris Peace Conference of 1919. The sequel, *The Fields of Force* (1968), spans his years as prime minister (1919–24, 1938–45) to his death in 1950. Hancock's biography bids fair to become one of the great biographies of the twentieth century. Three decades earlier, Hancock wrote *Australia* (1930), an enduring interpretation of Australian history as the mastering of a continent and the forging of an identity.

Huxley, Elspeth, *The Flame Trees of Thika: Memories of an African Childhood* (1959; Penguin, 2000). Huxley's parents arrived in Kenya, then known as British East Africa, in 1912 to start a small coffee farm. Thika is northeast of Nairobi on a branch of the Kenya-Uganda railway line, near the "Happy Valley," where in earlier times British aristocrats became famous for their decadent lifestyles. By contrast, Huxley experienced the hardships of rustic life and grew up among the Kikuyu and the Masai peoples. A biographer and novelist as well as a memoirist, Huxley wrote *White Man's Country: Lord Delamere and the Making of Kenya* (2 vols., 1935), a biography of a famous founding settler. An excellent account of the author's life is Christine Nicholls, *Elspeth Huxley: A Biography* (2002).

Mandela, Nelson, *Long Walk to Freedom: The Autobiography of Nelson Mandela* (1995; Little, Brown, 1995). The apartheid government of South Africa viewed Mandela as a terrorist and imprisoned him for 27 years on Robben Island. Mandela notes the psychological toll of incarceration: "There were many dark moments when my faith in humanity was sorely tested, but I would not and could not give myself up to despair." Under the inspired leadership of F. W. de Klerk, the government released him in 1990, and in 1994 he became the first black president of multi-racial South Africa. He stands with Gandhi and Martin Luther King as one of the twentieth's century's foremost anticolonial and antiracist leaders.

Soyinka, Wole, *The Man Died: Prison Notes* (1972; Vintage, 1994). An outspoken critic of repressive rule as well as a distinguished playwright and poet, Soyinka castigated African regimes, including Nigeria's, for "the oppressive boot and the irrelevance of the colour of the foot that wears it." He was imprisoned in 1967 during the Nigerian civil war and kept in solitary confinement for nearly two years. *The Man Died,* mainly written on toilet paper, is a testimony to the strength of the ideas running through his plays and poetry. In 1986 he became the first African awarded the Nobel Prize in Literature. Soyinka's versatility can be seen in his *Opera Wonyosi* (1977), an adaptation of Bertolt Brecht's *Threepenny Opera.*

Ancient World

Plutarch, *Parallel Lives* (2nd century AD; Oxford World's Classics, abridged as *Greek Lives*, 1998, and *Roman Lives*, 1999, both trans. Robin Waterfield). Drawing on earlier histories, anecdotes, inscriptions, and his own researches, including many sources no longer extant, Plutarch wrote 46 short, paired biographies of the most famous figures of the classical world. Plutarch was a favorite source for Shakespeare, an influence on Rousseau, and a staple of European education into the modern era. Especially recommended: the lives of Lycurgus, Pericles, Alexander, Julius Caesar, and Mark Antony.

Canada

English, John, *Just Watch Me: The Life of Pierre Elliott Trudeau, 1968–2000* (Penguin, 2010). In this second volume of Trudeau's life, John English establishes the force of Trudeau's intellect and political acuity. The theme is the way he maintained unity during the Quebec sovereignty movement and created a pan-Canadian identity. English wrote the biography with access to Trudeau's private papers and letters, giving him insight into Trudeau's flamboyant personality and the way in which he caused polarizing reactions throughout Canada because of his intellectual arrogance and his contempt for opponents. He took pride in fostering a Canadian identity and in helping defeat Quebec's secession movement, commenting that he "had never been so proud to be a Quebecer and a Canadian."

Levine, Allan, *King: William Lyon Mackenzie King* (2012; Douglas & McIntyre, 2013). Mackenzie King was prime minister of Canada for twenty-one years (1921–30, 1935–48), far and away the longest tenure of any Canadian leader. Levine's biography is significant because it is a balanced work in a field of controversial accounts that take King to task for such things as his spiritualism, his consorting with prostitutes, and his seeming neglect of French Canadians. King was an Anglophile but insisted on Canada's autonomy. During World War II, he increased the size of the Canadian armed forces from ten thousand to over a million. He got on well with both Roosevelt and Churchill while preserving his Canadian nationalism, which had a streak of anti-Americanism. He spoke with a slight Scottish burr.

Pearson, L. B. *Words and Occasions* (1970; Toronto, 1972). In this collection of writings, Lester "Mike" Pearson discusses his rise in Canadian politics, his part in the Suez crisis of 1956, and his success in keeping Canada out of the war in Vietnam. He won the Nobel Peace Prize in 1957 for organizing the United Nations Emergency Force in the Suez Canal crisis, but was denounced by some Canadians as having betrayed the British and the "mother country." Together with Secretary-General Dag Hammarskjöld, he forged the UN concept of peacekeeping. During Pearson's tenure as prime minister, 1963–68, Charles de Gaulle visited Canada and proclaimed, "Vive le Québec libre!" Pearson was enraged, telling de Gaulle, "Canadians do no need to be liberated!"

China

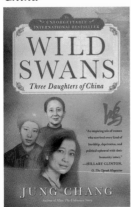

Chang, Jung, *Wild Swans* (1991; Touchstone, 2003). A history of China, 1909–78, based on personal experiences of three generations of women: grandmother (concubine to a warlord), mother (Maoist and victim of the Cultural Revolution), and daughter (the author, "re-educated" in the interior of China). The book takes the reader through the last days of the Manchu dynasty, the short-lived republic, the Japanese invasion, the horrors of Maoism, and the Deng reforms. For China, the story is about as important as anything else that happened in the twentieth century. Iris Chang's *The Rape of Nanking* (1997) is an unblinking history of the murder of 300,000 Chinese and the rape of 80,000 women by Japanese soldiers in 1937—it adds a further atrocity to the overall story covered by Jung Chang's *Wild Swans*.

Pakula, Hannah, *The Last Empress: Madame Chiang Kai-shek and the Birth of Modern China* (2009; Simon and Schuster, 2010). Soong Mei-ling, hot tempered, shrewd, and ruthless, was the wife of the Chinese nationalist leader Chiang Kai-shek. She spent part of her early years in the American South and spoke English with a southern accent. She became the symbol of Chinese resistance to the Japanese, but Chiang's post-1945 regime was authoritarian, corrupt, and ineffective. Was she the "last empress"? Jonathan Spence, the leading Western scholar of China, believes that she never had a coherent vision that could be called imperial and that her access to power was episodic. A good account of the life of her husband is Jay Taylor, *The Generalissimo: Chiang Kai-shek and the Struggle for Modern China* (2009).

France

Chateaubriand, François-René de, *Memoirs from Beyond the Grave, 1768–1800* (1849; NYRB, trans. Alex Andriesse, 2018). Writer, historian, and politician, Chateaubriand lived through the French Revolution, the Napoleonic era, and the restoration of the monarchy. Descended from an ancient family of Breton aristocrats, he hunted with King Louis XIV while a young man and later fled to America after seeing heads carried on pikes through the streets of Paris. In the United States, he gathered material for *Atala* and *René*, two pioneering works of French romanticism that made him internationally famous. The *Memoirs* have long been important in French cultural life; after resigning as head of the Provisional Government in 1946, de Gaulle said, "I don't care about anything. I am immersed in the *Memoirs from Beyond the Grave.*"

de Gaulle, Charles, *The War Memoirs of Charles de Gaulle* (1955–64; Carroll and Graf, trans. Richard Howard, 1988). These recollections encompass events from the fall of France in 1940 through the liberation of Paris to the aftermath of the war in 1946. Despite turbulent relations with Britain and, especially, the United States, de Gaulle emerges as the undisputed leader of the French Resistance. A stylist in the deliberate vein of Cicero, de Gaulle allows his personality to color every page, especially in his determination to restore France to its former glory. The overall impression is one of intense and controlled passion for one thing—the rebirth of France. De Gaulle, entirely sure of his place in history, saw himself as the symbol of his country.

Geyl, Pieter, *Napoleon: For and Against* (1949; Penguin, trans. Olive Renier, 1982). Geyl was the foremost Dutch historian of his time. Compelled to abandon his research after the Germans occupied Holland and interned him in the Buchenwald concentration camp, Geyl wrote about Napoleon with Hitler in mind. He explores the views of nineteenth- and early-twentieth-century French historians, and includes such quotations as Napoleon shouting to his chief diplomat, Talleyrand, that he was a "shit dressed in silk stockings." This book is historic for Geyl's own interpretation of Napoleon and for presenting the divergent views of French historians. David A. Bell's *Napoleon: A Concise Biography* (2015) portrays Napoleon as a self-promoting celebrity as well as the genius of the first total war.

Jackson, Julian, *A Certain Idea of France: The Life of Charles de Gaulle* (Penguin, 2018). This biography, which draws on a range of archival sources, focuses mainly on de Gaulle from World War II onward. De Gaulle had few resources during the war but, paradoxically, managed to place France at the center of world affairs. France, for example, was a coequal occupying power of Germany. One of the central passages relates de Gaulle's response to the danger of civil war breaking out over Algeria. Though often viewed as conservative, de Gaulle was a modernizer who, in Jackson's judgment, "celebrated scientific progress, economic and social reforms and the modernization of the armed forces." The biography leaves no doubt that de Gaulle was the greatest Frenchman since Napoleon.

Lacouture, Jean, *De Gaulle: The Rebel, 1890–1944* (1984; Norton, trans. Patrick O'Brian, 1993). Probably the best biography of the French leader by a French author, *De Gaulle* provides a clear assessment of the critical events culminating in the 1944 liberation of Paris. Rare for a book on de

Gaulle, it is impartial, not least in assessing his relations with Churchill, who found him exasperating, and Roosevelt, who humiliated him. He faced opposition among the French in occupied France and confronted considerable difficulty in organizing the Resistance. The book ends with de Gaulle's vindication when he marched into a liberated Paris. Throughout his life, de Gaulle was controversial, and there will always be anti-Gaullists in France. This biography helps explicate both the man's complexity and his stature.

Mitford, Nancy, *The Sun King: Louis XIV at Versailles* (1966; NYRB, 2012). A dual biography of sorts: the story of the epitome of absolute monarchs and of the monument he had built to celebrate his power. Though not trained as an historian—in fact, she was largely self-educated—Mitford acquired a mastery of primary sources and wrote with a vivid, conversational style that captured critics and readers alike. Mitford was one of five sisters, all of whom became either famous or notorious. Two were devoted to Hitler; another one became a muckraking journalist in America. Mitford started her literary career as a novelist, turning to biography later. Her other works in that field are are *Madame de Pompadour* (1954), *Voltaire in Love* (1957), and *Frederick the Great* (1970).

Reiss, Tom, *The Black Count: Glory, Revolution, Betrayal, and the Real Count of Monte Cristo* (2012; Penguin, 2013). During the French Revolution, Thomas-Alexandre Dumas, the son of a renegade French nobleman and a black Haitian slave, commanded 50,000 troops and then became one of Napoleon's most remarkable generals. His son was Alexandre Dumas; *The Three Musketeers* records some of his father's experiences (transposed to two centuries earlier). Reiss's clear and trenchant account places the "black count" in the wider context of France's role in the slave trade and colonial exploitation. An avowed aim of the Revolution was *égalité*—yet despite a brief moment of color blindness, the experience of General Dumas proved that racism was as ingrained in the French colonies as it was in the other European colonial empires.

Germany and Austria

Blanning, Tim, *Frederick the Great: King of Prussia* (2015; Penguin, 2016). The definitive biography in English of one of the most compelling figures of the eighteenth century. Frederick barely survived a sadistic upbringing under his father, Frederick William I. As king from 1740, he turned Prussia into a leading European power. He instigated the War of the Austrian Succession (1740–48) and deployed his armies across Europe during the Seven Years' War (1756–63), both to add to his territory and to weaken the Austrian Empire, an implacable foe. A minutely attentive administrator and a generous patron of the arts, as well as a talented flute player, Frederick became as famous for his tumultuous friendship with Voltaire as for his military successes—truly a man for his era.

Fest, Joachim, *Hitler* (1973; Harvest Mariner, 2002). Fest's biography was the first major biographical assessment of Hitler by a German writer to appear after Alan Bullock's *Hitler* in 1952, which maintains its own reputation as the classic work. Hitler's rise to power was essentially economic: ordinary Germans believed that he articulated their anxieties, and they accepted him as a leader who understood their mood, even recognizing themselves in him. Fest's other works include *Plotting Hitler's Death* (1997), which sustains his general argument that the German people willfully refused to accept the truth about Nazi rule until it was too late.

Hitler, Adolf, *Mein Kampf* (1925; Houghton Mifflin, 2009). Hitler was a gifted orator, not a writer, and *Mein Kampf* is rambling and repetitive yet wildly boisterous. One of his goals was to pillory the German leadership responsible for the country's defeat in World War I. The passages on the Jews, though only a small part of the book, make clear his anti-Semitism, which was connected with his belief that the destruction of the Soviet Union would give Germany the opportunity for territorial expansion, including, above all, land for settlers. He dictated the book, which helps explain how the cadence and emotion of his oratory were carried over into his prose; he sometimes burst into tears while reading particular passages. The book's mesmerizing rhetoric and impassioned plea to the German people eventually formed the ideological core of Nazism.

Jünger, Ernst, *Storm of Steel* (1920; trans. Michael Hoffmann, Penguin, 2004). Wounded at least fourteen times during World War I on the western front, Jünger seemed to many to be the personification of a German glorying in war as a mystical experience. As he recounts in this memoir, he instead saw himself as a soldier doing his duty as a patriotic yet conservative nationalist. He refused to join the Nazi party and lived to the age of 102, a towering figure in West German literature who wrote more than fifty books on subjects including poetry, philosophy, biology, and the use of LSD. In old age he renounced the German "ideology of war" as a "calamitous mistake."

Ritter, Gerhard, *Frederick the Great* (1936; California, trans. Peter Paret, 1975). The eighteenth-century king of Prussia stands in history as "Frederick the Great" for making Prussia a leading military power in Europe. He gained extensive battlefield experience in the wars he started and, like his father, maintained a large, highly trained standing army. He also supported the arts and increased freedom of the press and religion. He hoped to create "a lasting order of laws and peace." Ritter's book challenged Nazi ideology and was interpreted as a criticism, in one critic's words, of Hitler's "ideological fanaticism and insatiable lust for power." Ritter was later involved in the July 1944 plot against Hitler. He survived and continued to teach at the University of Freiburg until 1956.

Safranski, Rüdiger, *Martin Heidegger: Between Good and Evil* (2017). A sound biography as well as a comprehensive and clear account of Heidegger's philosophy. Contemporary sources described Heidegger as deceitful, ungenerous, and resentful, and he was a thoroughgoing Nazi from 1933 to 1945. Yet his major work, *Being and Time* (1927), has left an imprint on Western philosophy. He explicates a fundamental concept: the meaning of "being," or existence per se. Heidegger stands in the same rank as Kant and Hegel; and Sartre wrote *Being and Nothingness* under his influence. Did it matter, for the influence of his philosophy, that he was a Nazi? Those wishing to jump into the fray are warned that *Being and Time* is not for the faint of heart.

Speer, Albert, *Inside the Third Reich: Memoirs* (1969; Simon & Schuster, trans. Richard and Clara Winston, 1997). Speer was Hitler's chief architect and later his minister of armaments. His memoir, written while Speer was serving a twenty-year sentence in Spandau prison, provides a firsthand account of life among the Nazi elite. His book is notable for its frankness. Speer does not shy away, for example, from describing the hellish conditions of the slave laborers working on the V-1 program at Peenemünde and the V-2 rockets at Nordhausen. By contrast, the Nazi scientists Wernher von Braun and Walter Dornberger, who were brought to the United States after the war, wrote reminiscences that resolutely ignored the moral aspect of their work for Hitler and concentrated instead on the romance of rocketry.

Steinberg, Jonathan, *Bismarck: A Life* (2011; Oxford, 2012). The man of "blood and iron" not only unified the thirty-nine sovereign German states in 1871 but also kept the European peace for a quarter of a century. He had a volcanic temper but never allowed it to deflect him from his overall aim of dominating Europe while restraining France and Russia. Steinberg's method is to let the voices of those who knew Bismarck, and wrote down what he said, tell the story of his Rabelaisian monologues, his destruction of enemies and alienation of friends, his everyday subtlety and subversive humor, and above all his recognition of his own political limits. The best biography of Bismarck in English.

Zweig, Stefan, *The World of Yesterday* (1942; trans. Anthea Bell; Nebraska, 2013). Written when the Nazis were increasing their power and control in central Europe, Zweig's last book takes as a theme the wreckage of the Austro-Hungarian Empire as a result of World War I, and it includes Zweig's years of exile, which, as a pacifist, he spent in Switzerland and Brazil. He consistently expressed an emphatically European rather than national outlook, an aspect of his customary humanistic perspective. He sent the manuscript to the publisher the day before he committed suicide. Zweig's *Beware of Pity* (1939), the only novel the author published during his lifetime, relates the grim story of an Austrian military officer who performs an act of charity that inexorably ruins his life.

India

Chaudhuri, Nirad C., *The Autobiography of an Unknown Indian* (1951; NYRB, 2001). Chaudhuri dedicated his book "to the Memory of the British Empire in India," an attempt at mock-imperial rhetoric that nonetheless infuriated the Indian establishment. Iconoclastically relating the history of India before independence, he records his disenchantment with Indian nationalism and his gratitude to the British cultural legacy. Winston Churchill candidly wrote that the autobiography was among the best books he ever read; and V.S. Naipaul described it as the best account "of the penetration of one culture by another." Chaudhuri's *Passage to England* (1959) is an admiring yet sardonic view of all things British. He notes, as one reviewer commented, that the pursuit of love in England is as serious as the pursuit of money in India.

Gandhi, Mohandas Karamchand, *The Story of My Experiments with Truth* (1927–29; Beacon, trans. Mahadev Desai, 1993). In a slightly incoherent but engaging way, this account tells of Gandhi's struggle for India's freedom, including fasts, mass campaigns of civil disobedience, and imprisonment. Above all, he explains his principle of satyagraha, or nonviolent resistance, which gave inspiration to his followers throughout the world. They later included leaders of the American civil rights movement. The autobiography helps the reader to understand how he became a symbol of peaceful means to resolve conflict. The outstanding biography is *Gandhi: Prisoner of Hope* by Judith Brown (1991), especially good on Gandhi's aspiration to establish an anarchic utopia based on agriculture yet embracing "eternal truths in a changing world."

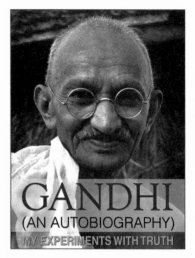

Gopal, Sarvepalli, *Jawaharlal Nehru: A Biography*, vol. 1 (3 vols., 1975–84). In a not uncritical account of Nehru's early years to the Partition of India in 1947, Gopal describes his subject as being brought into politics by Annie Besant at the time of World War I; his acceptance of Gandhi's moral principles, particularly civil disobedience; the development of his radical views in the interwar period; his imprisonment for anti-imperialist speeches in 1940; his writing of the cultural and historical *Discovery of India* while in prison; his negotiations with Jinnah and the realization that Partition was inevitable; and, as if reaching a climax in the first part of his career, his collaboration with Mountbatten in achieving independence in August 1947. A masterly work.

Israel

Oz, Amos, *A Tale of Love and Darkness* (2002; Houghton Mifflin, 2005). This book tells the story of the author's European background and loyalty to Israel, his childhood in the last days of the British mandate, and his mother's suicide in 1952. It is a double memoir of himself and Israel's early years, "Israel's violent birth pangs." Elias Khoury, the Palestinian writer, paid to have the book translated into Arabic and distributed in Beirut and other Arab cities in order to promote better understanding of "the Jewish people's national rebirth." Oz's writing reflects his belief in a two-state solution to the Israeli-Palestinian conflict. His allegorical novel *Judas* (2014) is a meditation on treason, betrayal, and idealism.

Teveth, Shabtai, *The Burning Ground: A Biography of David Ben-Gurion* (1971; Houghton Mifflin, 1989). In this highly readable and engaging biography, Teveth gives a full account of Ben-Gurion's life from his early years to the time he became the first prime minister of Israel, in 1948. Teveth is not an uncritical admirer, but he reflects on Ben Gurion's choices and asks questions about alternatives. The theme is Ben-Gurion's vision for a Jewish society and the building of institutional foundations. The biography comes to an end in 1948, when the next volume would have started had Teveth lived. Anita Shapiro's *Ben-Gurion: Father of Modern Israel* (2014) focuses on the period after 1948 and provides original insights into a complex man and his political leadership.

Weizmann, Chaim, *Trial and Error: The Autobiography of Chaim Weizmann*, ed. B. Horowitz (1949; Schocken, 1966). Weizmann was the Russian-born scientist and Zionist leader who became the first president of Israel. In this intellectually candid autobiography, he describes how he served two gods, the chemical laboratory and "Jews' street." Zionism represented to Weizmann a Jewish spiritual renaissance with a commitment to creating a Jewish state. He opposed Jewish terrorism in Palestine as a "cancer in the body politic" of Zionism. Though his autobiography sometimes reveals him as arrogant and manipulative, he succeeded in forging an alliance between the Zionist movement and the British Empire—and later in mobilizing the "Yankee Doodle Judaism" of American Jews. He played a vital part in persuading President Truman to recognize the Jewish state.

Italy
Cellini, Benvenuto, *Autobiography* (1563; Penguin, trans. George Bull, 1999). A sixteenth-century goldsmith and sculptor, Cellini composed his autobiography as a work of boisterous humor as well as a realistic description of prisons and palaces in Renaissance Italy—he was familiar with both. He was a braggart, blowhard, and murderer. Yet he was above all a distinguished sculptor, famous for works such as *Perseus with the Head of Medusa* and the *Cellini Salt Cellar*. He stands in literary history as a notorious Renaissance man who left an impression on widely diverse writers, including Ian Fleming, whose character Goldfinger was "a scientist in crime as great in his field as Cellini." *Cellini* (1985), the biography by John Wyndham Pope-Hennessy, is especially useful for its plates.

Levi, Primo, *If This Is a Man* (1947; Abacus, trans. Stuart Woolf, intro. Paul Bailey, 2003). Levi was arrested as a member of the Italian anti-Fascist resistance and imprisoned in Auschwitz in 1944–45. His account bears witness to the horrors of the Nazis' attempt to exterminate the Jewish people; yet the theme is humanity in the midst of inhumanity. Written with moral stamina and intellectual honesty, it is an unforgettable firsthand account of the Holocaust. "The camp was my university," he noted. Carole Angier's *The Double Bond: The Life of Primo Levi* (2002) is an intricate biography that is critical of Levi's "rational" response to the Nazis and also reveals his sense of guilt at having survived the camps.

Jamaica
Hall, Stuart, *Familiar Stranger: A Life between Two Islands* (with Bill Swartz, Penguin, 2017). Hall is sometimes called the godfather of postcolonial studies. As a Jamaican Rhodes Scholar in the early 1950s, he rebelled against Oxford's antiquarianism, hierarchical class culture, and racism. As one of the founding editors of the *New Left Review* and the director of Birmingham's Centre for Contemporary Cultural Studies, he combined literary theory, psychology, and social anthropology to forge the study of cultural identity Throughout his theoretical writings, he insists that cultural studies has the potential to resolve complexities of race, color, and class.

Latin America and South America

Arana, Marie, *Bolívar: American Liberator* (2013; Simon & Schuster, 2014). Inspired by the French and American revolutions, Simón Bolívar in the early nineteenth century aimed at a strong and united Latin America freed from the Spanish "triple yoke of ignorance, tyranny, and vice." He failed in his larger goal of unification but liberated the present-day countries of Venezuela, Bolivia, Columbia, Ecuador, Peru, and Panama. He later faced counterrevolutionary forces protesting his autocratic methods; but at the peak of his power, he ruled over a domain ranging from the Argentine border to the Caribbean. *Bolívar* gives a firm, comprehensive and acutely sensitive account of a man commonly regarded as the most revered figure in Latin American history.

Katz, Friedrich, *The Life and Times of Pancho Villa* (Stanford, 1998). One of the leaders of the Mexican Revolution (1910–20), Pancho Villa raised the largest revolutionary armies in Mexican history and became, as this comprehensive and perceptive book makes clear, a mythic figure. He was the first foreigner to attack the U.S. mainland since the War of 1812. He had a knack for guerrilla warfare, recruiting troops from the villages. In the people's view, he was a peasant's son driven to banditry, a hero who robbed the rich and righted the wrongs inflicted on the poor—a reputation he continues to hold in Mexican consciousness. Villa's popular image has been shaped in part by over two dozen Hollywood films, one starring Yul Brynner (1968).

Womack, John, Jr., *Zapata and the Mexican Revolution* (1969; Vintage, 1970). Womack's subject is the charismatic Emiliano Zapata, who led a peasant revolt during the Mexican Revolution of 1910–20, which radically transformed Mexican culture as well as government. Womack writes passionately and admiringly of Zapata as a courageous and just leader. His focus is on Zapata's dedication to land reform—he broke the back of the country's "Spanish feudal inheritance"—which made him a popular hero. Today Zapata is remembered as a visionary who fought for his countrymen in a spontaneous uprising that helped shape Mexico's national identity. According to Ernest R. May of Harvard, the book is "the best piece of narrative history that has been written about modern Latin America in any language."

Middle East

Burton, Richard Francis, *Personal Narrative of a Pilgrimage to El-Madinah and Meccah*, vol. 3 (3 vols., 1855–56; Cambridge, 2011). In 1853, Captain Richard Francis Burton traveled in disguise to the two holy cities of Islam. As a non-Muslim, he would have been executed if discovered. But he had mastered several Arabic dialects and the intricacies of Islamic ritual and etiquette—and even had himself circumcised—and so, despite several close calls, remained undetected. Besides mastering two dozen languages and exploring the Great Lakes of East Africa, he translated *The Arabian Nights* and the *Kama Sutra* into English and wrote numerous popular and scientific works on geography, cartography, ethnology, falconry, war, and sex. The best study is by Dane Kennedy, *The Highly Civilized Man: Richard Burton and the Victorian World* (2005).

Musaddiq, Mohammad, *Musaddiq's Memoirs* (JEBHE, intro. Homa Katousian, 1988). A charismatic leader, Musaddiq mobilized the Iranian nationalist movement in the early 1950s by challenging the country's corrupt, authoritarian political system and denouncing economic exploitation by the British. In 1951, he nationalized the Anglo-Iranian Oil Company. In 1953, joint intervention by the British and American intelligence agencies MI5 and CIA toppled his regime. His memoir helps explain why he is remembered as a revered figure in Iran's national history. The authority on Musaddiq's overthrow in 1953 is Mark J. Gasiorowski; see, for example, his *Mohammad Mosaddeq and the 1953 Coup in Iran* (2017, coedited with Malcolm Byrne), a milestone in the history of the subject.

Nafisi, Azar, *Reading Lolita in Tehran: A Memoir in Books* (2003; Random House, 2008). Despite the repression of Ayatollah Khomeini's Islamic Republic, an intrepid professor, Azar Nafisi, secretly met with female students to read Western classics. They read the works of Jane Austen, F. Scott Fitzgerald, Henry James, and Vladimir Nabokov. Taking inspiration from these works, they demonstrated resilience in the face of fundamentalist oppression. Their reactions varied widely: some objected to Austen more than *Lolita,* and others held highly individualistic views on "Islamic feminism" and the cultural upheavals of the 1970s. Readers find themselves seeing the world through the eyes of Shia Muslims caught up in a spiritual transformation, trying to save their country from falling into decadence.

Russia

Herzen, Alexander, *My Past and Thoughts* (1870. trans. Constance Garnett, intro. Isaiah Berlin, abr. Dwight Macdonald; California, 1992). Herzen came from a wealthy Russian landowning family. Much of his work was written in exile in London, and his ideas, particularly on agrarian populism, contributed to the emancipation of the serfs in 1861. His memoirs trace revolutionary developments from early Russian radicalism through the controversies over Russia's failure to modernize or to develop institutions of freedom. He wrote, "I have no liberty, I have no equality, I have no fraternity." His ideas are as relevant for Russia now as they were in his own time, and also for postcolonial Asia and Africa. Aileen Kelly's *The Discovery of Chance: The Life and Thought of Alexander Herzen* (2016) is an historically informed biography.

Kotkin, Stephen, *Stalin: Waiting for Hitler, 1929–1941* (Penguin, 2017). In the second volume of what will be a massive biography, Kotkin spares no details of Stalin as a murderer of millions. But his main purpose is to understand Stalin as a human being, a workaholic who read masses of reports but was also devoted to literature. Stalin's principal aim was to industrialize the Soviet Union, a goal he pursued inefficiently and at a horrendous cost of life. But by 1939 the Soviet Union was producing tanks and airplanes that would eventually turn the tide of the war. When the Germans attacked in 1941, they destroyed most of the Soviet air force and much of the army. Kotkin ends by pointing out that even worse was to come. An indispensable biography.

Kropotkin, Peter, *Memoirs of a Revolutionist* (1899; Black Rose, 1996). Born a Russian aristocrat in 1842, Kropotkin at an early age repudiated his princely title and denounced authoritarian institutions, including the state and the church. After joining the revolutionary movement in the 1870s, he spent most of his life in exile. In England, he became the leader of a movement known as "anarchist communism," which was based on self-sufficient societies free from central government control. He was invited to contribute the entry on anarchism to the *Encyclopedia Britannica* (11th ed.). He returned to Russia in 1917 but distanced himself from the Bolsheviks, opposing their authoritarian methods. Kropotkin acquired the lasting reputation of the best-known and best-liked figure in the anarchist movement, gregarious, knowledgeable, and irrepressible.

Taubman, William, *Khrushchev: The Man and His Era* (2003; Simon & Schuster, 2017). In 1953, Khrushchev famously denounced Stalin, an action both brave and reckless. He unmasked Stalin yet still admired him. Taubman quotes him as saying, "All of us taken together aren't worth Stalin's shit!" Khrushchev revived the Soviet Communist Party; he triumphed when *Sputnik* soared in orbit around Earth; he banged his shoe at the United Nations; and he misjudged the American response to the Cuban missile crisis. Taubman's Pulitzer Prize–winning work will long rank as the definitive biography. Taubman's *Gorbachev: His Life and Times* (2017) fully assesses the end of the Soviet Union, which saw Gorbachev praised in the West and despised in Russia.

Spain
Fernández-Armesto, Felipe, *Columbus* (1991; Oxford, 1996). This comprehensive and judicious biography challenges the legend of Columbus and provides an exact rendition of his travels of as well as a realistic assessment of his life. Fernández-Armesto places him in the context of the ongoing discovery of North and South America. Columbus was an autodidact who was intellectually aggressive but had only a rudimentary knowledge of navigation. He was not inspired by religion, turning to God only after the failures of his later expeditions. He died forlorn, without finding either gold or his long-sought passage to India. Written by an acknowledged authority on early European exploration, this is a sound and informative account that succeeds in separating fact from the romanticized Columbus.

Morison, Samuel Eliot, *Admiral of the Ocean Sea: A Life of Christopher Columbus* (1942; Little Brown, 1991). In a biography that portrays Columbus as a skilled navigator with strength of character, Morison demonstrates literary skill and exactitude (he sailed the routes of Columbus to ascertain details of the tempestuous voyages). He does not neglect the rapacious violence of the Spaniards' search for gold and slaves. Yet to historians of a later generation, Morison appears guilty of making cultural assumptions about the inferiority of the indigenous peoples and of ignoring how the barbarity of the Europeans would have appeared to their victims (for example, as described by Howard Zinn in *A People's History of the United States*).

Payne, Stanley G., and Jesús Palacios, *Franco: A Personal and Political Biography* (2011; Wisconsin, 2014). Biographies of Franco are usually biased or extreme in their interpretation. Payne and Palacios achieve an intricate balance, explaining how Franco's leadership in the civil war (1936–39) led to the nationalists' victory and the consolidation of his regime. Franco had gained extensive military experience while leading troops in North Africa, which helps explain the efficiency with which he oversaw the execution of thousands during the civil war, and his success in maintaining a military dictatorship from 1939 to 1975. The authors, among the first to gain access to the Franco archive, provide exacting detail about the decades of Franco's authoritarian rule, and a significant account of his support of the Axis during World War II.

Sweden

Urquhart, Brian, *Hammarskjold* (1972; Norton, 1994). Urquhart makes a fundamental contribution to the history of the United Nations with his biography of Dag Hammarskjöld, who served as secretary-general, 1953–61. He brought vitality to the UN and established the secretary-general as a major participant in world affairs. The biography is a substantial and enduring achievement, not least because it includes glimpses into a personality with wide interests in art and poetry, and religious beliefs bordering on mysticism. Hammarskjöld was widely respected as an intellectual. Major problems during his tenure included crises in Suez and the Congo. Urquhart provides a balanced account of Hammarskjöld's death in an airplane crash on his way to attempt to negotiate a cease-fire in the Congo. His leadership has never been equaled.

Vietnam

Brocheux, Pierre, *Ho Chi Minh: A Biography* (2007; Cambridge, trans. Claire Duiker, 2011). Brocheux was born in Vietnam to a French father and a Vietnamese mother. Sent to France at fifteen, he eventually became a lecturer at the University of Paris. That background is important for understanding the perspective in this accurate and sympathetic biography. His theme is Ho's steady preference for negotiation rather than confrontation. He tried to avoid conflict with the French; but he told a French general after World War II, "If we have to fight, we will fight." Brocheux describes Ho as having an abiding admiration for French culture, and a way of combining Leninist and Confucian thought. The standard work on Ho remains William Duiker, *Ho Chi Minh: A Life* (2000).

MacDonald, Peter G., *Giap: The Victor in Vietnam* (1993; Warner, 1994). General Vo Nguyen Giap of the People's Army of Vietnam played a decisive part, across four decades, in the fight for Vietnamese independence. He fought successively against Japanese, French, American, and Chinese forces, driving all of them from Vietnam. He is generally regarded as one of the great strategists of the twentieth century. Against the French in the 1940s and 1950s, and then the Americans in the 1960s and 1970s, he employed a combination of guerrilla and conventional tactics. MacDonald, a British general, was able to interview Giap. He writes clearly not only about Giap's military skills but also his part in securing the independence and unification of Vietnam.

Literature
Britain

17th century and earlier

Aubrey, John, *Brief Lives* (written 1669–96; first pub. 1813; Penguin, ed. John Buchanan-Brown, 2000). Aubrey, an antiquary, helped lay the foundations of modern biography. His interests included mathematics, astronomy, and archaeology, and he knew many of the scientists of his time; he became a member of the Royal Society in 1663. Gregarious and curious, Aubrey was acquainted with a wide swath of people, from high-ranking politicians to booksellers and merchants. The subjects of his short biographies include Francis Bacon, John Milton, Thomas Hobbes, Oliver Cromwell, Shakespeare, and Ben Jonson. Lively, even scandalous details are drawn from Aubrey's firsthand knowledge and wide reading as well as from anecdotes and folklore. *Brief Lives* is moreover significant for recording the details of everyday life, thereby providing a rounded, entertaining portrait of his era.

Bacon, Francis, *Essays* (1625; in Bacon, *The Major Works*, ed. Brian Vickers, Oxford, 2008). Bacon did not invent the essay form, but he was its earliest great practitioner in English. He wrote about whatever interested him, including revenge, envy, love, boldness, marriage, atheism, riches, and gardens, and then compressed and polished the essays until they glowed like gems. This heavily annotated edition explicates Bacon's references to the Bible and classical authors. Bacon was a phrasemaker ("hostages to fortune"), an aphorist ("What is truth? said jesting Pilate; and would not stay for an answer"), and an insightful commentator on numerous topics, including reading: "Some books are to be tasted, others to be swallowed, and some few to be chewed and digested."

Beowulf: A New Verse Translation, trans. Seamus Heaney (2000; Norton, 2001). In this Old English epic, Beowulf, hero of the Geats (western Swedes), successively wages battle against the monster Grendel, Grendel's mother, and (in Beowulf's old age) a dragon. The time of the poem is the sixth century; its date of composition is uncertain, but the only copy is part of a tenth-century manuscript. Old English poetry is notable for the use of kennings, compound terms for single ideas; examples in *Beowulf* include *whale-road* or *swan-road* for *sea*, *battle-sweat* for *blood*, and *raven-harvest* for *corpse*. Besides the poem's stark beauty, its power comes from the confrontation between human and monstrous forces—and the suggestion that humans might not always triumph.

Browne, Sir Thomas, *Religio Medici* and *Urne-Buriall* (1643, 1658; NYRB, ed. Stephen Greenblatt, 2012). Browne was a Norfolk physician with an idiosyncratic personality and a unique, ornate writing style. His *Religio Medici* (*Religion of a Doctor*), a psychological self-portrait, reveals a breadth of knowledge and curiosity about science, history, philosophy, and literature. He pursues especially the theme of faith, hope, and charity, not without subversive irony about the church and its rituals—which landed the work on the Vatican's *List of Prohibited Books*. *Urne-Buriall*, inspired by the local unearthing of Bronze Age funerary materials, is a comment on practices of interment, in effect a complement to the *Religio*. Virginia Woolf remarked that Browne paved the way for future writers of confessionals, private memoirs, and secret accounts of public affairs.

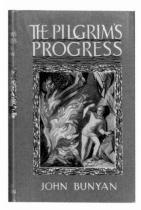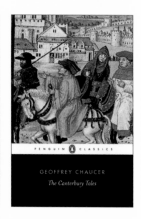

Bunyan, John, *The Pilgrim's Progress, from This World to That Which Is to Come* (1678; Oxford World's Classics, 2003). In the preeminent English allegory, the author dreams of Christian, weighed down by a burden of sin, who goes on a pilgrimage to the Celestial City. The journey takes him through, among other places, the Slough of Despond, the Valley of the Shadow of Death, Vanity Fair, and the Delectable Mountains. He is accompanied at times by the guides Faithful and Hopeful, yet encounters many enemies, including Mr. Worldly Wiseman, Lord Hate-Good, and the archdemon Apollyon. Bunyan's prose is steeped in biblical texts and cadences. Both Dickens and Thackeray paid tribute to it, as did many American writers, including Mark Twain and John Steinbeck.

Burton, Robert, *The Anatomy of Melancholy* (1621; NYRB, intro. William Gass, 2001). Burton was a seventeenth-century Oxford don who dabbled in mathematics and astrology. The *Anatomy*, his only published book, is rich in humor as well as encyclopedic detail on the subject of melancholia, a condition of low spirits that includes depression. Melancholia in Burton's sense is produced by an excess of black bile, which leads to bitterness and despondency. Anyone can be afflicted—scholars, lovers, statesmen, criminals. It affects virtually all human emotion and thought. Yet melancholia can frequently be a source of inspiration and creativity. This is hardly a book to be read from cover to cover, but dipping into it can be hilarious as well as enlightening about human emotions. And it makes one less melancholic.

Chaucer, Geoffrey, *The Canterbury Tales* (1478; Oxford World's Classics, 1985). In an ironic and critical portrait of English society, Chaucer's narrative, in poetry and prose, follows a group of thirty pilgrims traveling together from London to Canterbury to visit the shrine of St. Thomas à Becket. The group contains members from across English society: a knight, a merchant, a miller, a cook, a physician, a squire, etc. They pass the time by telling stories, which range from courtly romances to crude, bawdy revenge tales. Of this foundational work of English literature, Colin Powell once said that having knowledge of it and other classics helped him eventually become a four-star general in the U.S. Army.

Donne, John, *The Complete Poetry and Selected Prose of John Donne* (Modern Library, ed. Charles M. Coffin, 2001). Donne, a major poet of the seventeenth century, was renowned for love poems, sonnets, religious works, and satires. His poetry uses strong, surprising metaphors, irony, and unconventional rhythms to address corruption in English society, erotic themes, and questions of faith. In his own time, he was recognized as brilliant and learned. He became an Anglican priest and eventually dean of St. Paul's Cathedral. The titles of Ernest Hemingway's *For Whom the Bell Tolls* and Thomas Merton's *No Man Is an Island* were taken from Donne's "Meditation XVII." Recommended also: *Richard Burton Reads the Poetry of John Donne* (Saland, 2009).

Dryden, John, *The Major Works* (17th century; Oxford, ed. John Walker Keith, 2004). Dryden's poetry and literary criticism are marked by his knowledge of Greek and Roman literature. His translation of Plutarch's *Parallel Lives* was the standard for centuries. He earned fame as a playwright with works such as *All for Love* (1678) and *Marriage à la Mode* (1672), and with satiric verse, including *Mac Flecknoe* (1682), an attack on the poet Thomas Shadwell, and *Absalom and Achitophel* (1681), a political allegory. In 1688, he was made England's first poet laureate. In the nineteenth century, Coleridge, Keats, and Byron held him in high esteem, and his wit and style remain popular and highly regarded by students as well as judicious critics. For an account of the poet's life and times, see James Anderson Winn, *John Dryden and His World* (1987).

Ford, John, *'Tis Pity She's a Whore, and Other Plays* (c. 1629; Oxford 2008). The subject of the play, incest, perhaps explains why it was controversial from the outset and only rarely performed. Giovanni and Annabella, the compromised brother and sister at the center of the story, are not confused about their feelings for each other, but sense that their mutual desire is "evil." The rest of the action is Jacobean tragedy at its most overwrought: stabbings, poisonings, a blinding, and a burning at the stake. At one point, a human heart is impaled on a dagger and carried aloft. From the mid-twentieth century, the play has found success with audiences, who have taken a more tolerant view of Ford's failure to censure the two lovers.

Jonson, Ben, *Volpone* (1605; Norton, ed. Robert N. Watson, 2003). *Volpone*, a comedy, remains the most commonly performed play by Jonson. Volpone ("fox"), rich and childless, pretends to be dying in order to extract gifts from his potential heirs, Corvino ("crow"), Corbaccio ("raven"), and Voltore ("vulture"). Aided by his servant Mosca ("fly"), Volpone seems to triumph, but is punished in the end for his deceit. The others likewise face the heavy hand of justice—Mosca, for example, is sent to the galleys. The play is a species of beast fable, an allegorical literary form that uses animals to skewer human foibles, famously used by authors as diverse as Aesop and George Orwell (*Animal Farm*).

Langland, William, *Piers the Ploughman* (c. 1377; Penguin. trans. J. F. Goodridge, 1959). The work of a fourteenth-century cleric, *Piers the Ploughman* is one of the great poems of Middle English. The narrator, Will, has a series of eight visions while he sleeps. He first sees all humanity living between the Tower of Truth and the Dungeon of Falsehood. In the second vision, Piers leads a pilgrimage to Truth; in visions four and five, he performs Christlike acts of charity. In the third vision, Will sets out on his own search for Truth, consulting Thought, Wit, Study, Clergy, Scripture, Imagination, and Reason. The poem is both imaginative and dense with theological argument; the overarching theme is man's search for meaning in relation to eternity.

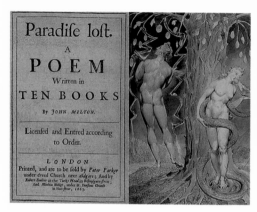 

Milton, John, *Paradise Lost* (1667; Penguin Classics, 2000). Milton's epic on "man's first disobedience, and the fruit / Of that forbidden tree" is an attempt to "justify the ways of God to men." It describes the revolt of the rebel angels, their defeat by the Son of God, their plot to corrupt mankind, the creation of Adam and Eve, the tempting of Eve, her sin and Adam's, God's judgment on them, and their expulsion from the Garden of Eden. Before everything goes wrong, Adam and the archangel Raphael discuss astronomy. The actions of God, Adam, and Eve are the focus, but Satan, charismatic to a fault, constantly upstages them. There is an excellent audio recording by Ralph Cosham (Blackstone).

More, Thomas, *Utopia* (1516; Penguin, 2003). The mercurial Henry VIII had More, his Lord High Chancellor, executed for refusing to accept the king as head of the Church of England. The circumstances of More's death were ironic in view of the society depicted in *Utopia* (Greek for "no place"), an island city-state characterized by religious tolerance and government by reason. Communal ownership supplants private property, and women are educated equally with men. Some four hundred years later, the pope canonized More as a Catholic martyr, and he was honored in the Soviet Union for describing a society without private property. A good biographical account of More is Peter Ackroyd's *The Life of Sir Thomas More* (1998), and the film *A Man for All Seasons* (1966), with Paul Scofield as More, compellingly dramatizes his conflict with the king.

Shakespeare, William, *Works* (1589–1613; Norton, 3rd. ed., 2015). The greatest playwright in English literature. Coiner of hundreds of words, including "obscene" (in *Richard II*), "assassination" (*Macbeth*), and "hint" (Othello), and innumerable now-common expressions, including "brave new world" (*The Tempest*), "give the devil his due" (*Henry IV, Part 1*), and "kill with kindness" (*The Taming of the Shrew*). The following plays provide a good introduction to his work; the recommended paperback versions of the individual plays are the current Arden editions.

A Midsummer Night's Dream (c. 1595; 2006): Theseus, duke of Athens, is set to marry Hippolyta, former queen of the Amazons. Oberon, king of the fairies, and his estranged queen Titania rest in a forest before the wedding. A group of tradesmen rehearse a play to be performed at the ceremony, but they get caught up in scheme by Oberon to embarrass Titania, as do two young couples wandering about in the forest. Love potions and mischief-making fairies roil the plot, but all comes right in the end.

Hamlet (c. 1600; 2016): One of the world's most renowned plays, *Hamlet* is a family drama, a revenge story, and an exploration of personal will. Prince Hamlet kills or loses everyone close to him: his mother, uncle (and stepfather), beloved, best friend, and adviser. Through it all, he meditates on what it means to be a man, to take action, to fashion oneself into complete person. A play within a play, more serious than the one in *Midsummer*, suggests that Shakespeare may have viewed life as a kind of performance.

Twelfth Night (c. 1601; 2008): Viola and her twin, Sebastian, are shipwrecked, and separated, off the coast of Illyria. Viola disguises herself as a young man and enters the service of Duke Orsino as a page. The duke is in love with Olivia, who rejects him. A great deal of miscommunication, misidentification, and misinformation brings the convoluted plot to the boiling point. On the other hand, a subplot involving a plan by Olivia's household to humiliate her officious steward, Malvolio, is charmingly clear.

King Lear (c. 1605; 1997): An old king misjudges his three daughters' love for him, with harrowing consequences. Lear loses his family, his kingdom, and eventually his sanity. The two nefarious sisters are undone by an even more malign character, Edmund, one of the author's supreme villains. Many, including Samuel Johnson, have viewed the death of Lear's faithful daughter, Cordelia, as almost unbearable. The play's bleakness is caught by the lines "As flies to wanton boys, are we to the gods; They kill us for their sport."

Macbeth (c. 1606; 2015): Three witches tell a Scottish nobleman that he is destined to be king. Urged on by his ambitious wife, he ensures that outcome by murdering the king. The king's sons escape, but Macbeth pursues one, killing his wife and children. Overtaken by fear and paranoia, Macbeth unleashes carnage on the kingdom, conceding: "I am in blood / Stepped in so far that, should I wade no more, / Returning were as tedious as go o'er." Civil war erupts, and Macbeth's reign of terror comes to an end.

The Tempest (c. 1610; 2011): In Shakespeare's last masterpiece, an old magician, Prospero, and his daughter, Miranda, live on an island with the sprite Ariel and the monstrous Caliban. Prospero causes the wreck of a ship carrying his usurping brother and a group of courtiers, including young Ferdinand. Separations, plots, and reversals—directed by Prospero's magic, with Ariel's help—confuse matters until, finally, Miranda and Ferdinand marry. At the end, Prospero breaks his staff and renounces magic.

In Harold Bloom's *Shakespeare and the Invention of the Human* (1999), one of America's most prominent academic critics argues that Shakespeare invented not only the modern English language but also modern consciousness.

Spenser, Edmund, *The Faerie Queene* (1590–96: Penguin, ed. Thomas P. Roche and C. Patrick O'Donnell, 1979). This epic allegory is dedicated to Elizabeth I, who is represented as the Faerie Queene, Gloriana. The narrative presents the struggle between good and evil by relating the tale of King Arthur and recounting the quest of twelve knights, who each symbolize a particular virtue. In the poem's symbolism, it tells of controversies over the colonization of Ireland as well as contemporary issues of social inequality, political corruption, and the use of violence in the name of justice. The work later captured the imaginations of poets from Milton to the Romantics. One of the longest poems in the English language, it is also one of the most memorable and distinctive.

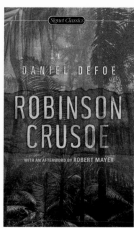

18th century

Blake, William, *The Marriage of Heaven and Hell* (1790; Bodleian Library, intro. Michael Phillips, 2011). In this book, told in the style of biblical prophecy, Hell is not so much a place of punishment as one where there is unrepressed energy and creative or debauched spontaneity— "The Road of Excess leads to the Palace of Wisdom"—as opposed to the regulated and authoritarian life in Heaven. In Blake's vision, the cosmos is unified, a place where "energetic creators," or devils, are as necessary as "rational organizers," the angels. Anthony Blunt's *The Art of William Blake* (1959) comprises six lectures on the development and meaning of Blake's paintings and engravings, including his "complex system of mystical symbolism."

Burns, Robert, *Selected Poems* (Penguin, ed. Carol McGuirk, 1994). The charismatic Burns is widely regarded as Scotland's national poet. Those who celebrate his work form a virtual cult. His most famous poems and songs include "Auld Lang Syne," "A Red Red Rose," "My Heart's in the Highlands," "To a Mouse" ("The best laid schemes o' mice an' men / Gang aft a-gley"), "To a Louse," "Tam o' Shanter" ("Nae man can tether time nor tide"), and "Scots, Wha Hae," an unofficial Scottish national anthem. Burns sympathized with the French Revolution and inspired the Romantic poets. Above all, his poetry expressed hope, as in the poem celebrating universal brotherhood: "That man to man, the warld o'er, / Shall brothers be for a' that."

Defoe, Daniel, *Robinson Crusoe* (1719; Signet Classics, intro. Paul Theroux, 1998). Defoe recounts the fictional autobiography of a castaway who spends twenty-eight years on a tropical island off the coast of Venezuela. The book was an important contribution to the "state of nature" debate in Enlightenment Europe; debate in Enlightenment Europe; Rousseau recommended it as the first book a boy should read. Crusoe survives and prospers through ingenuity, tenacity, and faith. He rescues a man, whom he names "Friday," from a group of cannibals, teaches him English, and converts him to Christianity. The novelist James Joyce commented that Crusoe is "the symbol of the British Empire," and the island a "British colony." An excellent study of Defoe and his works is presented in Paula R. Backscheider, *Daniel Defoe: His Life* (1989).

Fielding, Henry, *The History of Tom Jones* (1749; Penguin, 2005). The novel begins with the author declaring that it is a study in human nature. Tom Jones is a foundling brought up by a benevolent squire. A generous but wild and feckless country boy, he falls in love with the beautiful daughter of a neighboring squire. The plot then becomes complicated, almost unruly: banished from his home, Tom sets out to go to sea, gets caught up in the amorous machinations of some disreputable aristocrats, and almost goes to prison for killing a man in a fight. In the end, he is reconciled to the squire and reunited with his love. Details of his casual sexual encounters shocked readers at the time—Samuel Johnson among them—but now appear comical.

Jones, William, *Selected Poetical and Prose Works* (Univ. of Wales Press, ed. Michael John Franklin, 1993). Jones was a late eighteenth-century legal scholar and judge as well as a philologist who studied the relationship between European and Indian languages. He explicated the unmistakable similarities between Sanskrit, Greek, and Latin. His linguistic skills approached that of genius; by the end of his life, he had a working knowledge of some forty-eight languages. Politically, he was a radical, a friend of American independence and a champion of universal male suffrage. As a judge on the supreme court in Bengal, he codified Hindu and Muslim laws, laying the legal foundation of British rule in India. A good account of his life is Michael J. Franklin, *Orientalist Jones: Poet, Lawyer, and Linguist, 1746–94* (2011).

Pope, Alexander, *The Major Works* (Oxford, ed. Pat Rogers, 2009). Alexander Pope is eminently quotable: "A little learning is a dangerous thing," "To err is human; to forgive, divine," and "For Fools rush in where Angels fear to tread" all come from his *Essay on Criticism* (1711). Two of his great works are *The Rape of the Lock* (1712) and *The Dunciad* (1728), the former a mock-heroic poem about the theft of a lock of hair. The latter celebrates the goddess Dulness and her agents of imbecility, decay, and vulgarity. *The Dunciad*, which attacked political as well as cultural figures, caused such offense that Pope dared not go out without loaded revolvers. The definitive biography of the poet is Maynard Mack, *Alexander Pope: A Life* (1985).

Richardson, Samuel, *Clarissa: Or the History of a Young Lady* (1748; Penguin, 1986). *Clarissa*, which runs to more than a million words, has the reputation of being the longest novel in the English language. It is told entirely in letters. The heroine is under pressure from her family to marry a wealthy man whom she loathes. An untrustworthy rake named Lovelace tricks her into running away with him. Clarissa is beautiful, proud, and intelligent, but fatally attracted to Lovelace, who at one point confines her to a high-class brothel. Not entirely to reveal the long and complicated plot, but Clarissa attempts valiantly throughout to uphold her virtue. Though no doubt more talked about than read, *Clarissa* is one of the greatest English novels.

Stanhope, Philip, 4th Earl of Chesterfield, *Lord Chesterfield's Letters* (1774; Oxford, 2008). These earnest, well-intentioned letters from Chesterfield to his natural son were written weekly, sometimes daily, over a period of three decades, reaching a peak in the years 1748–52. They are witty, didactic, and often overbearing, always letting his son know that he was expected to avoid drinking, gambling, and low company, and that his father would be examining his life minutely. The condescending comments on women are of their time. Samuel Johnson commented at the time that the letters teach "the morals of a whore and the manners of a dancing master." On the other hand, Edward Gibbon sensed perceptively that they had the redeeming virtue of being "written from the heart."

Sterne, Laurence, *The Life and Opinions of Tristram Shandy, Gentleman* (1759–67; intro. Christopher Ricks, Penguin, 2003). This comic masterpiece, directly indebted to Cervantes, as well as to Montaigne, Swift, and Locke, combines satire, wild inventiveness (blank pages, diagrams, lines of asterisks), and humor both broad and gentle. The style anticipates that of the twentieth-century stream-of-consciousness novel as the narrative careers in all directions, interrupted by diversions and digressions on topics as various as military fortifications, travel in France, and a Latin treatise on noses. Tristram's birth is finally described in volume 3, where the belated preface to the novel also appears. Sterne's piercing wit and ribald perspective keep all this rollicking along—and always with bemused observations on the absurdities of life.

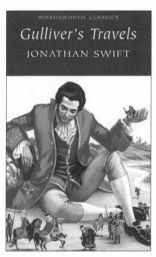

Swift, Jonathan, *Gulliver's Travels* (1726; Oxford World's Classics, 2008). In this satire, Lemuel Gulliver sails to uncharted lands, where he encounters tiny people, giant people, people more foolish than himself, and people much wiser. The tiny people—Lilliputians—hold him captive by tethering his arms and legs securely to the ground. The image has been adapted in countless ways, not least by Stanley Hoffmann in *Gulliver's Troubles*—which depicts the United States during the Vietnam War as a giant besieged by tiny enemies who nevertheless effectively shackle him. A representative sampling of Swift's shorter prose pieces can be found in *A Modest Proposal, and Other Writings* (Penguin, 2009), which includes essays, letters, and sermons, and the titular piece, about a culinary use for starving peasant children in Ireland.

19th century

Arnold, Matthew, *Culture and Anarchy* (1869; Oxford, 2009). Arnold was a mid-Victorian poet and critic, the son of the famous schoolmaster Thomas Arnold of Rugby. The essays in *Culture and Anarchy* address the problem of how to achieve high ideals. Arnold's targets are both the landed gentry ("Barbarians") and, particularly, the middle class ("Philistines"). The latter are accused of being overly complacent and yet intrusively vigilant, especially regarding the lower classes. His writing was intended to enhance civic life—"The men of culture are the true apostles of equality"—but was condemned as elitist. Spuriously populist criticism of Arnold revived in the late twentieth century and continues to the present. In *Matthew Arnold: A Critical Portrait* (2008), Stefan Collini provides a full, sympathetic, yet perceptively discerning account.

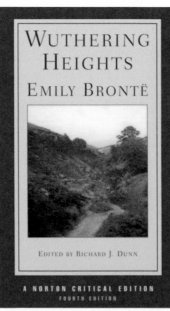

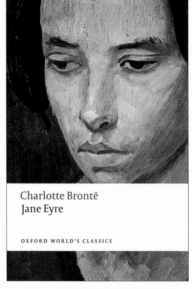

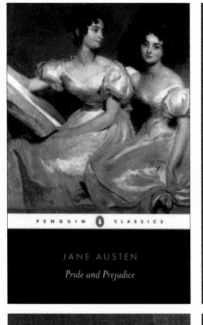

Austen, Jane, *Pride and Prejudice* (1813; Penguin Classics, 2003). A satirical account of an indolent country squire faced with marrying off five daughters, the second with a lively, deadly wit. In exposing the characters' vanity and pride, as well as detailing village gossip and snobbery, Austen proved to be a shrewd judge of human nature, which helps account for the book's reputation as one of the best, and best-loved, novels in the English language. The 1940 film adaptation was written by Aldous Huxley and stars Laurence Olivier and Greer Garson. In Austen's next novel, *Mansfield Park* (1814), the shy and impoverished Fanny Price grows up among rich, often thoughtless relatives whose prosperity rests on plantation slavery in Antigua.

Brontë, Charlotte, *Jane Eyre* (1847; Oxford World's Classics, 2008). A novel that hits the high notes of Victorian melodrama: a penniless, headstrong young girl is sent to a charity school and eventually finds a position as a governess in the household of a Byronic hero secretly married to a madwoman. Despite these overwrought elements, the story has an undeniable emotional power that accounts for its continued popularity. Jane's perseverance, undaunted whatever her circumstances, has inspired generations of readers. A companion piece of sorts, Jean Rhys's novel *Wide Sargasso Sea* (1966), recounts the life of the first Mrs. Rochester, the madwoman, imagining her as a Creole heiress in Jamaica, married off against her will and driven insane by her husband's mistrust and paranoia.

Brontë, Emily, *Wuthering Heights* (1847; Norton Critical Edition, 4th ed., 1994). A complex story of humiliation and lifelong revenge, set on the Yorkshire moors and told from multiple points of view, this novel swirls around Heathcliff, a character as implacable as a force of nature. An orphan taken in by a wealthy man, Heathcliff is tormented by his benefactor's son, runs away as a young man, and returns, mysteriously rich, to wreak havoc on everyone. Characters share names, family relations, and destinies in one of the most tangled, intertwined plots in English literature. A tour de force whose power never wanes. The acclaimed 1939 film version, directed by William Wyler, stars Laurence Olivier and Merle Oberon.

Browning, Elizabeth Barrett, *Aurora Leigh, and Other Poems* (1856; Penguin, 1996). By 1850, Elizabeth Barrett Browning's poetry had achieved such critical and popular fame that she was widely canvassed as a successor to William Wordsworth as poet laureate. In *Aurora Leigh*, she deals with social issues such as the lives of women in a world dominated by men, rape, and children born out of wedlock. Virginia Woolf later called *Aurora Leigh* a work of genius that should be admired for its "speed and energy, forthrightness and complete self-confidence." One of Browning's sonnets opens with the famous line "How do I love thee? Let me count the ways." At the time of her death, Robert Browning wrote that she possessed "the boldest of hearts that ever braved the sun."

Browning, Robert, *The Major Works* (Oxford, ed. Richard Cronin and Dorothy McMillan, 2009). Browning's work spanned the Victorian period. His epic, 21,000-line poem *The Ring and the Book* concerns an eighteenth-century murder trial but also contains thoughts on topics as varied as spiritualism and biological evolution. His most famous works include "Andrea del Sarto" ("A man's reach should exceed his grasp, / Or what's a heaven for?") and "Pippa Passes" ("God's in his heaven— / All's right with the world!"). In the early twentieth century, his reputation collapsed in the reaction against all things Victorian, though the critic Harold Bloom regards him as one of the great poets of the nineteenth century. Recommended also: recordings of his poems, especially "My Last Duchess," by "Tom O'Bedlam," available on YouTube.

Bulwer-Lytton, Edward, *Last Days of Pompeii* (1834). An epic tale of Roman dissipation and Christian martyrdom, culminating in the destruction of Pompeii by the eruption of Mount Vesuvius in AD 79. During Bulwer-Lytton's lifetime, his works were outsold only by those of Dickens, yet in the twentieth century his reputation plummeted. Nevertheless, he remains a literary curiosity for certain phrases, for example, his most famous words, from the play *Richelieu*:

> Beneath the rule of men entirely great
> The pen is mightier than the sword.

Today he is best remembered for the first line of his novel *Paul Clifford*: "It was a dark and stormy night; the rain fell in torrents." It inspired the annual Bulwer-Lytton Fiction Contest, in which contestants compete to write the opening sentence to "the worst of all possible novels."

Byron, George Gordon, *The Major Works* (Oxford, 2008). Lord Byron lived a life almost impossible to summarize. Prolific poet and playwright, member of the House of Lords, fighter for Greek independence, indefatigable writer of letters and journals—he had the superhuman energy of one of the heroes of his epic poems or dramas. He shot to fame with the publication of *Childe Harold's Pilgrimage* (1812–18) and found notoriety with *Don Juan* (1819–24; pronounced "Don *Jew*-en"). He was equally at home with irony ("Pleasure's a sin, and sometimes sin's a pleasure") and romance ("She walks in beauty, like the night / Of cloudless climes and starry skies"). All facets of Byron's life and work are covered in Jerome McGann's graceful, balanced, and informative essays collected in *Byron and Romanticism* (2002).

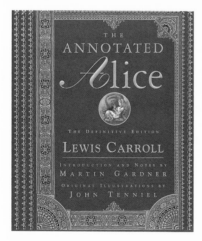

Carroll, Lewis, *Alice's Adventures in Wonderland* (1865; *The Annotated "Alice,"* ed. Martin Gardner, Norton, 1999). When Alice falls down a rabbit hole, she discovers a fantastical world where, among other amazements, life-size playing cards use flamingos as croquet mallets. She meets bizarre characters at every turn—the Mad Hatter, the disappearing Cheshire Cat, the homicidal Queen of Hearts—yet never loses her head. A trove of logic puzzles as well as a dense satire on nearly all things Victorian, the story can be enjoyed on numerous levels. An excellent recent biography of the author is Robert Douglas-Fairhurst, *The Story of Alice: Lewis Carroll and*

the Secret History of Wonderland (2015). On the controversial subject of Carroll and young girls, Douglas-Fairhurst suggests that the writer's affections were sentimental rather than sexual.

Coleridge, Samuel Taylor, *Selected Poetry* (Oxford, ed. H. J. Jackson, 2009). A radical poet in the age of the French Revolution, Coleridge collaborated with William Wordsworth, from whom he took inspiration, and vice versa, on the seminal collection *Lyrical Ballads* (1798). In addition to poetry, Coleridge wrote extensively on psychology, imagination, literature, politics, and religion. His best-known poems include the harrowing ordeal of the "Rime of the Ancient Mariner" ("Water, water, everywhere, / And all the boards did shrink; / Water, water, everywhere, / Nor any drop to drink") and "Kubla Khan," left unfinished after a visitor interrupted the opium-inspired poetic reverie of its composition. The best account of the poet's complicated life is the two-volume work by Richard Holmes, *Coleridge: Early Visions* (1989) and *Coleridge: Darker Reflections, 1804–1834* (1998).

Collins, Wilkie, *The Moonstone* (1868; Oxford, 2000) Regarded as the first modern detective novel, *The Moonstone* was initially serialized by Charles Dickens. The titular gem is a diamond given to the niece of a British army officer who had served in India. Such is its value, both material and religious, that three Hindu priests dedicate their lives to recovering it. Critical acclaim for the novel later included T. S. Eliot's assessment that it was "the first, the longest, and the best of modern English detective novels," and Dorothy Sayers, who referred to it as "probably the very finest detective story ever written." Collins's *The Woman in White* (1860), a fiendishly complicated mystery story, has a plot driven by the unequal status of women in marriage.

Conrad, Joseph, *Heart of Darkness* (1899; Oxford World's Classics, ed. Cedric Watts, 2008). Marlow journeys up the Congo River on behalf of a Belgian company. He encounters Kurtz, a trader who exercises sway over the inhabitants of the region through threats of dismemberment if they fail in the collection of ivory. Conrad implicitly raises the question of what constitutes a barbaric versus a civilized society. *Apocalypse Now* (1979), a film about the Vietnam War, is based on Conrad's novel. The author's cosmopolitan life (born in Poland, immigrated to England, traveled all over the South Pacific, the Caribbean, and the African coast) is fully captured in Maya Jasanoff, *The Dawn Watch: Joseph Conrad in a Global World* (2017).

 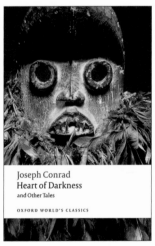

De Quincey, Thomas, *Confessions of an English Opium-Eater* (1822; Penguin, 2003). At Oxford, De Quincey failed to take his degree but discovered opium. Befriended by Samuel Taylor

Coleridge, he moved to the Lake District and became part of the Wordsworths' circle. In London, he consumed large amounts of laudanum—opium dissolved in alcohol—and recorded his wanderings in the city, along with his visions, hallucinations, and nightmares. *Confessions* conveys the effect of the drug in forging a link between self-expression and addiction. His account of mind-altering pleasures and pains—and perhaps more significantly, memory and dreams—helped create the literature of addiction and influenced later literary addicts such as William S. Burroughs. His tortured and tortuous life is described in Frances Wilson, *Guilty Thing: A Life of Thomas de Quincey* (2016).

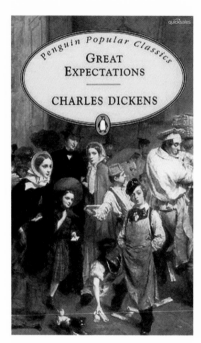 

Dickens, Charles, *Great Expectations* (1861; Penguin Classics, 2003). One of the last of Dickens's novels and perhaps his best. The orphaned Pip dreams of becoming a gentleman. The plot is one the author's intricate contraptions made up of chance meetings, improbable coincidences, and fortunes gained and lost. Among the indelible characters is Miss Havisham, permanently abandoned at the altar. The novel describes the Victorian urban scene. But Pip is neither an aristocrat nor a doomed capitalist, just a working-class boy who strives to achieve moral understanding. Jenny Hartley's *Charles Dickens: An Introduction* (2017) is a guide to the author that explores Dickens's complicated outlook on life—including his radical social views—in a way that lures readers back to his works with renewed enthusiasm.

Doyle, Arthur Conan, *The Complete Sherlock Holmes* (Barnes & Noble, 2009). Edmund Wilson once commented, "Sherlock Holmes *is* literature on a humble but not ignoble level . . . by virtue of imagination and style." The most significant literary influences on Doyle were Sir Walter Scott and, for technique, Guy de Maupassant. Doyle's life reveals some of his characters' antecedents.

Holmes's young assistants, the Baker Street Irregulars, were patterned after an Edinburgh street gang to which Doyle belonged. Holmes was drawn from one of Doyle's medical instructors, a master of deducing larger truths from tiny details. Over the course of Holmes's career, the stories grow increasing radical, dealing with social wrongs, official incompetence, and aristocratic privilege.

Eliot, George, *Middlemarch* (1871–72; Oxford World's Classics, 2008). This study of provincial life develops the central theme of the complexity of love and the meaning of marriage. Dorothea Brooke is involved in a disastrous union with the out-of-touch pedant Casaubon. Once her respect for him turns to pity, Dorothea allows her affections to be drawn to Casaubon's cousin Will. Other marriages and romances in the village are just as fraught with difficulties. Eliot's feminist views regarding education and women's social roles are apparent through the novel. Eliot's *The Mill on the Floss* (1860), her most autobiographical novel, tells the tragic story of a spirited young woman constrained in every part of her life by provincial narrow-mindedness.

Gaskell, Elizabeth, *Cranford* (1853; Oxford, 2011). In Cranford, a village near Manchester, the building of the railway has disrupted everyday life, a social as well as economic change viewed with dismay by some, yet by others as a chance for new and exhilarating opportunities. Presented with subtle satire, Gaskell's characters endure hardships such as bankruptcy, social restrictions on women, and unintended cruelty, against the background of the Industrial Revolution. Historians admire her treatment of class, and the novel holds a firm place in Victorian literature, although the author tends to be overshadowed by contemporaries such as Thackeray, Dickens, and Eliot. Gaskell based her *Life of Charlotte Brontë* (1857) on letters and other sources of literary and historical significance, but suppressed many of the racy details of Brontë's life.

Gissing, George, *New Grub Street* (1891; Penguin, 1976). In eighteenth-century London, Grub Street was home to low-end publishers and booksellers as well as swarms of aspiring and hack writers. Samuel Johnson and Henry Fielding, among many others, worked for a time on Grub Street. Gissing captures the timeless plight of embittered and impoverished writers attempting to make a living by their words. The plot contrasts the lives of Jasper Milvain, a prosperous, cynical, cutthroat journalist, and Edward Reardon, a hardworking, conscientious, but destitute novelist forced to work at subsistence level as a tutor in order to support his writing. George Orwell believed Gissing to be "perhaps the best novelist England has produced." Gissing's novel *The Private Papers of Henry Ryecroft* (1903) serves as a lightly fictionalized autobiography.

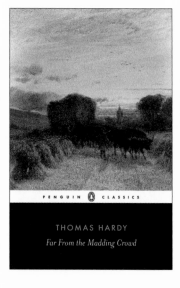

Hardy, Thomas, *Far from the Madding Crowd* (1874; Penguin Classics, 2003). Hardy's fourth novel pursues the themes for which his work became widely known. An idyllic but violent rural setting becomes madding, that is, frenzied, as three suitors pursue the headstrong and vain Bathsheba Everdene. The loyal shepherd Gabriel Oak, the lonely but prosperous William Boldwood, and the feckless Sergeant Troy cross paths and clash, sometimes violently. This work, which made Hardy famous, tells one of the great love stories in English literature. In *Tess of the D'Urbervilles* (1891), a young woman living in a "blighted" world is buffeted by deception and mischance, her opportunities for happiness continually thwarted. The novel was memorably adapted as a film, *Tess* (1979), by Roman Polanski.

Housman, A. E., *A Shopshire Lad, and Other Poems* (1896; Penguin, 2010). *A Shropshire Lad*, little regarded at first, came to represent all that was precious in England, a nostalgic, pastoral myth of rural landscapes and "blue remembered hills." A number of the poems have become classics, including "Loveliest of trees, the cherry now" and "To an Athlete Dying Young." Housman's imagined Shropshire—he first visited the county after the book was published—conjures an idyllic world whose subjects seem doomed. Wanting his poems to be published and distributed as inexpensively as possible, Housman refused royalty payments. During World War I, copies were found in the pockets of dead English soldiers on the western front. Peter Parker's *Housman Country: Into the Heart of England* (2017) sensitively explores what the poet means for his homeland.

Jerome, Jerome K., *Three Men in a Boat: To Say Nothing of the Dog!* (1889; Penguin, intro. Jeremy Lewis, 2004). Jerome's casual, sustained comedy distills British humor that is as alive today as it was in the late nineteenth century. Three friends decide to take a rowing holiday up the Thames to Oxford and back to London, accompanied by a dog named Montmorency. They hardly predict the troubles they will encounter with towropes, unpredictable weather, and camping mishaps. After one exhausting day, they look forward to the delicacy of chunks of pineapple in pineapple juice—only to discover that they have no can opener! Somewhere between a shaggy-dog story and a Victorian farce, the novel hilariously captures the spirit of the time.

Keats, John, *Selected Poetry* (Oxford World's Classics, ed. Elizabeth Cook, 2009). Keats, dead at twenty-five, left behind a large body of work that remains one of the glories of English literature. His poetry, especially the odes, is notable for sensual imagery through which he expressed extreme emotion. His best-known poems include "On First Looking into Chapman's Homer," "La Belle Dame sans Merci," "Ode on a Grecian Urn," and "Ode to a Nightingale," which, with other works, the critic Helen Vendler judged to be the "finest embodiment" of the English language. Tennyson considered him the greatest poet of the nineteenth century. Direct access to the poet's feelings and ideas can be found in his *Selected Letters* (2015).

Kingsley, Charles, *Westward Ho!* (1855; Scribner, 1992). Kingsley was an unconventional, radical Christian writer, passionately anti-Catholic and firm in his belief in the enlightened destiny of the British Empire. In the era of Sir Francis Drake and other sixteenth-century privateers, the ship *Westward Ho!* sails to the West Indies, where the crew reveals condescending and racist attitudes toward native peoples but battles the Spanish with rough sturdiness, physical courage, and moral decency. The ship returns to fight victoriously against the Spanish Armada. The depiction of muscular Christianity, combative manliness, and other British heroic virtues appealed to younger as well as older, patriotic readers. Kingsley dedicated the novel to John Eyre, the governor of Jamaica who later brutally suppressed the Morant Bay rebellion of 1865.

Lamb, Charles, and Mary Lamb, *Tales from Shakespeare* (1807; Penguin, 2010). In this engaging collection by a brother-and-sister writing team, a good selection of Shakespeare's comedies and tragedies are recast as prose narratives for children. The style is slightly dated, but nevertheless fluent and easy to read. Though intended for children, the paraphrases do not shy away from the violence and bloodiness of plays such as *King Lear* and *Macbeth*. The book is also useful for anyone wishing to have the gist of a play or to surmount the problem of Shakespeare's vernacular or simply to enjoy his genius. The overall tone is gentle thoughtfulness. David Cecil's *A Portrait of Charles Lamb* (1984) is a perceptive and readable study.

Lear, Edward, *The Owl and the Pussy-Cat* (1871; Penguin, illus. Jan Brett, 1996). "The Owl and the Pussycat" is a nonsense poem first published in 1871. Lear was a prolific writer and a talented landscape artist—he gave drawing lessons to Queen Victoria. He wrote that the owl and pussycat "dined on mince, and slices of quince, / Which they ate with a runcible spoon." He coined the word *runcible*, which thereafter came to mean a three-pronged fork used for pickles. In 2014, the British voted "The Owl and the Pussycat" as the nation's favorite childhood poem. The full flavor of Lear's inspired lunacy can be enjoyed in *The Complete Nonsense of Edward Lear* (Dover, 1951), with more than 500 illustrations by the author.

Scott, Sir Walter, *Ivanhoe* (1819; Oxford, ed. Ian Duncan, 1998). Set in the twelfth century, *Ivanhoe* depicts the tyranny of the Norman invaders, whose overthrow would represent the recovery of a golden age of English liberty. One of the main characters is Robin Hood, who embodies the struggle against injustice. Scott was the most successful writer of his time, and his reputation now rests mainly on his Scottish novels—rather than his poetry—in which clan warfare is part of a violent past. In a sense, Scott was a self-trained social anthropologist who believed that human beings were products of society and could be understood against a background of class, language, and national history.

Shelley, Mary Wollstonecraft, *Frankenstein; or, The Modern Prometheus* (1818; Barnes & Noble, 2003). The story is almost too well known: the young scientist Victor Frankenstein assembles and animates a gigantic, grotesque monster eight feet tall with penetrating yellow eyes and a breath of overwhelming stench. The name of the scientist is often confused with the creature itself, which is never given a name. Critics have seen aesthetic and moral qualities in the novel, or religious and metaphysical themes, and still others have subjected it to psychoanalytic and feminist criticism. In any event, it is a landmark of romantic and gothic literature, perhaps the first work of science fiction, and not least a good horror story. The groundbreaking 1931 film adaptation stars Boris Karloff as the monster.

Shelley, Percy Bysshe, *The Major Works* (Oxford, ed. Zachary Leader, 2009). Shelley was the heir to British and French revolutionary intellectuals of the late eighteenth century, and his writing from beginning to end carries with it a spirit of rebellion and radical vision. In 1816 he married Mary Wollstonecrfaft Godwin (his second wife), who later wrote *Frankenstein*. This collection includes his best-known poems, including "Ozymandias," "To a Skylark," "Ode to the West Wind," and "Adonaïs," an elegy on the death of Keats. Shelley drowned off the northwestern coast of Italy at a little less than thirty years of age. His angry antiwar idealism inspired generations of poets and nonviolent activists, including Thoreau and Gandhi.

Stevenson, Robert Louis, *The Strange Case of Dr. Jekyll and Mr. Hyde* (1886; Oxford, 2006). In this symbolic tale of good and evil, a kind and intelligent doctor, Henry Jekyll, experiments with a serum that transforms him into a self-indulgent brute, Edward Hyde. Jekyll uses Hyde to give free rein to his basest instincts and desires, but Hyde gets the upper hand, and eventually the transformations become involuntary. The term "Jekyll and Hyde," meaning a strongly two-sided personality, has become a commonplace in English. Stevenson was a masterly Victorian writer—his other novels include *Treasure Island* and *Kidnapped*—whose superb skill was attested to by Henry James, Graham Greene, and Jorge Luis Borges. Stevenson was also a poet, and his *A Child's Garden of Verses* (1885) is a beloved collection.

Stoker, Bram, *Dracula* (1897; Oxford, 1998). Count Dracula was originally more Irish than Transylvanian, embodying ideas drawn from Irish folklore of a red devil. In Stoker's hands, he became a blood-sucking monster who goes to England in search of fresh victims. Stoker's book was at first regarded simply as a horror story, but it gradually came to be seen as a masterpiece raising questions of identity, sanity, cultural "pollution," and Victorian sexuality. After the success of the 1931 Hollywood adaptation, starring Bela Lugosi, Dracula became the most filmed character after Sherlock Holmes, with well over 200 depictions. For the life of the author, see Barbara Belford, *Bram Stoker: A Biography of the Author of "Dracula"* (1996).

Tennyson, Alfred, *The Major Works* (Oxford, ed. Adam Roberts, 2009). Tennyson was poet laureate during most of Queen Victoria's reign. Contemporaries emphasized his melancholic temperament; he was sensitive to criticism. "In Memoriam," an elegy for his friend William Hallam, is often considered one of the great poems of the nineteenth century. Poems such as "The Charge of the Light Brigade," "The Crossing of the Bar," and the Arthurian retellings of *Idylls of the King* made him the most popular poet of his time, though his fame had begun to decline well before his death in 1892. Nevertheless, T. S. Eliot believed that he was one of the "greatest poets" because his poems possessed the qualities of "abundance, variety, and com-

plete competence." A thorough biographical and critical study can be found in Christopher Ricks, *Tennyson* (2nd ed., 1989).

Thackeray, William Makepeace, *Vanity Fair* (1848; Penguin, intro. John Carey, 2002). Thackeray took the title of his greatest and most famous novel from John Bunyan's *Pilgrim's Progress*, in which "Vanity Fair" is a place of continual sinful indulgence. The strong-willed and manipulative green-eyed Becky Sharpe is the antiheroine of sorts, juxtaposed with the more conventionally virtuous Amelia Sedley. During the period of the Napoleonic wars—the novel vividly describes the retreat from Waterloo—Becky's fortunes rise and fall, her machinations providing a satire on an English society shot through with hypocrisy. Thackeray again skewers his times in *The Newcomes: Memoirs of a Most Respectable Family* (1855), which portrays a colonel in the Indian Army who finds the snobberies and hypocrisies of Victorian England unsettling.

Trollope, Anthony, *The Way We Live Now* (1875; Wordsworth Classics, 2004). This novel holds a singular place in Trollope's overall work because, in his own words, he attempted to expose "a certain class of dishonesty, dishonesty magnificent in its proportions." The enormity of the financial confidence game at the heart of the story is echoed in the cynicism of the London marriage market and the shabbiness of literary society. Yet the novel succeeds also as a social comedy. Trollopians have enjoyed a resurgence of his reputation since World War II, in part because of general recognition of his sensitivity to the status of women in Victorian society. Trollope first gained literary fame as the author of the six-volume Barsetshire chronicles, which begin with *The Warden* (1855).

Wells, H. G., *The Time Machine* (1895; Penguin, 2005). Wells, along with Jules Verne, is sometimes called the "Father of Science Fiction." In *The Time Machine,* a Victorian scientist journeys around 800,000 years into the future and discovers a technological dystopia in which human beings have degenerated into two races: the Eloi, a leisured, effete type, and the Morlocks, an industrious subterranean breed resembling troglodytes. The groups' relationship seems to be master-servant in form, but turns out to be more akin to rancher-livestock. In *The War of the Worlds* (1898), seemingly invincible Martians attack England, destroying London. In 1938, Orson Welles broadcast parts of the novel as a news report of an alien attack on Grover's Mill, New Jersey, which led to panic among some of listeners.

Wilde, Oscar, *The Importance of Being Earnest* (first production, 1895; Harvard, 2015). This madcap farce about false and mistaken identities has been hailed by some as the greatest English comedy of all time. Lines of sparkling wit come thick and fast: "That must be Aunt Augusta. Only relatives, or creditors, ring in that Wagnerian manner"; "The good ended happily, and the bad unhappily. That is what fiction means"; "To lose one parent . . . may be regarded as a misfortune; to lose both looks like carelessness." The social skewering of flagrant hypocrisy continues to entertain audiences. The impeccable 1952 film version stars Michael Redgrave and Dame Edith Evans. Richard Ellmann's *Oscar Wilde* (1987) is still the indispensable, standard life.

Wordsworth, William, *The Prelude* (1850; ed. and intro. James Engell and Michael Raymond, Godine, 2017). Wordsworth was radicalized by the French Revolution but then horrified by the Terror, which brought to an end his political optimism. Feeling alienated in his own country and racked with despair and existential doubt, he turned inward. The posthumously published *Prelude,* intended as the first third of a gigantic epic poem, traces the growth of the poet's mind. He reconciles himself to the vicissitudes of life yet still finds joy and exaltation, as perhaps best summarized in his magnificent lines about the first days of the French Revolution: "Bliss it was in that dawn to be alive, / But to be young was very heaven!" Stephen Gill's *William Wordsworth: A Life* (1989) is a sturdy biographical account of the poet's long life.

20th century

Amis, Kingsley, *Lucky Jim* (1954; NYRB, 2012). Jim Dixon is a young lecturer in medieval history at a provincial, or "redbrick," British university in the early 1950s. In a series of comical mishaps, he rebels against the scholarly pretension of Professor Welch, a buffoonish, pedantic historian. In a drunken lecture to the faculty, Jim hilariously proclaims his contempt for the academic world, but in the end he proves to be "lucky." Christopher Hitchens described the book as one of the funniest in the second half of the twentieth century. In *One Fat Englishman* (1963), a caustic take on America and academic life, the title character teaches at Budweiser College in rural Pennsylvania; Amis peppers the novel with barbed observations on children, novelists, and deer.

Auden, W. H., *The Shield of Achilles* (Random House, 1955). It is difficult to single out just one collection of Auden's poems for recommendation, but *Achilles* is usually considered his best. The title poem is a dark reimagining of the scene from the *Iliad* in which Hephaestus forges an elaborately decorated shield for Achilles. In Auden's version, vineyards and olive trees are replaced by a featureless plain; instead of maidens dancing, there is a savage child "who'd never heard / Of any world where . . . one could weep because another wept." The poet's pacifism is on full display throughout the volume. Edward Mendelson's *Later Auden* (2000) is a study of the poems written from 1939 to 1973, by Auden's literary executor.

Ballard, J. G., *Empire of the Sun* (1984; Simon & Schuster, 2005). As a child, Ballard lived in Shanghai with his parents. Under the Japanese occupation, he was interned, at age eleven and without his parents, in a prison camp. These facts form the background for this semi-autobiographical novel. His attitude toward the Japanese guards is ambivalent. He admires their high spirits and camaraderie but sees clearly their savage cruelty. His account of the physical hardships of internment is detached, scientific. Yet he imaginatively enters the thoughts of the prisoners and guards. He is both compassionate and objective, a combination later called "Ballardian." The 1987 film adaptation, directed by Steven Spielberg and starring John Malkovich and Christian Bale, is excellent.

Bennett, Arnold, *The Old Wives' Tale* (1908; Penguin, 2007). In the decade before World War I, Bennett spent a half dozen years in France, where he fell under the influence of Guy de Maupassant. In a chance encounter in a Parisian restaurant, he found the inspiration for a story of two sisters, one who runs off to Paris and marries a "cad," while the other remains in England and marries a "mild-mannered shop assistant." They meet again many years later. The book, immediately acclaimed, established Bennett's reputation as a novelist. His fame was not merely literary: he created an omelet that bears his name in the Reform Club to the present. A full account of his life is given in Margaret Drabble, *Arnold Bennett: A Biography* (1974).

Betjeman, John, *The Best of Betjeman* (Penguin, ed. John Guest, 2000). When appointed poet laureate in 1972, Betjeman had acquired a popularity unrivaled since Kipling. Yet in the 1970s, literary critics came to regard him as a lightweight. His poetry expressed the ordinary, day-to-day experiences of his readers. He was also an accomplished amateur architectural historian, particularly of the Victorian era. Philip Larkin described his work as having a gaiety, a sense of the ridiculous, and affection for fellow human beings; Kingsley Amis wrote that his poetry, engaging and ebullient, reveals an impeccable ear. He gave the impression of being a bumbling fogey, but his comic and satirical verse, especially when he read it on radio or television, brought him great popularity.

Bradbury, Malcolm, *The History Man* (1975; Picador, 2012). Bradbury wrote nearly two dozen books, beginning with *Eating People Is Wrong* (1959). He is best known for *The History Man*, a campus novel set in 1972, satirizing the "glass and steel" universities that followed the redbricks. Howard Kirk, a professor of sociology, is a radical tutor at the time of the sexual revolution. One of his colleagues sleeps with men in whom she is professionally interested in order to elicit sociological information. Kirk and his wife, Barbara, each have multiple affairs. Mocking the absurdities of the era—Barbara supports the Children's Crusade for Abortion—the satire grows darker as Kirk becomes a corrupt and corrupting figure, causing sexual and intellectual havoc, all in the interest of keeping things "happening."

Buchan, John, *The Thirty-Nine Steps* (1915; Penguin, 2005). Richard Hannay, an expatriate Scot, returns to Britain before World War I after a long stay in Rhodesia. He discovers a German spy ring bent on stealing naval secrets. After an American agent is killed in Hannay's apartment, he flees to Scotland, pursued by English police and German conspirators. Unlikely coincidences and close escapes carry the plot along. Much is made of the Germans' failure to impersonate Englishmen successfully—"the cut of his collar and tie never came out in England," Hannay says of one. Buchan himself was a Scottish guardian of British values. The 1935 film adaptation by Alfred Hitchcock, co-written by Buchan and thrilling it its own right, bears little resemblance to the novel.

Burgess, Antony, *A Clockwork Orange* (1962; Norton, 1995). In a subculture of extreme hooliganism in England in the 1950s, the youthful antihero and sociopath Alex is captured after a short career of deadly mayhem ("ultraviolence"). Governmental officials force him to undergo aversion therapy to curb his brutal tendencies, but like a nightmare scored to Beethoven, the treatment renders him defenseless. When his programming is later undone, he declares, "I was cured, all right." Stanley Kubrick's film version (1971), itself an apogee of terrifying violence, perpetuated the popularity of the book. The range of Burgess's skill as a writer can be seen in *Earthly Powers* (1980), a panoramic novel spanning the twentieth century, told by a gay writer based loosely on Somerset Maugham.

Butler, Samuel, *The Way of All Flesh* (1903; Penguin, 2006). Butler's posthumously published novel describes four generations of the Pontifex family, mainly through the life of Ernest Pontifex, whose childhood and youth are a misery. His domineering father, a clergyman, and manipulative mother are based closely on Butler's own parents. The novel is a lacerating attack on Victorian family life and, in particular, the Church of England. Its admirers have included Orwell and Shaw, who called Butler "the only man known to history who has immortalized and actually endeared himself by parricide and matricide long drawn out." Butler made his name as a novelist with *Erewhon* (1872), a fantasy satirizing socialism and Darwinism. A good account of the author's life is P. N. Furbank, *Samuel Butler, 1853–1902* (1948).

Cary, Joyce, *Mister Johnson* (1939). As an Irishman in the British colonial service in Nigeria, Cary sympathized with the oppressed Africans but also with their British overlords. Johnson, an African clerk in the colonial administration, believes the British Empire represents progress and civilization. He regards the King of England as one of his friends. In reality, his British superior despises him as a member of an inferior race. Johnson's effort to be more English than the English leads not only to degradation but also to the possibility of the gallows. In Cary's *The Horse's Mouth* (1984), the hero, Gulley Jimson, despises conventional behavior and is regarded as a bad citizen but is a good artist. Alec Guinness wrote the screenplay and starred in the 1958 film adaptation.

Chesterton, G. K., *The Man Who Was Thursday* (1908; Penguin, 2011). Often called as a philosophical novel, *Thursday* could be classified also as a metaphysical thriller. Six detectives who believe they are fighting enemies eventfully discover that they are pitted against one another. The mastermind, Sunday, remains a mystery until the end. Chesterton wrote that the novel was intended "to describe the world of wild doubt and despair," "with just a gleam of hope." Shaw proclaimed Chesterton a "man of genius," in part because of *The Innocence of Father Brown* (1911). Brown is a priest with insight into human nature and criminal mentality; he was memorably portrayed by Alec Guinness in the film *Father Brown* (1954; released in the United States as *The Detective*).

Childers, Erskine, *Riddle of the Sands: A Record of Secret Service* (1903; Penguin (2001). Two friends sailing the North Sea, one a fastidious Foreign Office official, the other a sailing fanatic, reveal the danger of invasion from Germany, unmasking a traitor and identifying weaknesses in British coastal defenses. Childers himself had divided loyalties: initially a staunch supporter of the British Empire, he later embraced Irish nationalism. In 1922 he was captured and executed by Irish authorities for smuggling arms to the IRA. In Ireland, he is revered as one of the founders of the republic. His book prompted the Admiralty to build a naval base in Scotland to strengthen its North Sea defenses; less momentously, it helped inspire the *The Thirty-Nine Steps* by John Buchan (1915).

Christie, Agatha, *Murder on the Orient Express* (1934; William Murrow, 2011). Along with *The Murder of Roger Ackroyd* (1926) and *And Then There Were None* (1939), *Orient Express* is among Christie's most famous detective novels. The Belgian detective Hercule Poirot solves a murder on the famous train while giving the impression that he is confronted by a criminal mastermind, especially when it turns out that neither the victim nor any of the suspects are whom they appear to be. Christie gives readers clues, but only by applying Poirot's combination of logic and common sense can the mystery be worked out. Just as Arthur Conan Doyle eventually came to detest Sherlock Holmes and his inextinguishable fame, Christie turned on Poirot late in life, calling him "insufferable—a detestable, bombastic, tiresome, egocentric little creep."

Dahl, Roald, *Charlie and the Chocolate Factory* (1964; Puffin, 2007). In his most famous book for children, Dahl characteristically uses human vices, including grotesque gluttony and gruesome barbarity, to depict the adventures of Charlie Bucket, who enjoyed only one chocolate bar a

year and two helpings of cabbage as a special treat on Sunday. When Charlie meets the chocolate wizard, Willy Wonka, the dialogue reminds the reader of conversations in the works of
Hilaire Belloc and Lewis Carroll. Dahl's books, including *Charlie*, are controversial because of
his preoccupation with the dark side of human nature, not least revenge, cruelty, and greed.
Yet he remains one of the most popular children's writers of all time. The best account of the
author's life is Jeremy Treglown, *Roald Dahl: A Biography* (1994).

du Maurier, Daphne, *Rebecca* (1938; Everyman's Library, 2017). Although *Rebecca* is often described as a psychological thriller, du Maurier always said that it was a study in jealousy. The
brooding widower Maxim de Winter marries an unassuming young woman, who becomes
increasingly terrified while living at Manderley, his country estate in Cornwall, which seems
to be haunted by his first wife, Rebecca. The sinister housekeeper, Mrs. Danvers, drives the
heroine half mad with jealousy, intimidation, and fear. Things come to a head when a boat
with Rebecca's body is found in the waters offshore, and the truth surrounding her death—as
well as her life—is revealed. The 1940 film adaptation, directed by Alfred Hitchcock, stars
Laurence Olivier and Joan Fontaine.

Durrell, Lawrence, *The Alexandria Quartet* (1957–60; intro. Jan Morris, Faber, 2012). Durrell's
early work was influenced by Henry Miller's *Tropic of Cancer,* and the exploration of erotic
complications preoccupied him throughout his career. The *Quartet* is set in Alexandria before
and during World War II. Its first three volumes—*Justine* (1957), *Balthazar* (1958), and *Moun-
tolive* (1958)—present, from contrasting perspectives, the same events and characters, who are
caught up in sexual and political entanglements. The last volume, *Clea* (1960), moves the story
forward in time. The *Quartet* presents multiple perspectives, all perhaps true, on the intricacies
of love. Durrell once explained that the ideas behind the novels came from Einstein's relativity
and Freud's upending of the idea of stable personalities. For the life of the novelist, see I. S.
MacNiven, *Lawrence Durrell: A Biography* (1998).

Eliot, T. S., *The Waste Land, and Other Poems* (Signet, ed. Helen Vendler, 1998). "April is the
cruellest month": so begins *The Waste Land* (1922), an exploration of disillusionment in the
aftermath of World War I. The work is dense with poetic allusions and cultural references, as
is much of Eliot's later poetry. Another well-known poem, "The Love Song of J. Alfred Pru-
frock," seethes with indecision ("Do I dare / Disturb the universe?") and regret ("I have heard
the mermaids singing each to each. / I do not think that they will sing to me."). These works
helped secure Eliot's reputation as a towering figure of modern poetry. His *Four Quartets* (1943)
comprises late poems that reveal the author's religious preoccupations and conception of time.

Farrell, J. G., *The Singapore Grip* (1978; NYRB, 2005). A satire on the copulating, partying, condescending British in Malaya. who live in colonial bungalows and visit the opium dens and
brothels of Singapore. (The title is a slang phrase about Singapore prostitutes.) The focus is
on a rubber planter oblivious of the danger of a Japanese invasion. When it came, in February 1942, it was the worst defeat in the history of the British Empire. *The Singapore Grip* is the

last book in Farrell's Empire Trilogy, which includes *Troubles* (1970), dealing with the Irish insurrection in 1919, and *The Siege of Krishnapur* (1973), about the Indian Rebellion of 1857.

Ford, Ford Madox, *Parade's End* (4 vols., 1924–28; Penguin, intro. Julian Barnes, 2012). An allegory of the life of one man, Christopher Tietjens, who symbolizes old-fashioned Tory values. He experiences devastation on the western front and the transformation of the class system in England—the destruction of an era. Tietjens views the war as, notably, not the most important thing in his life, even when it is raging all around him. Estranged from his promiscuous wife, he turns to a pacifist suffragist, but redemption eludes him. Graham Greene commented, "There is no novelist of the twentieth century more likely to live than Ford Madox Ford." Ford's complicated personal and professional lives are detailed in Max Saunders, *Ford Madox Ford: A Dual Life* (2 vols., 1996).

Forester, C. S., *Lieutenant Hornblower* (1952; Penguin, 2011) and *Flying Colours* (1938; Penguin, 2006). Of the dozen novels by C. S. Forester about Horatio Hornblower, an officer in the Royal Navy in the Napoleonic era, these two are among the best. Throughout the sequence, Forester skillfully rescues Hornblower to go on missions requiring moral stamina and often leading to naval victories. *Lieutenant Hornblower* takes place in 1793, on the eve of the wars with France. *Flying Colours* finds Hornblower a captive of the French and facing execution. Forester's background included reporting on the Spanish Civil War and the German occupation of Czechoslovakia. His other novels include *The African Queen* (1935), made into a 1951 movie directed by John Huston and starring Humphrey Bogart and Katharine Hepburn.

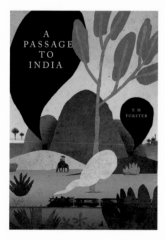

Forster, E. M., *A Passage to India* (1924; Penguin Classics, ed. Oliver Stallybrass, intro. Pankaj Mishra, 2005). Set against the background of the British Raj, the novel portrays a young English woman determined to escape the pretentions of the British community and discover the "real India"—but she finds herself at the center of a sexual scandal. Despite her good intentions, she realizes finally that her preconceptions and prejudices have distorted her views about the specific incident and India itself. The 1984 film version, directed by David Lean and featuring Alex Guinness, was hailed as "one of the greatest screen adaptations ever seen."

Galsworthy, John, *The Forsyte Saga* (1922; Oxford, 2008). In this trilogy of novels—*The Man of Property*, *In Chancery*, and *To Let*—for which Galsworthy won the Nobel Prize in Literature in 1932, the fortunes of an upper-middle-class family are linked with its inferior status as "new money." The main character, Soames Forsyte, becomes wealthy, but he and the rest of the family, despite their prosperous circumstances, find themselves torn over conflicts involving romance and love, property and inheritance. The ongoing phenomenon of the family saga in radio, film, and television adaptations derives from Galsworthy's success in telling the story within the wider developments of society, especially the changing position of women. The Forsytes' story was continued in two subsequent trilogies, *A Modern Comedy* and *End of the Chapter*.

Golding, William, *Lord of the Flies* (1954; Penguin, 2003). A group of boys is marooned on a desert island, which quickly becomes a microcosm of the world. Without civilized society to restrain their violent and cruel impulses, the boys descend into savagery, worshiping the "Lord of the Flies" (a translation of the Hebrew name "Beelzebub"). The novel reflects unrelenting distrust of rationalism and optimistic Christianity as well as disdain for the widely held post-war view that human nature is culturally determined by social circumstance. Since its publication, the novel has achieved global renown and influence—as well as a cultlike status among millions of readers—not least by inclusion on countless reading lists, like this one.

Grahame, Kenneth, *The Wind in the Willows* (1908; Modern Library, 2005). One of the beloved children's books of all time was based on bedtime stories Grahame told his son. Tales of the timeless figures of the swaggering, unpredictable Toad, the friendly and engaging Water Rat, the reclusive Badger, and the impulsive Mole impart a gentle, playful wisdom while occasionally revealing insights into Grahame's life. He had been denied the chance to study at Oxford; according to Mr. Toad:

> *The clever men at Oxford*
> *Know all that there is to be knowed.*
> *But they none of them know one half as much*
> *As intelligent Mr. Toad!*

Theodore Roosevelt helped Grahame find a publisher. A thorough, perceptive biography of the author is Peter Green, *Kenneth Grahame, 1859–1932: A Study of His Life, Work, and Times* (1959).

Green, Henry, *Loving* (1945; NYRB, 2016). In 1952, W. H. Auden commented that Green was "the best English novelist alive." The son of a wealthy industrialist, he developed a remarkable ear for the varieties of English speech, drawn from his experiences at Oxford, on the factory floor, and while working as a firefighter during the Blitz. *Loving*, set during World War II, depicts the dissolute life in a run-down Irish country house—bad behavior abounds upstairs and down—that is rather the opposite of Waugh's Brideshead. Waugh, a friend of Green's, notably (and wrongly) called *Loving* "an obscene book . . . about domestic servants." The best biography of the author is Jeremy Treglown, *Romancing: The Life and Work of Henry Green* (2001).

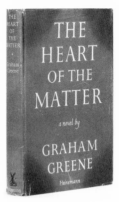

Greene, Graham, *The Heart of the Matter* (1948; intro. James Wood, Penguin, 2004). During World War II in Sierra Leone, Henry Scobie, a British colonial official, a just and honorable Catholic, compromises himself and contemplates suicide, a mortal sin. The novel builds in psychological and spiritual intensity as Scobie becomes increasingly involved in espionage, love, adultery, treachery, and betrayal in a colony characterized by heavy drinking and corruption as wells as rats, cockroaches, and vultures. One of Greene's best and most powerful novels. In *The Power and the Glory* (1940), a novel set in Mexico during the suppression of the Catholic Church in the 1930s, follows a whiskey-soaked priest as he attempts to elude a zealous police lieutenant intent on arresting him.

Hughes, Ted, *Collected Poems* (Faber & Faber, ed. Paul Keegan, 2005). A recurrent theme in the poetry of Ted Hughes is the violence of nature, often shown in close observations of animal life. Similarly, hunting and fishing are seen as ways for people to connect with nonhuman life. After the suicide of his wife, Sylvia Plath, in 1963, he wrote mainly for children. He returned to writing serious poetry with *Crow* (1970) and, late in life, *Birthday Letters* (1998), in which he finally exorcises the demon released by Plath's death. He served as poet laureate from 1984 until his death. Keith Sagar's *The Art of Ted Hughes* (2nd ed., 1978) is a full-length study of the major poems.

Huxley, Aldous, *Brave New World* (1932; Harper Perennial, foreword by Christopher Hitchens, 2005). In the future, planners oversee the conception and birth of children in laboratories, and predetermine their intelligence and social class. The two main cultural values are comfort and sex, both facilitated by pharmaceuticals. The cost, freedom and individuality, seems a reasonable price to pay in the opinion of most people. This dystopian "paradise" is disrupted when a twenty-year-old "barbarian"—someone born from a woman—is discovered. Huxley's *Point Counter Point* (1928), is a roman à clef (among the recognizable figures are D. H. Lawrence, Baudelaire, and Huxley himself) and dark satire of the English upper classes, whose members come across as self-obsessed, emotionally stunted cranks and fanatics.

Isherwood, Christopher, and W. H. Auden, *The Ascent of F6* (1936; Faber, 1958). Isherwood is most famous for his *Berlin Stories* (1945), which were adapted as the play *I Am a Camera* and the musical *Cabaret*. He wrote three plays with W. H. Auden, who called Isherwood one of the "great emotional milestones of his life." F6 is a fictitious Himalayan mountain. The central character, Michael Ransom, leads an expedition to the mysterious and haunted summit. All his men die during the climb, and he perishes at the peak, destroyed by his own ambition and conflicting emotions. The play is a parable about the nature of power and will, and Ransom is modeled in part on Lawrence of Arabia, the "Truly Strong Weak Man."

Ishiguro, Kazuo, *The Remains of the Day* (Vintage, 1990). The spirit of Jeeves hovers over the beginning of this novel about Stevens, a consummate English butler at a country estate. Like Jeeves, Stevens holds to the values of the 1920s and 1930s. But unlike Jeeves, Stevens is a victim of self-deception. He had believed that his aristocratic master worked for the good of humanity; in fact he tried to reconcile Britain with Nazi Germany in the years before the war. Contact with villagers who embody the democracy and decency of post-war Britain leads Stevens to believe that his life has been a sham. The novel concludes on the eve of the Suez crisis of 1956: the end of both imperial as well as personal illusions. Anthony Hopkins immortalized the butler in the film adaptation.

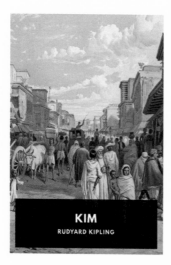 

Kipling, Rudyard, *Kim* (1901; Penguin Twentieth-Century Classics, intro. Edward Said, 1987). Kimball O'Hara, a vagabond orphan in Lahore, is taken up by the British secret police, educated, and sent to take part in the Great Game. While still a boy, he helps thwart the Russian advance in the Himalayas. Kim's life weaves together espionage and Buddhism as well as the world of the Indian bazaar and adventures on the Great Trunk Road. The book continues to attract a large readership, above all because Kim represents the meeting of East and West—one of Kipling's obsessions. For readers seeking details of the author's life, Thomas Pinney's edition of Kipling's autobiography, *Something of Myself, and Other Autobiographical Writings* (1937; Cambridge, 2013), restores many of the omissions and distortions that mar the original.

Koestler, Arthur, *Darkness at Noon* (1940; Scribner, 2006). Koestler was a Hungarian-British writer, a communist who became disillusioned with Stalin and broke from the party in 1938. His character Rubashov, an old Bolshevik, is swept up in Stalin's Great Purge. Considerations of his own past ruthlessness, along with interrogations conducted by an old friend, lead him to question having dedicated his life to bringing about a socialist utopia. In one harrowing scene, Rubashov is forced to listen to the screams of a prisoner being tortured in an adjoining cell. George Orwell drew inspiration from Koestler's figures while writing *1984*. Michael Scammell provides an excellent account of the author's life in *Koestler: The Literary and Political Odyssey of a Twentieth-Century Skeptic* (2009).

Larkin, Philip, *Collected Poems*, ed. Anthony Thwaite (1989; Farrar, Straus & Giroux, 2004). Philip Larkin was a famously meticulous, unprolific poet. His themes include loss and regret; as he said of himself, "Deprivation is for me what daffodils were for Wordsworth." Several of his poems achieved notoriety, including "This Be the Verse" ("They fuck you up, your mum and dad") and "Annus Mirabilis": "Sexual intercourse / began in nineteen sixty-three / (Which was rather late for me)." Perhaps surprisingly, no one more eloquently expressed the end of the British Empire than Larkin, in "Homage to a Government" (1969):

> *Next year we are to bring all the soldiers home*
> *For lack of money, and it is all right . . .*
> *Our children will not know it's a different country.*

James Booth's *Philip Larkin: Life, Art, and Love* (2014) is a necessary corrective to earlier, more hostile biographies of the poet.

Lawrence, D. H., *Lady Chatterley's Lover* (1928; Wordsworth Classics, 2005). Clifford Chatterley was paralyzed from the waist down in World War I, and his sexually frustrated wife seeks fulfillment with his gamekeeper, Mellors. With its four-letter words and explicit descriptions of sexual intercourse, Lawrence's last novel claimed a large underground readership. The British government's attempt to ban it led to the "Lady Chatterley trial" in 1960, which heralded the sexual revolution. Lawrence's earlier, autobiographical novel *Sons and Lovers* (1913), set among the mining communities of Nottinghamshire, describes the struggles of a son whose life is undone by his mother's excessive devotion. Mark Kinkead-Weekes, *D. H. Lawrence: Triumph to Exile, 1912–1922* (1996), shows how the author's life was turned upside down by his opposition to World War I.

Le Carré, John, *The Spy Who Came in from the Cold* (1963). From the time of Le Carré's first book (of nine) featuring the spymaster George Smiley, he has demonstrated that spy fiction can rise to the level of high literature. Smiley exists in a drab, jaded, and morally ambiguous world of crosses, double crosses, and triple crosses. In this novel, the British agent Alec Leamas is sent to East Germany on a disinformation mission. His girlfriend, an English communist, gets involved, and by the end the deceptions and deaths resulting from Leamas's actions reveal the tawdriness of Western counterintelligence, and its incongruity as a tool of democratic states. For the life of the novelist, see Adam Sisman, *John Le Carré: The Biography* (2015).

Lessing, Doris, *The Golden Notebook* (1962; Harper, 2008). Largely self-educated, Doris Lessing grew up in Southern Rhodesia. She moved to England after the Second World War and became active in anti-apartheid circles. She was a member of the British Communist Party until the Soviet invasion of Hungary. *The Golden Notebook,* her most famous work, describes a young woman's psychological and realistic encounter with colonial society and the communist movement. It has been regarded as a feminist classic—though Lessing refused to be known as a feminist author. She published more than fifty novels in all, as well as short stories, plays, and libretti. When she learned that she had received the Nobel Prize in Literature in 2007, her reaction was "Oh Christ!" Lessing's versatility can be seen clearly in her short, terrifying novel *The Fifth Child* (1988), a modern story of a changeling.

Lively, Penelope, *Moon Tiger* (1987; Penguin, intro. Anthony Thwaite, 2006). Lively was born in Cairo, and this novel is based partly on her recollections of Egypt. The protagonist, Claudia Hampton, was a war correspondent in Cairo—Moon Tiger was a brand of mosquito coil that she kept by her bed there—and later a popular historian. On her deathbed, she decides to write a history of the world that will include her personal history as well. She is worried that posterity will misjudge her character and misrepresent her life. She wants to be remembered as a freethinking woman of her time, but faces the possibility that her indifference as a mother, her private and public scandals, will in the end define her.

Lodge, David, *Changing Places: A Tale of Two Campuses* (1975; Penguin, 1995). The subtitle alludes to *A Tale of Two Cities*, by Dickens. The British campus is modeled on the University of Birmingham, and the American on the University of California, Berkeley (in the state of Euphoria). An Englishman, Philip Swallow, and an American, Morris Zapp, agree to a semester's exchange. Swallow is somewhat in awe of American academic life, while Zapp, modeled on the literary critic Stanley Fish, is at first contemptuous of British academic life. As a satire on the early 1970s, *Changing Places* can be hilarious in recounting the swapping of students and, inadvertently, wives, against the background of the sexual revolution, Vietnam, student sit-ins, smoking pot, and psychedelia.

Lowry, Malcolm, *Under the Volcano* (1947; Penguin, 2000). In the Mexican town of Quauhnahuac on the Day of the Dead in 1938, a British consul faces his last day. A submarine commander in World War I, he had been court-martialed for allegedly burning alive captured German sailors in the boiler of the vessel, but later was not only proved innocent but also decorated for valor and given this responsibility-free posting. He attempts to become an author, but alcohol dominates his life—in fact, kills him. In its portrayal of the perils of alcoholism, this story will send shivers down the spine of anyone who has ever imbibed a drop. The excellent 1984 John Huston film adaptation stars Albert Finney as the consul.

Mackenzie, Compton, *Whisky Galore* (1947; Vintage, 2004). Mackenzie, or "Monty," as he was known, wrote well over a hundred works, some of them completed by writing all night while sustained by Ovaltine. With a flamboyant personality and robust commitment to Scottish nationalism, he will be remembered above all for his novels dealing with the cultural and political mood of the twentieth-century Scottish Renaissance. *Whisky Galore*, his most popular work, is a fictionalized account of the grounding of the SS *Politician* off the coast of Scotland in 1941, with 28,000 cases of malt whisky on board. The valiant efforts of local villagers to save the precious cargo have a permanent place in twentieth-century folklore. The 1948 film stars Mackenzie as the skipper.

MacNeice, Louis, *Collected Poems* (2007; Wake Forest, ed. Peter McDonald, 2013). MacNeice was a poet and playwright whose work often reflected his childhood in Northern Ireland. He had a painter's eye for making sense of what he called the "drunkenness of things being various." During World War II and afterward, MacNeice worked for the BBC. Dylan Thomas acted in some of MacNeice's plays in the 1940s, and the two heavy drinkers became friends. MacNeice once wrote: "Poetry in my opinion must be honest before anything else and I refuse to be 'objective' or clear-cut at the cost of honesty." The first edition of his collected poems was published posthumously by E. H. Dodds, a fellow Irish poet and colleague at the University of Birmingham.

Manning, Olivia, *The Levant Trilogy* (1977–80; NYRB, 2014). The couple at the heart of Manning's earlier *Balkan Trilogy*, Harriet Pringle and her husband, Guy, a lecturer in English for the British Council, arrive in Egypt after fleeing the Nazi advance through Greece. In exacting detail, Manning depicts the British Army's North Africa campaign, which climaxes with the Battle of El Alamein in 1942, one of the turning points of the war. Sharp-eyed and sharp-tongued, Harriet is particularly contemptuous of the farcical response of civilians in Cairo to a likely German occupation. The author and critic Anthony Burgess described the trilogy as "the finest fictional record of the war produced by a British writer." Manning's *Balkan Trilogy* (1960–65; NYRB, 2010), set in Bucharest and Athens during the early days of the war, begins the story of Harriet and Guy.

Mansfield, Katherine, *Selected Stories* (1911–24; Oxford, 2002). Mansfield grew up in New Zealand and spent formative years in England. During a trip to Paris at the turn of the century, she became fascinated by, in her phrase, the *vie de bohème*. She went on to lead a life described by some as morally depraved yet by others as liberated. It included a series of lovers of both sexes and a tempestuous marriage to the critic John Middleton Murry. Her stories reflect fluctuating moods, revealing a lonely and tormented woman concerned with the vulnerable, the displaced, and the desolate. After dying from tuberculosis at age thirty-four, she became a cult figure, especially for younger women. Claire Tomalin vividly captures the author's eventful existence in *Katherine Mansfield: A Secret Life* (1987).

Mantel, Hilary, *Wolf Hall* (2009; Harper Collins, 2018). Set in the 1520s, the novel tells the story of Thomas Cromwell, a blacksmith's son who became the right-hand man of Cardinal Wolsey and, eventually, Henry VIII. Cromwell's nemesis is Thomas More, especially over the king's break with Roman Catholicism. There is an implicit historical parallel: many of the problems of Cromwell's era are the same as those in subsequent centuries: the tension between the individual, society, and state, and above all social mobility. Mantel explains that her work is separate from that of historians—though she pays scrupulous attention to historical detail—but no less true. Her chief concern is with the "interior drama" of her characters, which historians, along with her vast readership, can admire and enjoy.

Masters, John, *Bhowani Junction* (1954). In this novel, Robert Savage, a British officer commanding a Gurkha regiment, comes from a family that had long served in India (the author's background was similar). At Bhowani Junction in central India, Savage falls in love with Victoria, the Anglo-Indian daughter of a railroad worker. The British regard the Anglo-Indians as inferiors, calling them "wogs" and "chee-chee girls." Indian society regards them as half-breeds or "mongrels." Savage and Victoria are forced to confront their identities and their futures at the time of Indian independence in August 1947. The novelist Kushwant Singh commented that Kipling knew India but Masters knew Indians. In the 1956 film adaptation, Savage and Victoria are played by Stewart Granger and Ava Gardner.

Maugham, W. Somerset, *The Razor's Edge* (1944; Vintage, 2003). In one of Maugham's last novels, Larry Darrell, an American pilot traumatized by World War I, abandons a conventional life path and instead searches for enlightenment and meaning by working as a common laborer, studying, and traveling, eventually ending up in India and immersing himself in Hindu philosophy and religion. The "razor's edge" represents the peak of the difficult and dangerous path over which Larry must travel in his search for salvation. Several characters are based on real people of the period, not least Maugham himself, who pops up from time to time. A comprehensive and perceptive account of the author's life can be found in Selina Hastings, *The Secret Lives of Somerset Maugham: A Biography* (2012).

Milne, A. A., *Winnie-the-Pooh* (1926; Penguin, 2009) and *The House at Pooh Corner* (1928; Penguin, 1992). Inspired by Milne's son, Christopher Robin, the Winnie-the-Pooh books have sold in the millions and have been translated into over thirty languages. The characters are Pooh, named after a black Canadian bear in the London zoo; Piglet; Kanga and tiny Roo; Rabbit; Owl; and Eeyore, the melancholy donkey. Pooh is slow-witted but kind and good-natured, and sometimes comes up with clever ideas rooted in common sense. *The House at Pooh Corner* introduces the bouncing, lovable Tigger. Two of the most memorable books in children's literature, lighthearted and captivating, cherished by adults as well as younger readers. The best biography of the author is Ann Thwaite, *A. A. Milne: His Life* (1990).

Murdoch, Iris, *Under the Net* (1954; Penguin, 1977). The first of the author's twenty-six novels tells the picaresque story of Jake Donaghue, an Irish hack writer and translator living in London, who sets off a series of misadventures, including the theft of manuscripts. As in her other novels, Murdoch projects her ideas about good and evil, sexual relationships, and the importance of the "inner life" to moral action. Her philosophical works established her as one of the leading thinkers of her day. The philosopher Ray Monk lists *Metaphysics as a Guide to Morals* (1992) as one of the top ten philosophy books of the twentieth century. It argues that ethical judgments require a metaphysical basis. The author's life is told in Peter J. Conradi, *Iris Murdoch* (2001).

Naipaul, V. S., *A Bend in the River* (1979; Vintage, 1989). The story takes place in an abandoned village on the upper Congo, probably not far from the place visited by Conrad three-quarters of a century earlier. The protagonist, Salim, is an East African who earns a living by selling pens and pencils, pans, and pots. The mood of the country shifts, and Salim's life is transformed with the rise of the despotic Big Man, who bears an uncanny resemblance to Mobutu Sese

Seko, notorious for tyrannical corruption, nepotism, and embezzlement. The novel probably reflects Naipaul's view that post-colonial Africa is spiraling into hell. A thorough account of the author's life can be found in Patrick French, *The World Is What It Is: The Authorized Biography of V. S. Naipaul* (2008).

Opie, Peter, and Iona Opie, *The Oxford Book of Nursery Rhymes* (1951; Oxford, 1997). Renowned scholars of folklore, the Opies provide historical information about ballads, songs, lullabies, nonsense jingles, and simple rhymes by asking such questions as who was Mother Goose and whether particular rhymes originally portrayed real people. The 500 or so pieces include "A Frog He Would A-Wooing Go," "Baa, Baa, Black Sheep," "Old Mother Hubbard," and "Jack and Jill" as well as American rhymes and songs such as "Yankee Doodle Came to Town." The nearly hundred illustrations indicate the development of children's literature. It is a work that is equally a book for parents and children alike. Their scholarly masterpiece is *The Lore and Language of Schoolchildren* (1959; NYRB, 2001).

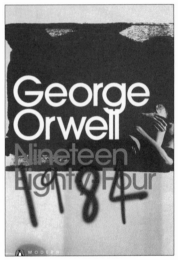

Orwell, George, *1984* (1949; Penguin, foreword by Bernard Crick, 2000). This novel is perhaps best viewed as a satire on authoritarian tendencies in England and elsewhere, not least the Soviet secret police. Orwell warns against the division of the world into spheres of influence by the great powers; the debasing of language by governments; and the rewriting of history for ideological purposes. More literally, the satire turns on the protagonist Winston Smith, who attempts to rebel but succumbs to torture and brainwashing. In a related work, Orwell's essay "Politics and the English Language" (1946) dissects the kind of political speech that, according to Orwell, is "designed to make lies sound truthful and murder respectable." In *Why Orwell Matters* (2002), Christopher Hitchens provides insight into his subject's life and work.

Osborne, John, *Look Back in Anger* (1956; Faber 1978). Jimmy Porter is a working-class jazz musician employed in a market stall. He lives with his wife, Alison, a colonel's daughter, in cramped quarters in the Midlands; their marriage is rent by class conflict and failed expectations. Jimmy swings between moods of violence and nostalgia for a past that never existed. He embodies the conflict between the pre- and post-war generations, the sense of alienation brought on by the tensions and inequities of the mid-1950s. Above all, the play conveys the sense that there are no crusades worth fighting for, which is ironic, since it was produced just before the Suez crisis of 1956, in a sense one of the last crusades of empire. Osborne recalls his life in a caustic and evocative memoir, *Looking Back: Never Explain, Never Apologize* (1999).

Owen, Wilfred, *The War Poems* (Chatto & Windus, ed. Jon Stallworthy, 1994). Owen admired Keats, and both died at age twenty-five. Like Keats, Owen had a piercing intelligence and scathing wit, though temperamentally he was naturally shy and aloof. After the outbreak of war in 1914, he wrote, "My subject is war, and the pity of war." He won the Military Cross for bravery under machine-gun fire, but was killed on the day the armistice was declared. His best-known war poems include "Dulce et Decorum Est" (with the lines "Men marched asleep. Many had lost their boots, / But limped on, blood-shod") and "Anthem for Doomed Youth" ("What passing-bells for these who die as cattle?"). The outstanding account of the poet's life is Jon Stallworthy, *Wilfred Owen: A Biography* (1974).

Potter, Beatrix, *The Tailor of Gloucester* (1902; Warne, 1903). A poor tailor works on a waistcoat for the mayor for Christmas morning but falls ill. When he returns to his shop, he is astonished to find it completed by grateful mice he had rescued from his cat. Some critics believe that *Tailor* is Potter's best work, and she regarded it as her favorite. In an illustration for the book, she went to extraordinary lengths to depict an authentic eighteenth-century cream satin waistcoat embroidered with colored silk. Potter kept a journal in code from the ages of fifteen to thirty-one; Leslie Linder broke the code and published *The Journal of Beatrix Potter* (1966). Both Graham Greene and Evelyn Waugh acknowledged that Potter exerted a formative influence on their writing.

Powell, Anthony, *A Question of Upbringing* (1951; Arrow, 2005), vol. 1 of *A Dance to the Music of Time* (1951–75). Powell's twelve-volume sequence is an absorbing, often comic narrative of English political, cultural, and military life, 1921–68. The first novel introduces the main characters at school and university. Nicholas Jenkins, the narrator, is a loose stand-in for the author, and the power-mad Widmerpool reminded some critics of Prime Minister Edward Heath. Powell's light comedy is pitched midway between P. G. Wodehouse's gentler frivolity and Evelyn Waugh's crueler humor. One of Powell's characters reviews books to make ends meet; Powell himself at age forty-six was reviewing a book a day. The best biography of the author is Hilary Spurling, *Anthony Powell: Dancing to the Music of Time* (2017).

Priestley, J. B., *The Good Companions* (1929). In this picaresque tale, a high-spirited trio of malcontents takes to the road, seeking adventure. Jess Oakroyd is a mill worker, Inigo Jollifant a frustrated music teacher, and Elizabeth Trant a wealthy spinster. They join a defunct performance troupe and, with the help of Trant's money, remake it under the name the Good Companions. With Jollifant at the piano, they meet with success, but a disastrous performance ends their good fortune. Their longings for acclaim and excitement satisfied, the threesome separates to fulfill their individual destinies. To the later generation of writers known as Angry Young Men, the novel was a noxiously unrealistic depiction of working-class Britain, the kind that they were rebelling against.

Ransome, Arthur, *Swallows and Amazons* (1930; Vintage, 2012). This novel, the first of twelve in a series, introduces two groups of siblings, known between themselves as Swallows and Amazons, vacationing in the Lake District. Their common enemy is the uncle of the Amazon children, whom they nickname Captain Flint, after the character in *Treasure Island.* In *The Last Englishman: The Double Life of Arthur Ransome* (2009), Roland Chambers recounts how Ransome worked for both MI6 and the Bolsheviks during and after the Russian Revolution. To Lenin, he was a trusted contact with the West; to British intelligence, he provided invaluable assessments on the temperament and aims of the Bolshevik leaders. In an obituary for Lenin, Ransome wrote that he had been "like a lighthouse shining through the fog."

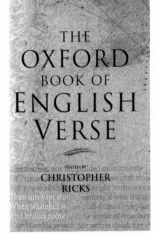

Ricks, Christopher, ed., *The Oxford Book of English Verse* (1999). Seven centuries of British poetry, from anonymous medieval lyrics through the work of Seamus Heaney. Major verse forms are well represented, but there are also limericks, nursery rhymes, epigrams, and squibs. For the first time, the volume includes translations that are now properly considered English poetry—Chapman's Homer, Dryden's Juvenal. Several classic long poems, such as Coleridge's *Rime of the Ancient Mariner* and Christina Rossetti's *Goblin Market,* appear in their entirety. This iconic anthology, updated for the first time since 1972, when Helen Gardner revised Arthur Quiller-Couch's original from 1900, remains the standard repository of the finest examples of the English poetic tradition.

Sassoon, Siegfried, *Memoirs of a Fox-Hunting Man* (1928; Penguin, 2013). In this semi-autobiographical novel, Sassoon tells of a pre–World War I country life of foxhunting, cricketing, and steeplechasing. The war ends all that. George Sherston, the protagonist, wanted war to be "terrible, but not horrible enough to interfere with [his] heroic emotions." But in the trenches he comes to realize that most lives are "an unlovely struggle against unfair odds, culminating in a cheap funeral." The novel is brutal in its depictions of both the front lines and the home front, where dreamed-of peace and rest elude returning soldiers. Sherston's story continues in *Memoirs of an Infantry Officer* (1930) and *Sherston's Progress* (1936). Max Egremont perceptively deals with the writer and his work in *Siegfried Sassoon: A Life* (2006).

Scott, Paul, *The Raj Quartet* (1965–75; Morrow, 1984). In this saga of a British military family in India, the reader is carried forward from the turbulence of the early days of World War II to the confused triumph of Indian independence in 1947. The historian Max Beloff once commented that one can learn more of the history and spirit of the British Raj by reading Paul Scott than by reading the works of all historians of India. An exaggeration, but Scott's creation of fictional characters such as the British-educated Hari Kumar and the complicated archvillain Ronald Merrick marks an achievement in the history and literature of Britain and India. Scott's sequel, *Staying On* (1977), was described by Ferdinand Mount as "an elegiac farewell to the Raj."

Sebald, W. G., *Austerlitz* (2001; Modern Library, 2011). In this novel, Jacques Austerlitz is an architectural historian who was adopted in Wales in 1939 as an infant refugee from Czechoslovakia, part of the *kindertransport,* which sent Jewish children to England ahead of the Nazi

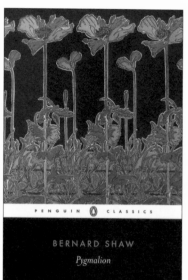

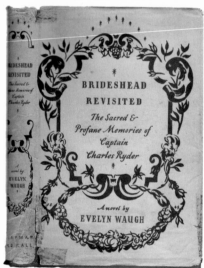

takeover of central Europe. As an adult, he diligently searches for clues about his biological parents. The journey takes him to the Theresienstadt concentration camp, Paris, Antwerp, and London. Sebald's overarching theme in this and other novels is Germans' willed forgetfulness about World War II, particularly in the late 1940s and 1950s. In an oblique style, partly historical and partly autobiographical, he reflects on German silence about the destruction of Warsaw, the atrocities committed at the camps, and similar traumas.

Shaw, George Bernard, *Pygmalion* (1914; Penguin Classics, 2003). Drawing on the myth of Galatea and Pygmalion, Shaw's didactic but highly entertaining play explores language, class, society, and relations between the sexes. Under the stern tutelage of a phonetics master, a Cockney flower girl acquires the elocution, and thereby the social standing, of a duchess. Shaw, one of the most gifted and prolific writers of the twentieth century, claimed that his writing style owed much to John Bunyan. *Pygmalion* is especially concerned with the articulation of sounds. Shaw left a bequest to finance the reform of the English language, including the creation of a forty-letter alphabet, representing every sound in the English language, to replace the present twenty-six-letter alphabet. Michael Holroyd's *Bernard Shaw* (one-volume ed., 2005) is the key biography.

Spark, Muriel, *The Prime of Miss Jean Brodie* (1961; Everyman's, intro. Frank Kermode, 2004). Miss Brodie is a demanding Scottish schoolmistress in the 1930s. She aims to bring out the best in her students by emphasizing ambition, independence, and dedication. At one point, she boasts that she is in her prime and will stop teaching only if assassinated. She acts as if she transcends morality, but when one of her students accuses her of promoting fascism, her career is brought to a crisis. David Lodge described Spark as "the most original and innovative British novelist writing in the second half of the twentieth century." The excellent film adaptation (1969) stars Maggie Smith as Miss Brodie. For the life of the novelist, see Martin Stannard, *Muriel Spark: The Biography* (2009).

Thompson, Flora, *Lark Rise to Candleford* (1945; Oxford, intro. Phillip Mallett, 2011). *Lark Rise* is a lightly fictionalized trilogy recounting Thompson's experiences as a child and young woman who at the age of fourteen got a job in a post office in Juniper Hill, the Oxfordshire hamlet where she was born. Largely self-educated by the use of a local library, she captured the mood and "decay" of an agrarian town in late-Victorian England. According to the poet and writer H. J. Massingham, her literary power brought passion to her descriptions of both sides of the social and economic divide, thus making her work not only memorable but also useful as a social history of the "vanished world" of rural culture.

Waugh, Evelyn, *Brideshead Revisited* (1945; Back Bay, 2012). England of the 1920s recalled from the vantage point of the morally decayed post–World War II era. The novel tracks the fortunes of an aristocratic Catholic family, but is famous above all for its description of effete yet extravagant decadence among students at Oxford in the interwar years. Waugh's *Sword of Honour* (*Men at Arms*, 1952; *Officers and Gentlemen*, 1955; *Unconditional Surrender*, 1961) tells the story of Guy Crouchback, a stand-in for the author, who grows increasingly disillusioned by his military experience in World War II. Guy is sent to Senegal, Egypt, Crete, and Yugoslavia, but finds neither heroism nor much honor anywhere. The series owes a literary debt to Ford Madox Ford's *Parade's End*, another fictionalized autobiographical account of wartime disappointment.

Wodehouse, P. G., *Right Ho, Jeeves* (1934; Penguin, 1999). Bertie Wooster, a wealthy, idle young Londoner, and his omnicompetent valet, Jeeves, figure in eleven novels. *Right Ho* presents the standard setup: at the country estate of one of Bertie's aunts, engagements are made, broken, and mended; trouble with the staff threatens; and Jeeves puts all to right. The climax comes when one of Bertie's friends gives a drunken, abusive speech while handing out prizes at the local grammar school. While interned by Germans during World War II, Wodehouse made lighthearted broadcasts from Berlin, believing they would indicate the "stiff upper lip" of someone making the best of bad circumstances; instead, he was widely regarded as a traitor. The best biography of the writer is Robert McCrum's excellent *Wodehouse: A Life* (2004).

Woolf, Virginia, *Mrs. Dalloway* (1925, jacket design by Vanessa Bell; Penguin Modern Classics, 2000). Upper-class Clarissa Dalloway spends a day in June preparing to give a party that evening. Simultaneously, a shell-shocked working-class veteran of World War I is committed to a psychiatric hospital, where he dies by jumping from a window. Hearing of his death at the party, Clarissa comes to admire his act of suicide, thinking, "Death was defiance." Woolf's *A Room of One's Own* (1929) contains the author's famous declaration, "A woman must have money and a room of her own if she is to write fiction." The essay celebrates what women had achieved as novelists despite the ongoing social and financial handicaps burdening them. Woolf calls for women's access to education to be greatly expanded—a vision that was still radical in the 1920s.

Literature
United States

19th century

Alcott, Louisa May, *Little Women* (1868–69; Penguin, 2014). The story of the four March sisters reflects Alcott's own family circumstances. She was a passionate abolitionist and served as a nurse during the Civil War. She held equally strong views about women's rights. Jo, Beth, Meg, and Amy experience the relative deprivations of family life during wartime, the agony of early death, and the quiet satisfaction of duty and commitment. Jo becomes a writer, initially of sensationalistic potboilers—something else she had in common with the author, who at one point supported a large household with earnings from her writings. *Little Women*, one of the best-selling novels in U.S. history, was followed by two sequels: *Little Men* (1871) and *Jo's Boys* (1886).

Cooper, James Fenimore, *The Last of the Mohicans: A Narrative of 1757* (1826; Scribner, 2013). Besides introducing the character Hawkeye (Natty Bumppo), who figures in each of the five volumes of Cooper's Leather-Stocking Tales, this novel established historical and literary themes that resonated through the twentieth century. Frontiersmen were fearless, strong, and resourceful. Indians were either noble savages or treacherous brutes. White women were at constant risk of capture by Indians. Set in upstate New York during the French and Indian War, the novel, an exemplar of romanticism, caught the public imagination on both sides of the Atlantic. The titular characters are Uncas and his father, Chief Chingachgook, a gallant, wise, and stoic "red man," the sole survivor of his race.

Crane, Stephen, *The Red Badge of Courage* (1895; Bantam, intro. Alfred Kazin, 2004). Crane, who had not been to war, drew mainly from newspaper accounts to give a realistic account of fighting during the Civil War. A young soldier hopes to receive a wound, a "red badge," in battle. Yet the one he eventually receives is unheroic, the result of being struck accidentally by a rifle butt. With suspense and irony, the book, which Civil War veterans swore could have been written only by a fellow soldier, has taken its place among the classics of American war literature. John Berryman's *Stephen Crane: A Critical Biography* (1950; 2001) is a life written by a fellow poet, especially valuable for its psychological insight.

Dickinson, Emily, *The Selected Poems of Emily Dickinson*, ed. Billy Collins (Penguin, 2000). Born in Amherst, Massachusetts, in 1830, Dickinson attended Amherst Academy. Outgoing and energetic as a student, she became increasingly reclusive afterward. She never married. Her poems are remarkable for emotional and intellectual energy, ironic wit, and themes of religious seeking and death. At the time of their first, posthumous publication, they caught the public eye, despite their distinctive, unconventional style—full of dashes and erratic capitalization—considered irregular and random by some. In the intervening century, she has come to be seen as one of the greatest American poets, of the stature of Walt Whitman.

Emerson, Ralph Waldo, *Nature, and Selected Essays* (1836–62; Penguin Classics, 2003). Emerson was perhaps America's first *American* philosopher, urging citizens of the young country to throw off the weight of European tradition, live harmoniously with nature, and guide their actions by a sense of personal integrity. The essay "Self-Reliance" stresses the importance of being resourceful and avoiding conformity. His influence on the ideas of Thoreau, who is the subject of one of the essays, comes through clearly, as does his commitment to the native mysticism of Transcendentalism. The life of the writer can be found in Lawrence Buell, *Emerson* (2003).

Harris, Joel Chandler, *Uncle Remus: His Songs and Sayings* (1880; Penguin, 1982). Harris, a Georgia newspaperman, created the character Uncle Remus, based on slaves he knew during the Civil War. Through Uncle Remus, Harris retold stories of African American animal folklore featuring Brer (Brother) Rabbit, Brer Fox, and Brer Bear. Brer Rabbit, a trickster figure, survives by his wits, outsmarting those who try to control (or eat) him. The tales likely have their origins in African and Caribbean folklore. In the most famous story, Brer Rabbit gets hopelessly stuck to a tar baby made by Brer Fox, but nonetheless finds a cunning escape. Lawrence Levine's *Black Culture and Black Consciousness: Afro-American Folk Thought from Slavery to Freedom* (1977) is a groundbreaking work on the rich oral tradition in African American culture.

Hawthorne, Nathaniel, *The Scarlet Letter* (1850; Penguin Classics, intro. Nina Baym, 2002). In Puritan Boston of the mid-seventeenth century, Hester Prynne is convicted of adultery and forced to wear a red letter *A* on her dress—a penance she accepts with dignity and even pride. An extended meditation on sin, guilt, hypocrisy, and the fall from grace, the novel is also a character study exploring pathways to redemption. Hawthorne's *House of the Seven Gables* (1851), a tale of lost legacies, family menace, and long-standing guilt, is based on a curse placed on the author's family when his great-grandfather was a judge at the Salem witch trials.

Irving, Washington, *The Legend of Sleepy Hollow, and Other Stories* (c. 1819; Modern Library, 2001). Irving was one of the first significant writers in post-revolutionary America. His two best-known stories are Americanized versions of European folktales. In "Sleepy Hollow," a superstitious, lovesick schoolmaster, Ichabod Crane, encounters the Headless Horseman while riding home through the woods one night. In "Rip van Winkle," the titular character falls asleep in the Catskill Mountains and wakes up twenty years later—having missed the American Revolution. The reader can imagine waking from a long sleep and missing the era of Donald Trump. Contemporary critics, including Edgar Allan Poe, dismissed Irving as an inferior writer, but his stories hold an iconic status in American literature.

James, Henry, *The Portrait of a Lady* (1881; Signet Classics, 2007). Isabel Archer, a beautiful young American, travels to England, where she attracts the attention of a group of suitors. Gilbert Osmond wins her, but marriage turns out to be anything but the leisured idyll she expected. The novel is replete with acute observations, yet never succumbs to the oppressiveness of some of the late major works. *The Ambassadors* (1903), a dark comedy of manners that James regarded as his finest novel, deeply plumbs his perennial subject, the clash between European and American sensibilities. Lambert Strether is sent to Paris by his fiancée to retrieve her son, Chad, who has overstayed his time there. Unsurprisingly, Chad, who much prefers Paris to small-town Massachusetts, has no intention of returning.

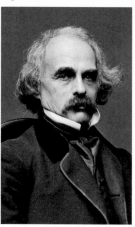

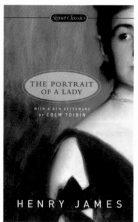

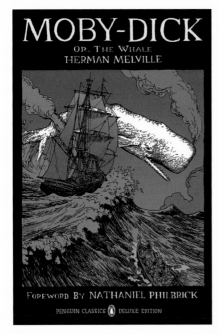

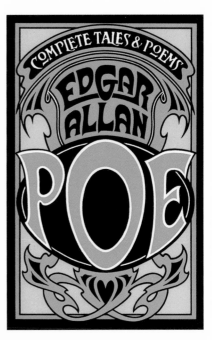

Longfellow, Henry Wadsworth, *Selected Poems* (Penguin, ed. Lawrence Buell, 1988). Generations of American schoolchildren were introduced to poetry through Longfellow's works. His poems were immensely popular in England as well as America—some 10,000 copies of *Miles Standish* were sold in London on a single day. But critics have not been kind. Edgar Allan Poe, for example, dismissed him as a "determined imitator." After his death, his reputation declined still further, yet no poet was more read in his time. "Paul Revere's Ride," *Evangeline*, and *The Song of Hiawatha* helped shape the perception of American history and the national character. Edward Wagenknecht's *Henry Wadsworth Longfellow: Portrait of an American Humanist* (1966) is a scholarly and unusually sympathetic account.

Melville, Herman, *Moby-Dick* (1851; Penguin, 2000). Obsessed Captain Ahab relentlessly pursues the great white whale, even to the point of annihilation. Though the novel can be read as a straightforward sea story, it has been generally seen as a commentary on any number of dualities, including freedom and fate, and, perhaps most persuasively, belief and unbelief. Its grip on the imagination of its readers is like the hold that Moby-Dick exercises on Ahab. The life of the writer is described in Laurie Robertson-Lorant, *Melville: A Biography* (1998). *Typee* (1846), the author's first book, and the one that made his name, is based in part on his experiences in the South Pacific; it became a sensation for describing incidents of cannibalism.

Poe, Edgar Allan, *Complete Stories and Poems* (1849; Doubleday, 1966). For a good sense of the author's work, start with "To Helen," which has been called one of the most beautiful love poems in the English language; "The Raven," about a distraught lover who receives the answer "Nevermore"; and "The Gold-Bug," which influenced Arthur Conan Doyle's creation of Sherlock Holmes, and the plot of Robert Louis Stevenson's *Treasure Island*. Poe was also a fearless critic, "using prussic acid instead of ink." Poe's one novel, *The Narrative of Arthur Gordon Pym* (1838), is a sea tale that later influenced Herman Melville and Jules Verne. According to Alfred Hitchcock, "It's because I liked Edgar Allan Poe's stories so much that I began to make suspense films."

Stowe, Harriet Beecher, *Uncle Tom's Cabin* (1852; Penguin, intro. Anne Douglas, 1981). The story of Tom has been denounced as racist, condescending, and sentimental; but the critic Alfred Kazin described it as "the most powerful and enduring work of art ever written about American slavery." The theme is Christian love and its ability to overcome enslavement. The saintly Tom, a middle-aged man with a wife and children, is sold to the plantation owner Simon Legree and eventually whipped to death for refusing to betray an escaped slave. The book popularized stereotypes about black people, including Uncle Tom himself, who came to symbolize a "subservient fool who bows down to the white man." The book became the second best-selling book in English, after the Bible, in the nineteenth century.

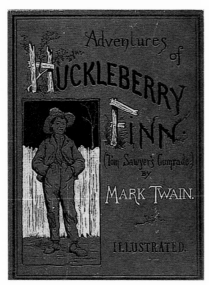 

Twain, Mark, *The Adventures of Huckleberry Finn* (1884; Barnes & Noble Classics, intro. Robert O'Meally, 2016). Ernest Hemingway famously had one of his characters say, "All modern American literature comes from one book by Mark Twain called 'Huckleberry Finn.'" On a raft on the Mississippi, Huck wrestles with his feelings about Jim, a slave he has helped escape. He grows to consider Jim a true friend. When warned that associating illegally with a runaway slave could lead to eternal damnation, Huck replies, "All right, then, I'll go to Hell." Twain chronicles a different sort of waterborne adventure in *The Innocents Abroad* (1869), an account of cruise around the Mediterranean. He recounts visits to barely habitable hotels, dealings with deceptive guides, and a meeting with the Russian royal family that left him awestruck.

Whitman, Walt, *Leaves of Grass* (1855; Penguin, intro. Harold Bloom, 2005). Whitman believed that poetry should be read by all Americans, poor as well as rich, and written in the language of the people. This can be seen in the famous first lines of "Song of Myself":

> *I celebrate myself, and sing myself,*
> *And what I assume you shall assume,*
> *For every atom belonging to me as good belongs to you.*

Some critics deplored the book's overtly sexual descriptions, one dismissing it as "trash, profane, and obscene," but Whitman gained fame as a poet "whose body is as good as the soul." Two of his elegies for Abraham Lincoln, "O Captain! My Captain!" and "When Lilacs Last in the Dooryard Bloom'd," sustained his popularity as America's "poet of the people."

20th century

American crime fiction. Chandler, Raymond, *The Big Sleep* (1939; Vintage, 1988); Ross Macdonald, *The Galton Case* (1959; Vintage, 1996); Elmore Leonard, *52 Pickup* (1974; Morrow, 2013). The style of crime fiction known as hard-boiled detective fiction typically features a private investigator who works for himself and is bound by a self-imposed moral code. The first great, early practitioner in the field was Raymond Chandler, whose hero, Philip Marlowe, worked the sun-blasted streets of Los Angeles. In *The Big Sleep*, Marlowe must untangle a fiendishly complex web of deception involving blackmail, drugs, pornographers, and several killings. Chandler's heir was Ross Macdonald (the pen name of Kenneth Millar). His nineteen Lew Archer novels are set mainly in Southern California, and all of them are fueled by the uncovering of long-buried family secrets. In *The Galton Case*, Archer's search for a man missing for twenty years leads him into a dark labyrinth of false identities, fraud, and violated innocence. Elmore Leonard's early crime novels are set in the decay of his native Detroit. The main character in *52 Pickup* is blackmailed by three men who have filmed him with his mistress. The man, unwilling to go to the police, must figure out for himself how to deal with the criminals.

American science fiction. Heinlein, Robert, *Stranger in a Strange Land* (1961; Ace, 1987); Frank Herbert, *Dune* (1965; Ace, 1990); Philip K. Dick, *Do Androids Dream of Electric Sheep?* (1968; Del Rey, 1996). Science fiction started in Europe, with H. G. Wells and Jules Verne, but caught on quickly in the United States. In the 1960s, American sci-fi grappled with problems racking the country, including environmental degradation and the sexual revolution. In Robert Heinlein's *Stranger in a Strange Land*, Valentine Michael Smith, a human raised from birth on Mars by Martians, is returned to Earth, where his presence causes mayhem. The novel is famous for its frank treatment of sex and for *grok*, a Martian word meaning "to understand profoundly and intuitively." Frank Herbert's epic *Dune* is set on the desert planet Arrakis, the sole source in the universe of the substance that makes interstellar travel possible. Not least of the book's accomplishments is its convincing depiction of a desert world and its nomadic tribes. Philip Dick's *Do Androids Dream of Electric Sheep?*, the basis of the film *Blade Runner* (1982), is set in a future where virtually all nonhuman animal life on Earth is extinct. The main character,

Deckard, is a policeman who hunts escaped replicants, androids so lifelike that they can pass for human. The novel is an extended meditation on ecology, religion, and identity.

Anderson, Sherwood, *Winesburg, Ohio* (1919; Norton, 1995). Anderson was a midwestern businessman who in 1912 suffered a nervous breakdown that enabled him, according to his numerous accounts of it, to become a writer and to introduce new insights from psychology. During World War I, he met Gertrude Stein in Paris. In the words of the critic Irving Howe, she "did not bend Anderson to her style, she liberated him for his own." In precise and unsentimental style, the stories in *Winesburg* reveal the frustrations, loneliness, and longings of the townspeople, who relate their "tales"—Anderson's deliberate word—which a young reporter binds sympathetically together. In 1926, H. L. Mencken proclaimed Anderson "America's most distinctive novelist." For the life of the novelist, see Kim Townsend, *Sherwood Anderson* (1987).

Bellow, Saul, *Herzog* (1964; Penguin, 2003). Sitting alone in a dilapidated house, Moses Herzog thinks, "If I am out of my mind, it's all right with me." He gives some credence to this possibility by writing numerous unmailed letters to the living and the dead, including Dwight Eisenhower, Martin Heidegger, and Friedrich Nietzsche. His life, which seems caught in a holding pattern, is complicated by entanglements with his ex-wives, his mistresses, and his brother, who fail to understand him. The book contains echoes of Bellow's *The Adventures of Augie March* (1953), in which the protagonist finds that intelligence and ebullient ideas lead to nothing without ambition and self-understanding. Zachary Leader's *Life of Saul Bellow: To Fame and Fortune, 1915–1964* (2015) covers Bellow's career up through the writing of *Herzog*.

Berryman, John, *77 Dream Songs* (1964; Farrar, Straus & Giroux, 2014). Berryman was born in McAlester, Oklahoma, in 1914 and studied in the 1930s at Columbia University under Mark Van Doren. He gained widespread recognition with *77 Dream Songs*, a series of eighteen-line poems telling the life story of drunk, depressed, irrepressible Henry, Berryman's alter ego. Jazzy and slangy in style, the poems use free verse and irregular rhyme schemes to portray Henry's thoughts almost photographically. Confessional in nature, the poems had much in common with those of Berryman's good friend Robert Lowell. The sequence was continued in *His Toy, His Dream, His Rest* (1968), which brought the number of dream songs to 385. Improbably enough, Lyndon Johnson once invited Berryman to lunch at the White House.

Bishop, Elizabeth, *The Complete Poems, 1927–1979* (Farrar, Straus & Giroux, 1983). While a student at Vassar in the 1930s, Bishop revealed her independent spirit by founding an underground literary magazine with the writer Mary McCarthy. She later lived for many years in Brazil. Her poetic themes involve landscape and the human connection with the natural world, as, for example, in "Geography III." Throughout much of her life she suffered from acute shyness, depression, and alcoholism. The critic Alfred Corn described her poems as works of "radiant patience" and "philosophic beauty and calm." Bishop's *One Art: Letters* (1994), especially the correspondence with the poets Marianne Moore and Robert Lowell, and with Lowell's wife, the writer Elizabeth Hardwick, gives unvarnished access to the poet's responses to her travels and personal struggles.

Bowles, Paul, *The Sheltering Sky* (1949; Ecco, 2014). Three Americans, a husband and wife and their friend, travel through the Sahara. The husband, Port, finds his fate in the desert; his wife, Kit, glimpses the chaos of life outside the illusory shelter of the sky. The minor characters are one of the strengths of the book: French officers in garrison towns, Arab prostitutes, and a comically stupid pair of American tourists, mother and son. The prose is as dispassionate as the desert itself. Bowles lived for more than five decades in Tangier, Morocco. He and his wife, Jane, also a novelist, came to symbolize expatriate life in North Africa. The 1990 film version, directed by Bernardo Bertolucci, features Bowles in a cameo role.

Burroughs, Edgar Rice, *Tarzan of the Apes* (1914; Penguin, intro. John Seelye, 1990). Tarzan is a man of physical strength and moral courage who was raised by apes. As he grows into manhood, he rescues Africans menaced by exploitative whites, though he does not have a high opinion of the Africans themselves. He emerges as a consistent and chivalrous opponent of colonial oppression, but with some exceptions: he takes Israel's side against the Arabs, especially the arch-villain Gamal Abdel Nasser. The Tarzan series consistently pursues themes of honesty and bravery and has never lost popularity. Tarzan stands as an archetype of the modern hero. There have been over twenty sequels, translated into fifty-eight languages, with total sales estimated at thirty million copies.

Burroughs, William S., *Naked Lunch* (1959; restored text, Grove, 2007). The composition of *Naked Lunch* was inspired by the writings of Paul Bowles and assisted by Allen Ginsberg and Jack Kerouac, mainly in Tangier. It consists of fragmentary episodes assembled into a nonlinear text dealing mainly with drugs, sex, violence, and death. The book draws on Burroughs's addiction to heroin and other drugs as well as his contempt for what he believed to be hypocritical and vicious in American life. Burroughs led a dissolute life, but he had graduated from Harvard with a major in English and could defend his style of writing by quoting from Matthew Arnold. A sturdy account of a notably chaotic life is Ted Morgan's *Literary Outlaw: The Life and Times of William S. Burroughs* (1988).

Cather, Willa, *My Ántonia* (1918; Mariner 1995). A novel about the daughter of Bohemian immigrants, Ántonia, and an orphaned boy, Jim, who belong to pioneer families in Black Hawk, Nebraska, at the end of the nineteenth century. It stands as Cather's masterpiece. H. L. Mencken wrote in 1920 that it was "the best piece of fiction ever done by a woman in America." And Sinclair Lewis was certainly right when he wrote that *My Ántonia* made Nebraska known "as no one else has done" by portraying immigrants as pioneers forging their lives and enduring hardships on the American plains. Cather's *Death Comes for the Archbishop* (1927) concerns the lives of Catholic priests in New Mexico and the building of the cathedral in Santa Fe.

Cummings, E. E., *e. e. cummings: Complete Poems, 1904–1962*, ed. George James Firmage (1994; Liveright, 2016). Early on, Cummings attracted attention by his eccentric use of grammar, punctuation, and capitalization. He aimed at precise, compressed language put in the rhythms of common speech, for example, "may I feel said he / I'll squeal said she." By the 1930s, he had become a cynical, abrasive critic of American society, portraying prostitutes, drunks, gangsters, bums, and Salvation Army workers. By the 1950s his political views had become reactionary. His critical reputation never matched his popularity, yet his poems show wit, ingenuity, and occasional beauty. The definitive biography is Richard S. Kennedy, *Dreams in the Mirror: A Biography of E. E. Cummings* (1980).

DeLillo, Don, *White Noise* (1985; Penguin, 2009). In this novel, Jack Gladney is a professor of Hitler studies at a small midwestern college. He and Babette (his fourth wife) and a brood of children and stepchildren are subjected to an "airborne toxic event" that forces them to evacuate their home. The terror of death that Jack and Babette feel results in a search for ways to alleviate it: first an experimental drug designed for that purpose, and later the possibility of killing another person to give one a sense relief. Both "cures" for existential dread are among the kinds of artifice pervading the characters' lives. DeLillo followed *White Noise* with *Libra* (1988), which tells Lee Harvey Oswald's story from his early days up through the Kennedy assassination—a tour de force of historical re-creation.

Didion, Joan, *Slouching towards Bethlehem: Essays* (1968; Farrar, Straus & Giroux, 2008). In the title piece, Didion's aim is to understand the 1960s counterculture, especially as it manifested in San Francisco's Haight-Ashbury district. Though she dislikes hippies and disapproves of student radicals, she talks to runaways, dropouts, and aging Beats, determined to figure out what they are rebelling against and what they are looking for. There are also essays dealing with, among other topics, Joan Baez and John Wayne, Hawaii and the Sacramento Valley, Nevada weddings and California murders. Didion's novel *Play It as It Lays* (1970), about a young actress's experience of the curdled promise of the 1960s, is set in the morally arid landscapes of Hollywood and Las Vegas.

Dos Passos, John, *USA* (1930, 1932, 1936; Library of America, 1996). Dos Passos thought of himself as a social revolutionary who saw the United States as divided into two countries, rich and poor, the latter dehumanized and ground down by capitalism. In *The 42nd Parallel, 1919,* and *The Big Money,* which make up *USA,* Dos Passos uses a collage of narrative styles—including "Newsreels," which grab headlines, newspaper articles, and song lyrics of the day—to follow the lives of a dozen characters, including the author himself, in the early decades of the twentieth century. He won praise from such diverse personalities as

Norman Mailer, who praised the work as "a Great American Novel," and Jean Paul Sartre, who called Dos Passos "the greatest novelist of our time." The life of the novelist is detailed in Virginia Spencer Carr, *Dos Passos: A Life* (rev. ed., 2004).

Dreiser, Theodore, *Sister Carrie* (1900; Penguin, intro. Alfred Kazin, 1995). Carrie Meeber, a teenager from rural Wisconsin, runs off with George Hurstwood, a married man and embezzler. (The story is based on a similar affair of Dreiser's sister.) The pair end up in New York, where Hurstwood degenerates into a derelict on the Bowery while Carrie pursues fortune and fame through occasional flings and a talent for the stage. Upon publication, the novel was condemned as immoral, but H. L. Mencken admired Dreiser as a man of "unshakable courage" and the book itself, a victim of "puritanical repression," as the greatest of American big-city novels. The 1952 film adaptation, titled *Carrie*, stars Laurence Olivier and Jennifer Jones.

Ellison, Ralph, *Invisible Man* (1952; Vintage, 1995). A nameless narrator who believes himself to be invisible to white America because of the color of his dark skin seeks recognition at the most basic, human level. He confronts intellectual as well as social issues that African Americans faced in the early twentieth century.Over the course of his life, he is met by failure in education, revolutionary politics, and religion. He finally retreats to a brilliantly lit underground lair, visible at least to himself. This story of serial disillusionment denies the possibility of easy redemption for America's original sin. Ellison's *Collected Essays* (1995) amounts to a fragmentary autobiography found in the gathered interviews, personal pieces, and commentaries; the preface, by Saul Bellow, a friend of Ellison's, offers firsthand insights.

Faulkner, William, *Light in August* (1932; Vintage, 1991). A pregnant young woman looking for the father of her child arrives in Jefferson, Yoknapatawpha County, Mississippi. Her arrival is the catalyst for a chain of events leading to murder, arson, betrayal, and lynching. She leaves town in the end, and order is restored. In Jefferson's hardened racial attitudes, narrow religiosity, and straitened economic life, Faulkner depicts an almost feudal society closed off from the larger world. Faulkner's *The Sound and the Fury* (1929), perhaps the first American stream-of-consciousness novel, tells, from multiple points of view, the story of the dissolution of the Compson family, of Jefferson, Mississippi, through three generations. Several themes of southern Gothic fiction—debauchery, incest, suicide—are on full display.

Fitzgerald, F. Scott, *The Great Gatsby* (1925; Scribner, 1988). A clear-eyed, unsentimental examination of the great American themes of self-reinvention and the divide between rich and poor. Aloof, mysterious Jay Gatsby pursues beautiful, married Daisy Buchanan. Their affair, slow to begin, unravels quickly, disastrously on a night scarred by three killings. Fitzgerald traces the rigid class boundaries in American society, which are often impervious even to great wealth, and the ceaseless pull of the past. Fitzgerald deals with another wealthy, troubled American couple in *Tender Is the Night* (1934), set in a posh Swiss psychiatric clinic and the French Riviera. For an account of the novelist's short, tumultuous life, see David S. Brown, *Paradise Lost: A Life of F. Scott Fitzgerald* (2017).

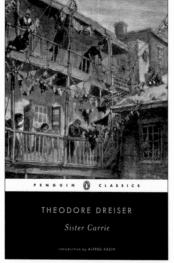

THEODORE DREISER

Sister Carrie

Introduction by ALFRED KAZIN

RALPH ELLISON

Invisible
Man

WILLIAM FAULKNER

Light in August

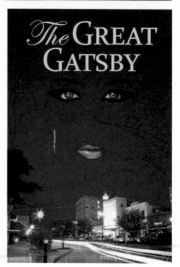

The GREAT
GATSBY

Frost, Robert, *The Poetry of Robert Frost*, ed. Edward Connery Lathem (1979; Holt, 2002). Frost became famous for his "Yankee spirit" and his realistic depictions of rural life—he worked as a farmer for years. His poetry adheres to traditional forms; he once disdainfully likened free verse to "playing tennis without a net." After reading such poems as "The Road Not Taken," Ford Madox Ford assessed his achievement as a poet as "much finer than Whitman's." In "The Death of the Hired Man," Frost famously defined "home" as the place where, "when you have to go there, they have to take you in." For a generous assessment of the poet and his work, see W. H. Pritchard, *Frost: A Literary Life Reconsidered* (1984).

Gaddis, William, *The Recognitions* (1955; Dalkey Archive, 2012). Counterfeits, masks, forgeries, false names, and other simulations of all kinds fill William Gaddis's sprawling first novel, set in the late 1940s and 1950s. The central character, a talented painter, finds his metier in forging Dutch Old Masters. He moves in a world of unscrupulous art dealers, untalented writers, and uninspiring muses. The one true artist in the story, a musician, dies horribly. The exuberance of the plot, the huge swirl of characters, and the author's ironic, poetic, elliptical prose keep the strands of the multifarious story moving. Gaddis later took dead aim at the mindless rapacity of U.S. capitalism in *JR* (1975), about an international business conglomerate run by an eleven-year-old from the pay phone at his school.

Ginsberg, Allen, *Howl, Kaddish, and Other Poems* (1956, 1961; Penguin, 2009). "I saw the best minds of my generation destroyed by madness": so begins *Howl*, Ginsberg's most famous poem. Regarded as pornographic upon publication, it denounces capitalism, conformity, militarism, and bureaucracy, and was vindicated at a trial for obscenity. It became an icon of the Beat generation of the 1950s and 1960s—Ginsberg shows up in another of those iconic works, Jack Kerouac's *On the Road*, as Carlo Marx—not least because of its opposition to sexual repression and embrace of drugs and Eastern religions. Among Ginsberg's formative influences, he counted Lionel Trilling's course at Colombia on great books, and the poetry of Walt Whitman and Emily Dickinson. He once had a hallucination while reciting William Blake's *Marriage of Heaven and Hell*, which he referred to as his "Blake vision."

Hammett, Dashiell, *The Maltese Falcon* (1930; Vintage, 1992). Hammett published five novels, which made his reputation, in 1929–34. For *The Maltese Falcon*, he created the private investigator Sam Spade, who became the iconic hard-boiled detective, the forerunner of Raymond Chandler's Philip Marlowe and Ross Macdonald's Lew Archer. The intricate plot involves a search by half a dozen people to find a jeweled-encrusted gold statue of the titular bird. The book's style is notable for refusing to explore the characters' thoughts and for its utter lack of sentimentality. The 1941 film version, directed by John Huston and starring Humphrey Bogart, Mary Astor, Peter Lorre, and Syndey Greenstreet, is justly celebrated. Hammett's other best-known novel is *The Thin Man* (1934), which features the detective team of Nick and Nora Charles.

Heller, Joseph, *Catch-22* (1961), a bleakly comic satire set on a U.S. air force base off the coast of Italy during World War II. The protagonist, Captain John Yossarian, a bombardier, spends most of his time just trying to stay alive, despite what seem like the best efforts of his fellow officers—including Lieutenant Milo Minderbender, Major Major Major Major, and General Scheisskopf—to kill him. The title has entered English as a term for any problem whose solution is made impossible by the conditions of the problem: for example, an actor needing show business experience in order to get an agent, but being unable to get work in show business without an agent.

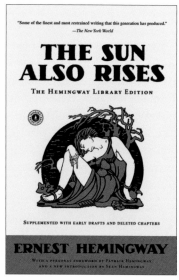

Hemingway, Ernest, *The Sun Also Rises* (1926; Scribner, 2006). From the nightclubs of Paris to the running of the bulls in Pamplona, this novel follows disaffected members of the "Lost Generation" as they search for thrills and sensation, having given up belief in anything else. The characters Jake Barnes and Brett Ashley remain among Hemingway's most indelible creations. Hemingway recast the ending thirty-nine times, which helps explain his reputation as a stylist who influenced most American writers of the twentieth century. Hemingway's *A Farewell to Arms* (1929) is a romance between an English nurse and an American serving in the Italian ambulance corps in World War I, set against the monotonous horrors of the fighting in northern Italy.

Hughes, Langston, *The Collected Poems of Langston Hughes* (Vintage, ed. Arnold Rampersad, 1995). Hughes was known as the poet laureate of the Harlem Renaissance of the 1920s. His first book of poetry, *The Weary Blues* (1926), became famous for its innovative style, described as "jazz blues." This anthology includes the well-known pieces "The Negro Speaks of Rivers," "I, Too," "Summer Night," and "Montage of a Dream Deferred," along with verse for children and previously uncollected poems. His writing over some four decades reflected humor and a buoyant spirit. In 2002, the U.S. Postal Service issued a commemorative stamp in his honor. The standard biography of the poet is Arnold Rampersad, *The Life of Langston Hughes*, 2 vols. (1986, 1988).

Hurston, Zora Neale, *Their Eyes Were Watching God* (1937; Harper, 2013). Hurston was an African American writer whose writings did not directly address racism or seek to present blacks in the best possible light. Independent and idiosyncratic, she studied with Franz Boas (whom she called "Papa Franz") at Barnard College and under his direction did anthropological research in Harlem. In her second novel, *Their Eyes Were Watching God*, she tells the story of Janie Crawford, mainly through her three marriages, each one leading her closer to happiness and fulfillment. Hurston was a pioneer in writing both lyrically and frankly about female sexuality and in describing black women's fraught relationships with men. Hurston's *Dust Tracks on a Road* (1942) is the rollicking autobiography of her first fifty years.

Jarrell, Randall, *The Woman at the Washington Zoo: Poems and Translations* (Atheneum, 1960). In 1956–58, Jarrell was "consultant in poetry" at the Library of Congress—essentially, poet laureate. Known for his wit and erudition, Jarrell was widely regarded as the best poetry critic of his generation. This collection was strongly influenced by his reading of William Wordsworth, from whom he took inspiration to mix joys and terrors, along with the injunction that poems must be as "convincing as speech." The translations include adaptations of Goethe. He drew on his experience in the Army Air Forces to pen his most famous poem, "The Death of the Ball Turret Gunner," which ends with the line: "When I died they washed me out of the turret with a hose." Jarrell's *Collected Essays* (1999, ed. Brad Leithauser) includes selections from the four volumes of essays published during Jarrell's lifetime.

Kerouac, Jack, *On the Road* (1957; Pelican, 1999). An iconoclastic, fictionalized autobiography, *On the Road* came to symbolize the Beat and countercultural generation of the late 1940s and 1950s. Kerouac emphasized his style as a sort of improvisational jazz expressed in "spontaneous writing." He typed out the bohemian trans-country hitchhiking, freight-train-jumping, and Greyhound-bus-riding adventures of Sal Paradise and Dean Moriarity on a continuous roll of paper 30 feet long, telling of friendship, poetry, and drugs in a search for revelation. Kerouac's other road novels include *The Dharma Bums* (1958), *The Subterraneans* (1958), and *Tristessa* (1960); *The Lonesome Traveler* (1960) collects travel essays from Mexico and Europe. For the life of the author, see Tom Clark, *Jack Kerouac: A Biography* (2001).

Kingsolver, Barbara, *The Poisonwood Bible* (1998; Harper Perennial, 1999). In a novel with a dual religious and political theme, Kingsolver tells the story of an American Southern Baptist missionary family that moves to the Congo to convert the natives to Christianity. Flickers of Joseph Conrad illuminate the story, but instead of the heart of darkness, the characters face only ants, hookworms, torrential storms, and green mamba snakes. The daughters in the family lose their Christian faith but discover another. Politically, the novel is set against the background of the Congo's independence in 1960, the plans of the CIA to murder Patrice Lumumba, and the kleptocracy and villainous tyranny of his successor, Mobutu.

Lee, Harper, *To Kill a Mockingbird* (1960; Harper, 2010). Set in the Great Depression in a small town in Alabama, the novel tells the tale of six-year-old Scout Finch; her older brother, Jem; her father, Atticus; her friend Dill; and the reclusive Boo Radley. Atticus, a lawyer, is appointed to defend Tom Robinson, a Negro accused of rape. He is innocent of the crime, and Atticus heroically tries to clear his name, but Robinson was "a dead man the minute [his accuser] opened her mouth and screamed." On the basis of this single book—her only published work until 2015—Lee was awarded the Presidential Medal of Freedom in 2007. The film version (1962) stars Gregory Peck in an iconic performance as Atticus.

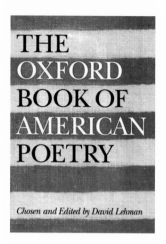

THE OXFORD BOOK OF AMERICAN POETRY

Chosen and Edited by David Lehman

Lehman, David, ed., *The Oxford Book of American Poetry* (3rd ed., 2006). A large selection (1,200 pages) from more than 200 poets, stretching from Anne Bradstreet (b. 1612) to David Yau (b. 1950), weighted toward poetry of the twentieth century—though Walt Whitman receives the most coverage. Poets added since publication of the previous (1976) edition include W. H. Auden, Charles Bukowski, Paul Lawrence Dunbar, Kenneth Koch, Emma Lazarus, Howard Moss, James Schuyler, Gertrude Stein, James Weldon Johnson, and Louis Zukofsky. Female poets, African American poets, and song lyricists are better represented than before. The emphasis is on breadth rather than depth: more poets, fewer poems by each. Like most chronologically arranged anthologies, it gives a good sense of the development and changing styles of its subject.

Lewis, Sinclair, *Babbitt* (1922; Oxford, 2010). Thanks to Sinclair Lewis, a "Babbitt" means a person who conforms to middle-class standards, which he satirized with wit and perception. George F. Babbitt decides that his life as a businessman in the midwestern town of Zenith is not only pointless but also boring and vacuous. He decides to pursue a bohemian lifestyle—only to discover that bohemians have rigid standards of their own. Lewis was regarded by critics as antibusiness and anti-American, but in fact he was a sharp social critic with an ear for the American idiom. Always sensitive to academic criticism, he commented after receiving the Nobel Prize in 1930 that "our American professors like their literature clear and cold and pure and very dead."

London, Jack, *The Call of the Wild* and *White Fang* (1903, 1906; Bantam, 1991). Set in the Yukon during the Klondike gold rush of the 1890s, these novels portray dogs fighting for survival in the arctic North. The savagery of life in the wild is unsparingly detailed. London wrote on subjects as diverse as assassination, ecology, folklore, penal reform, and germ warfare against China. A longtime alcoholic, he lived as a sailor, hobo, and boxer; he was also a skilled photographer. He professed strongly racist beliefs, and George Orwell considered him a fascist; yet he was a passionate advocate of workers' rights. His lifestyle was a seminal influence on Ernest Hemingway and Jack Kerouac. London provides a searing autobiographical account of his struggles with out-of-control drinking in *John Barleycorn: "Alcoholic Memoirs"* (1913).

Lovecraft, H. P., *The Call of Cthulhu, and Other Weird Stories* (c. 1915–35; Penguin, 1999). Horror and science fiction tales from one of Edgar Allan Poe's literary descendants. Lovecraft once wrote, "The oldest and strongest emotion of mankind is fear, and the oldest and strongest kind of fear is fear of the unknown"; these frequently terrifying stories attest to the truth of that observation. The malign influence of the unholy *Necronomicon* crops up repeatedly, and many of the stories take place within a cosmology governed by the "Elder Gods," pitiless extraterrestrial beings of vast age and vaster malevolence. The settings of the tales, no less creepy than the goings-on, range from fictional Arkham, Massachusetts, home of Miskatonic University, to New York City (which Lovecraft despised) to the Antarctic wastes.

Lowell, Robert, *For the Union Dead* (1964). The titular poem, Lowell's most famous work, juxtaposes heroic black Union soldiers with civil rights activists fighting for integration in the 1950s. His poems often reflect the themes of political resistance and historical memory. The poet Stanley Kunitz wrote in 1985 that Lowell's *Life Studies* (1959) was the most influential book of modern verse "since T. S. Eliot's *The Waste Land.*" Lowell was frequently hospitalized for mental illness. One of his last poems compares Richard Nixon with the mad George III. Lowell's *Collected Prose* (1987), compiled by his longtime editor, Robert Giroux, includes essays, reviews, and autobiographical pieces. Kay Redfield Jamison's *Robert Lowell: Setting the River on Fire; A Study of Genius, Mania, and Character* (2017) is a perceptive study by a psychiatrist.

Mailer, Norman, *Armies of the Night: History as a Novel, the Novel as History* (1968; Penguin, 1985). Combining the techniques of a novelist, journalist, and historian, Mailer relates the October 1967 anti–Vietnam War march on the Pentagon, by a crowd estimated at 100,000. He describes the hippies, yippies, radicals, anarchists, fundamentalist Christians, feminists, Weathermen, and intellectuals who came together in a three-day protest that culminated in a clash with military police—Mailer was the second person arrested. Those of the younger generation had in common a rebellion against authority. What all the protesters had in common was a demand for an answer to the central question, "Why are we in Vietnam?" Mailer's overall achievement was to portray the country's deep, irreconcilable division over the war.

McCarthy, Cormac, *Blood Meridian, or, The Evening Redness in the West* (1985; Vintage, 1992). In the Texas-Mexico border regions in the 1850s, the U.S. Army paid a bounty for every Indian scalp brought in, a forerunner of sorts to the "body count" strategy it used in Vietnam. McCarthy fictionalizes the horror of this ultraviolent setting through the experiences of the Kid, a nameless Tennessee teenager who finds himself part of a group of marauders that includes Judge Holden, an unforgettable embodiment of pure malevolence. The violence depicted can be hard to fathom, taking in, as it does, women, children, and even puppies; it does not help to know that McCarthy based many of the incidents on true events. This is the story of the West at its darkest.

McCarthy, Mary, *The Group* (1963; Mariner, 1991). The "Group" in this satirical novel consists of eight young women who graduate in 1933 from the socially prestigious Vassar College. With razor-sharp descriptions, McCarthy portrays the characters as confronting, each in her own sometimes hilarious way, career and marriage, sex and contraception, fidelity to husbands versus loyalty to friends, psychoanalysis and, not least, sexual double standards. The book was banned in Ireland, Australia, and Italy. Norman Mailer attacked it in a 4,000-word jeremiad in the *New York Review of Books*, describing the male characters in particular as "feverish, loud-talking, drunken, neurotic, crippled, and jargon-compensated louts." Yet he gave it one well-justified compliment: *The Group* succeeded as a *sociological* portrayal of young women in the tempestuous decade of the 1930s.

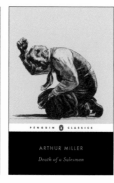

McCullers, Carson, *The Heart Is a Lonely Hunter* (1940; Penguin, 2000). In this novel of loss and failed connections, set in small-town Georgia, a teenage girl finds solace in music as she yearns for love. John Singer, a deaf man whose only friend has been committed to a nearby asylum, takes a room in her family's house. A disparate group of people, including a philosophical drifter and a black physician, find themselves drawn to the empathetic Singer, who nonetheless feels isolated. The death of his friend sets off a chain of events leaving ruin and shattered dreams in their wake. Graham Greene wrote: "Mrs. McCullers and Mr. Faulkner are the only writers since the death of D. H. Lawrence with an original poetic sensibility. I prefer Mrs. McCullers." Recommended also: the 1968 film adaptation, starring Alan Arkin and Sondra Locke.

Mencken, H. L., *The Vintage Mencken: The Finest and Fiercest Essays of the Great Literary Iconoclast* (1955; comp. Alistair Cooke, Vintage, 1990). Mencken, a harsh yet supremely witty critic of American life and letters, brought such passion and virtuosity to his writing that Edmund Wilson called him "our greatest practicing literary journalist." With sharp humor and a contrarian spirit, the "Sage of Baltimore" coined such phrases as "monkey trial" (referring to the 1925 Scopes case) and "Bible belt" while writing on topics including the failure of democracy, the foibles of females, and the dangerous puritanism that he thought was suffocating American life. The best biography of Mencken is Terry Teachout, *The Skeptic: A Life of H. L. Mencken* (2002).

Millay, Edna St. Vincent, *The Selected Poetry* (Modern Library, ed. Nancy Milford, 2002). During World War I, Millay attended Vassar College, where she acquired the reputation of a saucy and defiant feminist, red-haired and beautiful. Her poetry reflects the intellectual stimulation of Greenwich Village in the interwar years, often bittersweet and sorrowful, though, in the words of one of her critics, with the voice of eternal youth. Her sonnets are among the most beautiful in American poetry, and she will probably be forever remembered for her quatrain

> *My candle burns at both ends;*
> *It will not last the night;*
> *But ah, my foes, and oh my friends—*
> *It gives a lovely light!*

A good account of the poet's unconventional life is Nancy Milford, *Savage Beauty: The Life of Edna St. Vincent Millay* (2001).

Miller, Arthur, *Death of a Salesman* (1949; Viking, 1996). In a country where everyone is expected to do great things, it is a tragedy to be ordinary. Capturing an American sensibility made up of nostalgia, sports worship, groundless optimism, and financial anxiety, Miller, in the person of the traveling salesman Willy Loman, turned a spotlight on the dark side of the American Dream. The 1985 televised film version stars Dustin Hoffman and John Malkovich. Miller's next play, one of his best known, is *The Crucible* (1953), an intense imagining of the Salem witch trials, intended as a reflection on the paranoia and fear generated by Joseph McCarthy's witch hunts for communists in the U.S. government.

Miller, Henry, *Tropic of Cancer* (1934; Penguin, 2015). Writing in 1930 to a friend, Miller commented on his arrival in France and his plans: "I start tomorrow on the Paris book: First person, uncensored, formless—fuck everything." It became the most famous banned book in the world. Besides relating his experiences with the down-and-out painters and writers in Montparnasse, it details his sexual adventures, obscenely yet sometimes hilariously. Contrary to many views at the time, it was highly regarded by fellow writers, including, for example, Edmund Wilson and T. S. Eliot, who praised it as a "magnificent piece of work." Legal proceedings in the United States in 1961 finally permitted its publication, which came to represent the virtual end of American censorship.

Morrison, Toni, *Song of Solomon* (1977; Vintage, 2004). This novel tells a complex yet engrossing story of Macon "Milkman" Dead III, a young black man in Michigan. His personal and familial history includes a welter of people with biblical and mythological names (Hagar, Pilate, First Corinthians, Circe), rumors of buried treasure, and a large infusion of African American folklore. People close to Macon—his best friend as well as a second cousin who is infatuated with him—repeatedly try to kill him. Morrison skillfully moves a complex narrative backward and forward through time, revealing Macon's heritage gradually but inexorably. The Swedish Academy praised the novel, along with the highly acclaimed *Beloved* (1987), in awarding the author the Nobel Prize in Literature in 1993.

Nabokov, Vladimir, *Lolita* (1955; Vintage, 1997). Humbert Humbert, in his forties, develops an obsessive passion for twelve-year-old Dolores Haze, whom he refers to as a "nymphet." Humbert considers himself a sophisticated European, and his erotic attachment to a coltish, unformed teenager mirrors in some way Nabokov's fascination with a raw America full of roadside diners, resorts, and roller rinks. The novel scandalized the conservative reading public of the 1950s but nonetheless became a huge best seller. Writing in *Encounter*, Lionel Trilling provocatively asserted that the novel "is not about sex, but about love." *The Annotated "Lolita"* (1991), edited by Alfred Appel Jr., clarifies Nabokov's intricate wordplay and dense allusions. Nabokov's *Ada or Ardor* (1969) is another story of obsessive, transgressive love, this one beginning in adolescence and continuing for a lifetime.

O'Connor, Flannery, *The Complete Stories* (1971; Farrar, Straus & Giroux, 1972). Flannery O'Connor was a devout Catholic who lived in a society dominated by primitive forms of Protestantism. Religion features strongly and unsparingly as a theme in almost all her stories, whether by its presence or its absence. Her most famous (or infamous) story, "A Good Man Is Hard to Find," about a family outing gone horrifyingly wrong, gives a clear picture of her version of a world without God. Race forms part of the general atmosphere of her fiction, and sometimes comes to the fore, as in "The Artificial Nigger." Another motif, the collision of rural southern whites with the larger world, is given a twist in "The Displaced Person," in which a family of Polish refugees is settled on a Georgia farm as workers. This collection, published posthumously, won the National Book Award in 1972.

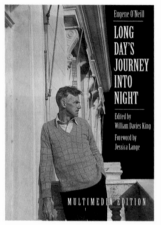

O'Neill, Eugene, *Long Day's Journey into Night* (1956; Yale, intro. Harold Bloom, 2002). O'Neill had a troubled childhood and education, including an apocryphal story of being expelled from Princeton for throwing a beer can through the window of the university's president, Woodrow Wilson. *Long Day's Journey*, a play so searingly autobiographical that O'Neill would not allow it to be produced while he was alive, reveals a family locked in a ferocious struggle over the mother's morphine addiction, the father's stinginess and alcoholism, and the two brothers' raw emotions—yet with all of them yearning for tenderness, affection, and encouragement. The excellent 1962 film adaptation stars Katharine Hepburn and Ralph Richardson.

Pirsig, Robert, *Zen and the Art of Motorcycle Maintenance* (1974; Harper, 2006). This fictionalized autobiography is only indirectly concerned with Buddhism and the mechanics of motorcycle repair. But a motorcycle trip—Pirsig and his son go on a seventeen-day jaunt from Minnesota to California—is the point of departure. Their philosophical discussions along the way include "shortcuts to living right"—tips on avoiding frustration, loneliness, and boredom. The novel resonated with readers disillusioned by Watergate and Vietnam—and it continues to have a wide readership, perhaps not least because of its embrace of technology: Buddha "resides quite as comfortably in the circuits of a digital computer . . . as he does . . . in the petals of a flower."

Plath, Sylvia, *The Bell Jar* (1963; Harper, 2013). Published shortly before Plath's suicide, *The Bell Jar* is a semi-autobiographical novel about a young college student working for a New York fashion magazine as a summer intern. Overcome by personal and professional difficulties, she attempts suicide, but recovers to sort out her problems and return to college. Harper and Row initially had reservations about publishing the book, describing it as "disappointing, juvenile, and overwrought." Nevertheless, it won critical acclaim; it has been translated into a dozen languages; and it perennially appears on book lists like this one. Perhaps the novel's purpose was best expressed by Plath herself: she wanted to show "how isolated a person feels when he is suffering a breakdown."

Porter, Katherine Anne, *Ship of Fools* (1962; Little Brown, 1984). Porter was born in Indian Creek, Texas, and her ashes are buried there. *Ship of Fools* takes place on a ship bound from Mexico to Germany in 1931. The passengers include a couple of Mexican Catholic priests, a drunken German lawyer, a divorced American woman, and a Spanish aristocrat—along with hundreds of Spanish workers in steerage—all of whom in one way or another reveal the racist pride and nationalist arrogance of the early 1930s. Treachery and passion also play a prominent part. Although headed for Europe, the ship has the more complex and symbolic destination of eternity. Also noteworthy is Porter's *Collected Short Stories* (1965), which won the Pulitzer Prize and the National Book Award.

Pound, Ezra, *Selected Poems* (New Directions, 1957). The literary critic Hugh Kenner once wrote that no poet is less read than Pound but no one appeals more through "sheer beauty of language." Pound's poetry includes elevated language and common slang, classical allusions and advertising slogans. He translated works from Anglo-Saxon and ancient Chinese. His worldview was shattered by World War I. Believing fascism to be the only way to stabilize international relations, he drifted into the orbit of Mussolini. During World War II, he criticized the United States, Roosevelt, and the Jews in radio broadcasts from Rome. After the war he was tried for treason and committed to St. Elizabeth's mental hospital on grounds of insanity. Released in 1958, he returned to Italy, where he continued to work on his masterpiece, the *Cantos*. Before his death, he told Allen Ginsberg that his worst mistake was his anti-Semitism.

Pynchon, Thomas, *Gravity's Rainbow* (1973; Penguin, 2006). In London during the close of World War II, Tyrone Slothrop, an American serviceman, becomes a person of great interest to a shadowy intelligence organization. For reasons unknown, his sexual exploits predict rocket attacks by the Nazis. Slothrop is turned loose in the Zone (post-war Europe) to see what else his actions might foretell. Pynchon's masterwork deals with the control and manipulation of information, one of his recurrent themes, within a dominant mood of paranoia. A short novel by Pynchon dealing with many of the same ideas is *The Crying of Lot 49* (1966), in which the disposing of a complicated business empire plays out against a California landscape in full flight from reality; paranoia, psychiatry, and postal systems figure prominently in the proceedings.

Rand, Ayn, *The Fountainhead* (1943; Signet, 1996). Rand was a Russian-born American novelist who developed a neo-Aristotelian philosophy known as Objectivism, the main thrust of which is ethical egoism. *The Fountainhead*, the story of an idealistic architect based loosely on Frank Lloyd Wright, established her reputation. Her popularity soared with the publication of *Atlas Shrugged* (1957), a novel about a revolt of society's productive members, and she eventually attracted a cultlike following. Alan Greenspan, later chairman of the Federal Reserve, became a member of Rand's inner circle. She appeared on a U.S. postage stamp in 1998. Jennifer Burns's *Goddess of the Market: Ayn Rand and the American Right* (2009) delves into Rand's long-standing influence on American conservatism.

Roth, Philip, *American Pastoral* (1997; Vintage, 1998). In a story narrated by Nathan Zucker-man, Roth's frequent alter ego, a tall blond Jewish athlete in Newark becomes the all-Amer-ican boy, marries outside his faith, and settles into an upper-middle-class suburban life. His family's idyllic existence is overtaken by the chaos of the late 1960s, the "indigenous American berserk," and left in ashes. A pitiless look at the perils of assimilation—"She's post-Catholic, he's post-Jewish, together they're going to . . . raise little post-toasties"—by a preeminent American novelist. In *Goodbye, Columbus* (1959), the author's first book, the title novella deals with upper-middle-class Jewish assimilation to post-war suburban consumerism and materialism, with a dash of plastic surgery thrown in for good measure.

Salinger, J. D., *The Catcher in the Rye* (1951; Little, Brown, 1991). The opening sentence of this novel has become famous: "If you really want to hear about it, the first thing you'll probably want to know is where I was born, and what my lousy childhood was like, . . . and all that David Copperfield kind of crap, but I don't feel like going into it, if you want to know the truth." Instead, sixteen-year-old Holden Caulfield rambles on at length about his misadventures in Manhattan after getting kicked out of an expensive prep school. The pervasive adolescent narcissism, combined with the sentimentality of trying to reclaim lost innocence, can make the book, for anyone past the age of sixteen, seem a little overdone.

Sinclair, Upton, *The Jungle* (1906; Penguin, 2006). Sinclair prompted a public outcry with this muckraking novel that exposed labor conditions in the meatpacking industry. Through the protagonist, Jurgis Rudkus, Sinclair dealt with not only the exploitation of workers in unsan-itary and inhumane conditions but also dangerous slaughtering methods and the processing of diseased cattle for food. President Theodore Roosevelt regarded Sinclair as a "crackpot" but nevertheless invited him to lunch at the White House to congratulate him for his part in bringing about passage of the Pure Food and Drug Act and the Meat Inspection Act. Sinclair went on to write some 100 books, usually iconoclastic in urging radical change to improve the lives of victims of capitalism.

Singer, Isaac Bashevis, *A Crown of Feathers, and Other Stories* (1973; Farrar, Straus & Giroux, 1981). These stories, first written in Yiddish and full of wit, mysticism, and a search for the truth, usually end with a surprise. Singer's writings are often compared with those of Anton Chekhov and Guy de Maupassant. Ghost stories and fables are set in Polish-Jewish villages, prewar Warsaw, and post-war New York. Characters adhere to unusual Jewish religious practices and grapple with religion itself. The critic Alfred Kazin wrote of the collection that it "represents the most delicate imaginative splendor, wit, mischief and, not least, the now unbelievable life that Jews once lived in Poland." Singer received the Nobel Prize in Literature in 1978.

Sontag, Susan, *Against Interpretation, and Other Essays* (1966; Picador, 2001). This first collection of Sontag's criticism made her reputation. Besides the titular piece, it includes such well-known essays as "On Style" and "Notes on Camp." There are essays on individual writers (Simone Weil, Jean-Paul Sartre, Albert Camus, Claude Levi-Strauss), on the theatre (Eugene Ionesco, the death of tragedy), and on film (Robert Bresson, Jean-Luc Godard). The overall impression is of a voracious, exacting intellect fully at home in all fields of culture. Sontag's *The Volcano Lover* (1992) is an historical novel that explores the early nineteenth-century love triangle between Sir William Hamilton, the naval hero Admiral Horatio Nelson, and Hamilton's wife, Emma. The 1941 film *That Hamilton Woman*, with Laurence Olivier and Vivien Leigh, deals with the same events.

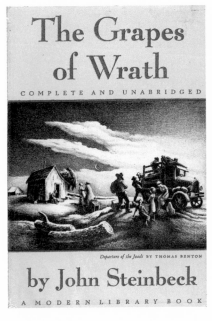

The Grapes of Wrath

COMPLETE AND UNABRIDGED

Departure of the Joads BY THOMAS BENTON

by John Steinbeck

A MODERN LIBRARY BOOK

Steinbeck, John, *The Grapes of Wrath* (1939; Penguin Modern Classics, 2001). The Joads, a family trapped in the Dust Bowl in Oklahoma in the 1930s, set out on Route 66 for work and a better life in California. A story of almost unremitting tragedy—family members die or drift away, food is scarce, work is nonexistent or paid at slave wages—ends in a vision of charity and compassion that transcends conventional boundaries of kinship and society. Deep compassion is found also in Steinbeck's short novel *Of Mice and Men* (1937), about two migrant ranch hands in California. In awarding Steinbeck the 1962 Nobel Prize in Literature, the prize committee described *The Winter of Our Discontent* (1961) as having "attained the same standard which he set in *The Grapes of Wrath*."

Stevens, Wallace, *The Collected Poems of Wallace Stevens* (1954; Vintage, ed. John N. Serio and Chris Beyers, 2015). A career insurance executive, Stevens became famous for such poems as "The Emperor of Ice-Cream," "Sunday Morning," and "Thirteen Ways of Looking at a Blackbird." His unexciting job and calm demeanor hid an exuberant imagination and sometimes belligerent personality—he once got in a drunken fistfight with Ernest Hemingway in Key West. His poetry combines precise descriptions with allusive images to convey meanings that often hover just on the edge of understanding. The critic Harold Bloom describes Stevens as "the best and most representative American poet." For a "full commentary" on nearly all the poet's works, see Bloom's *Wallace Stevens: The Poems of Our Climate* (1980).

Styron, William, *The Confessions of Nat Turner* (1967; Vintage, 1992). Styron imagines Turner, who led a slave revolt in Virginia in 1831, as a figure with a vision of a struggle between black and white angels, intent on leading the black race in a holy war to destroy all whites. Yet during the rebellion, he begins to doubt his mission, with unexpected consequences. Many African American writers denounced Styron for portraying Turner as a caricature and a racial stereotype; but the novelists Ralph Ellison and James Baldwin defended him, and the (white) historians Eugene Genovese and C. Vann Woodward viewed the novel as historically authentic. Genovese's *Roll, Jordan, Roll: The World the Slaves Made* (1974), is a landmark history of southern slavery.

Traven, B., *The Treasure of the Sierra Madre* (1927; English trans. by the author, 1935; Farrar, Straus & Giroux, 2010). B. Traven is the pen name of an author about which almost nothing certain is known. In this novel, three down-and-out American prospectors set out to discover gold in the remote Sierra Madre. They succeed, but after they find the gold, a gang of bandits, pretending to be Federal Police, threatens to murder them. Real *Federales* show up and arrest the bandits, and the Americans carry off the gold. But a continual series of complications, betrayals, and reversals still await them. The faithful 1948 film adaptation, directed by John Huston, stars Humphrey Bogart and Walter Huston.

Vidal, Gore, *United States: Essays, 1952–1992* (1993; Broadway, 2001). A career-spanning collection by America's most gimlet-eyed critic. Vidal casts a pitiless gaze on literature, politics, films, and himself. Some of the essays have achieved near-classic status, such as "The Top Ten Best Sellers," in which he reviews, honestly but with devastating wit, the ten fiction books leading the *New York Times* list in early 1973. His more appreciative efforts take in writers as diverse as Michel de Montaigne and Italo Calvino. His attempt, in Cairo, to secure an interview with General Nasser in 1963 captures Egyptian society and the intractable problems of the Middle East coolly and almost casually, but with great force. Jay Parini's *Empire of Self: A Life of Gore Vidal* (2015) describes a writer who lived on his own terms.

Vonnegut, Kurt, *Cat's Cradle* (1963; Dell, 1998). Vonnegut's dark satire on religion and the arms race. The title refers to the children's string game in which a series of *X*s produces, in fact, "no damn cat, and no damn cradle." The plot involves ice-nine, a compound that causes adjacent water molecules to freeze solid, and Bokonism, a nihilistic religion that no one believes in but millions follow. The combination of the two produces an apocalypse. Vonnegut's long-standing outrage at militarism can be seen most clearly in *Slaughterhouse-Five* (1969).

The novel's protagonist, Billy Pilgrim, a survivor of the pointless firebombing of Dresden in 1945, constantly relives both the atrocity and his abduction by aliens, possibly as a result of a condition like post-traumatic stress disorder.

Wharton, Edith, *The Age of Innocence* (1920; Signet Classics, 2008). In New York in the 1870s, Newland Archer, a well-to-do young lawyer, falls in love with his fiancée's cousin, and she with him. But the strictures of Gilded Age society make it impossible for them to act on their feelings. The novel consolidated Wharton's reputation as an acute critic of class distinctions and lavish lifestyles. The 1993 film version, directed by Martin Scorsese and starring Daniel Day-Lewis and Michelle Pfeiffer, faithfully conveys the complexities of the story. Wharton had earlier dealt with the power of social convention to blight aspirations in *The House of Mirth* (1905), whose heroine, Lily Bart, gambles on cards and on love, and always loses. The best biography of the author is Hermione Lee, *Edith Wharton* (2007).

White, E. B., *Charlotte's Web*, illustrations by Garth Williams (1952; Harper Collins, 2012). White tells the story of a spider, Charlotte, who saves her friend, Wilbur, a piglet who was the runt of a litter and therefore destined for early slaughter. Charlotte lives in a barn and writes messages praising Wilbur in order to persuade the farmer to let him live. Other characters include Templeton, a rat that helps Charlotte despite being mainly out for himself, and Fern, a young farm girl who befriends Wilbur. A novel of friendship, love, and death, written in a dry, low-key manner. The 1973 animated version, with Debbie Reynolds's supplying the voice of Charlotte, and Paul Lynde doing the same for Templeton, is well worth seeing.

Wilder, Thornton, *The Bridge of San Luis Rey* (1927; Harper, 2003). In this novel, a bridge in Lima, Peru, collapses in 1714, killing five unrelated people. A monk who witnesses the catastrophe (and was about to cross the bridge himself) decides to prove that the five deaths were part of God's providential plan for the victims. The evidence he compiles forms the story's narrative. Wilder believed that one should carry on resolutely in the face of sudden reversals. In the play *Our Town* (1938), set in Grover's Corners, New Hampshire, he affirms his belief in the dignity, beauty, and mystery of everyday life—paradoxically, a perspective fully grasped only by those no longer living.

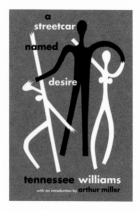

Williams, Tennessee, *A Streetcar Named Desire* (1947; New Directions, 2004). Williams uses the word "desire" to mean a longing for a spiritual or psychological state of bliss. In the play, desire saturates the cramped working-class apartment in New Orleans where Blanche DuBois, a faded southern belle, visits her sister and brother-in-law, Stella and Stanley Kowalski. Blanche lives in a world of pretension and fantasy; Stanley is earthy to the point of brutality. Their collision leads to Blanche's psychotic break and commitment to a mental hospital. The powerful 1951 film adaptation, directed by Elia Kazan, stars Vivien Leigh and Marlon Brando. Williams first achieved success with *The Glass Menagerie* (1944), an autobiographical story of a family undone by a mother's delusions, her daughter's fragility, and her son's flight.

Williams, William Carlos, *Selected Poems* (Penguin, ed. Charles Tomlinson, 2000). Late in life, Williams summed up his approach to writing by saying that he had "attempted to fuse poetry and painting." The poet and critic Randall Jarrell commented that he was "magically observant." He had a long career as a doctor while writing stories and novels as well as poetry; many of his poems were first scribbled on prescription pads. In 1923 he published his seminal book of poetry *Spring and All*, written in colloquial American English, at the same time that T. S. Eliot rose to fame with *The Waste Land*. He influenced younger poets and acted as a mentor, writing, for example, the introduction to Allen Ginsberg's first book, *Howl*. Williams tells the story of his life in *The Autobiography of William Carlos Williams* (1951).

Wister, Owen, *The Virginian: A Horseman of the Plains* (1902; Penguin, 1998). Wister dedicated *The Virginian* to Theodore Roosevelt, whom he had known while at Harvard. In one of the first memorable works about the American West, the lanky, soft-spoken hero bridges the differences between life in the raw West and the traditional East. In Wyoming in the 1880s, the aristocratic Virginian encounters the villain Trampas. When Trampas accuses him of cheating at cards, pulls his pistol, and says, "You son-of-a-. . .," the Virginian makes a famous reply: "When you call me that, *smile*!" The Virginian, a quietly courageous figure, honorable and chivalrous, became an archetypal westerner, a type that endured in countless stories told through radio, television, and film as well as novels.

Wolfe, Thomas, *Look Homeward, Angel* (1929; Scribner, 2006). Wolfe, a major practitioner of the autobiographical novel, gives a fictionalized account of his upbringing in North Carolina in a troubled family. Presented with the enormous, ramshackle manuscript of the novel, Maxwell Perkins, an editor at Scribner's, ruthlessly cut it and kept the focus on the protagonist. Wolfe published one other novel during his lifetime, *Of Time and the River* (1935), and two posthumously: *The Web and the Rock* (1939) and *You Can't Go Home Again* (1940). The critic Harold Bloom judged Wolfe's work to have "no literary merit whatsoever," yet William

Faulkner greatly admired his talent. Wolfe at his best has a magnetic, lyrical quality that reveals the despair as well as the hope of the common man in the 1930s.

Wolfe, Tom, *The Bonfire of the Vanities* (1987; Picador, 2008). A common theme of Wolfe's writing is people's concern for status. *Bonfire* is a piercing satire on the extravagances and pretensions of status-conscious New Yorkers in the 1980s—Sherman McCoy, the protagonist and self-described "master of the universe," laments that he is "going broke on a million dollars a year." In the racially charged turbulence of the city, McCoy is brought down by newspaper hacks, alcoholic politicians, an opportunistic preacher, and a Bronx judge. Wolfe's urban social novel, told in his distinctive, hilarious voice, looks back to those of Dickens and Zola. Wolfe first made his name as a groundbreaking journalist, with works such as *The Electric Kool-Aid Acid Test* (1968), about the LSD-fueled adventures of Ken Kesey and the Merry Pranksters.

Wouk, Herman, *The Caine Mutiny* (1951; Back Bay, 1992). This Pulitzer Prize–winning novel is based in part on Wouk's experience in the U.S. Navy in World War II. Lieutenant Commander Philip Queeg commands the *Caine*, a decrepit minesweeper with a slovenly crew. A petty tyrant full of irritating quirks and bizarre fixations, he loses the respect of the crew and, more critically, the loyalty of his officers, who regard him as a coward after giving orders to desert a battle area. Although any attempt to relieve him of duty would be seen as mutiny, one of the officers takes command to prevent the loss of the ship—with consequences leading to a dramatic court-martial. In the 1954 film adaptation, Humphrey Bogart gives a superb rendition of Queeg.

Literature
Europe

Central and Eastern Europe

Eliade, Mircea, *Bengal Nights* (1933; Chicago, trans. Catherine Spencer, 1995). Eliade was a Romanian scholar of religion as well as a novelist. The semi-autobiographical *Bengal Nights* tells the story of Alain, a young French engineer who falls in love with an Indian poet, the inscrutable Maitreyi, a former student of the poet and nationalist Rabindranath Tagore. (The character is based on the Bengali writer Maitreyi Devi.) Their erotic passion violates the moral codes of Indian society, whose conventional inhibitions the novel exposes and condemns. Eliade's *The Myth of the Eternal Return: Cosmos and History* (1949) explains the beliefs and practices of a wide range of archaic religions. He argues for their importance in contributing to a full understanding of what it means to be human.

Hašek, Jaroslav, *The Good Soldier Švejk and His Fortunes in the World War* (1921–23; Penguin, trans. Cecil Parrott, 2005). Švejk appears to be a cheerful idiot, but in fact he undermines military authority through feigned stupidity. Though often read as absurdist farce, the novel is also a dark comedy about the Austrian Empire during World War I. Soldiers fight in a war they do not understand, for a regime to which they have no loyalty. Švejk plays cards, gets drunk, and uses natural cunning in dealing with police, clergy, and military officers. The Nazis burned *Švejk* in 1933. Among the writers who admired it, Bertolt Brecht regarded it as one of his favorite books, and Joseph Heller said he could not have written *Catch-22* without the inspiration of Švejk.

Hrabal, Bohumil, *Closely Watched Trains* (1965; Northwestern, trans. Edith Pargeter; 1995). The Czech writer Hrabal was widely regarded, at least in Czechoslovakia, as one of the best writers of the twentieth century. During the Nazi occupation, he worked as a railroad laborer and dispatcher. In *Closely Watched Trains*, a young, naive railroad apprentice braces himself against cruelty and grief by imagining himself hypnotizing the Nazis into retreating. In the real world, he becomes a member of the resistance and attempts to blow up a German ammunition train. Critics compare it as an antiwar story (and film, 1968) with *All Quiet on the Western Front*.

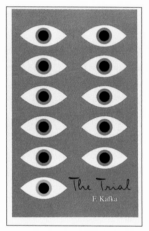

Kafka, Franz, *The Trial* (1925; Schocken, trans. Breon Mitchell, 1999). Josef K., a bank clerk, is arrested by two unidentified policemen from an unknown branch of government for an unspecified crime. Interrogated, summoned to court, saddled with an unhelpful lawyer, K seems caught up in a widening conspiracy against him involving everyone he knows and an overpowering, corrupt legal system. The novel has the claustrophobic, disorienting feel of a nightmare. In *The Metamorphosis* (1915), perhaps Kafka's most famous work, Gregor Samsa, a traveling salesman, finds himself transmogrified into a very large beetle-like insect. His thoughts and feelings remain those of a human, intensifying the horror of his condition. Reiner Stach's *Kafka: The Early Years* (2016) is a compelling account of the writer from birth to age twenty-seven.

Krúdy, Gyula, *The Adventures of Sinbad* (1911; NYRB, trans. George Szirtes, 2011). Sinbad, related in spirit to the *Arabian Nights* character, is a charismatic rogue, traveling from Budapest to the provinces and back again in search of love in the waning days of the Hapsburg Empire. Nor, in these stories, is he constrained by time, moving through past centuries as easily as the present. Krúdy was a popular Hungarian writer in the years before World War II, his tales of Budapest likened to Joseph Roth's contemporaneous ones of Vienna. The character Sinbad, who appeared in numerous short stories and several of Krúdy's fifty novels, functioned as the author's alter ego, engaging in exploits and romances similar to his own.

Lem, Stanislaw, *Solaris* (1961). The planet Solaris is almost completely covered by an ocean—which is sentient. A research team in an orbiting space station studies the ocean, with little success, and it studies the humans in turn. When the team resorts to harsh methods of probing the watery being, it strikes back in ways that are psychologically devastating to the humans. Lem, a prolific Polish novelist, exposes the hubris behind the notion of human communication with nonhumans, particularly if they are extraterrestrial. The three (to date) film adaptations of the book have generally ignored this idea. Even darker is the world presented in Lem's *Memoirs Found in a Bathtub* (1961), a dystopia of bureaucracy and paranoia run amok to the point that every perception is treated as a message.

Milosz, Czeslaw, *Selected and Last Poems, 1931–2004* (Ecco, trans. Anthony Milosz, intro. Seamus Heaney, 2011). Milosz, a Polish poet, won the Nobel Prize in Literature in 1980. Born in Lithuania in 1911, he served in the Polish resistance movement during World War II, and in 1951 fled from communist Poland to France, later teaching at the University of California, Berkeley. His poems address the Bolshevik revolution, the Nazi invasion and occupation of Poland, and Soviet post-war control of the country's government. In his own words, his poetry describes "the wreckage of a civilization" in Poland. Milosz's *The Captive Mind* (1953) is an analysis of, among other things, the lure of Stalinism for intellectuals; its devastating indictment led to comparisons with *1984* and *Darkness at Noon*.

Szabó, Magda, *The Door* (*Az ajtó*, 1987; NYRB, trans. Len Rix, 2015). One of Hungary's best-known and best-selling novelists, Szabó writes compellingly about relationships between women. In *The Door*, a married writer named Magda and her housekeeper, Emerence, form a bond that over decades develops into friendship and mutual dependence. Emerence has seemingly inexhaustible energy and an indomitable will. She refuses to let anyone, even relatives and friends, enter her house. Near the end of the story, Emerence becomes so ill that Magda forcibly takes her to the hospital. Then Magda does something that destroys the closeness between the two women. Other novels by Szabó available in English translation include *Katalin Street* (1969), about life in Budapest in the years before, during, and after World War II.

Szymborska, Wisława, *View with a Grain of Sand: Selected Poems* (1993; HBJ, trans. Stanisław Barańczak and Claire Cavanaugh, 1995). Winner of the Nobel Prize in Literature in 1996, Szymborska is known for poems that combine cool irony with a deep sense of humanity. Her themes include war or terrorism ("After every war / someone has to clean up. / Things won't / straighten themselves up, after all"), the animal world ("Though hearts of killer whales may weigh a ton, / in every other way they're light"), and even statistics ("Out of every hundred people, / those who always know better: / fifty-two"). This collection provides a thorough overview of her work, drawing on seven books published from 1957 to 1993.

Vazov, Ivan, *Under the Yoke* (1888; JiaHu, 2015). In the late nineteenth century, Ottoman rule in Bulgaria stimulated Ivan Vazov to write of a peaceful town in which the villagers prepare for rebellion. The protagonist, Boicho Ognyanov, recently escaped from prison, returns to his hometown, old friends, and the woman he loves. Collectively they discuss the oppression of the Turks. They make plans for what became known as the April Uprising of 1876, which the Ottomans brutally suppressed. *Under the Yoke*, the most famous piece of classic Bulgarian literature, has been translated into more than thirty languages. For the historical context there is a useful account by Davide Rodogno, *Against Massacre: Humanitarian Interventions in the Ottoman Empire, 1815–1914* (2014).

  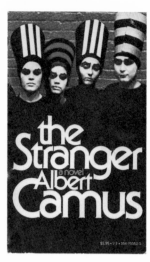

France

Balzac, Honoré de, *The Human Comedy: Selected Stories* (1829-47; NYRB, 2014). Like Dante, Balzac aspired to universal scope. His massive series *La Comédie humaine* comprises close to 100 works—novels, stories, and essays—describing all aspects of French life, mainly in the years 1815–47. This selection of nine stories gives the flavor of the feast. Balzac acknowledged the influence of Sir Walter Scott, Rabelais, and Cervantes on his work; among the many later writers paying tribute to his own example and legacy, including Dostoyevsky and Proust, foremost was Henry James in *French Poets and Novelists* (1878). An excellent concise account of the writer's frenetic life is V. S. Pritchett, *Balzac* (1973).

Baudelaire, Charles-Pierre, *Selected Poems* (1850s; Penguin, trans. and ed. Carol Clark, 1996). Baudelaire's reputation as an innovative poet rests mainly with *Les Fleurs de Mal* ("the flowers of evil"), published in 1857. Its unsettling and explicit imagery of debauchery and corruption was regarded as so scandalous that it was condemned as "an insult to public decency." Baudelaire was fined but not imprisoned. His poems portray the seedy and violent side of Parisian life, including beggars, thieves, whores, and gamblers. Baudelaire was also a critic of art and literature, and a translator of Edgar Alan Poe and Thomas De Quincey. He died at age forty-six. Marcel Proust regarded him as among the two or three great poets of the nineteenth century.

Camus, Albert, *The Stranger* (1942; Vintage, trans. Matthew Ward, 1989). Meursault, the protagonist, shoots an Arab in Algiers who was involved in a dispute with (and an attack on) a friend. Excoriated during his trial for his apparent lack of remorse—he failed to cry at his mother's funeral a few days before, he shows no guilt over the killing—he rebels unwaveringly against conventional morality. It is while awaiting execution that he finds meaning in his life. A good introduction to Camus's philosophical writings is *The Myth of Sisyphus, and Other Essays* (1955), which deals with the problem of finding meaning in a world without God or eternal truths. While such existential bleakness might imply that suicide is the answer, Camus insists that it instead requires revolt.

Corneille, Pierre, *Le Cid* (1636; in *Le Cid, Cinna, The Theatrical Illusion*, trans. John Cairncross, Penguin, 1975). Along with Molière and Jean Racine, Corneille was one of the three supreme French dramatists of the seventeenth century. *Le Cid* is based, ultimately, on an epic poem about an eleventh-century Spanish warrior. Don Rodrigue loves the daughter of his sworn enemy. He kills the enemy in a duel, and the daughter thereafter seeks his death. Even Rodrigue's glory on the battlefield against the Moors fails to dissuade her. Yet as in other plays by Corneille, challenges to integrity and bravery do not end in destruction and death but in persistent moral commitment. Voltaire described Corneille as doing for the French language what Homer did for Greek.

Diderot, Denis, *The Nun* (1796; Oxford, 2008). Diderot was a prominent Enlightenment figure, best known as the chief editor of the *Encyclopédie*, a revolutionary publishing enterprise extending to all branches of knowledge. In this novel, a young girl, Suzanne, is forced against her will into a convent, where she encounters intrigue, persecution, and pettiness. The novel denounces religion as a social system, claiming, for example, that convents subject their inhabitants to cruelty and lesbian exploitation, leading to madness. The spirited Suzanne denounces the traditional role of women in society, the hypocrisy of religious orders, and the fanaticism of the Catholic Church. *The Nun* remains one of the most incisively original works of eighteenth-century France. P. N. Furbank's *Diderot: A Critical Biography* (1992) provides an excellent account of the writer's life.

d'Ormesson, Jean, *The Glory of the Empire* (1971; trans. Barbara Bray, intro. Daniel Mendelsohn; NYRB, 2016). D'Ormesson was a prolific French novelist, the director of the conservative newspaper *Le Figaro* (1974–75), and dean of the Académie française. In 1971, the academy awarded him the Grand Prix for *The Glory of the Empire*. This fictional history traces the course of an imaginary empire resembling Persia or Byzantium—its rulers have names such as Basil, Arsaphes, and Alexis—and comes complete with footnotes to real writers and books. The Empire is place of great beauty and great cruelty (blindings are common), whipsawed by the whims of its leaders but bolstered by the toil of peasants and artisans. The story acutely satirizes both fiction and history.

Dumas, Alexandre, *The Count of Monte Cristo* (1844; Penguin, trans. Robert Buss, 2003). Upon publication, *The Count of Monte Cristo* gained a reputation as the most popular novel in Europe. It tells the story of a criminal conspiracy in the aftermath of the Napoleonic wars. Edmond Dantes, a young merchant sailor wrongly convicted and imprisoned on an island in the Mediterranean, escapes, acquires a fortune, and returns to Parisian society as the Count of Monte Cristo. He ruins the upper-class schemers who betrayed him, but finds that revenge does not lead to happiness or contentment. The novel is perhaps the epitome of melodramatic romance, with themes of greed, injustice, and vengeance. Along with *The Three Musketeers*, it is one of Dumas's most significant novels.

Feydeau, Georges, *A Flea in Her Ear* (1907; Oberon, trans. John Mortimer, 2011). Feydeau was a master of French farce, a genre built on the upending of social conventions. The fiendishly precise, complicated plot, impossible to summarize briefly, involves suspected affairs, attempted affairs, unintended affairs, and successful affairs, all occurring at top speed at the same hotel. The humor has a hard edge, but in the end everything is set right, including a certain confusion between a husband and his doppelgänger, a drunken hotel porter. The film *What's Up, Doc?* (1972) is an uproarious American screwball comedy with many elements of a French farce: a hotel setting, mistaken identities, multiple overlapping story lines, and a manic pace.

Flaubert, Gustave, *Madame Bovary* (1857; Signet, trans. Mildred Marmur, 2012). Beautiful, bored, and unhappy, Emma Bovary tries to escape the emptiness of provincial life through adultery. The book, Flaubert's masterpiece, reflects on the problem of finding love and meaning in the modern world. It was attacked upon publication for obscenity by critics and public prosecutors, who compared Emma to "a woman who throws off all garments."
In Flaubert's novel *Sentimental Education* (1869; a better translation of the title would be *The Education of the Sentiments*), Frédéric Moreau lives a generally aimless life except for his constant attachment to an older woman. Flaubert was an acclaimed stylist, a perfectionist always seeking *le mot juste*. A good account of the novelist's life is Frederick Brown, *Flaubert: A Biography* (2007).

France, Anatole, *The Revolt of the Angels* (1914; Eng. trans. Mrs. Wilfrid Jackson; Dover, 2015). "With a passion for liberty and intellectual honesty" and a style that was "indefatigably pornographic"—George Orwell's phrases—Anatole France tells the story of an archbishop's guardian angel leading a revolutionary movement against God, who is surprised at some of the hilarious plots against his tyrannical rule. The insurgents realize in the end that success would raise the question, what to do next? Unsurprisingly, the Catholic Church placed the book on its *List of Forbidden Books*. France received the Nobel Prize in 1921 in recognition of his having "a nobility of style, a profound human sympathy, grace, and a true Gallic temperament."

Gide, André, *The Counterfeiters* (1926; Eng. trans., Dorothy Bussy, 1927; Vintage, 1973). In *The Counterfeiters*, a group of schoolboys are faced continually with discerning the genuine from the only apparently so. Paternity, friendship, and romance all reveal their false aspects as the young men are subjected to corrupt influences. And there is an actual ring of counterfeiters. Gide won the Nobel Prize in Literature in 1947—*The Counterfeiters* was specifically commended—but a year after his death, the Vatican put his works on the *List of Forbidden Books*. A good biography of the novelist is Alan Sheridan, *André Gide: A Life in the Present* (1999).

Hugo, Victor, *The Hunchback of Notre-Dame* (1831; Wordsworth, 1998). In the late Middle Ages, a deformed, nearly deaf, half-blind bell ringer at the cathedral of Paris, Quasimodo, falls in love with Esmeralda, a beautiful gypsy who showed him kindness. The plot is a convoluted romance of love, jealousy, and betrayal set within a top-to-bottom portrait of medieval Paris and culminating in a harrowing climax at Notre-Dame. The 1939 film adaptation stars Charles Laughton as a compassionate Quasimodo, and Maureen O'Hara as a bewitching Esmeralda. Hugo's other masterpiece, *Les Misérables* (1862), is a sprawling story of the convict Jean Valjean, imprisoned for stealing a loaf of bread and pursued by the satanic Javert. A detailed account of the author's tumultuous life can be found in Graham Robb, *Victor Hugo: A Biography* (1999).

La Fayette, Marie-Madeleine de, *La Princesse de Clèves* (1678; Oxford, trans. Terence Cave, 2009). *La Princesse de Clèves* was written by a woman of minor but wealthy nobility who published it anonymously. Set in the late 1550s, it tells a story of unrequited love and heartbreak. At the court of Henri II, a young heiress settles for the prince de Clèves, an undistinguished suitor, but almost immediately thereafter falls deeply in love with a duke. Although the would-be lovers do not act on their feelings, the prince pries a confession from the princess. Everything then falls apart. It is usually regarded as one of the first psychological novels—the princess's inner thoughts and feelings are examined minutely—as well as a classic work of French literature.

Malraux, André, *Man's Fate* (*La Condition humaine*, 1933; Eng. trans. 1934; Penguin, 2009). Written by the French critic and historian of art who became de Gaulle's minister of culture, the novel deals with the 1927 communist rebellion in Shanghai. The leader of the revolt and his comrades face certain death. The exception is a French merchant, Baron Clappique, who helps the insurrectionists with a shipment of weapons, but gets involved with gamblers, racketeers, opium addicts, prostitutes, and coolies. Malraux's *The Voices of Silence* (*Les Voix du silence*, 1953) is less a history of art than a passionate art lover's exploration of themes and ideas pursued across centuries and cultures; Edmund Wilson called the original edition "one of the really great books of our time."

Maupassant, Guy de, *Selected Works* (Norton, ed. Robert Lethbridge, trans. Sandra Smith, 2016). Maupassant is widely regarded as an early master of the short story, and he helped establish features of the form that readers came to expect: memorable characters, clear plots, unexpected endings. Gustave Flaubert inspired him and helped start his career as a writer. From 1870 to his death in 1893, he wrote some 300 short stories, including such famous works as "The Necklace" and "Boule de Suif." Certain themes recur in imaginative ways: the futility of war, the pervasiveness of hypocrisy, the weight of social expectations, and lives that end in disillusion. Maupassant was admired by writers as diverse as Nietzsche and Tolstoy for his psychological insight.

Molière (Jean-Baptiste Poquelin), *The Misanthrope, and Other Plays* (1666; Penguin, 2000). Molière had one of the greatest gifts for comedy in Western literature. In *The Misanthrope*, Aleste possesses such an obsession with honesty that it ruins his own relations and those of people around him, demonstrating that fanatical devotion to truth can be more destructive than lying. Jean-Jacques Rousseau attacked Molière for ridiculing Aleste's sincerity. In *Tartuffe* (1664), the title character uses a pretend piety—*tartuffe* comes from an Italian word for "hypocrite"—to insinuate himself into a bourgeois household, seduce the master's wife, banish his son, and take possession of his house. The play's portrayal of religious hypocrisy caused it to be banned for five years in conservatively Catholic France.

Montaigne, Michel de, *The Essays: A Selection* (1580–88; Penguin Classics, trans. M. A. Screech, 2004). Often described as the inventor of the essay, Montaigne explores what it means to be human and to live well. Among the best known of this series of informal, autobiographical reflections are "On fear," "On idleness," and "On solitude." "On the Cannibals," in the 1603 translation by John Florio, influenced Shakespeare's writing of *The Tempest*. Montaigne was admired and imitated by a diverse group of later writers and thinkers including Descartes, Rousseau, Emerson, and Nietzsche. Among the numerous biographies of the essayist, see Philippe Desan, *Montaigne: A Life* (2017).

Proust, Marcel, *Swann's Way* (1913; Penguin Classics, 2004), vol. 1 of *In Search of Lost Time* (7 vols., 1913–27). *Swann's Way* introduces the narrator of the story and many of the other prominent characters in this large, comprehensive account of the middle and upper reaches of French society given in *Search*. *Swann's Way* follows the narrator from childhood through his first unhappy romance—with the daughter of Swann, a family friend in many ways uncannily like the narrator. The other six volumes carry the narrator's story through World War I and his decision to write *In Search of Lost Time*. An excellent biography of the author, Jean-Yves Tadié's *Marcel Proust: A Life* (2000), strictly separates the life from the work by relying only on the biographical and historical record.

Rabelais, François, *Gargantua and Pantagruel* (1532–64; Penguin, trans. and intro. M. A. Screech, 2006). Through the lives and adventures of two giants, Gargantua and his son Pantagruel, Rabelais, a physician and Benedictine monk, satirizes religion, law, and scholarly pretension as well as the follies and superstitions of his time. The comedy takes place in Utopia, where bawdy jokes, vulgar insults, obscene and colorfully coarse language, and description of the bodily functions are

commonplace. Rabelais used scatology for comic condemnation so effectively, according to Screech, that it embodies ribald *gaulois* humor, which became a permanent element of the French national character. A detailed, perceptive study of the novel and its author is M. A. Screech, *Rabelais* (1979).

Racine, Jean, *Phèdre: A Play* (1677; Farrar, Straus & Giroux, trans. Ted Hughes, 2000). The story of Phaedra, Theseus, and Hippolytus has been adapted by Euripides, Seneca, and Eugene O'Neill, among many others. In Racine's telling, Phèdre, wife of Thésée, king of Athens, is in love with her stepson, Hippolyte, but he loves the princess Aricie. In a delirium, Phèdre tells Hippolyte her feelings for him; horrified, he rejects her. So that Phèdre can save face, Hippolyte is falsely accused of rape. He ends up being killed by sea monsters, upon Thésée's request to Neptune. Racine brings psychological insight to the conflict between uncontrollable emotion and rational thought. The translation by Ted Hughes, Britain's poet laureate at the time, received widespread praise.

Sartre, Jean-Paul, *Nausea* (1938; Penguin, trans. Robert Baldick, intro. James Wood, 2000). In Sartre's conception, "nausea" conveys a sense of disgust at all people, things, and situations that curtail personal freedom. The author regarded this novel, his first, as his best work. Its story of a bored, aimless historian passing the time in a French seaside town makes clear the principles of existentialism: the uniqueness and isolation of the individual in an indifferent, hostile world. The novel stresses freedom of choice and responsibility for one's own actions even though human existence is inexplicable. *Nausea* is a landmark in existentialist fiction and probably the easiest point of access to Sartre's fundamental ideas.

Song of Roland, The, trans. Dorothy L. Sayers (c. 1100; Penguin, 1957) *La Chanson de Roland* is oldest epic poem in French. The subject is an encounter between the armies of Charlemagne and the Saracens, Islamic enemies of Christianity who controlled much of Spain and the Mediterranean. Deceived by the Muslims' offer to surrender, Charlemagne begins returning to France, leaving his rear guard under the command of his nephew, Roland. The Saracens ambush the army at the pass of Roncevaux. Courageous to a fault, Roland waits to summon aid from Charlemagne until it is too late. Roland was an iconic figure in medieval Europe, appearing in numerous poems. *The Song of Roland* was recognized as France's national epic when an edition was published in 1837.

Stendhal, *The Red and the Black* (1830; Penguin Classics, trans. Margaret Shaw, 1953). This historical and psychological novel chronicles the attempts of Julien Sorel, a poor young man from the provinces, to rise socially through a combination of intelligence, hard work, and brilliant deceit. A volatile mixture of Napoleonic shrewdness and Rousseauian sentiment,

Sorel campaigns and seduces his way to the top. Through his adventures, the novel satirizes the aristocracy, army, and clergy. Stendhal's other major work, *The Charterhouse of Parma* (1839), relates the eventful life of Fabrice del Dongo. At seventeen he fights for Napoleon at Waterloo, later becomes a priest (despite having no interest in celibacy), kills a romantic rival, is imprisoned for murder, and escapes. He eventually finds true love, but in the end loses everything.

Verne, Jules, *Around the World in Eighty Days* (1873; trans. G. M. Towle and N. d'Anvers; Wordsworth, 1997). At the Reform Club, Phileas Fogg accepts a wager for £20,000, about £2 million in 2017, to complete a journey around the globe in eighty days. The opening of the Suez Canal in 1869 and the completion of transcontinental railroads in India and the United States at about the same time made the possibility of such a speedy journey just feasible. On October 2, 1872, he and his resourceful French valet, Passepartout, set out. *Around the World* became one of the most widely read novels of the late nineteenth century and played a significant part in shaping Western attitudes toward the non-European world.

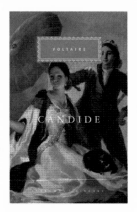   

Voltaire, *Candide, and Other Stories* (1759; Oxford World's Classics, trans. Roger Pearson, 2008). The most widely read of Voltaire's many works. Candide is a young man influenced by his moral tutor, Dr. Pangloss, who believes that all is for the best—including the Lisbon earthquake of 1755, which killed tens of thousands—in this best of all possible worlds. Candide's disillusionment reveals Voltaire's sharp wit and black humor as well as his practical advice, in summary, "we must cultivate our own garden." In the masterly study *Voltaire's Politics: The Poet as Realist* (1959), Peter Gay analyzes Voltaire's religious beliefs—his Deism and hostility to Christianity—his complicated relations with figures such as Frederick the Great, and his politics, which were consistently monarchist.

Zola, Emile, *The Dreyfus Affair: "J'accuse" and Other Writings* (1898; Yale, trans. Eleanor Levieux, 1998). Zola, a successful French novelist, protested when Captain Alfred Dreyfus was court-martialed, convicted of treason for giving military secrets to the Germans, and banished to Devil's Island in French Guiana. Zola accused the French government of anti-Semitism and obstruction of justice. A victim of the same forces, he was convicted of libel, and fled to England to avoid imprisonment. His writings became symbolic of the power of the intelligentsia to influence public affairs. In *For the Soul of France: Culture Wars in the Age of Dreyfus* (2010), Frederick Brown argues that *J'Accuse!* represents the peak of Zola's campaign against social injustice and reaction, and simultaneously revived his waning creativity.

Germany and Austria

Brecht, Bertolt, *The Threepenny Opera* (1928; Methuen, 2005). A socialist satire on the capitalist society of Weimar Germany in the 1920s, based on John Gay's *The Beggar's Opera* (1728). Brecht's drama introduces the criminal antihero Macheath, who is condemned to be hanged, against the background of Kurt Weill's jazz score and the unforgettable song "Mack the Knife," which became one of the most recorded songs of the twentieth century. The play was the biggest hit of 1920s Berlin, presenting the Weimar Republic as a society at the height of decadence and on the verge of chaos.

Fontane, Theodor, *Effi Briest* (1896; Penguin, trans. Hugh Rorrison and Helen Chambers, 1996). Thomas Mann once said that if he reduced his library to six novels, *Effi Briest* would be one of them. Fontane was the supreme champion of Prussian values. When the young and lonely protagonist, Effi, commits an act of adultery, her family disowns her. Her husband decides that he must kill the seducer or die himself. It is a testament to Fontane's skill as a novelist that he convinces the reader that neither Effi nor her husband has choice other than to conform to the Prussian ethical code. Fontane's novel *Before the Storm* (1878) deals with the growth of German nationalism in the early nineteenth century.

Goethe
Faust
Part One
A new translation by David Luke
OXFORD WORLD'S CLASSICS

Goethe, Johann Wolfgang von, *Faust*, part 1 (1808; Oxford World's Classics, trans. David Luke, 1987). Faust is the protagonist of the classic German legend of the scholar who makes a pact with the Devil. He exchanges his soul for unlimited knowledge and worldly pleasures, thus surrendering moral integrity in order to achieve power and success. There is a magnificent Deutsche Grammophon recording of the poem (in German). The standard biography in English is Nicholas Boyle, *Goethe: The Poet and the Age* (2 vols., 1992, 2000), a rigorous work that is accessible to the general reader and does not assume a knowledge of German literature or history. Rüdiger Safranski's *Goethe:*

Life as a Work of Art (2017), translated from the German, is a biography that makes Goethe's thought accessible without sacrificing subtlety.

Grass, Günter, *The Tin Drum* (1959; Mariner, trans. Breon Mitchell, 2010). A novel in the form of a memoir written from an insane asylum. Phantasmagorical throughout, the story largely resists summary. At the age of three, Oskar Matzerath hears his father declare that the boy is destined to be a grocer. Horrified, Oskar wills himself not to grow up—or at least not to grow any larger than a three-year-old. Accompanied always by a toy tin drum, the diminutive Oskar, born in Danzig, lives through the rise of Nazism, World War II, and devastated post-war Germany. The acclaimed film version of the novel (1979), directed by Volker Schlöndorff, won an Academy Award for Best Foreign Language Film.

Grimm, Jacob, and Wilhelm Grimm, *The Original Folk and Fairy Tales of the Brothers Grimm* (1812–15; Princeton, trans. and ed. Jack Zipes, 2014). This annotated and unexpurgated edition includes all the traditional favorites, such as "Little Red Riding Hood," "Hansel and Gretel," and "Sleeping Beauty." Despite a consistent religious and spiritual motif, the tales are filled with so much violence—cannibalism is common—and brutality that American educators debated the extent to which children should be shielded from them. The Grimms were influenced by the ideas of Johann Gottfried Herder, who believed that folklore provided a pillar of German cultural and national identity. The Third Reich used the tales to foster nationalism, but American film adaptations of the time, such as *Snow White and the Seven Dwarfs* (1937), instead popularized the triumph of good over evil.

Hesse, Hermann, *Siddhartha* (1922; Penguin, 2002). The German-born Swiss writer Hermann Hesse acquired an early knowledge of Indian poetry and culture from his missionary parents and later immersed himself in Indian philosophy in a quest for transcendental enlightenment. In this novel, Siddhartha leaves home in search of nirvana, becomes an ascetic, and renounces all possessions. But does he find enlightenment? In the 1960s, the novel became a surprising countercultural best seller, and Hesse, according to a critic at the time, "became a cult figure for those seeking spiritual self-discovery." In Hesse's novel *Steppenwolf* (1929), his most autobiographical work, the protagonist struggles against bourgeois conformity and his own despair.

Kleist, Heinrich von, *The Marquise of O, and Other Stories* (1808; Penguin, 1978). In a dramatic story that combines psychological insight and humorous asides, a German aristocrat, the marquise, is raped while unconscious. Finding herself pregnant, she places a newspaper advertisement asking the father to identify himself so that she can marry him. As in other works by Kleist, the initial circumstances produce complex consequences in which luck, chance, and coincidence play a part. Yet there was also the serious theme of German nationalism in Kleist's work. In his time, he believed that the individual should place himself in the service of the *Volk*, or nation, against Napoleon—a principle that was anachronistically co-opted by Nazi propagandists.

Mann, Thomas, *Death in Venice* (1912; Vintage, trans. H. T. Lowe-Porter, 1989). Mann's short novel is of interest to writers as well as students, among other reasons because the protagonist suffers from writer's block. He travels to Venice to find artistic renewal and spiritual fulfillment, but instead becomes obsessed with a young Polish boy, who is "supremely beautiful, like a Greek sculpture." A work of great psychological intensity. Mann's first novel, *Buddenbrooks* (1901), minutely describes the decline of a wealthy German merchant family over the course of four generations; the Swedish Academy singled out the book when awarding Mann the Nobel Prize in Literature in 1929. Mann's other masterwork, *The Magic Mountain* (1924), tells of Hans Castorp's seven-year stay in a sanatorium in Davos, Switzerland.

Musil, Robert, *The Man Without Qualities*, vol. 1 (1930; Vintage, trans. Sophie Wilkins, 1996). In Vienna before and during World War I, a young mathematician named Ulrich feels so objectively detached from everything happening around him that he loses the qualities of selfhood. His sense of life's pointlessness grows exponentially when he is put in charge of a committee organizing a celebration for the emperor. Swirling with characters and close observations, the novel offers psychological and philosophical insight into the moral and intellectual decline of the Austro-Hungarian Empire. Thomas Mann, when asked about the outstanding novel of his time, did not hesitate to choose *The Man Without Qualities*. Musil's novel *Young Törless* (1906; Eng. trans. 1955), the story of an Austrian military academy where order is maintained through sadism and scapegoating, was later seen as anticipating the rise of European fascism.

Remarque, Erich Maria, *All Quiet on the Western Front* (1928; Ballantine, trans. A. W. Wheen, 1987). In a strong story simply told, one of the most powerful antiwar novels ever written follows the experiences of Paul Bäumer during World War I. The German title, *Im Westen nichts Neues*, more accurately conveys the stagnation, bitterness, and hopeless loss of life in the trenches. Soldiers of the same generation are pitted against one another in nameless battles, wearing different uniforms but alike in choking on poison gas and becoming emotionally drained and shaken while their officers enjoy fine cigars. The book was one of the first to be publicly burned by the Nazis.

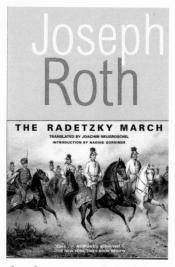

Roth, Joseph, *The Radetzky March* (1932; Overlook, trans. Joachim Neugroschel, intro. Nadine Gordimer, 2002). Field-Marshal Radetzky was an Austrian hero, immortalized by Johann Strauss, Sr., in 1848 with a march that became a sort of national anthem. Roth, an Austrian novelist of the interwar years, saw, with psychological insight, the subtle differences in anti-Semitism in Austria and Nazi Germany. *The Radetzky March* develops the theme of the decline and death of the Austro-Hungarian Empire—and the moral collapse of Austrian society—by following the fortunes of the Trotta family before and during World War I. Its members find the failure and collapse of the Austro-Hungarian Empire in 1918 incomprehensible. The story of the Trottas' decline continues in Roth's *The Emperor's Tomb* (1938), which ends with the Nazi takeover of Austria.

Schiller, Friedrich, *The Robbers* and *Wallenstein* (1781, 1800; Penguin, 1980). Schiller was a poet, philosopher, and playwright approaching the stature of Goethe, with whom he maintained a tempestuous relationship. He claimed to need the decaying scent of rotten apples to be able to write. *The Robbers*, an early work, reflects themes of liberty, fraternity, and betrayal. *Wallenstein*, a trilogy set during the Thirty Years' War, is perhaps his masterpiece; Goethe directed the premiere. The work can seen as Schiller's way of projecting himself as a nationalist or proto-revolutionary; his embrace of revolutionary ideals led to an honorary membership in the French Republic. Beethoven used a choral arrangement of Schiller's "Ode to Joy" as the final movement of his Ninth Symphony.

Schnitzler, Arthur, *The Road into the Open* (1908; Northwestern, trans. Horace Samuel, intro. William M. Johnston, 1991). Schnitzler studied psychology and psychiatry in Vienna, but he devoted most of his time to writing about the society around him. *The Road into the Open* portrays a talented but unmotivated young composer who spends most of his time in cafés, talking with others like himself. He has a troubled love affair with a socially inferior girl, but the interest of the novel lies in the brilliant description of the Vienna of Freud and Mahler, and the steady encroachment of anti-Semitism.. Hitler described Schnitzler's novels as "Jewish filth." *The Road into the Open*, along with his other books, was tossed into the flames by Austrian Nazis in 1933.

Werfel, Franz, *The Forty Days of Musa Dagh* (1933; Eng. trans. by Geoffrey Dunlop and James Reidel, 1934; Verba Mundi, 2012). Werfel, an Austrian-Bohemian writer, in 1929 visited Damascus, where he met Armenian refugees from Turkey. They inspired him to write about the atrocities they suffered during World War I. On Musa Dagh, a mountain in southern Turkey on the Mediterranean coast, Armenian villagers held out against an evacuation order, repelled Turkish army units, and desperately hoped for rescue by Allied forces fighting at the Dardanelles. Werfel's novel drew international attention to the genocide. Banned in Nazi Germany, it was later viewed as foreshadowing the Holocaust. In 1941, Werfel published *The Song of Bernadette*, about a French teenager who in 1858 saw visions of the Virgin Mary in Lourdes, France.

Ireland

Beckett, Samuel, *Waiting for Godot* (1953; Faber, 2006). Two men sit on a rickety bench beside a desolate road waiting for Godot, whose identity remains as mysterious as the reason they hope to see him. Nothing happens. The conversation is commonplace. Perhaps Godot represents God? Perhaps someone who fights oppression and brutality, which would help explain the play's popularity both in South Africa in the era of apartheid and in the Jim Crow South. Beckett himself once exclaimed, "If I knew who Godot was, I would have said so in the play." The mystery endures, whether absurd from the outset or existentialist in ultimate meaning. James Knowlson's *Damned to Fame: The Life of Samuel Beckett* (1996) is a first-rate biography by a longtime friend of Beckett.

Donleavy, J. P., *The Ginger Man* (1955; Abacus, 1997). Banned upon publication in Ireland and the United States as obscene, *The Ginger Man* tells the story of an Irish American, Sebastian Dangerfield, who is a law student at Trinity College, Dublin, in the late 1940s. "Feckless, unwashed, charming, and penurious," Dangerfield indulges in drunken debauches and sexual misadventures. The novel resembles a funnier version of Henry Miller's *Tropic of Cancer*. The publishing history of *The Ginger Man* is itself worthy of a novel. Donleavy persuaded Maurice Girodias of the Olympia Press to publish it, but was infuriated when it appeared as part of a pornographic series. After twenty years of lawsuits, Donleavy bought out Girodias at a bankruptcy sale and found himself the owner of a publishing house.

Heaney, Seamus, *Death of a Naturalist* (1966; Faber & Faber, 1987). The first major work by the Irish poet who won the 1995 Nobel Prize in Literature. Heaney began writing poetry in college, spurred on after reading the work of Ted Hughes. The poems in this collection deal often with the natural world, rural life, and death—sometimes sensually ("the warm thick slobber / Of frogspawn that grew like clotted water / In the shade of the banks"), and sometimes brutally, as when describing the drowning of unwanted kittens and puppies on a farm. One of Heaney's most famous and most moving poems, "Mid-Term Break," tells of the death of his younger brother: "No gaudy scars, the bumper knocked him clear. / A four foot box, a foot for every year."

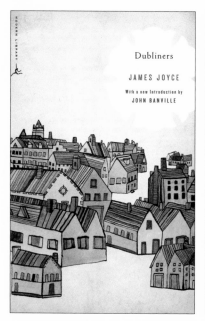

Joyce, James, *Dubliners* (1914; Penguin, 1993). The stories in *Dubliners* pursue Joyce's lifelong themes of the conflict between art and morality, and his ambivalent views of his native Ireland. It depicts life in and around Dublin in the early years of the twentieth century, when Irish nationalism was gaining full momentum. The stories famously display Joycean epiphanies: moments of revelation and enlightening understanding. Joyce's novel *Portrait of the Artist as a Young Man* (1916) tells of the religious and intellectual awakening of young Stephen Dedalus, an anti-hero and Joyce's alter ego. Joyce's masterpiece, *Ulysses* (1922), is a wandering, kaleidoscopic tour—patterned loosely on Homer's *Odyssey*—through Dublin on June 16, 1904, told through the consciousnesses of, primarily, Stephen Dedalus, Molly Bloom, and her husband, Leopold Bloom.

O'Brien, Edna, *The Country Girls* (1960; Plume, 2002). Denounced and banned upon publication—and publicly burned by the author's parish priest—*The Country Girls* deals with romance and sex in Irish society during the era of social repression following World War II. Kate and Baba, two young country girls who spent their childhood together, leave the safety of their convent school in search of life and love. O'Brien charts their inner thoughts and dilemmas in responding to men, breaking the taboo of silence in Ireland on sexual and social issues. The story of Kate and Baba is continued in *The Lonely Girl* (1962) and *Girls in Their Married Bliss* (1964). O'Brien deals with a war criminal in Ireland in *The Little Red Chairs* (2015).

O'Brien, Flann, *The Third Policeman* (1967; Dalkey Archive, 2002). "Flann O'Brien" was a pen name of the Irish writer Brian O'Nolan. He wrote *The Third Policeman* in 1939–40, but it was not published until after his death. The plot seems simple: the unnamed narrator and another man conspire to kill a third and steal his money. But things go awry, and the narrator winds up someplace that is not exactly Ireland, confounded at every turn by two policemen who speak in non sequiturs and are obsessed with bicycles. When the narrator finds the third policeman, all becomes clear. O'Brien's first novel, *At Swim-Two-Birds* (1939), is a novel about a man writing a novel about another man writing a novel, an intricate knot of stories recalling the playfulness of Sterne's *Tristram Shandy.*

Trevor, William, *The News from Ireland, and Other Stories* (1981; Penguin, 1987). An Irish writer long resident in England, Trevor became known as a twentieth-century master of the short story, often compared to Chekhov. The ordinary lives of his ordinary characters are undone by misinterpreted remarks, small betrayals, a realization of the hidden meaning of events. In the titular story, set in Ireland during the famine of the 1840s, the new English owners of an estate remain resolutely unaware of the suffering surrounding them, until their butler forces the "news" on them. Trevor was also a superb novelist. In *The Story of Lucy Gault* (2002), an English family flees Ireland in 1921 ahead of the threat of violence, unintentionally leaving behind their nine-year-old daughter, a tragic misunderstanding that echoes for decades.

Yeats, William Butler, *The Collected Poetry of W. B. Yeats*, ed. Richard J. Finneran (Scribner, 1996). Over a fifty-year career, Yeats wrote poems in a range of styles: mystical and supernatural, courtly and heroic, vernacular and colloquial. Some of his lines have become well known—"In the foul rag-and-bone shop of the heart," "Things fall apart; the centre cannot hold," "The best lack all conviction, while the worst / Are full of passionate intensity," "And what rough beast, its hour come round at last, / Slouches towards Bethlehem to be born?" Yeats was also a playwright, essayist, and autobiographer, but his continued popularity rests on his poetry, for which he was awarded the Nobel Prize in Literature in 1923, the first Irish writer so honored.

Italy

Ariosto, Ludovico, *Orlando Furioso*, part 1 (1532; Penguin, trans. Barbara Reynolds, 1975). The adventures of Roland, Charlemagne's favorite knight, became the subject of many poetic works from the Middle Ages onward. This epic by the Italian poet Ariosto was meant to continue the story begun in Matteo Boiardo's unfinished *Orlando Innamorato* (1495). But Ariosto throws in surprising elements—a sea monster, a flying horse—not found in earlier, often pious accounts of Roland. The two chief love stories feature religious mismatches: Roland and Angelica (a pagan princess), and Bradamante (a female Christian warrior) and Ruggiero (a Muslim). Orlando's unrequited love makes him frenzied (*furioso*), and he recovers his wits only after they are brought back in a bottle from the moon. Ariosto treats ideas of chivalry ironically, an attitude characteristic of an age of rising humanism.

Boccaccio, Giovanni, *Tales from the Decameron* (1353; Penguin, trans. Peter Hainsworth, 2016). Three young men and seven women escape from plague-ridden Florence to a nearby villa. For ten days, each tells a story based on a theme for that day: tragic love stories, the mutability of fortune, the power of human will, etc. Boccaccio collected the 100 tales from other sources, but adapted them to reflect a fourteenth-century setting and outlook. Despite satirizing the Church, celebrating deceit and trickery, and containing numerous bawdy passages, the witty tales affirm moral values and a humane outlook, marking a clear break with medieval dogmatism. *Decameron* stories were used as source material by many later authors, not least Chaucer and Shakespeare.

Calvino, Italo, *If on a winter's night a traveler* (1979; HBJ, trans. William Weaver, 1981). In this novel about the experience of reading novels, the Italian novelist Italo Calvino regularly addresses "you," the reader of the book, narrating your reading of *If on a winter's night a traveler*. Two other characters are reading the same book, but also pick up and start ten other novels, whose first pages are included in the text. These kinds of metafictional hijinks can seem pointless and solipsistic, but Calvino's light touch and playful humor keep the story bouncing along like a soap bubble on a breeze. A different sort of self-consciousness is on display in Calvino's novel *Mr. Palomar* (1983): the titular character strives to view the world with complete objectivity, but his "I" refuses to be silenced.

Dante, *Inferno* (1320; Penguin Classics, trans. Mark Musa, 1984). The first part of the 14th-century epic poem *Divine Comedy* tells of Dante's journey through the nine circles of Hell, a realm of grotesque suffering located within the earth. The trip begins at gates marked "Abandon all hope, ye who enter here" and descends through levels of increasing iniquity. At the core of Hell, Satan gnaws eternally on the heads of Judas Iscariot, betrayer of Christ, and Brutus and Cassius, assassins of Julius Caesar. The poet's journey is continued in the *Purgatorio* and the *Paradiso*. For a biography of the poet, see Marco Santagata, *Dante: The Story of His Life* (trans. Richard Dixon, 2016).

Eco, Umberto, *The Name of the Rose*, trans. William Weaver (1980; Eng. trans., William Weaver, 1983; Houghton Mifflin, 2014). In 1327, a group of churchmen arrive at an Italian monastery to argue a theological dispute. Several unaccountable deaths among the monks attract the attention of a Franciscan named William of Baskerville (a clear allusion to Sherlock Holmes) and his young assistant. The deaths are linked, and the key to the mystery lies in the monastery's magnificent, labyrinthine library and a long-lost book. Along with the detective story, the novel includes lengthy discussions of such topics as heresy, the Inquisition, and the conflict between religious teaching and science. Eco gave the Richard Ellmann Lectures at Harvard in 2008, which were published as *Confessions of a Young Novelist* (2011).

Lampedusa, Giuseppe Tomasi di, *The Leopard* (1958; Vintage Classics, trans. Archibald Colquhuon, 2007). In this posthumously published novel, the Prince of Salina, the descendant of an ancient Sicilian aristocratic family, is known as the "Leopard" (after the stone leopards adorning his palace). He finds himself caught in civil war and revolution in the 1860s during the Sicilian portion of Garibaldi's campaign to unify Italy. Skeptical and disillusioned, clear-eyed and melancholic, but without self-pity, he impassively watches the destruction of his class and his wealth. as well as the resilience of the peasantry. Burt Lancaster gave a memorable performance in the 1963 film adaptation, directed by Luchino Visconti.

Manzoni, Alessandro, *The Be-trothed* (1827; trans. Bruce Penman, Penguin, 1984). Often referred to as the most famous and widely read Italian novel. In northern Italy in the 1620s, two young lovers, Renzo and Lucia, are prevented from marrying when Don Rodrigo, a petty Spanish overlord, threatens a cowardly parish priest with violence if he performs the ceremony. They  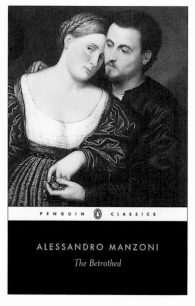 are cruelly separated, and then suffer through the bubonic plague, war, and bread riots, all three of which were visited on Milan at the time of story, as well as imprisonment. They face calamity with such tireless determination, faith, and courage that the novel inspired readers' patriotism and the quest for a unified Italy, parts of which at the time, were controlled by the Austrian Empire.

Sciascia, Leonardo, *The Day of the Owl* (1961; NYRB, 2003). Sciascia was a Sicilian novelist who wrote bravely and damningly about the Mafia at a time when many Italians doubted whether it even existed. In this crime novel, an inspector from Parma is sent to Sicily to investigate the murder, in broad daylight, of the owner of a small construction company. None of the dozens of witnesses claims to have seen anything. Every lead turned up by the inspector widens the pool of suspects and the number of related crimes. Sciascia's *To Each His Own* (1966), another murder mystery involving the Mafia, shows pervasive corruption to be contagious, infecting the attitudes and morals, even if not the actions, of those exposed to it.

Silone, Ignazio, *Bread and Wine* (1937; Signet, trans. Darina Silone, intro. Irving Howe, 2005). Silone's masterpiece was written in 1937, at the height of Mussolini's power. A communist revolutionary disguises himself as a village priest in order to avoid arrest. He acquires an understanding of the simple ways of the peasants, whose material sustenance consists of bread and wine but who yearn for spiritual community as well. Silone, a founder of the Italian Communist Party, became disillusioned with Stalinism—and implacably opposed to Mussolini—which becomes clear not only in *Bread and Wine* but also in the major work on the loss of faith in that ideology, Richard Crossman's *The God That Failed* (1949).

Low Countries

Couperus, Louis, *Eline Vere* (1889; Archipelago, trans. Ina Rilke, 2010). If there is a Dutch national novel, it is *Eline Vere*. Cooperus, a member of the Dutch social and political elite in the late nineteenth century, was critical of the politics and conventions symbolized by The Hague. Inspired by Tolstoy and Flaubert, Couperus created Eline Vere, a young dreamy heiress given to somber moods yet also philosophical and ethereal. She is known as an eccentric because of her long solitary walks and her conversations with a disreputable, vagabond cousin. When pressed to marry a friend of the family, she becomes desperate, with an overpowering desire to escape the confines of The Hague and depressingly conventional Dutch society.

Maeterlinck, Maurice, *The Life of the Bee* (1901; Dover, trans. Alfred Sutro, 2006). Maeterlinck was a Belgian playwright, poet, and essayist. In 1911 he won the Nobel Prize in Literature, mainly for his early plays, most of which deal with death and the meaning of life. In *The Life of the Bee,* the theme is the bee's orderly and intricate achievement, which in Maeterlinck's imaginative vision includes self-sacrifice. The essay deals with mystical fatalism so memorably that it contributed to Maeterlinck's reputation as a sage and an embodiment of melancholy-tinged European idealism before World War I. In retrospect, his inspired gloom seemed to catch a stoic mood of 1914.

Multatuli (Eduard Douwes Dekker), *Max Havelaar: Or the Coffee Auctions of the Dutch Trading Company* (1860; Penguin, trans. Roy Edwards, 1995). The pen name "Multatuli" is from the Latin, "I have suffered much." Dekker was famous for denouncing the abuses of Dutch colonial rule, especially on the islands of Java and Sumatra. In this novel, Max burns with a desire to end the oppression of the native peoples of the East Indies, who suffer from poverty and starvation not only because of crippling taxes but also because the Dutch sell opium to the natives, keeping them addicted and poor. The novel contributed to Dutch colonial reforms. After World War II, nationalist leaders, including Sukarno, cited the novel as an inspiration for colonial independence.

Simenon, Georges, *Maigret and Monsieur Charles* (1972; David and Charles, 1973). Although a Belgian, Simenon spent much of his life in Paris. While working as a journalist, he started writing novels, using as least twenty pseudonyms. He consorted with prostitutes, drunkards, and others on the fringe of society, and they often feature in his writing. His famous fictional detective, Jules Maigret, first appeared in 1931. Of the almost 500 novels Simenon wrote, 76 center on Maigret, of which *Maigret and Monsieur Charles* is the last. In it, the alcoholic wife of a wealthy lawyer asks Maigret to investigate the disappearance of her husband, who is eventually fished out of the Seine, murdered. Blackmail, another murder, and the revelation of a seedy past lead to the bittersweet resolution of the case.

Portugal

Lobo Antunes, António, *The Inquisitor's Manual* (1996; Grove, trans. Richard Zenith, 2004). The Portuguese novelist Lobo Antunes tells the story of the overthrow of the dictator António de Oliveira Salazar in 1974. During the Portuguese colonial war in Angola underway since 1961, a younger generation of army officers instigates what became known as the "Revolution of the Flowers"—no shots are fired and carnations appear in rifle barrels, ending over four decades of authoritarian rule. In a larger sense, the novel relates the regeneration of a morally and spiritually vitiated Portuguese society. Lobo Antunes, the author of over twenty novels, was described by Harold Bloom as "one of the living writers who will matter most."

Saramago, José, *The Gospel according to Jesus Christ* (1991; Mariner, 1994). In 2003, Harold Bloom proclaimed the Portuguese writer Saramago "the most gifted novelist alive in the world today." *Gospel* portrays Christ as all too human: he lives with Mary Magdalene and tries to avoid the crucifixion. Catholics were outraged, especially at his description of God as fallible, even cruel. When Saramago received the Nobel Prize in 1998, the Vatican denounced it as a political award. Saramago replied that the Church should stick to its prayers and leave others in peace. In Saramago's *The History of the Siege of Lisbon* (1989), another assault on historical truth, a lowly proofreader adds a negative to one sentence in an account of the twelfth century, and Portugal is not the same afterward.

Russia

Babel, Isaac, *Red Cavalry, and Other Stories* (1926; Penguin, trans. David McDuff, 2005). Babel was an acknowledged literary genius, popular at the time of the Russian Revolution and afterward. Red Cavalry, perhaps his masterpiece, portrays the wars on the frontiers of the Soviet Union in the early 1920s as so brutal and violent that his account seems at variance with his own gentle nature. He was executed on Stalin's order in 1940. His mistress, who had requested the return of his unpublished work, was subsequently visited by two KGB agents. When she accused them of coming to tell her that his writings had been destroyed, they replied, "How could you think such a thing? We came here to commiserate. We understand how precious Babel's manuscripts would be."

Brodsky, Joseph, *To Urania: Selected Poems* (1988; Farrar Straus & Giroux, 1992). The Russian poet and critic published this book of poetry the year after he received the Nobel Prize in Literature, which cited his "clarity of thought and poetic intensity." He was expelled from the Soviet Union in 1972 after serving prison sentences of hard labor and being confined in a psychiatric institution. He taught in several American universities, and in 1991 became U.S. poet laureate. W. H. Auden described his poetry as drawing on wide-ranging reflections on "the human condition, death, and the meaning of existence." Unsurprisingly, his major themes include exile, wandering, and loss. Lev Loseff's *Joseph Brodsky: A Literary Life* (2010) is a biography by a close friend of the poet.

Bulgakov, Mikhail, *The Master and Margarita* (1967; Penguin, trans. Richard Pevear and Larissa Volokhonsky, 2001). Bulgakov eked out a meager living by helping run an art theater. He was protected by Stalin, who, reportedly, saw one of his plays fifteen times. In the 1930s, Bulgakov wrote a novel he knew could never be published in his lifetime, a biting satire indicting the corruption, greed, and paranoia of Soviet society. In it, the devil visits atheistic Moscow and consorts with, among others, a talking cat and a beautiful naked witch. Bulgakov died in 1940. His novel was published in 1967, to wide acclaim and influence—Salman Rushdie, for example, stated that it was the inspiration for *The Satanic Verses*.

Chekhov, Anton, *The Cherry Orchard* (1904; in The Plays of Anton Chekhov, Harper Perennial, trans. Paul Schmidt, 1998). Chekhov's last great play, *The Cherry Orchard* deals straightforwardly with the decline of the Russian aristocracy and the rise of the formerly downtrodden. A landowner returns to her debt-encumbered estate, but makes no move to save it. The son of a former serf buys it, and the play ends with the sound of axes felling the estate's famous  orchard. Perhaps surprisingly, Chekhov intended the play to be a comedy, with elements of farce, but it is generally treated as a tragedy. V. S. Pritchett's *Chekhov: A Spirit Set Free* (1988) is a biography and critical appreciation of Chekhov's short stories by an English master of the form.

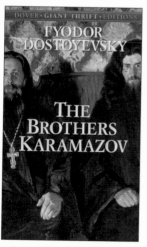

Dostoyevsky, Fyodor, *The Brothers Karamazov* (1880; Farrar, Straus & Giroux, trans. Richard Pevear and Larissa Volokhonsky, 2002). A gigantic novel built around the author's recurring themes: God, free will, belief, and its absence. The story of a "nice little family" involves patricide too. The three brothers could have been reduced to types—the sensualist, the rationalist, and the spiritualist—by a lesser writer, but in Dostoyevsky's they become full-blooded and indelible. The book is famous for the "Grand Inquisitor" section, in which a priest confronts the returned Jesus. The author's philosophically knotty short novel *Notes from the Underground* (1864) is presented as the ramblings of a retired civil servant. His concerns anticipate those in Dostoyevsky's masterpiece *Crime and Punishment* (1866), a penetrating exploration of nihilism, sin, and redemption.

Gogol, Nikolai, *Dead Souls* (1842; Penguin, trans. Robert A. Maguire, 2004). Gogol was a seminal figure in Russian literature. In his most famous novel, the antihero Chichikov sets out to buy "dead souls," deceased serfs who impose a tax burden on their former owners. His transactions reveal the corruption of landowners, peasants, and, especially, petty officials. In a comic account that captures the failures of mid-nineteenth-century Russia, Gogol presents dead souls, those of the departed serfs and the morally inert living, that cannot be seen but are ever present. In one sense, it can be read as a comedy of the absurd, yet in another as a Russian *Inferno*. *Dead Souls* immediately established Gogol as one of the great writers in the Russian language.

Goncharov, Ivan, *Oblomov* (1859; Penguin, trans. David Magarshack, 2005). Oblomov is a descendant of Russia's dying aristocracy, a man so torpid that he gives up his job in the civil service and is in danger of losing the young woman with whom he has fallen in love. He does little except insult his friends and neglect his ambition to be a writer. He lives in self-indulgent squalor, fueled by cigars and vodka, not leaving his bed for long stretches and attended by an almost equally lazy servant. Nevertheless, he is an engaging figure: he suffers from the foibles that plague all writers. Ivan Turgenev stated at one point that "as long as there is even one Russian alive, Oblomov will be remembered."

Gorky, Maxim, *The Collected Short Stories of Maxim Gorky* (1894–1924; Citadel, ed. Avram Yarmolin-sky and Moura Budberg, 1998). Gorky ranks with Tolstoy and Chekhov among Russia's greatest writers. A playwright, novelist, and poet, he achieved fame in pre-revolutionary Russia for short stories in which he described the lives of the oppressed, their hardships and humiliations but also their energy and dignity. He supported the Bolsheviks in 1917 but grew to distrust Lenin as a cold-blooded tyrant. After spending the 1920s mainly in Italy, he returned to the Soviet Union in 1932 at Stalin's personal invitation. Stalin later proclaimed Gorky's short story in the form of a fairy tale, "A Girl and Death," to be "stronger than Goethe's Faust." For an account of the writer's life, see Tovah Yedlin, *Maxim Gorky: A Political Biography* (1999).

Grossman, Vasily, *Life and Fate* (1960; first pub. 1980; NYRB, trans. Robert Chandler, 2006). Grossman, a Ukrainian Jew, was a correspondent for the Soviet army newspaper *Red Star* during World War II. He reported mainly from the eastern front, covering the siege of Stalingrad, the fall of Berlin, and Treblinka. Those experiences form the basis of *Life and Fate*, a gigantic novel comparable to the large-scale works of Tolstoy and Solzhenitsyn. The story follows the fortunes of Viktor Shtrum and his in-laws, the Shaposhnikovs, whose members are scattered from Berlin to Siberia, during the war. Confronted with unrelenting horrors, they nonetheless manage to hold on to hope. A fine selection of Grossman's journalism is collected in *A Writer at War* (2005), edited and translated by Anthony Beevor and Luba Vinogradova.

Pasternak, Boris, *Doctor Zhivago* (1957; Everyman, trans. Manya Harari and Max Hayward, intro. John Bayley, 1991). The physician-poet Yuri Zhivago, his wife and children, his lover, and a large group of supporting characters are swept up in the events of the Russian Revolution of 1917 and the subsequent civil war between the White army and the Bolshevik Reds. The intricate narrative, driven by repeated clashes between irreconcilables, moves from Moscow to Siberia to the Russian countryside, giving a panoramic view of society during the early years of communist rule. The Soviet Union banned publication and forced Pasternak to refuse the Nobel Prize in Literature in 1958.

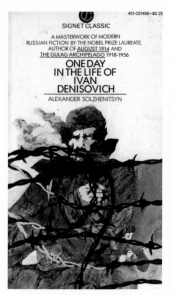

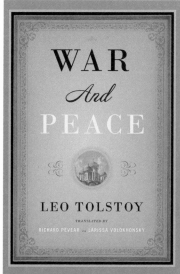

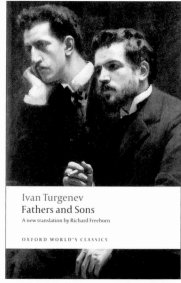

Pushkin, Alexander, *Eugene Onegin: A Novel in Verse* (1833; Penguin, rev. ed., trans. Charles Johnston, 2003). It has been said that Pushkin is to Russia as Shakespeare is to England and Goethe is to Germany, and that *Eugene Onegin* is the father of all Russian novels. The title character is a young dandy from St. Petersburg who retreats to his country estate after becoming bored with the social whirl. He spurns the affections of a local young woman, the sister of a friend's fiancée, and ends up killing the friend in a duel. Years later in St. Petersburg, the young woman, by then married to an aged prince and playing a leading role in society, turns the tables on Onegin when he professes his love for her.

Serge, Victor (Victor Lvovich Kibalchich), *Midnight in the Century* (*S'il est minuit dans le siècle*, 1933; NYRB, trans. Richard Greeman, 2014). As a consequence of his unflinching honesty and his conviction that Stalin had betrayed the revolution, Rodion, a semi-autobiographical figure based on the author, is arrested in 1934, interrogated, and held in solitary confinement. Released, he spends two years in exile in the remote district of Chenor (a stand-in for Orenburg, on the border of Kazakhstan). His banishment is shared by unrepentant Russian Orthodox believers as well as other men and women whose fidelity to the revolution of 1917 led to their imprisonment and torture. Rodion finds deliverance in a radical form of resistance. For a life of the novelist, see Susan Weissman, *Victor Serge: A Political Biography* (2013).

Solzhenitsyn, Aleksandr, *One Day in the Life of Ivan Denisovich* (1962; Noonday, trans. H. T. Willetts, 2005). The best introduction to the author's work, this short novel distills the inmate experience in Stalin's gulags from the events of a single day: the hunger, the cold, the casual brutality, the long hours of pointless drudgery, the bureaucratization of suffering. Solzhenitsyn wrote from personal experience, as he did in his later three-volume epic, *The Gulag Archipelago* (1973), about the Soviet system of forced labor camps, which were strung across vast distances like a chain of islands. Solzhenitsyn's experience as a captain in World War II is reflected in his *August 1914* (1971), a novel culminating in the Battle of Tannenberg, a catastrophic defeat of the Russian army by the Germans.

Tolstoy, Leo, *War and Peace* (1869; Vintage, trans. Richard Pevear and Larissa Volokhonsky, 2007). An epic novel about the lives of five aristocratic families during Napoleon's invasion of Russia in 1812. Among the book's famous set pieces are descriptions of the Battle of Austerlitz and the Battle of Borodino, the deadliest day of the Napoleonic Wars. Tolstoy's *Anna Karenina* (1877; Penguin, trans. Pevear and Volokhonsky, 2004) revolves around the doomed love of Anna, married to the much older Karenin, for Count Vronsky. Set against a Russian society adjusting to the sweeping reforms enacted by Tsar Alexander II in the 1860s, the novel details the lives of senior civil servants, minor nobles, military officers, landowners, and serfs—a realistic portrait of an entire society.

Turgenev, Ivan, *Fathers and Sons* 1862; trans. Richard Freeborn, Oxford, 2008). *Fathers and Sons* outstandingly portrays conflict between traditionalist Old Russia and the Russia headed toward revolution. Two friends, Arkady Kirsanov and Yevgeny Bazarov, set out on their lives after university. Barazov, a medical student and nihilist, describes himself as "a man who does not bow before any authority whatever." Arkady becomes something of his disciple. Both young men struggle unsuccessfully against the pull of family ties and convention. Turgenev had considerable influence on the next generation of novelists, including Joseph Conrad and Henry James. Turgenev's *A Sportsman's Notebook* (1852; Everyman's, 1992) is a set of stories and vignettes linked by hunting excursions and walks in the country; the introduction, by Max Egremont, is particularly perceptive.

Yevtushenko, Yevgeny, *The Collected Poems, 1952–1990* (1991; Holt, ed. Albert Todd and James Ragan, 1992). Yevtushenko was famous for his verse of public protest, which he often declaimed in the streets. He inspired a generation of young Russians in the struggle against Stalinism during the Cold War, expressing the hope but also the fear of those with tangled emotions about the "mad tyrant" and his successors. He once joked that his closest readers were the Moscow censors, who were expert at catching his nuances. A populist, he preferred Oklahoma to New York when visiting America. His poetry dealt above all with love and patriotism, as expressed in the line "I caress the Red Flag and cry."

Scandinavia and Finland

Andersen, Hans Christian, *Fairy Tales: A Selection* (1835–61; Oxford, 2009). Andersen's fairy tales appeal to adults as well as children because of their insight into human nature, although with a pervasive grimness. The Tin Soldier stoically accepts whatever happens to him, including incineration; the Ugly Duckling endures solitude and ridicule; the Little Match Girl freezes to death in an alley while dreaming of warmth and kindness; the Little Mermaid gives up her undersea life for one of ceaseless pain in order to be with a prince. Even the stories known for their humor, such as "The Emperor's New Clothes," carry a serious message. Without sermonizing, the tales present lessons of resilience and virtue in the face of adversity.

Dinesen, Isak, *Seven Gothic Tales* (1934; Vintage, 1991). The Danish writer Karen Blixen, who published under the name Isak Dinesen, came to prominence with *Seven Gothic Tales* when it was picked up by the Book of the Month Club as a main selection. The title is misleading: most of the individual tales contain additional stories: characters stranded by a flood tell stories to pass the time, a ghost tells stories to the living, three men tell a woman stories about a beautiful woman, not realizing that it is she. Dinesen and her husband ran a coffee plantation in Kenya, which she wrote about in her best-known work, *Out of Africa* (1937); the 1985 film adaptation, starring Robert Redford and Meryl Streep, was highly acclaimed.

Ibsen, Henrik, *A Doll's House* (1879; Oxford World's Classics, 2008, with *Ghosts, Hedda Gabler,* and *The Master Builder*). In this play, as in others, Ibsen deals with financial desperation and the moral conflicts inherent in a male-dominated society. Nora Helmer commits a desperate act to help save her husband's life, but ends up leaving him and their children after realizing that he will always think of her as stupid and helpless. *A Doll's House* was universally condemned at the time of its production, but Ibsen's attack on entrenched beliefs and attitudes influenced many

later playwrights, including Oscar Wilde, Arthur Miller, and Eugene O'Neill. George Bernard Shaw's essay *The Quintessence of Ibsenism* (1891) provides extended analyses of Ibsen's works, using them to criticize English society.

Laxness, Halldór, *The Atom Station* (1948; Methuen, 1961). Laxness believed that Iceland had been torn from its moorings by the American occupation during World War II. The *Atom Station* is a satire written as a protest against a post-war U.S. base that housed atomic bombs. The principal figure is Ugla, a girl from northern Iceland who is steeped in Icelandic sagas of the Middle Ages. She comes to Reykjavik, the capital, where she meets communists and anarchists and learns to play the organ. She believes the American presence threatens the Icelandic way of life. In 1955, Laxness became the only (to date) Icelander to receive the Nobel Prize in Literature—for his "vivid epic power which has renewed the great narrative art of Iceland."

Strindberg, August, *Plays: One—The Father, Miss Julie,* and *The Ghost Sonata* (1887–1907; Methuen, trans. Michael Meyer, 1976). Strindberg was a Swedish playwright, novelist, poet, and painter. *The Father* pursues his theme that war between the sexes is driven by a psychological battle for dominance; *Miss Julie,* his most famous play, is another Darwinian struggle for supremacy, spiced by sexual passion and differences in social position; *The Ghost Sonata* is perhaps best described as phantasmagoric. A common theme throughout is hostility to the family, the military, the church, and the monarchy. After his death, Eugene O'Neill voiced a sentiment shared by writers as diverse as Tennessee Williams and Maxim Gorky when he wrote that Strindberg was "the greatest genius of all modern dramatists."

Undset, Sigrid, *Kristin Lavransdatter* (1920, 1921, 1922; Eng. trans., 1923–27; Penguin, 2005). This trilogy by the Norwegian writer who won the Nobel Prize in Literature in 1928 traces the life of a headstrong woman in fourteenth-century Norway. The daughter of a prosperous nobleman-farmer, Kristin defies her family and flouts local customs in ways large and small. She marries an impulsive, reckless landowner, and they eventually have eight sons. Despite Kristin's many acts of rebellion, she remains a devout Catholic, fortified by her faith at critical points in her life. The narrative ends with the arrival of the Black Death in Norway in 1349, which killed over 60 percent of the population. A strength of the novels is their historical and ethnological accuracy, which was attested to early on.

Waltari, Mika, *The Egyptian* (1945; trans. and abridged by Naomi Walford, 1949; Chicago Review, 2002). The most successful of Waltari's historical novels, it is set in ancient Egypt during the era of Akhenaten and the young Tutankhamun. The book was praised at the time for its historical accuracy and detailed descriptions of ancient Egyptian everyday life. Written in Finland during World War II, it conveys a pessimistic message about human nature throughout the ages, perhaps reflecting Finland's fate during the war. The theme of war-weariness evoked a wide response in readers around the world in the late 1940s; the book was translated into forty languages and became a number one best seller in the United States.

Spain

Alas y Ureña, Leopoldo (also known as Clarín), *The Regent's Wife* (1885; trans. John Rutherford, Penguin, 1999). After its publication, *La Regenta* acquired a reputation as a landmark in Spain's cultural and moral regeneration in the nineteenth century. Ana Ozores is married to the retired judge of Vetusta (a stand-in for Oviedo), in northern Spain. Bored with her monotonous life, she seeks fulfillment through religion but becomes entangled with a priest, as well as with a handsome man-about-town. Both compete for her body and her soul. The novel skewers the stultifying, hypocritical world of the upper class. The atmosphere of the narrative is set from the beginning when the priest climbs the church tower to survey the local people with his telescope.

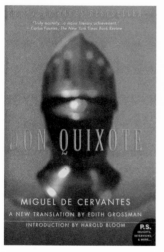 

Cervantes, Miguel de, *Don Quixote* (1605, 1615; Harper, trans. Edith Grossman, intro. Harold Bloom, 2005). Unhinged by an infatuation with knightly romances, Quixote sets off on a chivalric quest, at one point attacking a windmill, imagining it to be a giant. His companion, the simple farmer Sancho Panza, possesses an earthy common sense that parodies and balances Quixote's high-flown rhetoric. In the second half of the book, Quixote relishes the published account of his adventures—that is, the first part of *Don Quixote*—as if the novel itself were self-aware. *Quixote* inspired writers as varied as Flaubert, Melville, Dickens, and Faulkner. A recent study of the author and his work is William Egginton, *The Man Who Invented Fiction: How Cervantes Ushered in the Modern World* (2016).

Delibes, Miguel, *The Heretic* (1999; Overlook, trans. Alfred MacAdam, 2006). The novel begins with the birth of Cipriano Salcedo in Valladolid, Spain—on the day in 1517 that Luther nailed his Ninety-five Theses to a church door in Wittenberg. Salcedo becomes a wealthy Protestant merchant. He and a small group of coreligionists secretly conduct their services in the forbidding shadow of the Inquisition. The novel tries to catch the motivation of the inquisitors, men dedicated to bringing the recalcitrant back to orthodoxy but blinded by fanaticism. *The Heretic* evokes the spirit of sixteenth-century Spanish life, particularly in Valladolid where a holy brothel spends its profits on helping the poor and sick.

Galdós, Benito Pérez, *Fortunata and Jacinta* (1887; trans. Lester Clark, intro. Hugh Thomas, Everyman, 2018). In his time, Galdós was considered the greatest Spanish writer since Cervantes. *Fortunata and Jacinta* tells the turbulent story of two women in Madrid in the 1870s, both in love with Juanito, a feckless playboy. Fortunata is a girl from the slums, generous and feisty; she has a child by Juanito. Jacinta marries him, but remains childless. Galdós catches all levels of Madrilenian society: spirited coffeehouses, noisy cafes, boisterous markets, bourgeois drawing rooms, and stinking tenements. The creative authority of the author makes *Fortunata and Jacinta* one of the most memorable and distinguished Spanish novels of the nineteenth century. The excellent introduction by Hugh Thomas helps provide the historical context.

Goytisolo, Juan, *Count Julian* (1970; Dalkey Archive, trans. Helen Lane, 2007). The Spanish writer Juan Goytisolo spent most of his life in exile from Franco's Spain. He spent his last years in Morocco, which is also where the protagonist of this epic novel of revenge resides. The narrator celebrates the life of the quasi-mythical Don Julián, the vilest traitor in Spanish history, who aided the Moors' conquest of Iberia in the eighth century, in revenge for the rape of his daughter by the king. At one point, he applauds Julián's scheme to infect all of Spain with syphilis. Ferociously anti-Catholic as well as anti-Spanish, the novel, like all of Goytisolo's works, could not be published in Spain until after Franco's death.

Life of Lazarillo de Tormes, The (1554; NYRB, trans. W. S. Merwin, 2005). This short work by an anonymous Spanish author is the first picaresque novel, the progenitor of later works as varied as *Tom Jones* and *Huckleberry Finn*. Lazarillo, a poor boy from Salamanca, is apprenticed to a succession of roguish figures: a shrewd blind beggar, a priest, a squire, a friar, and several others. Lazarillo assimilates their tricks and stratagems, making his way in the world as a *pícaro*, or rascal. The story is strongly anticlerical—none of the religious characters come off well—and so the author chose to remain unidentified. Unsurprisingly, the book was banned by the Spanish court and placed on the Vatican's *List of Prohibited Books*.

Literature
Africa, Asia, the Middle East

Africa

Achebe, Chinua, *Things Fall Apart* (1958; Anchor, intro. Kwame Anthony Appiah, 1994). Set in the Nigerian homeland of the Igbos in the 1890s, the novel pits the protagonist, Okonkwo, against British missionaries. When the missionaries arrive, Okonkwo fails to persuade his fellow villagers that their society will disintegrate if they exchange their culture for that of the British. *Things Fall Apart* is Achebe's most famous novel. In 1975, he explained that the novel was meant to be the antithesis of Conrad's *Heart of Darkness*—in his view, a racist novel portraying Africans as savages and dehumanizing them as "niggers." As Achebe put it, "Conrad had a problem with niggers. His inordinate love of that word itself should be of interest to psychoanalysts."

Coetzee, J. M., *Waiting for the Barbarians* (1980; Penguin, 1988). The Magistrate, a colonial officer in a frontier settlement of the Empire, is unsure whether the Barbarians, or natives, are, as alleged, enemies planning an attack. When the Magistrate stands up to the security forces' torturing of Barbarian prisoners, he is denounced as a man of unsound mind and a collaborator. Despite his years of service to the Empire, he too is humiliated and tortured. The Barbarian invasion never comes; in fact, the Empire may be in a state of dissolution. Coetzee's themes are timeless and universal. Graham Greene rightly characterized the book as "remarkable and original." Coetzee's *Disgrace* (1999), a Booker Prize winner, deals with the violence and racial complexities of the new South Africa.

Gordimer, Nadine, *July's People* (1981; Penguin, 1982). Nadine Gordimer was a South African writer and a friend of Nelson Mandela. Racial and economic inequality are themes running through her novels. *July's People*, which the government banned, takes place during a revolution to end apartheid. Whites are driven out of their homes or hunted down and murdered. A liberal white couple in Johannesburg is saved by their former servant, July, who shelters them in his village. There they encounter further race hatred, violence, and, perhaps worst of all, humiliation. Susan Sontag praised Gordimer as a "matchless story-teller" who "articulated an admirably complex view of the human heart." *Burger's Daughter* (1979) is another of Gordimer's novels that was banned upon publication, this one set in the time of the Soweto uprising.

Ngũgĩ wa Thiong'o, *The River Between* (1965; Heinemann, 2008). Set in the mountains of Kenya around 1930, this novel deals with topics still timely: female circumcision, Christian missionaries in Africa, clashes between religions, and the struggles of modernity. Two Ki-kuyu communities are separated by a river, and much more. An idealistic young leader, educated in white Christian mission schools, returns to his village as a teacher, hoping to negotiate a balance between tradition and change. Complicating matters is his love for the daughter of the leader of the rival village. Ngũgĩ's *Decolonising the Mind: The Politics of Language in African Literature* (1986) is a bold, even subversive work in which the author calls on African writers to abandon English and "do for our languages what Spenser, Milton, and Shakespeare did for English."

Paton, Alan, *Cry, the Beloved Country* (1948; Vintage, 2002). In a remote part of the Natal province, a Zulu pastor, the Reverend Stephen Kumalo, travels to Johannesburg to help his sister and to be reunited with his son. His son is arrested for murder after a botched robbery; his sister, who became a prostitute, disappears. They represent the social instability facing black Africans after the breakdown of the tribal system. The book was published in the year when apartheid was enacted. The *New Republic* hailed it as "the greatest novel to emerge out of the tragedy of South Africa, and one of the best novels of our time." In Paton's novel *Too Late the Phalarope* (1953), an Afrikaner policeman faces retribution for breaking the law against miscegenation.

Schreiner, Olive, *The Story of an African Farm* (1883; Penguin, intro. Dan Jacobson, 1983). Schreiner was, in her own phrase, pro-Boer and a suffragette, an antiwar campaigner as well as a novelist. *African Farm*, set in the Karoo region of the Cape Province, is often recognized as one of the first feminist novels. It tells the story of a girl on an isolated farm struggling for her independence in the face of rigid social conventions. The novel abounds in vitality; its topics include agnosticism, pacifism, premarital sex, pregnancy out of wedlock, a bumptious Irish liar and sadist, and above all the elemental nature of life on the colonial frontier. For the background of Afrikaner nationalism, *New Babylon, New Nineveh: Everyday Life on the Witwatersrand, 1886–1914* (2001) by Charles van Onselen is useful.

Asia

Anand, Mulk Raj, *Untouchable* (1935; Penguin, 2014). In this novel, Anand focuses on a single day in the life of Bakha, an eighteen-year-old untouchable who cleans latrines in the mid-1930s in British India. Anand implicitly argues that Bakha is an example of why untouchability must end. It is an inhumane, unjust system of oppression. Bakha believes that salvation lies in modern plumbing: human waste would be flushed away, thus freeing him from his inherited task. B. R. Ambedkar's *Annihilation of Caste* (1936) is an historic book written at nearly the same time by a Dalit, or untouchable, who, after enduring indignities, humiliations, and hardships, became one of the principal architects of independent India's constitution.

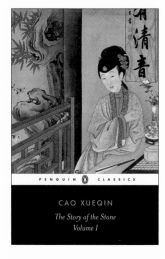

Cao Xueqin, *The Story of the Stone; or The Dream of the Red Chamber*, vol. 1, (mid-18th century; Penguin, trans. David Hawkes, 1973). Bao Yu is the personification of a stone that the goddess Nu-wa did not use when repairing a rift in the heavens. With no practical skills, he devotes his life to poetry and refinement in the company of a group of young women, and is too inhibited to profess his love for his cousin Dai Yu. The backdrop of the story is the dissolution of a wealthy family during the Qing dynasty. The huge novel follows forty or so main characters and over four hundred minor ones. The story is so complex that a field of study, Redology, is devoted to its explication.

Du Fu, *Selected Poems* (8th century AD; Columbia, trans. Burton Watson, 2002). There are some 1,500 extant works of Du Fu, known in China as a poet-saint and poet-sage. He is a central figure in Chinese poetic history, and his compassionate and straightforward poetry incorporates the philosophical thought of Confucius. His poems are often charged with emotion as well as historical awareness and an ethical sense of duty. He mastered all forms of Chinese poetry, and used diction that varied from the colloquial to the self-consciously literary. At the time of the Chinese Revolution in 1949, the concern for the poor expressed in his work made him a literary icon for the communists. William Hung, *Tu Fu: China's Greatest Poet* (1952) is a study of the poet's life and work.

Hua, Yu, *To Live* (1993; Anchor, trans. Michael Berry, 2003). A rich young man in southern China gambles away his family's wealth. After serving in the national army during the Chinese civil war, he returns home to find things in ruins: his mother is dead, and his daughter has become deaf and mute. Over the course of the novel, all his family members—wife, son, daughter, son-in-law, and grandson—die. Reduced to poverty, he travels the countryside, accompanied by an ox, collecting folk songs and legends. In the midst of all the grimness in his personal life, the man hears horrific stories of what happened in the country during the Great Leap Forward and the Cultural Revolution.

Kawabata, Yasunari, *The Master of Go* (1954; Vintage, trans. Edward Siedensticker, 1996). In 1938, a respected Japanese Go master played his last match, against a younger opponent. Kawabata covered the contest for a newspaper and then fictionalized it in this novel. Complex themes pulse beneath its spare, lyrical style, much as extensive calculations lie behind the seemingly simple moves of Go. Not least is a lament for the passing of old traditions: "From the way of Go, the beauty of Japan and the Orient had fled. Everything had become science and regulation." Kawabata began writing the story during World War II, a cataclysm that deeply affected him, and the novel can be interpreted as a subtle commentary on Japan's defeat. In 1968, Kawabata became the first Japanese Nobel literature laureate.

Mishima, Yukio, *The Temple of the Golden Pavilion* (1956; Eng. trans. 1959; Vintage intro. Nancy Wilson Ross, 1994). The story of a Buddhist priest burning down a magnificent historic temple, *Golden Pavilion* initially shocked Japanese readers. Part of the narrative involves a drunken American soldier and his pregnant Japanese girlfriend at the time of the outbreak of the Korean War in 1950. The protagonist, Mizoguchi, embodies complex themes, including a riddle about Japan's defeat in 1945 and the destruction of beauty despite knowledge. The introduction by Nancy Wilson Ross adds to the enjoyment of the novel by Western readers.

Mistry, Rohinton, *A Fine Balance* (1995; Vintage, 2001). Set in India during the "Emergency," the tumultuous period in 1975–77 when Indira Gandhi ruled the country by decree, this novel relentlessly depicts the plight of poor Indians—not just the endlessly degraded lives of the lower castes, but also what it takes to survive as a beggar in a large city (it helps to be on good terms with the Beggarmaster), what it feels like to have your house destroyed without warning for an urban beautification project, and what it is like to be forcibly castrated as part of a national "family planning" campaign. The characters that manage to survive do so by drawing together for support and solidarity.

Murasaki, Shikibu, *The Tale of the Genji* (c. 1008; trans. Dennis Washburn, Norton, 2017). Lady Murasaki, as she is known in English, was a Japanese novelist who wrote against the background of the feudal court and nobility in Heian-kyo, present-day Kyoto. The sprawling novel—around 400 individual characters are described in its 1,400 pages—develops the theme of "the tyranny of time and the inescapable sorrow of romantic love." The protagonist, Prince Genji, is a nobleman who takes a series of mistresses and wives. He discovers the disappointments and complexities of love, but never finds fulfillment. The dominant sentiment is the fragility of human relationships, a theme that has made it a Japanese classic with a worldwide readership.

Ōe, Kenzaburo, *A Personal Matter* (1964; Grove, 1994). In this novel, a Japanese teacher learns that his newborn son is brain damaged, but will probably survive. Overwhelmed by feelings of rage (at the senseless injustice of his son's condition), grief (for what the catastrophe means for his own life), and guilt (at hoping his son will die), he turns to whiskey and adultery in an attempt to blot out his thoughts. The protagonist's circumstances closely track those of the author, whose eldest son has a severe brain malady. Ōe was awarded the Nobel Prize in Literature in 1994.

Roy, Arundhati, *The God of Small Things* (1997; Random House, 2008). This winner of the Booker Prize is set in Kerala, India, in the late 1960s, when political movements have shaken the caste system and the local economy. The multigenerational story follows fraternal twins whose lives are hemmed in by social taboos in which only "small things" are said. Small things can nonetheless have unexpected significance, as the shocking heart of the story reveals. The author's clear language is invigorated by a sense of foreboding and inevitability befitting an intricate story of crime, punishment, and the destruction of a prosperous Indian family.

Roy's *The Ministry of Utmost Happiness* (2017) is a polemic disguised as a novel: the new India has been built on the backs of the poor.

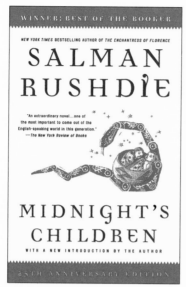 

Rushdie, Salman, *Midnight's Children* (1981; Random House, 2006). This novel tells the story of Saleem, born in Bombay at midnight on August 15, 1947, India's independence day. His life becomes tied up with the fate of his country, especially the events of Partition and the rule of the Gandhi family. The elements of magical realism that suffuse the novel recall the fantastical events of the *Arabian Nights.* Rushdie's *Satanic Verses* (1988) is a novel ostensibly about a physical struggle between an angel and a demon. The book proved so controversial that riots broke out in the Muslim world, two of the book's translators were murdered, and the Iranian government put a price on the author's head, causing him to spend around a decade under the protection of the British government.

Singh, Khushwant, *Train to Pakistan* (1956; Grove, 1994). During the Partition of India in August 1947, ten million people, Muslims, Hindus, and Sikhs—fled from India to Pakistan or in the opposite direction. In this novel, the remote Indian village of Mano Majra, near the frontier, remains calm; Sikhs and Muslims have lived together there in peace for hundreds of years. But when a train arrives with the butchered bodies of hundreds of refugee Hindus, the villagers give in to religious hate. A single man attempts to save a train full of Muslims from murder and rape, a solitary person representing integrity in the moral confusion of a slaughter that consumed as many as two million lives.

Sōseki, Natsume, *Kokoro* (1914; Penguin, trans. Meredith McKinney, 2010). Sōseki is commonly regarded as the greatest writer in Japanese history—his portrait appears on the front of the Japanese 1,000 yen note. In *Kokoro,* the word means "heart" or "the heart of things," an unnamed college student and an older man known only as Sensei (teacher) take turns telling the story. Sensei, lonely and sensitive, is torn between tradition and modernity; the novel covers the wrenching period when Japan moved from semi-feudalism to modernization. He struggles with guilt and the loss of belief in human goodness, and falls into despair, a process mirrored in the student's growing awareness.

Tagore, Rabindranath, *Selected Poems* (Penguin, trans. and ed. William Radice, 2005). Tagore is known above all as the poet who reshaped Bengali literature in the late nineteenth century. In 1913 he became the first non-European to win the Nobel Prize in Literature, largely for his collection *Gitanjali* (*Song Offerings*); and in 1915 he was awarded a knighthood, which he renounced in 1919 after the Jallianwala Bagh massacre. He traveled widely in Europe and America, where he was greeted as a guru and prophet. Tagore's output was enormous, including more than 2,200 songs. His poetry, which often deals with relations between the divine and the human, moved from traditional Bengali forms to free-form colloquial styles to modernist techniques.

Tanizaki, Junichiro, *The Key* (1956; Vintage, trans. Howard Hibbett, 1991). An aging professor encourages his decade-younger wife to commit adultery—first in fantasy, later in reality—in order to rejuvenate his sexual vitality. They even implicate their daughter in their erotic machinations. Both keep diaries of all that transpires, which not only inform the reader but also describe Japanese class subtleties and cultural identities. At one point, they suspect each other of reading the other's diary; from then on, there is the suggestion that each may be writing primarily for the other's benefit. One of Japan's most esteemed writers, Tanizaki was nominated for the Nobel Prize seven times but never won.

Toer, Pramoedya Ananta, *This Earth of Mankind* (1980; Penguin, trans. Max Lane, 1996). Toer was an Indonesian novelist whose writings span the era of Dutch rule in the nineteenth century, the occupation by Japan during World War II, the struggle for independence, and the postcolonial authoritarian regimes of Sukarno and Suharto. He was imprisoned by the Dutch (1947–49) and by Suharto (1969–79). *This Earth of Mankind* is part one of the Buru Quartet, which tells the story of Minke, a Javanese student in the late nineteenth century. *This Earth* covers his early life through his marriage. Minke refuses to condemn Dutch education and culture, yet is staunch in upholding Javanese traditions, believing that their merging will lead to a "new historical consciousness."

Wu, Cheng'en, *Journey to the West*, 4 vols. (16th cent.; Chicago, rev. ed., trans. Anthony Yu, 2012). A Buddhist priest, his horse (a former dragon prince), the Monkey King, Pig, and Friar Sand (a river ogre) travel to the West (Central Asia and India) to obtain Buddhist scriptures. Based on a real seventeen-year pilgrimage, the novel incorporates numerous traditional folk stories and mythological elements. The most memorable character is the Monkey King, thrown out of heaven for destroying a wedding feast. He is violent, immature, and self-centered; but he gains maturity and then enlightenment. Two visually dazzling, energetic, and amusing film adaptations are *Journey to the West: Part I, Conquering the Demons* (2013) and *Part II, The Demons Strike Back* (2017).

Middle East

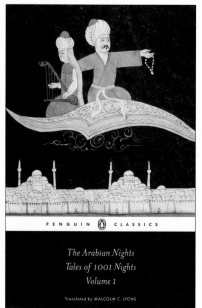

The Arabian Nights: Tales of 1,001 Nights, vol. 1 (Penguin Classics, trans. Malcolm C. Lyons, intro., by Robert Irwin, 2010). To delay her execution by a vengeful king, Shahrazad (Scheherazade) tells him stories such as "Ali Baba and the Forty Thieves," "Aladdin's Lamp," and "Sinbad the Sailor." Each tale ends in suspense, leading the king to delay her execution in order to hear the continuation. The inspired, imaginative tales, which originated in India and Persia, are sheer pleasure, although they have been denounced in Arabic culture as vulgar and badly written. They have had an immense acknowledged influence on, for example, Goethe, Tolstoy, and Proust. Robert Irwin, *The Arabian Nights: A Companion* (2004) is an invaluable guide to the individual stories and the collection as a whole.

FitzGerald, Edward, *Rubáiyát of Omar Khayyám* (1859; Oxford, 2010). Omar Khayyám was a medieval Persian poet. FitzGerald was a Victorian poet and writer whose fame rests on his translation of the *Rubáiyát* (quatrains). He once remarked that all his relatives were mad, and that he himself was insane but at least knew it. His translation, little noticed at first, eventually became known as a masterpiece. Many of its phrases are frequently quoted, such as "A Jug of Wine, a Loaf of Bread—and Thou" and "The Moving Finger writes; and having writ, moves on." The introduction discusses FitzGerald's life as well as the Victorian context of the translation. There has been prolonged debate about the accuracy of both the rendering and the philosophy of the poem.

Grossman, David, *A Horse Walks into a Bar* (2014; Vintage, trans. Jessica Cohen, 2017). At a local dive in a small Israeli town, an audience expecting to be entertained watches a comedian disintegrate as he relates a life torn between his family and his dearest friends. He tells of his beautiful mother, a Holocaust survivor, and his father, an uncomprehending bully. He relates treachery and guilt as he flays himself unsparingly, leaving his audience to respond with both empathy and revulsion, at times with laughter but also with tears. By telling of his decisions that have caused distress and suffering, he conveys how cruelty can spread from tightly knit families to society at large. The novel won the Man Booker International Prize for 2017.

Idris, Yusuf, *The Essential Yusuf Idris: Masterpieces of the Egyptian Short Story* (American University in Cairo Press, trans. and intro. Denys Johnson-Davies, 2009). Besides being a master of the short story, Idris was a playwright and novelist. He trained as a doctor, but was drawn to literature and politics. His stories depict ordinary, poor people who, though inarticulate, reflect his own political aims. Famous for his newspaper columns as well as for his carefully crafted stories, he held outspoken views about Israel. A prominent Egyptian nationalist, he initially supported Nasser, but in 1954 was imprisoned for opposing him. Idris's *Tales of Encounter* (2012) comprises three novellas set in Vienna, New York, and a Nile Delta village, the first two sharing a theme of East-West confrontation.

Iqbal, Muhammad, *Poems from Iqbal*, trans. Victor Kiernan (1955; OUP Pakistan, 2004). Iqbal was one of the foremost poets writing in Urdu, acclaimed in Pakistan as the nation's "Spiritual father." He viewed Muhammad Ali Jinnah as the only leader capable of uniting Muslims to create the state today known as Pakistan. As both a poet and a philosopher, he denounced political divisions and believed in the spiritual unity of Muslims throughout the world. The translator, Victor Kiernan was a prominent Marxist historian of the British Empire. For an examination of Iqbal's critique of nationalism, an ideology that he called "the greatest enemy of Islam," see Iqbal Singh Sevea, *The Political Philosophy of Muhammad Iqbal: Islam and Nationalism in Late Colonial India* (2012).

Johnson-Davies, Denys, ed., *The Anchor Book of Modern Arabic Fiction* (Penguin, 2006). Johnson-Davies, who died in 2017, was described by Edward Said as "the leading Arabic translator of our time." This collection of work from seventy-nine authors ranges across the Arabic-speaking world, from Morocco in the west to Iraq in the east, and from Syria in the north to Sudan in the south. The writers include Tawfik al-Hakim, a pioneer of the Arabic literary renaissance; the short story writer Mahmoud Teymour, on the comedy of death; the Lebanese writer Hanan al-Shaykh, on a daughter's view of her parents' divorce; and the Iraqi writer Mohamed Khudayir, with a story about watches, sailors, and horses.

Kemal, Yashar, *Memed, My Hawk* (1955; NYRB, trans. Edouard Roditi, 2005). Kemal, a Kurd, was one of Turkey's most famous writers, and this novel is his most famous work. Memed is a boy growing up in an Anatolian village whose inhabitants are practically enslaved by the local landowner. Memed escapes with his beloved, but is caught and tortured. He escapes once more into the mountains and becomes a bandit, intent on vengeance. Kemal worked as a farmer, public letter writer, and journalist before turning to creative writing full-time. A tireless advocate for Kurdish causes and the poor, he joined the Workers Party of Turkey, but left it after the 1968 Soviet invasion of Czechoslovakia. Memed's adventures are continued in *They Burn the Thistles* (1969) and two subsequent novels.

Khoury, Elias, *Broken Mirrors: Sinalcol* (Archipelago, trans. Humphrey Davies, 2016). Elias Khoury, a Lebanese writer who worked for the Palestine Liberation Organization, was seriously injured—temporarily blinded—during the Lebanese civil war of 1975–90. The complex political themes of his novels raise questions of character and ethics in a land ravaged by decades of war. One strand of the multilayered *Broken Mirrors* follows an architect who razes buildings in downtown Beirut, thereby destroying memories of both the elegant city built by the French and the civil war. Against this willed cultural amnesia, Khoury's protagonist asserts the claims of history and collective memory. Khoury's novel *Gate of the Sun* (2007) caused critics to describe him as an Arab combination of Dickens, Dostoyevsky, and Zola.

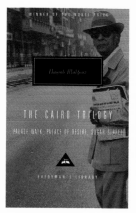

Mahfouz, Naguib, *The Cairo Trilogy* (1956, 1957; Anchor, 1990–92). Three generations of an Egyptian family from the revolution in 1919 to the Nasser-led coup against the monarchy in 1952. Through the intertwined lives of his characters, Mahfouz traces the evolution of Cairo, paying particular attention to the changing roles of women. The author's admiration for Proust can be seen in the novels' treatment of time, which moves imperceptibly from a child's viewpoint, but flashes by in the lives of adults. Mahfouz's *Arabian Days and Nights* (1979) is a subtle critique of corrupt, modern Cairo set in a medieval Islamic city where warring fundamentalist religious sects and political parties—above all, the Waft—coexist with genies escaped from bottles.

Pamuk, Orhan, *My Name Is Red* (1998; Vintage, trans. Erdag Göknar, 2002). In this novel by a Turkish writer, the sultan of the Ottoman Empire in 1591 brings together a group of gifted artists to create a book celebrating his reign. But the Islamic prohibition on religious imagery looms over their task. When one of them is murdered, the plot takes on the aspect of a mystery. Each chapter uses a different narrator, including Satan, dervishes, and the color red, all of which pose philosophical puzzles relevant to the murder. Spiritual questions are considered: do the souls of the dead remain on earth to listen to the living? The novel, which has been translated into sixty languages, was instrumental in Pamuk winning the Nobel Prize in Literature in 2006.

Rumi, Jalal al-Din, *Rumi: Swallowing the Sun* (Oneworld, trans. Franklin D. Lewis, 2013). Rumi (1207–1273) was a Persian poet, mystic, and Sufi whose family fled to Baghdad and then Anatolia ahead of a Mongol invasion. In the last twelve years of his life, Rumi dictated around 100,000 lines of poetry, mostly in Persian but also in Arabic, Turkish, and Greek. Many of the poems convey religious ecstasy, expressing a desire for union with like-minded mystics and with God. Some of the poems were meant to be sung or recited while dancing. In this collection by a leading Rumi scholar, poems are grouped by theme: praise and invocation, faith and observance, poetry and music, and so forth. After Rumi's death, his followers formed the mystical Order of Whirling Dervishes.

Saadawi, Ahmen, *Frankenstein in Baghdad* (2013; Penguin, trans. Jonathan Wright, 2018). Like the monster in Mary Shelley's *Frankenstein*, the Iraqi writer Ahmen Saadawi's creature feels that he is misunderstood. He does not slaughter at random but seeks revenge, killing the men whose bombs killed him and thousands more. Set in the aftermath of the U.S. invasion of Iraq, the novel shows Baghdad reduced to a charnel house. The bodies and body parts of victims cover its streets. The putrefying, rampaging monster perfectly embodies the surreal, pointless war. Ultimately evoking Kafka more than Shelley, the novel works because Saadawi writes with a rare style that simultaneously conveys magnanimity, cruelty, and black humor to create a "dystopian hellscape." It won the 2014 International Prize for Arabic Fiction.

Salih, Tayeb, *Season of Migration to the North* (1966; NYRB, trans. Denys Johnson-Davies, intro. Laila Lalami, 2009). After seven years in England, a young Sudanese returns to his village, but finds he belongs to neither country. An older man relates his own experience in London and his spiteful, tragic entanglements with English women. His sense of displacement brings further misery to himself and the villagers, including the (unnamed) narrator. This novel, published ten years after Sudan's independence and initially banned in that country, shows a society struggling to come to grips with the legacy of former British control overlaid on Islamic tradition. Laila Lalami, *The Moor's Account* (2014), pursues a similar theme of an "Arab Negro" caught between different cultures.

Shalev, Meir, *Blue Mountain,* (1988; Canongate, trans. Hillel Halkin, 2010). Shifting back and forth in time, this novel, written by one of Israel's most celebrated writers, portrays the pioneering life of Jewish families in the decades before and after the birth of the State of Israel. The settlers before World War I stand in contrast to the arrivals of Russian-Jewish immigrants three generations later. The story begins with the narrator telling how he, at age two, survived a bomb thrown by Arab terrorists that killed his sleeping parents. The finely drawn characters of Zionist folklore include an accomplished musician, a religious fanatic, and a mortician, all heroic and absurd at the same time. Shalev shows a more contemporary storytelling side in *My Russian Grandmother and Her American Vacuum Cleaner* (2009).

Tamer, Zakaria, *Tigers on the Tenth Day, and Other Stories* (1978; Quartet, trans. Denys Johnson-Davies, 1985). A Syrian born in Damascus in 1931, Tamer is one of the most widely read writers in the Arab world. His short stories, which often draw on folktales, are famous for conveying political and social complexities with a simplicity of style. Inhumanity in the Arab world is his overarching theme: oppression of the rich by the poor, of women by men, of the weak by the powerful. The oppressed likewise hold inhumane views of their oppressors. He deals also with the breaking of sexual taboos and the brutality of the police. According to one critic, "Tamer's world is Orwellian though unmistakably Arab." These same themes continue in his story collection *Breaking Knees* (2002).

Literature
Ancient World

Aeschylus, *Agamemnon* (458 BC; in *The Oresteia*, Penguin, trans. Robert Fagles, 1984). In the absence of law or justice, there is only vengeance. *Agamemnon*, the first play in the only extant trilogy of Greek tragedies, tells of the homecoming of the Greek commanding general at Troy. When he arrives at his palace, his wife, Clytemnestra, murders him, along with Cassandra, a Trojan princess brought back as a war trophy, in retaliation for Agamemnon sacrificing their daughter Iphigenia ten years earlier. The chorus of townspeople prays for the return of Orestes to punish his father's murderer, and thus to continue the cycle of vengeance. For the continued relevance of Aeschylus in Western culture, see Hugh Lloyd-Jones, *Blood for the Ghosts: Classical Influences in the Nineteenth and Twentieth Centuries* (1982).

Aristophanes, *The Complete Plays* (Penguin, trans. Paul Roche, 2005). In the plays of Aristophanes—the epitome of ancient Greek comedy—satire, invective, and obscenity are put to serious ends. *Acharnians* and *Lysistrata* lambast the folly of war between Athens and Sparta. Two of his most famous plays are *Clouds* and *Birds*. In the former, Socrates appears as a typical sophist, ready to supply a winning argument to either side in a debate. *Birds* is a direct assault on Greek religion, in which the birds build a walled city for themselves, "Cloud-cuckoo-land," and nearly starve the Olympian gods to death. The plays' use of ridicule and bawdy humor has lost none of its bite. The translator, Paul Roche, was one of the last of the Bloomsbury group.

Epic of Gilgamesh, The (18th century BC; Penguin, trans. Andrew George, 2003). The poem of Gilgamesh, the king of Uruk, takes place in ancient Mesopotamia, circa 2100 BC. It tells the story of Gilgamesh, who is two-thirds divine, and Enkidu, a wild man of superhuman strength created by the gods to stop Gilgamesh from oppressing his people. He challenges Gilgamesh to a test of strength, after which the two become friends. They set out on a series of adventures that end up angering the gods, Ishtar in particular. In the end, the gods sentence Enkidu to death. Gilgamesh then goes on a quest for immortality. The poem is notable for including an account of a world-destroying flood, much like the one recounted in Genesis.

Euripides, *Medea* (431 BC; Oxford, trans. and ed. James Morwood, 1998). The enchantress Medea leaves her home and family to marry Jason, enables him to steal the Golden Fleece,

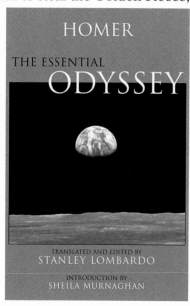

bears him two sons, and, at Jason's request, causes the murder of his uncle. The family flees to Corinth, where Jason decides to marry the local king's daughter, knowing that this will mean certain banishment and possible death for Medea and their sons. Scorned and humiliated, Medea unleashes a vengeance almost unmatched in its savagery. In the end, she escapes safely off to Athens in a flying chariot, leaving Jason bereft of wife, children, everything. A modernized film adaptation, *A Dream of Passion* (1978), stars Ellen Burstyn and Melina Mercouri, who performs parts of *Medea* in Greek.

Homer, *Odyssey* (c. 750 B.C.; Hackett, trans. Stanley Lombardo, 2000). The greatest poem about homecoming. After ten years of war, Odysseus and his soldiers set off for home, but curiosity leads them astray, wild winds scatter them, and many fall victim to magic and monsters. Odysseus returns alone, recovers his home by violence, and rejoins his wife, Penelope, and his son,

Telemachus. The other epic by Homer, the *Iliad* (c. 750 B.C.; California, trans. Peter Green, 2015) is set during the tenth year of the Trojan War. It tells of the "wrath of Achilles" and its consequences for Greeks and Trojans. It explores themes of fate, courage, love, and mortality in an all-encompassing portrait of Bronze Age culture in the eastern Mediterranean, a place ruled by kings, gods, and fate.

Horace, *The Odes of Horace* (23 BC, 13 BC; Farrar, Straus & Giroux, trans. David Ferry, 1998). The four books of Horace's odes established his reputation as one the greatest Latin lyric poets. The second ode of book 3 contains the famous line: "Dulce et decorum est pro patria mori" ("Lovely and honorable it is to die for one's country"). Describing this sentiment as the "old lie," Wilfred Owen in World War I used the phrase in an antiwar poem in response to a gas attack. It shows up also in a poem by Ezra Pound and on a tombstone in *Gone with the Wind*.

Ovid, *The Erotic Poems* (1st century BC–1st century AD; Penguin, trans. and ed. Peter Green, 1983). The classicist Peter Green selects Ovid's poems dealing with sexual desire, from noble declarations of eternal love to ingenious persuasion to commit adultery to confessions of guilt. The poems, which were immensely popular, on the whole provide a guide to seduction and promiscuity. In AD 8, the Emperor Augustus banished Ovid, for reasons that remain mysterious. Some of his love poetry may have fallen afoul of recent legislation regarding marriage. Historically, there was no doubt, for example, in the mind of Thomas Whitgift, the archbishop of Canterbury, that Ovid was an immoral influence—he ordered Christopher Marlowe's translation of the love poems to be burned publicly in 1599.

Pliny the Younger, *Fifty Letters of Pliny*, ed. A. N. Sherwin-White (AD 97–109; Oxford, 2nd ed., 1969). Pliny the Younger was a Roman statesman whose private letters illustrate public life at the peak of the Roman Empire. He wrote on social and literary topics—his friends included the writers Tacitus, Suetonius, and Martial—and corresponded with the Emperor Trajan. Two famous letters describe the eruption of Mount Vesuvius that destroyed Pompeii; others record his reaction to early Christians—for example, as "a desperate sort of cult carried to

extravagant lengths." His uncle, Pliny the Elder, was a keen observer of nature. His thirty-seven-volume *Natural History* (AD 77; Penguin, abr. ed., trans. John Healy, 1991) is a comprehensive source of ancient beliefs about the world.

Sophocles, *Antigone* (c. 441 BC; Hackett, trans. Paul Woodruff, 2001). Antigone's brother Polyneices was executed for waging civil war against their city, Thebes. Though forbidden to bury the corpse, Antigone does so anyway. That act leads to an all-out bloodbath of the kind common in Greek tragedy. The play raises a question of up-to-the-minute topicality: are there atrocities so unforgivable that their perpetrators lose the right to be treated as human, even in death? Controversies over the disposition of the bodies of slain terrorists suggest that we are still struggling with an answer. Simone

Weil (pictured on the cover) closely identified herself with Antigone. The play is often treated as part of a trilogy with Sophocles's *Oedipus Rex* and *Oedipus at Colonus*, which tell of the tortured life of Antigone's father.

Virgil, *The Aeneid* (29–19 BC; Vintage Classics, trans. Robert Fitzgerald, 1990). In the character of Aeneas, Virgil portrays the virtues of a heroic warrior who devotes his life to duty and sacrifice, yet is also driven by passion and emotion. He flees the ashes of Troy to lead his people to safety, eventually founding the city of Rome. The poem is a sweeping epic of arms and heroism. Considered the masterpiece of Roman literature, it is no less than a triumphant statement of Roman civilization. Yet there is an underlying, muted question: might Aeneas succumb to ambition and become a malign despot? Since the poem was a favorite of Emperor Augustus—Virgil read parts of it to the imperial family—the question was better left unanswered.

Xenophon, *Education of Cyrus* (4th century B.C.; Cornell, trans. Wayne Ambler, 2001). The first historical novel and a powerful influence on Machiavelli, this fictionalized account of the life of Cyrus the Great functions as a great adventure story, a manual on how to take over the world, and a profound meditation on the character of political ambition and the inevitable disappointments that the most ambitious people are bound to encounter, even—or especially—when they are successful.

Literature
Miscellaneous

Australia and New Zealand

Cook, Kenneth, *Wake in Fright* (1961; Text Publishing, 2012). This Australian classic takes its title from an ancient curse: "May you dream of the Devil and wake in fright." On the way to Sydney for a holiday, a schoolteacher spends the night in a hardscrabble outback town. In a drunken spree, he loses all his money, which propels him toward destruction in an alcoholic, sexual, and spiritual nightmare. This descent into barbarism, conveyed with a tone of menace and suspense, ends in a state of hypnotic, brutal, hallucinatory purgation. The 1971 film version, comparable to *A Clockwork Orange*, was described by the *New Yorker* as having achieved "cult status" by portraying the unforgettably perverse Australian "mateship" in the outback.

Mulgan, John, *Man Alone* (1939; Penguin 1990). A New Zealander, Mulgan wrote this existentialism-themed novel while working as an editor at Oxford University Press. The protagonist, Johnson, an Englishman who fought in World War I, goes to New Zealand during the Great Depression. There he works a series of jobs, including a long stint as a farmhand. After accidentally killing his employer, he flees to the wilds of the hill country, where, alone in an indifferent universe, he ponders such things as the white man's conquest of New Zealand and the killing of an individual Maori. Purified by his time in the wilderness, he decides to fight in the Spanish Civil War. *Man Alone* is a classic of New Zealand fiction, often called the "great Kiwi novel."

Shute, Nevil, *On the Beach* (1957; Vintage, 2010). In Australia, people await radioactive fallout being blown south after a nuclear war in the Northern Hemisphere that has devastated most of the rest of the world. The government provides citizens with free suicide pills and injections so that they can avoid prolonged suffering from radiation poisoning. The characters neither indulge in self-pity nor express intense emotions. *The Economist* in 2013 called *On the Beach* "still incredibly moving after nearly half a century." The title comes from T.S. Eliot's poem "The Hollow Men":

> *In this last of meeting places*
> *We grope together*
> *And avoid speech*
> *Gathered on this beach of the tumid river.*

The somber 1950 film adaptation stars Gregory Peck, Ava Gardner, and Fred Astaire.

White, Patrick, *Voss* (1957; Penguin, 2009). Based on a nineteenth-century German explorer who disappeared during an expedition to the Australian outback, John Voss tries to cross the continent with a small party of settlers and two Aborigines as guides. They encounter desert, drought, and floods; Voss faces betrayal and mutiny. The outback comes to represent an existential challenge to Voss's vision and spiritual quest, though the soul of the Aborigines is inextinguishable. White received the Nobel Prize in Literature in 1973, and *Voss* has become known as the Great Australian Novel. White's novel *The Vivisector* (1970) tells the story of an Australian painter's rise from destitution to success; "Great Vivisector" is his term for God.

Canada

Atwood, Margaret, *The Handmaid's Tale* (1985; Anchor, 1988). The phrase "Canadian literature," Atwood once recalled, used to bring yawns of boredom, even contemptuous ridicule—but according to critics and the public, certainly not in the case of *The Handmaid's Tale*. In the Republic of Gilead, near what used to be Boston, a totalitarian theocracy has reduced women to subservience, illiteracy, and sexual slavery. The only hope of freedom is to escape to Canada.

Harold Pinter wrote the screenplay for the 1990 film adaptation. Atwood's Booker Prize–winning *The Blind Assassin* (2000) tells, through three nested novels, the tightly intertwined life stories of two sisters.

Davies, Robertson, *The Cornish Trilogy* (1981, 1985, 1988; Penguin, 1992). In some sense a campus novel, this sprawling masterwork by one of Canada's great storytellers relates the life and afterlife of Francis Cornish, along the way touching on Rabelais, failed academic promise, sexual role-play, Gnosticism, allegory, art forgery, opera, King Arthur, musical-instrument restoration, and the Tarot. The first volume, *The Rebel Angels*, follows the travails of Cornish's executors as they attempt to sort out his over-bounteous legacy. *What's Bred in the Bone* backtracks to give a detailed account of Cornish's remarkable career. *The Lyre of Orpheus*, mainly concerned with the production of an opera, provides an appropriately over-the-top, operatic conclusion to the whole affair. A work brimming with brio and *sprezzatura*.

Gallant, Mavis, *Paris Stories* (NYRB, selected by Michael Ondaatje, 2002). Gallant was a Canadian writer from Montreal who lived most of her life in Paris. Known mainly for her short stories—she published 116 in the *New Yorker* alone over a period of five decades—she sympathetically explored themes of exile, expatriation, and disillusion. In addition, she grappled intensely with the psychological appeal of fascism—"its small possibilities in people"—particularly for French collaborators with the Nazis. Her most famous story in this regard is "Speck's Idea," included in this collection. The flowering of Gallant's talent can be traced in *The Cost of Living: Early and Uncollected Stories* (NYRB, 2009), which includes works published from 1951 to 1971.

Munro, Alice, *A Wilderness Station: Selected Stories, 1968–1994* (Vintage, 2015). Munro is a Canadian writer of short stories, many of which are set in Huron County, Ontario. In 2013 she won the Nobel Prize in Literature, the citation calling her a "master of the contemporary short story." Her stories are often compared with Chekhov's: the plot is secondary to epiphany or revelation. Her themes are apparent in the title of one of her collections, *Hateship, Friendship, Courtship, Loveship, Marriage* (2001). Munro's work bears a perhaps surprising resemblance to that of American practitioners of southern Gothic, including William Faulkner and Flannery O'Connor: all three favor closed-off, repressive communities as settings, and they rely to varying degrees on figures of the grotesque.

Ondaatje, Michael, *The English Patient* (1992; Vintage, 1993). A Canadian poet and novelist, Ondaatje was born in Ceylon of Dutch, Sinhalese, and Tamil ancestry, which perhaps helps explain his understanding of multicultural encounters. In this novel, a French-Canadian, an Italian-Canadian, a Sikh, and a Hungarian wind up at an Italian villa near Tuscany toward the end of World War II. The "English patient," nameless and grotesquely burned, has memories of suffering, rescue, and betrayal. A nurse, Hana, looks after him obsessively and likewise suffers from emotional damage inflicted by war and love. *The English Patient* won the Man Booker Prize, establishing Ondaatje as one of Canada's most renowned writers. It was adapted into a 1996 film directed by Anthony Minghella and starring Ralph Fiennes.

Caribbean

Carpentier, Alejo, *The Kingdom of This World* (1949; Farrar, Straus & Giroux, 1989). This novel, the Cuban author's second, was quickly recognized as a masterpiece of Caribbean literature. During the Haitian Revolution of 1791–1804, the country's first black king presides over a regime of terror and suffering. The novel explores voodoo and sexual predation as well as the repeated patterns found in all revolutionary violence. Further, Carpentier develops his idea of the "marvelous real," the observation that events in Latin America are often so extreme as to appear magical or supernatural. Carpentier's novel *The Lost Steps* (1953) follows a disillusioned, depleted composer as he flees from New York to, ultimately, the upper reaches of a great South American river, in search of revitalization.

Césaire, Aimé, *The Collected Poetry* (California, trans. Clayton Eshleman, 1984). Césaire was born on Martinique in 1913 and became one of the founders of the negritude movement in France and in French Africa. His poetry expresses the ambiguities of Caribbean life and culture as well as the cultural identity of black Africans in France. His work includes *Une Tempête* (1969), a radical adaptation of Shakespeare's *Tempest* for a colonial audience. In the interwar years, he taught Frantz Fanon, whose work was inspired by Césaire. Not least, Césaire is the author of a biography of the Haitian revolutionary Toussaint Louverture (1962). His poetry and political writings hold a distinguished place in Francophone literature. Césaire's *Discourse on Colonialism* (1955, trans. Joan Pinkham) is one of the foundations of post-colonial literature.

Guillén, Nicolás, *Cuba Libre* (Anderson & Ritchie, trans. Langston Hughes, 1948). Guillén is best known as the national poet of Cuba, but he was equally a political activist. The American poet and activist Langston Hughes felt a kinship with writers of the African diaspora in the Americas. Guillén's first poems appeared in the 1920s. After being jailed and released in 1936, he fled to the United States, joining the Communist Party. He returned to his homeland after the Cuban revolution of 1959. His poetry reflects the rhythms of American jazz and blues as well as Afro-Cuban dance and songs. He used Cuban folklore and music to express his protest, above all, against racial inequality.

Rhys, Jean, *Wide Sargasso Sea* (1966; Penguin, 2000). On Jamaica, shortly after the ending of the slave trade, a Creole heiress marries an Englishman. He takes her to England, declares her insane, and locks her away. She becomes the "madwoman in the attic"—a character remarkably similar to the first Mrs. Rochester in Charlotte Brontë's *Jane Eyre*. Hated by black Jamaicans, who called her a "white nigger," and exploited by her husband, she finds refuge nowhere. As in Brontë's novel, she dies while getting revenge on her faithless husband. The titular sea, an area of the North Atlantic hemmed in on all sides by strong currents and full of animal and plant life deposited by them, nonetheless contains water of exceptional clarity and beauty—the symbolism is straightforward.

Walcott, Derek, *Dream on Monkey Mountain, and Other Plays* (1970; Farrar, Straus & Giroux, 1971). Walcott was a poet and playwright from Saint Lucia—in his own emphatic phrase, "absolutely a Caribbean writer." Much of his work reflects the complex colonial history of the region and the "deep colonial damage" done to Caribbean culture. In *Dream on Monkey Mountain*, a drunken carouser winds up in jail and has hallucinations of becoming an itinerant healer tending to the sick and poor; after waking, he tries to transform himself. Robert Graves wrote that Walcott "handles English with a closer understanding of its inner magic than most, if not any, of his contemporaries." He won the Nobel Prize in Literature in 1992, mainly for his poetry. A wide selection can be found in *The Poetry of Derek Walcott, 1948–2013* (2014).

Latin America and South America

Asturias, Miguel, *Mulata* (*Mulata de tal*, 1963; Avon, trans. Gregory Rabassa, 1982). A phantas-magoric novel by the Guatemalan writer who won the Nobel Prize in Literature in 1967. To aid his pursuit of a mulatto woman, a poor farmer makes a deal with the Corn-Husk Devil: in exchange for being granted the arts of sorcery, he will cause all the women in a nearby town to receive the host at Mass while in an impure state—a mortal sin. From that point, the novel becomes a Hieronymous Bosch–like dreamscape full of Rabelaisian touches. For example, a priest is turned into a giant black-robed spider and then must battle a giant hedgehog in church. The novel's pervasive hybridity, seen in creatures such as spider-parrots, finds a parallel in its mix of Mayan mythology and Catholic imagery.

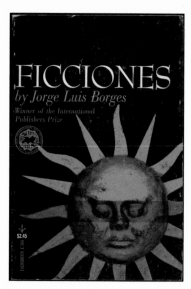

Borges, Jorge, *Ficciones* (1944; English trans., Grove, 1969). Seventeen stylistically and thematically inventive stories, including such well-known ones as "Tlön, Uqbar, Orbis Tertius," "The Library of Babel," "The Garden of Forking Paths," and "Funes, His Memory." Combining vividness with the bizarre, they deal with maps of nonexistent countries, pirates, spies, surreal labyrinths of books, and Nazi firing squads. The worlds they create are far larger than their delicate and diminutive scale would suggest. Borges's essay collection *Other Inquisitions, 1937–1952* (1952; Eng. trans., 1964) contains brief, pointed assessments of many of his favorite authors, including Coleridge and Cervantes, Hawthorne and Whitman, Wilde and Chesterton, Kafka and Keats.

Cortázar, Julio, *Hopscotch* (1963; trans. Gregory Rabassa, 1966; Pantheon, 1987). The masterwork of an Argentine writer, *Hopscotch* can be read, as its title implies, by jumping around throughout the story (a helpful "table of instructions" is supplied). The plot moves between Paris and Buenos Aires as the main character lives variously as an intellectual, a salesman, a circus performer, and an attendant in a mental hospital, without much plan or purpose. A selection of Cortázar's equally fantastic short stories is found in *Blow-Up, and Other Stories* (1967), the title piece of which was the basis for Michelangelo Antonion's film of the same name.

Fuentes, Carlos, *The Old Gringo* (1985; trans. Margaret Peden; Farrar, Straus & Giroux, 2007). In this novel, a young American woman named Harriet Winslow travels to Mexico to discover the truth about her father's disappearance during the Mexican Revolution of 1910–20. Along the way she meets Tomás Arroyo, a revolutionary general, and Ambrose Bierce, the elderly American journalist also known as the "old gringo." The theme is corruption of revolutionary ideals in a cycle of repression and rebellion. Harriet discovers an uncomfortable truth about her father, and the general and the gringo encounter a fate determined by one of the great leaders of the revolution, Pancho Villa. The 1989 film adaptation stars Jane Fonda as Winslow, Jimmy Smits as Arroyo, and Gregory Peck as Bierce.

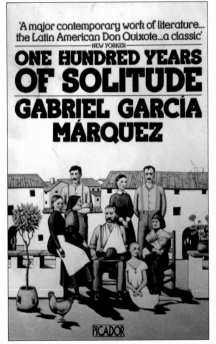

'A major contemporary work of literature... the Latin American Don Quixote...a classic'
— NEW YORKER —
ONE HUNDRED YEARS OF SOLITUDE
GABRIEL GARCÍA MÁRQUEZ
PICADOR

García Márquez, Gabriel, *One Hundred Years of Solitude* (1967; HarperCollins, trans. Gregory Rabassa, 2006). A novel in which ghosts abound, a village is struck with insomnia, and a woman ascends to heaven while doing laundry. Seven generations of the Buendía family live in a town in Colombia built by their founding patriarch. Their lives seem almost fatalistically unable to escape the past, and events in the town become a microcosm of Colombian history and that of Latin America generally. The author's *Love in the Time of Cholera* (1985) spins a tale of unrequited love that endures for half a century; it is saved from sentimentality by the fully human characters and the succession of surprises they provide.

Güiraldes, Ricardo, *Don Segundo Sombra* (1926; translated by Harriet de Onis as *Shadows on the Pampas*, New American Library, 1966). The central character is a mythical gaucho, a national symbol and folk hero of Argentina. For the book's description of the restless gaucho lifestyle, Güiraldes drew on his own experience. He spent his boyhood on a ranch near Buenos Aires, where he learned horse taming and participated in rodeos. He broadened his experience with trips to Paris, where he became acquainted with avant-garde writers of the time. His stylistic idiosyncrasies eventually became recognized as the forerunner of post–World War I literary innovation in Argentina. *Don Segundo Sombra* celebrates the gaucho as the exemplar of a free, stoic, lonely, and silent life.

Guzmán, Martín Luis, *The Eagle and the Serpent* (1928; trans. Harriet de Onis, Dolphin, 1965). Guzmán served under Pancho Villa in the Mexican Revolution of 1910. The novel, which reflects the author's exploration of Mexican national identity, is often regarded as the best fictional account of the purpose and course of the revolution. Its unflinching portrayal of Pancho Villa depicts his brutality as well as his vision. The narrative carries the reader on the march from the northern states to Mexico City while Emiliano Zapata's forces approach from the south. Guzmán's witty and gripping story provides insights into the betrayals as well as the dedication of the revolutionaries, rendering the common people as well as the heroes comprehensible in the broad sweep of Mexican history.

Harris, Wilson, *Palace of the Peacock* (1960; Faber, 2010). Harris, a poet and novelist from Guyana, wrote about the struggles of colonized peoples. In *Peacock*, he tells the story of a multiracial expedition venturing upriver into Guyana's interior, through the jungles to the savannahs, to find indigenous people for cheap labor on a plantation. The journey takes on spiritual significance, ending with the forest tribes finding sanctuary and the members of the expedition discovering that death does not bring an end to the soul. Wilson's *Jonestown* (1996) is a fictionalized retelling of the mass murder in Guyana of 900-plus followers of the religious cult leader Jim Jones in 1978. Most were killed by drinking cyanide-laced Flavor Aid—which gave rise to the erroneous expression "drinking the Kool-Aid."

Machado de Assis, Joaquim Maria, *Dom Casmurro* (1900; trans. Helen Caldwell; Farrar, Straus & Giroux, 2009). In a blackly comic novel that illuminates, with great psychological insight, the culture and history of Brazil, the untrustworthy narrator, Bento Santiago, becomes convinced that his wife has been seduced by his best friend. His jealousy grows until he seems to be suffering from paranoia; crimes of vengeance follow. Though Machado's work did not gain popularity outside Brazil during his lifetime, his novels have now been translated into multiple languages, and he is widely regarded as the greatest writer of Brazilian literature. The author's *Epitaph of a Small Winner* (1880) is a biographical tale told by a corpse, who dedicates it to "the first worm that gnawed my flesh."

Mutis, Álvaro, *The Adventures and Misadventures of Maqroll* (1993; NYRB, trans. Edith Grossman, 2002). Mutis, a Colombian poet and novelist long resident in Mexico City, published seven novellas about Maqroll, a man of indeterminate origin and age who restlessly travels the world alone. He searches for love and knowledge, but never finds enough of either to satisfy him. He is known as Maqroll the Gaviero, the "Lookout," though *gaviero* also suggests *gavia*, seagull, a restless flyer over sea and land. Maqroll's creator, Mutis, worked in public relations for Standard Oil and in sales for Twentieth Century Fox while trying to make a living as a writer. His work, which is widely popular across Latin America, was championed by Octavio Paz and his fellow Colombian Gabriel García Márquez.

Neruda, Pablo, *100 Love Sonnets* (*Cien sonetos de amor*, 1959; Texas, trans. Stephen Tapscott, 1986). Neruda, a Chilean poet who won the Nobel Prize in Literature in 1971, wrote these sonnets for his wife Matilde Urrutia. The sequence is divided into times of day: morning, afternoon, evening, and night. The poems are celebrated for their sensuality and their evocations of life on Isla Negra, off the Chilean coast. Neruda served for decades in the Chilean diplomatic corps, in postings that included India, Java, Singapore, Barcelona, and Mexico City. He died in 1973 under suspicious circumstances suggesting that he may have been poisoned on the orders of Augusto Pinochet, who had staged a coup d'état a few days earlier. Thousands ignored a curfew and crowded the streets of Santiago in mourning.

Puig, Manuel, *Eternal Curse on the Reader of These Pages* (1980; Minnesota, 1999). Written in English by an Argentine novelist, *Eternal Curse*, which is told entirely through dialogue, starts as a straightforward account of Larry, an academic washout, taking care of Ramirez, an elderly Argentine expatriate, in Greenwich Village. Though ostensibly strangers, the pair seem to know things about each other's pasts. As they construct ever more elaborate lies to keep this knowledge secret, the story becomes a study in deception and deciphering—not least because Ramirez encoded his memoirs in three French novels, including *Les Liaisons Dangereuses* and *La Princesse de Clèves*. In style, the book recalls Puig's *Kiss of the Spider Woman* (1976), another novel told entirely through misleading, self-deceiving dialogue between two men.

Rulfo, Juan, *The Burning Plain, and Other Stories* (1967; Texas, 1971). Rulfo was a prominent screenwriter and photographer as well as a novelist, distinguished especially for capturing the sheer violence of the Mexican Revolution and its consequences for the common people. The protagonist of "The Burning Plain" is Pedro Zamora, a charismatic, populist leader with piercing eyes and a commanding presence. He combines political and military strength, a caudillo who is courageous on the battlefield yet ignorant of such consequences of war as raped women and orphaned children. In portraying the cult of violence and the suffering it engenders, Rulfo raises basic questions about social as well as political upheavals. The stories leave the reader with a haunting sense of ambivalence toward revolutions in general.

Vargas Llosa, Mario, *Aunt Julia and the Scriptwriter* (1977; trans. Helen R. Lane, 1982; Picador, 2007). A romantic, comic novel (based on the author's first marriage) by the winner of the Nobel Prize in Literature in 2010, *Aunt Julia* tells parallel stories, set in Lima in the 1950s, of a May–December romance (he is eighteen, she is thirty-two) and of a frenzied writer of radio soap operas. The plotlines weave in and out as the scriptwriter's tales affect, and are affected by, the lovers' ups and downs. Vargas Llosa's second novel, *The Green House* (1965), is a larger, darker work set on the Peruvian coast and in the Amazon jungle; its complex plot, which unfolds non-chronologically, follows the intersecting lives of prostitutes (working in the titular brothel), smugglers, soldiers, and priests.

Literary Criticism
Auerbach, Erich, *Mimesis: The Representation of Reality in Western Literature* (1953; Princeton, trans. Willard R. Trask, intro. Edward W. Said, 2013). Auerbach was a Berlin Jew who in 1935 fled from Germany to Turkey, where he wrote one of the great works of literary and historical scholarship. He ranges from antiquity to the twentieth century, from Homer to Virginia Woolf. He finds that the Old Testament, for example, reveals the real life of common people, and that

what smacks of the reality of everyday language is superior to other types of literature. One critic praises his work for being "vulgar, vigorous, dynamic, grotesque, and historical." This is a scrupulous literary survey that places each work in its exact, populist, and historical context.

Bloom, Harold, *The Visionary Company: A Reading of English Romantic Poetry* (1961; rev. ed., Cornell, 1971). In this elucidation of romantic poetry, Bloom, one of America's leading literary critics and most entertaining curmudgeons, provides close readings of poems by Blake, Byron, Coleridge, Keats, Shelley, and Wordsworth as well as the less well-known poets John Clare, Thomas Beddoes, and George Darley. They incarnated the spirit of an age. They all shared a religious background of Protestant dissent. Britain's repressive response to the French Revolution formed their political and cultural milieu, and their work is filled with calls for independence of mind and freedom of spirit. Bloom traces the interplay of imagination and nature in their poetry, and tracks the friendships and rivalries among them.

Empson, William, *Seven Types of Ambiguity* (1930; Penguin, 1995). Empson had an extraordinary career. He was expelled from Cambridge when condoms were found in his room, and he subsequently taught in Japan and China before returning to England. He uses the term *ambiguity* to refer to "any verbal nuance, however slight, which gives room for alternative reactions to the same piece of language." In this sense, metaphor is the most familiar kind of ambiguity. Most other kinds arise from conflicts within an author. Empson was described in an obituary as giving the impression of "something between a slightly batty retired colonel and a Taoist sage." The critic F. R. Leavis believed him to be a true successor to John Donne, whom Empson took as his model.

Epstein, Joseph, ed., and Barry Moser, illus., *Literary Genius: 25 Classic Writers Who Define English and American Literature* (Paul Dry, 2007). Twenty-five contemporary or recent critics assess twenty-five classic writers, their books as well as their styles and insights. The entries include Tom Shippey on Chaucer, Dan Jacobson on William Wordsworth, Hilary Mantel on Jane Austen, John Gross on James Joyce, and Epstein himself on Henry James. The collective aim is to penetrate the genius behind the books. Epstein quotes Melville: "Genius, all over the world, stands hand in hand, and one shock of recognition runs the whole circle round." A book about books, it combines criticism of the authors with the context and significance of the books themselves. Barry Moser provides distinctive engraved portraits and illustrations.

Fussell, Paul, *The Great War and Modern Memory* (1975; Oxford, 2000). Fussell describes literary consequences of combat experience of soldiers in World War I, especially trench warfare. Soldiers suffered cultural and deep psychological shock. Romantic ideas of war gave way to harsh perceptions of its futility. This movement from fantasy to reality could be seen in the poetry of Edmund Blunden, Robert Graves, Wilfred Owen, Siegfried Sassoon, and many others. Although these poets were unrepresentative of British society as a whole, their work captured universal themes of despair and disillusion. Fussell wrote a sequel of sorts in *Wartime: Understanding and Behavior in the Second World War* (1989), which takes account of the author's experiences fighting in France as well as the literature of the period.

Leavis, F. R., *The Great Tradition* (1948; Faber, 2011). As a Fellow of Downing College, Cambridge, Leavis championed moral depth and intellectual responsibility in literature. He therefore, for example, criticized what he regarded as the dilettante elitism of the Bloomsbury group. He often expressed his views dogmatically and belligerently—one critic called him "a sanctimonious prick." In *The Great Tradition*, he recognized as pre-eminent novelists Jane Austen, George Eliot, Joseph Conrad, and Henry James, although Austen is not discussed in the book. To Leavis, those authors upheld rigorous intellectual and moral standards and were, in his own phrase, "the touchstone of creativity." The best study of Leavis is by Ian Mackillop, *F. R. Leavis: A Life in Criticism* (1997).

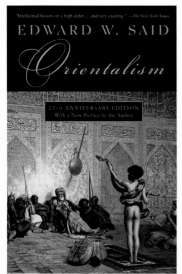

Said, Edward, *Orientalism* (1978; Penguin Modern Classics, 2003). Said, a Palestinian American, held consistently that Western scholarship on the region remains distorted, and that public attitudes about the Arab world continue to be ingrained with a condescending attitude. The preface, written shortly before the author's death, takes into account criticism of his work. His other books include *The Question of Palestine* (1979). His diatribes overshadowed his work as a professor of English at Columbia and his reputation as an accomplished pianist. Robert Irwin's *For Lust of Knowing: The Orientalists and Their Enemies* (2006) is a detailed rejoinder to Said's "long and persevering polemic."

Shattuck, Roger, *Forbidden Knowledge: From Prometheus to Pornography* (1996; Harvest, 1997). Are there things that humans should not know—or not even seek to know? Shattuck, an acclaimed literary critic, addresses this question from all sides. The breaking of long-standing limits and taboos inevitably involves the idea of evil. Shattuck's detailed exploration of evil leads him into regions of extremity: the book comes with two warnings about the unsuitability, for children or minors, of the chapter on the marquis de Sade. Shattuck discusses literary works that warn against the dangers of wanting to know too much, including *Paradise Lost, Frankenstein, Dr. Jekyll and Mr. Hyde,* and *The Stranger*. Science, too, is interrogated: does the Human Genome Project offer the chance to fulfill Dr. Frankenstein's dream?

Steiner, George, *The Death of Tragedy* (1961; Yale, 1996). Steiner's theme is that Western culture no longer produces tragedies in the classical sense. By this sort of tragedy, he means "the dramatic representation or, more precisely, the dramatic testing of a view of reality in which man is taken to be an unwelcome guest in the world." Put another way: "Tragedy springs from outrage," and it denies the possibility of consolation or amelioration. Steiner's definition of tragedy excludes many ancient Greek plays usually called tragedies, all of Shakespeare except *King Lear* and *Timon of Athens,* and the plays of Samuel Beckett. Among modern dramatists, only Racine qualifies as a consistent tragedian. Clearly written and strongly argued, the book explores what is lost when a sense of the tragic disappears.

Trilling, Lionel, *The Liberal Imagination* (1950; NYRB, intro. Louis Menand, 2008). A collection of mainly literary essays that takes a close look at society and politics as well. Trilling warns about the dangers of complacent liberalism and a naïve belief in progress. He pursues those themes in observations on things as varied as Kipling's works, the novels of Henry James, the *Kinsey Report*, and Americans' attitudes toward money. The essays give a flavor of the concerns of the New York Intellectuals, a loosely defined circle of friends and colleagues that included, at times, Lionel and Diana Trilling, Jacques Barzun, Hannah Arendt, and Daniel Bell. Alexander Bloom's *Prodigal Sons: The New York Intellectuals and Their World* (1986) is a joint biography of the group.

Philosophy

Ancient and Medieval

Aristotle, *Nicomachean Ethics* (4th century B.C.; Chicago, trans. Robert C. Bartlett and Susan D. Collins, 2012). In this practical guide to living the best life, Aristotle shows that the highest goal of human activity is *eudaimonia*, or happiness and human flourishing. Excellence requires people to exercise reason: cultivate knowledge and exercise good judgment. They must also develop moral virtues such as courage, generosity, and fair-mindedness. Reason governs human action, but so does desire. Aristotle proposed what became known as the Golden Mean, for example, a point midway between complete self-denial and giving in to temptation. Interestingly, the book deals at length with *akrasia*, weakness of the will, especially as manifested in doing what one knows is bad for oneself.

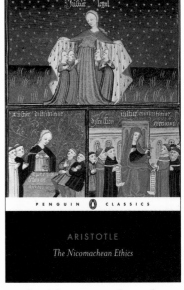

Confucius, *Analects* (5th century BC; Hackett, trans. Edward Slingerland, 2003). Confucius believed that the welfare of a country depended on moral and ethical principles of dutifulness. Political leaders should conduct themselves with gravity, speak with respect for others, and demonstrate integrity as well as basic honesty. The *Analects* ("selected passages") have been as widely read in China as the Bible has in the West. They uphold the ideals of self-knowledge, courage, and, above all, an ethical code of leadership that commands obedience by example. Raymond Dawson provides a good, short introduction to the philosopher in *Confucius* (1982), in Oxford's Past Masters series.

Cartledge, Paul, *Democritus* (Routledge, 1999). The reputation of the ancient Greek philosopher Democritus (c. 460–c. 370 BC) rests mainly on his having been the first recorded person to theorize the existence of the atom as the irreducibly smallest thing. He taught and wrote also on mathematics, aesthetics, ethics, and politics. None of his writings have survived; what is known about them comes from fragments copied in secondhand sources. He stated that "equality is everywhere noble" (though equality did not extend to women or slaves). One reason he remains significant is his example of intellectual ambition and imaginative reach, and not least his well-attested habit of laughing at human folly. He set an example, still worth emulating, for scholars to try to remain cheerful at all times.

Epicurus, *The Epicurus Reader* (1994, Hackett, trans. Lloyd Gerson). These short, powerful, mostly aphoristic sayings are the only surviving writings of the first philosopher to win a wide following. Proclaiming that death is "nothing" and not to be feared, that our natural needs are simple and easy to meet, and that most of what we strive for contributes only to suffering, Epicurus reveals that his teachings on happiness are not at all what the term "epicurean" has come to suggest—namely, they encourage self-knowledge, not hedonism.

Lucretius, *De Rerum Natura: The Nature of Things* (c. 54 B.C.; California, trans. David R. Slavitt, 2008). A Roman poet and philosopher, Lucretius puts forward a materialistic account of the world and makes an Epicurean argument that seeks to relieve people of a sense of guilt and the fear of death. In a long exposition of the atomic theory of nature, the poet demonstrates that the soul is mortal. Following Epicurus, he promotes pleasure, found in peace of mind and freedom from fear, as the object of life. Thanks to the occasional "swerve" by the atoms that make up everything, man has free will. Stephen Greenblatt's *The Swerve: How the World Became Modern* (2011) argues that the fifteenth-century rediscovery of Lucretius changed the course of history.

Maimonides, *Eight Chapters on Ethics*, in *Ethical Writings of Maimonides* (12th century; Dover, trans. Raymond Weiss and Charles Butterworth, 1983). This volume provides a good, short introduction to the thought of Maimonides, probably the most important Jewish Torah scholar and philosopher of the Middle Ages. Drawing on the Hebrew Bible, *Eight Chapters* offers lessons on ethics and divine law, and reflections on the relation between reason and revelation and between human freedom and divine will.

Marcus Aurelius, *Meditations* (ca. 175; Oxford World's Classics, trans. Robin Hard, 2011). In this widely influential classic, the author, a Roman emperor, reflects on how to use the principles of Stoicism to find equanimity in the midst of natural disaster and human conflict. His goal is to live according to nature, namely, accepting the suffering and death that are an inescapable part of life, detaching oneself from things that one cannot control, and focusing attention on doing one's own part as well as possible. Earlier, Epictetus, a former slave in the time of Nero and Domitian, taught Stoic ethics—principally, that people are responsible for their actions, which they can control through self-discipline—and his precepts were compiled into a short handbook, the *Enchiridion*, by his disciple Arrian.

Mo Zi, *The Book of Master Mo* (5th century BC; Penguin, ed. Ian Johnston, 2014). Mo Zi was an artisan in ancient China, also skilled in designing fortifications. His philosophical writings cover topics such as ethics, epistemology, and logic as well as military engineering. His powerful, radical message was "universal love," in the sense of caring for all people equally. At the time, devotion to family and clan was paramount in Chinese society. His straightforward moral instruction emphasized self-reflection and authenticity rather than Confucian obedience to ritual. Sun Yat-sen centuries later used Mo Zi's "universal love" as a foundation for Chinese democracy. Chris Fraser's *The Philosophy of the Mozi: The First Consequentialists* (2016) is a full explication of Mohism.

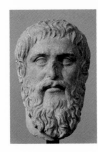 **Plato**, *Dialogues* (c. 4th century BC). The ancient Greek philosopher Plato was a student of Socrates in Athens. A decade or so after his teacher's death, Plato established the Academy, a school where aspiring philosophers met to discuss and debate questions of ethics, epistemology, logic, politics, and the like. Plato published his works as dialogues, fictional accounts of a group of characters arguing about important topics in philosophy. Socrates is the leading figure in most of the dialogues. He is shown asking probing questions in a way that gave rise to what is now called the Socratic method.

Apology (in *Four Texts on Socrates*, rev. ed., Cornell, trans. Thomas West and Grace West, 1998). "Apology" here means defense, and the book records Socrates's self-defense while on trial for impiety and corrupting the youth of Athens. Among his claims are that his only wisdom consists in knowing that he knows nothing, that his actions are done in obedience to Apollo, and that "the unexamined life is not worth living." Unimpressed and unpersuaded, the jury finds him guilty and sentences him to death.

Euthyphro (in *Four Texts on Socrates*, rev. ed., Cornell, trans. Thomas West and Grace West, 1998). The action of this dialogue takes place just before the events in the *Apology*. Socrates and Euthyphro, a seer, explore the nature of piety. Is something pious because the gods love it, or is it loved by the gods because it is pious? Socrates questions whether piety should involve more than asking the gods for things and giving things to them, implying that such a shallow form of religious devotion should not be considered pious.

Phaedo (Hackett, 2nd ed., trans. G. M. A. Grube, 1977). Socrates's conversation with his friends on his final day, ending with the famous scene in which Socrates drinks hemlock. In the course of arguing that the soul is immortal and that death should not be feared, Socrates introduces the theory of forms, according to which sensible things have to participate in perfect and unchanging forms or ideas—a theory that became the basis for philosophical idealism and exerted enormous influence on Western philosophy.

The Republic of Plato (Basic, 2nd ed., trans. Alan Bloom, intro. Adam Kirsch, 2016). The *Republic* asks, "What is justice?" The dialogue focuses on the construction of a just state. Plato's ideal polity, a sort of totalitarian utopia overseen by philosopher-kings, would require the banishing of poets, because their works lead to indulgence in damaging emotions. The *Republic* contains Plato's famous allegory of the cave, which purports to demonstrate that humans are little better than prisoners chained in an underground cell.

Symposium (Chicago, trans. Seth Benardete, 2001). During a drinking party, seven guests offer speeches on the nature of love or the god Eros. Aristophanes, in an account that became famous, depicts love as a search to find one's "missing half" in order to feel whole. Socrates explains that, ideally, love starts with an attraction to physical beauty and then rises through stages to an intellectual love of the beautiful and the true. This notion of the superiority of nonsexual love became known as Platonic love.

Sun Tzu, *The Art of War* (6th cent. BC; Barnes & Noble Classics, trans. Lionel Giles, 2003). Sun Tzu, a Chinese general and military strategist, believed that comprehensive knowledge of the enemy was necessary in order to achieve the ultimate goal of control through psychological domination. Ho Chi Minh commanded his officers to study its relevance to the war in Vietnam. During the Gulf Wars of the 1990s, General Norman Schwarzkopf Jr. remarked that he applied Sun Tzu's doctrine of deception, speed, and striking at the enemy's weak points.

Modern

Austin, J. L., *Philosophical Papers*, 3rd. ed. (1961; Clarendon Press, ed. J. O. Urmson and G. J. Warnock, 1979). Austin developed the idea of performative language, namely, that to say certain kinds of sentences in certain circumstances is to perform an action—a speech act, in Austin's terminology—and not just to "say" something. In this posthumously published collection of clear and witty essays, he brilliantly looks at distinctions in ordinary language to illuminate and sometimes solve philosophical problems dealing with such issues as truth, facts, and excuses. Austin can be grouped with Ludwig Wittgenstein, Gilbert Ryle, H. L. A. Hart, and others as a philosopher interested in determining meaning through the way that words are ordinarily used.

Ayer, A. J., *Language, Truth, and Logic* (1936; Penguin, 2001). Upon returning to Oxford from studying in Vienna, the twenty-six-year-old Ayer wrote what he thought would be an introduction to logical positivism, the first one in English. It came to be recognized as a classic statement of the philosophical assertion that metaphysical, religious, and ethical sentences were not cognitively meaningful. Respectable philosophy needed to confine itself to analyzing concepts. Everything depended on the principle of verifiability, namely, that the meaning of an expression is its method of verification. Unfortunately for positivism, that principle itself was neither verifiable nor trivial. Ben Rogers's *A. J. Ayer: A Life* (1999) is a sharp, informative, and entertaining biography that portrays Ayer as an eccentric personality in an antiauthoritarian tradition.

Bentham, Jeremy, and John Stuart Mill, *Utilitarianism, and Other Essays* (Penguin, 1987). Bentham set out the "fundamental axiom" of the philosophy that became known as utilitarianism: "It is the greatest happiness of the greatest number that is the measure of right and wrong." As a political reformer, he had immense influence in law and politics for generations. Yet he was almost incapable of publishing his writings—thus, he shares this volume with John Stuart Mill, who elaborates on Bentham's axiom with imagination and reason. Bentham was well ahead of his time in speaking for complete equality between sexes and especially for proposing reform of the anti-homosexual laws in England.

Cassirer, Ernst, *An Essay on Man: An Introduction to a Philosophy of Human Culture* (1944; Yale, 1962). Cassirer discusses how humanists have conceived of history, literature, and philosophy. He vindicates man's ability to resolve human problems by self-realization: a study of cultural achievements can lead to an understanding of man's capacity for both good and evil. His views were shaped by his experience as a Jew in Germany before his departure in 1933 for Oxford and, eventually, Yale. One of his themes is the irrationality of the myth of the state as put forward by Nazi Germany. Irrationality can be combatted by rejecting the notion of destiny, but it is important to keep in mind that myths underpin every regime, not just fascist ones.

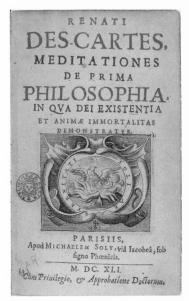

Descartes, René, *Meditations on First Philosophy: In Which the Existence of God and the Immortality of the Soul Are Demonstrated* (1641; Penguin, trans. Michael Moriarty, 2008). Worried that the new science of Copernicus and Galileo had thrown all human knowledge into doubt, Descartes took the first-person perspective of doubting everything. He discovered that "If I doubt, then I exist" must be true. On the basis of this realization, Descartes tried to construct an edifice of knowledge. The last of the six meditations presents the mind-body problem, a conundrum that continues to vex philosophers and scientists. In the *Discourse on the Method* (1637), Descartes attempted to apply the mathematical ideal of certainty to scientific and philosophical thought and thereby unify all knowledge.

Erasmus, Desiderius, *Praise of Folly* (1511; Oxford, trans. Betty Radice, 2004). A Renaissance humanist, social critic, and theologian, Erasmus gave voice in this satire to the goddess Folly, who ridicules superstition and religious rigidity. Apart from wise and learned men, most people do foolish things—get drunk, indulge in lewd thoughts, commit licentious acts. Indeed, all human beings are created by acts of folly. Erasmus believed in faith, piety, and grace; he was renowned in his lifetime for immense learning, wisdom, and criticism of religious doctrine. He sympathized with Protestant reformers, though he remained a Catholic priest. He dedicated *Praise of Folly* to Thomas More, another scholar whose name is synonymous with learning, humanity, and wit.

Guénon, René, *The Crisis of the Modern World* (1927; Sophia Perennis, trans. Marco Pallis, Arthur Osborne, and Richard C. Nicholson, 2004). A major French writer contemplating the aftermath of World War I, Guénon argued that Western traditions had fallen into decline and social chaos—an age of darkness. He responded metaphysically, encouraging Western intellectual leaders to meet to restore the West to its spiritual roots, perhaps through a revitalized Christianity. He found his own solution by studying under esoteric Islamic scholars, becoming

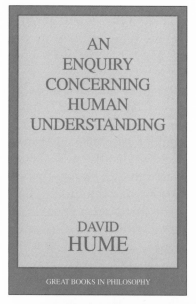

AN
ENQUIRY
CONCERNING
HUMAN
UNDERSTANDING

DAVID
HUME

GREAT BOOKS IN PHILOSOPHY

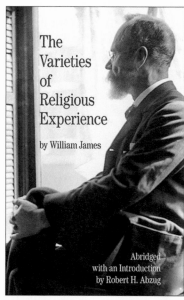

The
Varieties
of
Religious
Experience

by William James

Abridged
with an Introduction
by Robert H. Abzug

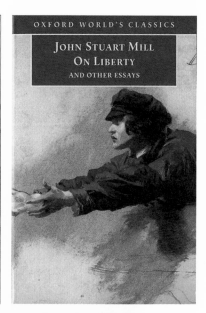

OXFORD WORLD'S CLASSICS

JOHN STUART MILL
ON LIBERTY
AND OTHER ESSAYS

a Sufi and gaining the title Shaykh 'Abd al-Wahid Yahya. For Guénon's ideas on the spiritual roots of Western societies, see Graham Rooth, *Prophet for a Dark Age: A Companion to the Works of René Guénon* (2008).

Herder, Johann Gottfried, *J. G. Herder on Social and Political Culture* (1969; Cambridge, trans. F. M. Barnard, 2010). One of the major figures in eighteenth-century social and cultural thought, Herder was critical to the development of the concepts of nationalism and patriotic identity. He argued, like Goethe, that the German language and cultural practices had created a nation. Above all, folklore, art, music, dancing, and other traditions bound together the German people, or *Volk*. In the eighteenth century, the use of the idea of the *Volk* in a positive sense, not as the "rabble," was imaginative and unifying. Virtually all ideas about the cultural, literary, and political, movement toward a unified Germany can be traced to Herder.

Hume, David, *An Enquiry Concerning Human Understanding* (1748; Oxford World's Classics, 2007). Following up on the empiricism of Locke and Berkeley, Hume rigorously examines the basis of human knowledge and is led to a thoroughgoing skepticism concerning notions such as the self, causality—he uses the example of one billiard ball striking another to demonstrate that our experience of causation is always learned and can never be innate—and God. His work had a profound influence on Immanuel Kant, who claimed Hume had awakened him from his "dogmatic slumber," and on later philosophers such as Bertrand Russell, Ludwig Wittgenstein, and A. J. Ayer.

James, William, *The Varieties of Religious Experience* (1902; Bedford, abridged ed., intro. Robert H. Abzug, 2013). One of the foremost American intellectuals establishes both the reality and the psychological nature of transcendent experience, thus providing a way to understand and evaluate styles and beliefs embedded in religious life. A touchstone for students of religion, psychology, and intellectual history. Jacques Barzun's *A Stroll with William James* (1983) provides an appreciation of James's character, portraying him as an old-fashioned Yankee stoic but with an artistic temperament, skeptical yet morally sound, open-minded and kindly, always yearning for a faith he knew he would never really find, but fundamentally at peace with himself.

Mill, John Stuart, *On Liberty, and Other Writings* (1859; Cambridge, ed. Stefan Collini, 1989). Mill championed individual rights, privacy, and maximum liberty—as long as it did not harm other people. By ensuring the good of the individual, society would achieve "the greatest happiness for the greatest number," the utilitarian formula for "acting rightly" and creating a just society. He defended the British Empire by arguing that a fundamental distinction existed between civilized and barbarous peoples, and that it was Britain's duty to improve the latter. His conception of the freedom of the individual in opposition to unlimited state and social control led the critic Gertrude Himmelfarb to hold Mill responsible for the unraveling of society in the 1960s, when increased liberty became license for rebellion.

Moore, G. E., *Principia Ethica* (1903; Dover, 2004). Moore, a Cambridge don, was one of the founders of analytical philosophy. He influenced the intellectual secret society known as the Apostles and later the Bloomsbury group of writers and artists. The key to the *Principia* and Moore's influence is his commonsense argument that knowledge of facts must be supplemented by an intuition of the "goodness" of such things as beauty and friendship. Informed intuition provides the basis of human reasonableness and decency. Leonard and Virginia Woolf believed that the *Principia* and the example set by Moore's personality and moral character provided an anchor of stability in an otherwise meaningless world. For Moore's thought and influence, the key work is Paul Levy, *G. E. Moore and the Cambridge Apostles* (1979).

Niebuhr, Reinhold, *Moral Man and Immoral Society: A Study in Ethics and Politics* (1932; Westminster John Knox, 2013). The book's thesis holds that people are more likely to violate standards of ethical behavior as groups than as individuals. His views grew in influence with the rise of fascism in the 1930s. During World War II and the post-war era, his book provided moral bearings in a world of perpetual social and political conflict—hard-hitting, ironic, Niebuhrian guidance. Niebuhr was the author of the Serenity Prayer, made famous by Alcoholics Anonymous. For the life of the author, see Richard Wightman Fox, *Reinhold Niebuhr: A Biography* (1985).

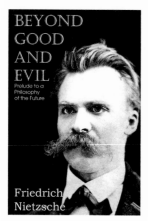

Nietzsche, Friedrich, *Beyond Good and Evil: Prelude to a Philosophy of the Future* (1886; Penguin Classics, trans. R. J. Hollingdale, 1990). According to Nietzsche, the traditional morality of Judeo-Christian religion is slave morality, to be used by the weak against the strong, who live by master morality. In addition to taking on past philosophers—for example, Descartes, Spinoza, and Kant—the book returns to the author's aphoristic style, for example, "He who fights with monsters might take care lest he thereby become a monster. And if you gaze for long into an abyss, the abyss gazes also into you." In *Thus Spoke Zarathustra* (1883–91), Nietzsche uses the character Zarathustra, an Aryan prophet, to put forward the concept of the *Übermensch*: a superior human whose existence would justify mankind.

Pascal, Blaise, *Pensées* (1670; Penguin, trans. A. J. Krailsheimer, 1995). Pascal was a brilliant mathematician and physicist, but his most celebrated work is his *Penseés*, a posthumously published collection of philosophical fragments, notes, and essays in which he reflects on human nature and human depravity and provides a classic apology for the Christian faith. Above all, Pascal explores the contradictions of the human condition, in psychology as well as theology. Believing that religious principles can be grasped only through intuition, he emphasizes the necessity for submission to God while searching for truth. Jeff Jordan, *Pascal's Wager: Pragmatic Arguments and Belief in God* (2006), is a penetrating, analytical book by a leading religious philosopher.

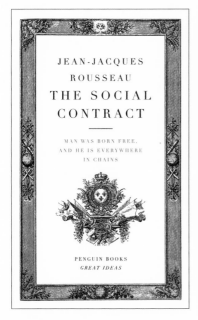

Rousseau, Jean-Jacques, *The Social Contract* (1762; Oxford World's Classics, trans. Christopher Betts, 2008). "People are born free; yet everywhere they are in chains." Rousseau argues that people are freed from the chains of repressive government when they are represented by a government that expresses their general will. Those who resist that will may have to be "forced to be free." Rousseau's *Confessions* (1764–70), sometimes credited with inaugurating the modern genre of autobiography, describes his childhood—and its importance for the rest of his life—at length and continues through his early love affairs, his career as a writer, his numerous quarrels and feuds, and his years in exile. The definitive biography is the three-volume life by Maurice Cranston (1982, 1991, 1997).

Russell, Bertrand, *The Problems of Philosophy* (1912; Oxford 1997). Russell was a mathematician and social activist as well as a philosopher, altogether one of the twentieth century's most influential public intellectuals. He was a founder of the method of analytic philosophy, which emphasizes conceptual and argumentative clarity and precision. *The Problems of Philosophy*, perhaps his most accessible work, is a short guide to perennial questions in the field, with an emphasis on theories of knowledge. Ray Monk's *Bertrand Russell, 1872–1920* (1996) covers the first half of the philosopher's long, tumultuous life. Russell was at once a philosopher, logician, mathematician, social critic, historian, writer, political activist, and Nobel laureate. Not least, he also advocated nuclear disarmament and attacked the United States for the war in Vietnam.

Ryle, Gilbert, *The Concept of Mind* (1949; Chicago, intro. Daniel C. Dennett, 2000). Ryle, who had a reputation for using plain words, regarded himself as language philosopher. He once quipped that his subject was "talk about talk." Though an authority on the philosophical tradition from Plato to Collingwood, he was concerned especially with the ordinary use of language.

He attacked the idea of a fundamental distinction between mind and body, calling it the "ghost in the machine," that is, the lingering tradition of the distinction between mind and matter. The mind of a person is *not* an independent non-material entity that only temporarily inhabits and governs the body. Arthur Koestler carried the subject further in his distinctive style in his book about philosophical psychology, *The Ghost in the Machine* (1967).

Santayana, George, *The Life of Reason*, 5 vols. (1905–6; abridged ed., Prometheus, 1998). Santayana, born in Madrid, retained his Spanish citizenship despite teaching in the philosophy department at Harvard for more than two decades. He retired early to Rome, acquiring the reputation of a cosmopolitan intellectual, philosopher, literary critic, and poet. In this book, he explains how reason emerges in five dimensions of thought: common sense, society, religion, art, and science. Santayana was an elegant stylist and aphorist. One of his statements is quoted so frequently that it is in danger of becoming a cliché, but conveys an abiding truth: "Those who cannot remember the past are condemned to repeat it." His correspondence, collected as *The Letters of George Santayana*, ed. Daniel Cory (1955), was described by Lionel Trilling as "of classic importance."

Schopenhauer, Arthur, *The Essential Schopenhauer: Key Selections from "The World as Will and Representation," and Other Writings* (1819–51; Harper, ed. Wolfgang Schirmacher, 2010). Schopenhauer was a major figure in nineteenth-century philosophy, a member of Goethe's Weimar circle, and a visionary skeptic. Famous for his pessimism about the fundamentally painful human condition, he argued that—in a world filled with endless strife—tranquility and a beneficent frame of mind could be achieved by artistic and ascetic forms of awareness. Rüdiger Safranski's *Schopenhauer and the Wild Years of Philosophy* (1987, trans. Eward Osers, Harvard, 1991) is a useful companion. In examining Schopenhauer's seminal works, including *The World as Will*, Safranski presents a rounded interpretation of his ideas and his influence on writers as diverse as Tolstoy, Wittgenstein, Zola, and Beckett.

Spinoza, Benedict de, *Ethics* (1677; Penguin, intro. Stuart Hampshire, 2005). Drawing on principles derived from Descartes, Hobbes, ancient Stoicism, and medieval Jewish rationalism, Spinoza shaped an original body of ideas that encompassed a definition of the nature of God and the possible control of the passions, leading to virtue and happiness. His eclectic, inventive thought advanced democratic theory and challenged religious doctrines. The Catholic Church placed his work on the *List of Forbidden Books*. The introduction by Hampshire elucidates the complex elements of Spinoza's thought as the backbone of the Enlightenment and suggests its enduring relevance. Spinoza's pivotal role in the international philosophical movement that became the Enlightenment is detailed at length in Jonathan I. Israel, *Radical Enlightenment: Philosophy and the Making of Modernity, 1650–1750* (2002).

Weil, Simone, *The Need for Roots: Prelude to a Declaration of Duties towards Mankind* (1949; trans. Arthur Wills; Routledge, 2002; preface by T. S. Eliot). A mystic and political activist trained as a philosopher, Weil was a pacifist until the fall of France, when she joined the Resistance. She died of tuberculosis in London at age thirty-four. The theme of this posthumous work is the psychological uprootedness plaguing modern society. A balance between rights and obligations, along with honoring the "spirituality of work," was the solution. Weil's followers believe she reached a level of mystical insight that places her among the great religious figures of all time.

Wittgenstein, Ludwig, *Philosophical Investigations* (1953; Wiley-Blackwell, trans. G. E. Anscombe, 2009). Wittgenstein studied under Bertrand Russell, who described him as "passionate, profound, intense, and dominating." His ideas touched several fields, but foremost was his study of logic and the meaning of words, which he believed could best be understood according to their use. In fact, the gist of *Philosophical Investigations* is that many long-standing philosophical problems result from confusion about how language is used. In this, he took the radical step of challenging his own early assumptions about traditional philosophy. In 1999, a survey of philosophers ranked *Investigations* as the most important book of twentieth-century philosophy. In *Ludwig Wittgenstein: The Duty of Genius* (1990), Ray Monk gives a perceptive account of the philosopher's life.

Religion

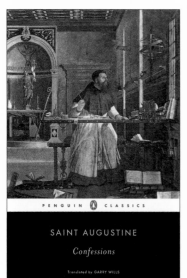

Augustine of Hippo, *Confessions* (A.D. 400; Oxford World's Classics, trans. Henry Chadwick, 2009). Augustine was a Christian theologian and philosopher from the Roman province of Africa whose writings influenced the development of Western Christianity and Western philosophy. Theories of a "just war" can be traced to his ideas. He describes his inner life, much of which shows an obsession with sinfulness. He believed that he had sinned in infancy when crying at his mother's breast. As a young man, he famously prayed, "Give me *chastity* and continence, but not yet." Peter Brown's *Augustine of Hippo: A Biography* (rev. ed., 2000), based on Augustine's writings and those of his contemporaries, describes his life and thought in the context of the late Roman Empire.

Bhagavad Gita (c. 500 B.C.; Three Rivers, trans. Stephen Mitchell, 2002). Forming one section of the epic Mahabharata, the Bhagavad Gita (The Song of the Lord) tells the story of Prince Arjuna and Lord Krishna, his spiritual guide and charioteer, on the eve of a great battle. As the prince seeks to overcome his doubts, Krishna engages him in a philosophical dialogue about duty, life, divinity, and self-mastery. In *Hindu Myths: A Sourcebook Translated from the Sanskrit* (2004), Wendy Doniger collects stories from the Rig Veda and the Mahabharata, among other sources, that recount the exploits of gods such as Vishnu and Shiva, and the avatars Rama and Krishna. Although there are many contradictions in the sources on Hinduism, its greatness as a religion can be found in its idiosyncratic qualities.

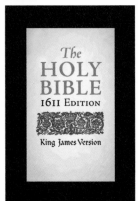

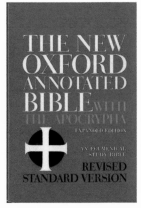

Bible

King James Version (1611). The version of the scriptures that embodied Protestant religious belief and has influenced English prose for 400 years. The source of hundreds of commonplace phrases, for example, "God save the king," "A man after his own heart," "the skin of my teeth," "To everything there is a season," "The race is not to the swift, nor the battle to the strong," "swords into plowshares," and literary titles—*East of Eden, The Little Foxes,* and *Absalom, Absalom,* to pick just three—the King James Version is an essential document for understanding the religious heritage of the English language.

The New Oxford Annotated Bible, 4th ed. (Oxford, 2010). A fundamental work for understanding not only religion but also the literature, history, art, politics, and philosophy of Western culture. A good way to approach this multifarious, complicated work is to start with Genesis, Exodus, Job, and Psalms, all in the Old Testament, and Mark, Matthew, and First Corinthians in the New Testament. Also helpful are the separate translations, with commentaries, of Genesis (1996) and Psalms (2007) made by Robert Alter.

Blavatsky, H. P., *The Secret Doctrine* (1888, TarcherPerigee, ed., Michael Gomes 2016). Helena Petrovna Blavatsky, of Russian origin, became a Buddhist. She believed in reincarnation and claimed to have studied esoteric mysteries in Tibet. In 1875 she founded the Theosophical Society, the purpose of which included the "study and elucidation of Occultism." Her numerous followers in Britain and America believed in her powers to communicate with the dead. The best critical study of her is the *Oxford Dictionary of National Biography* entry by Richard Davenport-Hines, who concludes that she had exceptional creative energy but must be considered a charlatan. Blavatsky's career in the United States is captured in Peter Washington's *Madame Blavatsky's Baboon: A History of the Mystics, Mediums, and Misfits Who Brought Spiritualism to America* (1995).

Bonhoeffer, Dietrich, *Letters and Papers from Prison* (1951; Touchstone, ed. Eberhard Bethge, 1997). Bonhoeffer was a young German pastor and anti-Nazi dissident who openly denounced Hitler's persecution of the Jews. He organized underground religious meetings and worked with the German resistance. In a speech in April 1933, he claimed that it could become necessary for Christians "not just to bandage the victims under the wheel" of injustice, but to jam the spokes of the wheel itself. He was hanged by the Gestapo in the Flossenbürg concentration camp in Bavaria in April 1945 two weeks before its liberation by U.S. troops. In *The Cost of Discipleship* (1937), Bonhoeffer provides an exposition of the Sermon on the Mount that is notable for its distinction between "cheap" and "costly" grace.

Book of Common Prayer (current edition, 1662; Penguin, intro. James Wood, 2012). As archbishop of Canterbury (1533–55), Thomas Cranmer laid out the original liturgical structure of the new Church of England under Henry VIII. Under Edward VI, he wrote and compiled the first two editions of the Book of Common Prayer, a complete liturgy of services and prayers to replace those of the Roman Catholic Church. Cranmer's phrase-making skill was second perhaps only to Shakespeare's. Examples include "peace in our time," "ashes to ashes, dust to dust," "the world, the flesh, and the devil," and "with this ring I thee wed." The historian Diarmaid MacCulloch describes the prayer book as "one of the handful of texts to have decided the future of a world language."

Buber, Martin, *I and Thou* (1923; Touchstone, trans. Walter Kaufmann, 1971). A classic of modern religious thought by one of the major Jewish thinkers of the twentieth century. Buber's basic insight was that human life finds meaning in relationships, with other human beings and with the Eternal Thou, meaning God. Politically, Buber was a Zionist. He left Germany in 1939 and settled in Jerusalem. He supported a bi-national solution in Palestine, believing that the Jews had to work with the Arabs, even at the cost of the Israelis remaining a minority. The goal was an Israeli-Arab regional federation. Buber's life and thought are detailed in Maurice Friedman, *Encounter on the Narrow Ridge: A Life of Martin Buber* (1991), written by Buber's chief expositor in the United States.

Buddhist Scriptures (Penguin Classics, ed. Donald S. Lopez Jr., 2004). Buddhism originated with the teachings of Siddhartha Gautama (6th–5th centuries BC), who acquired the title "Buddha," or "Enlightened One." The religion does not have a central text like the Bible or the Qu'ran. Instead, starting about four centuries after Siddhartha's death, Buddhist works considered sacred were written throughout South and East Asia, in languages such as Pali, Sanskrit, and Japanese. Buddhism teaches that enlightenment begins with the realization that unnecessary desires are the root of unhappiness, and provides instructions for extinguishing these desires and coming to understand the nature of reality. The religion is practiced worldwide by about 500,000,000 people, most of them in Asia.

Calvin, John, *Institutes of the Christian Religion* (1536; Hendrickson, 2007). Written originally by Calvin as an introduction to the Bible, the *Institutes* (the Latin original can also be translated as "instruction") develops the theme of the absolute sovereignty of God in saving the human soul from eternal damnation. Organized according to the Apostle's Creed, the book seeks to provide knowledge of both God and humankind. Calvin's thought, however, went beyond theology: he believed in the rights and freedom of ordinary people. Justification was through faith alone, but nonetheless everyone was obligated to work. Economic success could be seen as a sign of God's grace. This strain of Calvin's thought was one of the foundations of Max Weber's theory about the rise of capitalism.

Gauchet, Marcel, *Disenchantment of the World: A Political History of Religion* (*Le Désenchantement du monde*, 1985; Princeton, trans. Oscar Burge, foreword by Charles Taylor, 1999). Gauchet places religion at the center of the human condition and argues that Western history has been marked by a retreat from religious society. Primeval religion was pervasive, all-encompassing. Monotheistic religion, beginning with prophetic Judaism, was a revolution: God became all-powerful but remote, and people became free. This revolutionary movement accelerated under Christianity, leading to the rise of the political state. Gauchet believes that religion will continue to play a part in shaping Western politics and political conceptions. But in the foreword, Taylor asks a critical question: does it have a place in the future of Western society?

Ignatius of Loyola, *Personal Writings* (c. 1522–55; Penguin, trans. Joseph A. Munitiz and Philip Endean, 1997). The founder of the Jesuit Order, Ignatius was a Basque military officer from Loyola. His *Reminiscences* give an account of his turbulent and intense emotional state of mind at the time of his conversion, when he resolved to commit himself to the austerities of the saints. The *Spiritual Exercises* were written to guide penitents in seeking to discover God's will for their lives. The *Spiritual Diary* records Ignatius's daily encounters with God during a period of personal struggle. His writings reveal a private, gentle, and brave figure who became revered for his kindness and wisdom. William Meissner's *Ignatius of Loyola: The Psychology of a Saint* (1992), written by a Jesuit and psychoanalyst, provides a psychological portrait of its subject.

John of the Cross (Juan de Yepes y Álvarez), *Dark Night of the Soul* (c. 1578; Penguin, 2003). The sixteenth-century Spanish mystic Saint John of the Cross is one of the foremost poets in the Spanish language. While imprisoned in a small cell in a monastery, he wrote the *Spiritual Canticle*, an adaptation of the Song of Solomon. After escaping from his captors, he fell into a state of ecstasy, or "mystical intoxication," and wrote *Dark Night of the Soul* to give guidance to others searching for communion with God. One of the most famous works in Spanish literature, it has endured as a landmark of writing on spiritual growth and Christian mysticism.

Kierkegaard, Søren, *Fear and Trembling* (1843; Penguin Classics, trans. Alastair Hannay, 2003). Kierkegaard elaborates on the biblical account of God commanding Abraham to sacrifice Isaac, his only son, at a place to which God would direct him. In several scenarios, the author imagines what Abraham thought about during their three-day journey and also in the moments leading up to the planned killing. Kierkegaard's analysis of duty and obedience, choice and freedom, marks him as the first existentialist, antedating Jean-Paul Sartre, Albert Camus, and others by almost a century. For an explanation why Kiekegaard is regarded as the most important religious thinker of the modern age, see Dapne Hampson, *Kierkegaard: Exposition and Critique* (2016).

Küng, Hans, *On Being a Christian* (1974; Bloomsbury, trans. Edward Quinn, 2008). Küng, a Swiss Catholic priest and distinguished theologian, holds candid, often controversial views. He rejects the doctrine of papal infallibility, criticizes the Church for sexual abuse, believes that people have the right to end their own lives, and acknowledges that the Christian faith has lost rather than gained credibility. He nonetheless affirms the positive vitality and unique quality of Christianity. His unorthodox convictions, for which the Church banned him from teaching Catholic theology, have attracted the attention of intellectuals, agnostics, atheists, and others who would ordinarily ignore spiritual guidance. For readers wishing a sophisticated vision of Christianity and its robust meaning in relation to Buddhism and Islam, this is the book.

Laozi, *Daodejing* (c. 6th century BC; Oxford 2008). Laozi (Lao-tzu, Lao-tse) was the founder of Taoism, one of the pillars of ancient Chinese thought. It represents a philosophical tradition as well as an organized religion based on humility and piety. Laozi was revered as a deity. The *Daodejing* (*Tao Te Ching*) expresses his ideas through paradoxes that emphasize passivity, quietism, and mysticism. He was a proponent of limited government, to the extent that he denied serving any ruler at any time. The nineteenth-century Russian philosopher Peter Kropotkin believed that he was among the earliest proponents of anarchist thought. Next to the *Bible*, the *Daodejing* is the most widely translated work in world literature. A good guide to the philosopher and his works is Max Kaltenmark, *Lao Tzu and Taoism* (1969).

Lewis, C. S., *The Screwtape Letters* (1942; Harper, annotated ed., 2013). Screwtape, a senior demon, writes to a junior demon about ways to secure the damnation of an average young Englishman. A satirical masterpiece, it explains human foibles in a comic yet serious way, but the demons cannot comprehend God's love for man. They raise questions with inadvertent answers about temptation and repentance, good and evil, and offer guidance on how to live good Christian lives. The spiritual writings of Lewis, a Christian apologist, have attracted a cultlike devotion. Anthony Burgess perhaps best caught one of the reasons for his popularity: he is the "ideal persuader . . . for the good man who would like to be a Christian but finds his intellect getting in the way."

Mather, Cotton, *On Witchcraft* (1692; Dover, 2005). An influential, deeply religious Puritan minister, Mather was convinced that he had been called to serve God and New England. He is remembered mainly for his role in the Salem witch trials of 1692–93, which he supported out of a strong belief in witches and devils. His book includes advice on how to recognize witches and how to resist their temptations. His part in the trials can be read as a warning against mass hysteria—there is a thin line between Mather's conviction and self-deception. A good companion volume is Brian Levack's study *The Witch-Hunt in Early Modern Europe* (1987; 3rd ed., 2006). For a brief biography of Mather, see Rick Kennedy, *The First American Evangelical: A Short Life of Cotton Mather* (2015).

Müller, F. Max, *Introduction to the Science of Religion* (1873). Müller was one of the principal founders of the Western academic field of Indian studies and the discipline of comparative religion. A master of Sanskrit, Arabic, and Persian as well as Greek and Latin, he reconstructed the earliest roots of Sanskrit, which helped explain the development of pagan religions and religious beliefs generally. He became a leading figure in Victorian public life, debating and lecturing on topics such as "What Can India Teach Us?" He never visited India, but was recognized there for his pioneering achievements. The history of Müller's fifty-volume project of translated texts is given in Arie L. Molendijk, *Friedrich Max Müller and the "Sacred Books of the East"* (2016).

Nasr, Vali, *The Shia Revival: How Conflict with Islam Will Shape the Future* (Norton, 2007). The value of this passionately written book is the insight into the layered world and ancient conflict between Shia and Sunnis. The Shia crescent—countries with a Shia-majority population or a strong Shia minority—extends from Lebanon and Syria to Azerbaijan and Iran. Nasr presents a vigorous argument from the Shia perspective, helping explain why the Shia regard themselves as historic underdogs and how they regard the Iranian Revolution of 1979 as an inspirational resurgence.

Paine, Thomas, *The Age of Reason*, part 1 (1794; in *The Thomas Paine Reader*, Penguin, ed. Michael Foot and Isaac Kramnick, 1987). Paine makes a case for Deism, subverting belief in miracles and challenging the divinity of the Bible. In clear, straightforward language, he attacks Christianity as corrupt for its involvement in politics and denounces churches as having been "set up to terrify and enslave mankind." He advocates reason in place of revelation, and intellectual freedom in place of superstition. Paine's presentation of his views to a mass readership in an irreverent and engaging style led the British government to believe he might provoke a revolution. He had earlier come close to doing just that with his pamphlet *Common Sense* (1776), a stirring call for independence for the American colonies.

Qur'an (Oxford World's Classics, trans. M. A. S. Abdel Haleem, 2005). The Qur'an is the holy book of Islam, revealed to the Prophet Muhammad. The religion demands unquestioning submission to the commands of Allah, Arabic for "God." Peace is the first virtue, but warfare is permitted for self-defense or retribution. Many passages in the Qur'an are variations on stories from the Torah and the Bible. The most satisfactory introduction to the Qur'an is Karen Armstrong, *Islam: A Short History* (2000). William H. McNeill, a distinguished historian and unsparing critic, commented: "I found her account of the dedicated following that formed around the prophet Muhammad particularly fresh and powerfully persuasive . . . a valuable corrective to the hostile caricatures of Islam that circulate in the English-speaking world."

Schama, Simon, *The Story of the Jews: Belonging, 1492–1900* (Penguin, 2017). *Belonging* develops the theme of the Jews' search for security. Jews were not trusted as a minority, even less so when they adopted the culture or religion of the majority. The Jews who managed to thrive made themselves sometimes indispensable in trade and finance—but their success was held against them, and they remained outsiders. Schama's felicitous dealing with such themes can be attributed to his talent for finding colorful personalities filled with human contradictions: rogues as well as eccentrics worthy of Dickens. The book ends with a rather gloomy Theodor Herzl hoping for a Jewish homeland in Palestine, and, at the same time, the ever-enduring theme of anti-Semitism in the closing episode of the Dreyfus affair.

Teresa of Avila, *The Life of Saint Teresa of Avila* (c. 1567; Penguin, trans. J. M. Cohen, 1987). Teresa was a sixteenth-century Roman Catholic Spanish mystic. She combined strenuous activity—she founded more than a dozen convents in Spain as well as the order that became the Discalced Carmelites—with fervent contemplation. Some of her mystical experiences lasted up to two years. Famously, she envisioned the piercing of her heart by a spear of divine love, a moment captured in a rapturous sculpture by Bernini. Her autobiography is one of Spain's most widely read classics. Vita Sackville-West compares her life with that of a later Carmelite saint in *The Eagle and the Dove: St. Teresa of Avila and St. Therese of Lisieux* (1943).

Thomas à Kempis, *The Imitation of Christ* (c. 1420; Penguin, ed. and trans. Robert Jeffery, 2013). "Imitation" here means the practice of following the example of Jesus, a fundamental aim of Christian life. Thomas à Kempis was a fifteenth-century Dutch monk who copied the Bible no fewer than four times in order to make it more widely available. *The Imitation of Christ* is usually regarded as the most influential work in Christian literature apart from the Bible, its appeal due to the straightforward language and direct address to the individual. On the other hand, atheists dismiss it out of hand. Frederick Nietzsche once said it was a book he could not bear to hold in his hand because of its "perfume," which was "strictly for Frenchmen—or Wagnerians."

Thomas Aquinas, *Thomas Aquinas: Selected Writings* (Penguin, trans. and ed. Ralph McInerny, 1999). McInerny, who taught philosophy and medieval studies at Notre Dame for more than half a century, introduces the general reader to the thirteenth-century theologian and philosopher Thomas Aquinas. Influenced above all by the rational thought of Aristotle, Aquinas synthesized ancient philosophy and medieval theology. He was also a great systematizer, setting out the four cardinal virtues (prudence, temperance, justice, and fortitude), the three theological virtues (faith, hope, and charity), and the seven deadly sins. McInerny sums up the thought of St. Thomas by emphasizing his belief that wisdom and truth can be reached only through divine revelation. The range and depth of his intellect and faith place him as perhaps the greatest medieval philosopher.

Tillich, Paul, *The Courage to Be* (1952; Yale, 2nd ed., 2000). Tillich was a central figure in the intellectual and religious life of his time. A refugee from Nazi Germany, he taught at the Union Theological Seminary in New York and later at Harvard, where he was popular because of his willingness to engage undergraduates on questions of psychology and philosophy in relation to religion. In *The Courage to Be*, he argues that psychoanalysis and existentialist philosophy can enhance religious or ethical convictions. Here and elsewhere, he persuasively presents the *restraint and reasonableness* of the Christian faith. At a time when discussions of God and faith often led to an undermining of traditional religious beliefs, he seemed to many to be the last major spokesman for a vanishing Christian culture.

Wesley, John, *John Wesley,* ed. Albert C. Outler (Oxford, 1980). Wesley was one of the major figures in eighteenth-century Christianity. What he started as a small group of Oxford students doing charitable works on a set schedule (ridiculed as "Methodism") became a radical off-shoot of the Anglican Church marked by open-air worship services of evangelical passion and female preachers. Methodism proved wildly popular among the poor in Britain and America. Wesley was also an abolitionist, a friend of William Wilberforce. This collection of his writings reveals a logical thinker who expressed his ideas forcefully but not dogmatically. He initially thought that Methodism would help revive the Church of England; his followers believed that he saved England from another civil war and provided hope for those uprooted by the Industrial Revolution.

Anthropology, Economics, Psychology, Sociology

Anthropology

Benedict, Ruth, *Patterns of Culture* (1934; Houghton Mifflin, 1957). Benedict's experience in diverse cultures led her to believe that peoples should be judged by their own values. As an anthropologist, she studied the Zuni Indians in the southwestern United States, the Kwakiutl of the Pacific Northwest, and the Dobu of New Guinea. She concluded that cultural configurations and underlying mental patterns define different cultures. She held a nonjudgmental attitude, believing in the "the relativity of cultural responses." In the *Chrysanthemum and the Sword* (1946), which she wrote during World War II to make Japanese culture comprehensible to American readers, she helped those in the U.S. government and Army understand the place of the emperor in Japanese society.

Boas, Franz, *Anthropology and Modern Life* (1928; Transaction, intro. Herbert S. Lewis, 2003). Boas exposes the fallacy of racial, cultural, or ethnic superiority, and supports the principle of cultural relativism—the view that cultures cannot be ranked as higher or lower, advanced or primitive. His research was later used to refute the Nazis' idea of Aryan supremacy. Boas did not flinch from comparing American discrimination against blacks with European prejudice against Jews. Two of his students, Ruth Benedict and Margaret Mead, achieved worldwide fame by pursuing his belief that encouragement of human differences could enrich society—and that anthropology can improve the human condition. In *The Mind of Primitive Man* (1911), Boas mounted an early challenge to eugenic claims regarding race and intelligence.

Evans-Pritchard, E. E., *Witchcraft, Oracles, and Magic among the Azande* (1937; Oxford, 1976). The Azande, a tribe in southern Sudan, routinely appealed to "witchcraft" in their daily lives. To Europeans, their behavior seemed to reveal the "irrationality of primitive people." But Evans-Pritchard demonstrated that their beliefs were coherent and closely reasoned. He famously disavowed the assumption, common as late as the post-1945 era, that anthropology was a natural science, holding rather that it should be understood as a subject of the humanities closely related to history. As part of his bohemian lifestyle, "E.P." liked to exchange ideas in Oxford pubs as much as in his college, All Souls.

Firth, Raymond, *Elements of Social Organization* (1951; 3rd ed., Routledge, 2005). A social anthropologist at the London School of Economics, Firth, a New Zealander, devoted himself to the study of Polynesian society. Keeping to the general theme that ceremonies and rituals are more important than self-interest, he wrote ten books on the people of Tikopia, a tiny island in the southern Solomons, four miles long with 1,200 inhabitants. His most significant general work deals with social organization, assessing people's economic motives and moral dilemmas. He resisted the jargon of structuralism, remained skeptical of theory, and argued lucidly that the structure of any society is the outcome of continually revised organization based on coordination and agreement. He was still writing books at age 100.

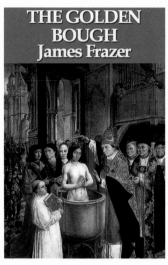

Frazer, James, *The Golden Bough: A Study in Magic and Religion* (12 vols., 1898–1915; one-volume abridgment, Oxford, 2009). Frazer was an anthropologist, often regarded as one of the founders of the discipline. In a comparative study of people's beliefs and superstitions, he argued that man progresses intellectually and psychologically from magic through religion to scientific thought. His work was initially pervasive among anthropologists, Bronislaw Malinowski writing, for example, that he was "bound to the service of Frazerian anthropology." Later anthropologists were exceedingly critical. Yet the concepts of myth and ritual, of secular thought versus Christianity—above all, humanity's upward struggle toward an understanding of itself and the world—had immense literary influence on figures as diverse as Robert Graves, T. S. Eliot, and James Joyce.

Geertz, Clifford, *The Interpretation of Cultures: Selected Essays* (1973; Basic, 2000). Geertz, a cultural anthropologist, began his career in Indonesia and produced detailed studies on cultural and social change. He argues that social issues are larger than themselves—they speak to broader patterns of human interaction and basic meaning in life. For example, in his famous essay "Deep Play: Notes on the Balinese Cockfight," Geertz concludes that cockfighting ultimately embodies the network of familial and village social relationships underlying Balinese life. Cultural understanding makes comprehensible patterns and concepts that connect in the humanities, the social sciences, and religion as well as anthropology. In *Islam Observed: Religious Development in Morocco and Indonesia* (1968), Geertz traces the deep differences underlying the practice, in two widely separated countries, of what is nominally the same creed.

Kenyatta, Jomo, *Facing Mount Kenya* (1938; Vintage, 1962). Kenyatta is generally known as the charismatic African nationalist who was imprisoned by the British for nearly a decade yet afterward presided over Kenya's transition to independence in 1963 and became the country's first president. His autobiographical book is mainly anthropological, reflecting his training at the London School of Economics under Bronislaw Malinowski. He examines in detail the life of the Kikuyu tribe before the coming of white settlers, who later believed, erroneously, that

Kenyatta commanded the Mau Mau revolt, calling him the "leader to darkness and death." In fact, he became the symbol of Kenyan nationalism and unity, presiding over the new state with a spirit of generosity and reconciliation up to his death in 1978.

Lévi-Strauss, Claude, *Tristes Tropiques* (1955; Penguin, trans. John Weightman and Doreen Weightman, 2012). On the basis of wide-ranging visits to the Amazonian rain forest in the late 1930s, Lévi-Strauss argued that the "savage" mind was as sophisticated as the "civilized" mind of Western societies. His work, which dealt with common aspects of humanity, served as the foundation of a school of thought in which universal elements or structures give shape to distinct cultures. He wrote *Tristes Tropiques* in the mid-1950s in an outburst against "Europe's rape of the tropics." He eventually achieved the reputation, in a phrase often used to describe him, of "the father of modern anthropology."

Malinowski, Bronislaw, *Sex and Repression in Savage Society* (1927; Routledge, 2001). Malinowski played a critical part in the development of anthropology, especially ethnography, the scientific description of human customs. During World War I, he did fieldwork in the Trobriand Islands, off the coast of New Guinea. Living among the people and speaking their language, he studied sexuality, family dynamics, and similar matters in relation to power. His research placed him in fruitful conflict with the theory of psychoanalysis. Malinowski denied that the Oedipus complex was universal, and in the 1920s he referred to analysis as "a popular craze of the day." He concluded on the basis of his extensive work in the Trobriands that *power*, not sex, was the source of conflict in human society.

Mead, Margaret, *Coming of Age in Samoa: A Psychological Study of Primitive Youth for Western Culture* (1928; Harper, 2001). In 1923, Mead began her research in Samoa. Her study of girls in three villages showed that the experience of adolescence depends on one's cultural upbringing. Her findings advanced the understanding of child rearing, not least for concluding that adolescence for American girls need not be a time of stress. Mead's *Culture and Commitment: A Study of the Generation Gap* (1970) argued that younger Americans of the 1960s dealt better with a changing world than had their parents—thus endearing her to youthful protesters and the counterculture. Jane Howard, *Margaret Mead: A Life* (1989), is a journalistic account drawing on extensive interviews, lively and valuable as a document of record.

Taussig, Michael, *Shamanism, Colonialism, and the Wild Man: A Study in Terror and Healing* (1987; Chicago, 1997). Taussig provides an original though controversial account of the exploitation of the Putumayo River region on the upper Amazon by British "rubber barons" in the late nineteenth and early twentieth centuries. The indigenous inhabitants, or Indians, were forced to extract rubber under a system of brutal terror much like the one used in King Leopold's Congo. Economically, the system was inefficient in the extreme; the British justified torturing the Putumayo by dehumanizing them as cannibalistic savages. Taussig has degrees in medicine and anthropology; his work is significant among other reasons because it polarizes his fellow anthropologists, one of whom describes Taussig's recondite writing as being "like Alan Ginsberg's on a bad day."

Tilak, Bal Gangadhar, *The Arctic Home in the Vedas* (1903; Arktos, 2011). Tilak was the most widely known Indian nationalist before Gandhi, referred to by the British as "the father of Indian unrest." A Sanskritist and mathematician, he drew on astronomical, geological, and archaeological evidence to prove that the ancient scriptures known as the Vedas (the oldest Hindu texts) were written by Aryan bards in the Arctic. An ice age drove the Aryans south to Eurasia and ultimately to India. Tilak, an extreme Hindu nationalist, was among the first to propose that Hindi should be the sole language of India. Tilak's political career is described in D. V. Tahmankar, *Lokmanya Tilak: Father of Indian Unrest and Maker of Modern India* (1956).

Economics

Frank, Andre Gunder, *Capitalism and Underdevelopment in Latin America: Historical Studies of Chile and Brazil* (1967; rev. ed., Monthly Review Press, 1969). A controversial, uncompromising economist, Frank was best known for his contribution to dependency theory, which holds that poor states are impoverished because of exploitation by rich states. In this book, his most influential work, he argues that the polarizing consequences of exploitation in Latin America and elsewhere gave rise to nationalist, ethnic, and religious fundamentalist movements that would eventually undermine capitalist culture and control. He was an indefatigable activist and writer, producing 40 books and 1,000 other publications. Despite his negative analysis, Frank believed that change for the better was possible. His best work, *Reorient* (1998), distills his views and argues that the disadvantaged will continue to resist.

Friedman, Milton, *Capitalism and Freedom* (1962; Chicago, 2002). Friedman received the Nobel Prize in Economics in 1976. His collaborations with Anna Jacobson Schwartz, *A Monetary History of the United States* (1963) and two subsequent volumes, are often cited as some of the most important works on economics in the twentieth century, surpassed only by John Maynard Keynes's *General Theory* (1936). *Capitalism and Freedom*, aimed, in his own phrase, at the "educated layperson," makes his more technical work accessible in clear and readable language. His general thesis is that capitalism is a necessary condition for a high degree of personal freedom. An example of his ability to express complex ideas colloquially is his use of the adage "There ain't no such thing as a free lunch."

Galbraith, John Kenneth, *The Affluent Society* (1958; Mariner, 1998). Galbraith, one of the most famous and influential economists of his generation, in the late 1950s criticized the large U.S. national defense budget while pointing out the appalling neglect of schools, roads, and the environment. His work now seems prophetic in calling attention to damaging effects of the huge disparities in wealth between the rich and the poor. He acknowledged as critical to his social and economic thought the influence of Keynes, Veblen, and Schumpeter.

George, Henry, *Progress and Poverty* (1879; Schalkenbach Foundation, 1997). A tax theorist who acquired a cultlike following, George upheld the principle of "land value taxation." He believed that economic growth would bring "poverty for the many and wealth for the fortunate few"—unless a tax was levied on landowners. Technological and social advances increase the value of land, particularly in cities, even for landowners who contributed nothing to the improvements. Government should tax land to prevent owners from profiting by its mere possession. Taxing the unearned income of land is a proposition endorsed by economists from Adam Smith to Milton Friedman—but it is Henry George's name that symbolizes it. One of his followers invented the game of Monopoly to demonstrate the evils of untaxed land.

Hayek, F. A., *The Road to Serfdom* (1944; Chicago, intro. Milton Friedman, 1994). Writing toward the end of World War II, Hayek warned that the socialist idea of empowering government with increasing economic control would inevitably lead to regimes similar to Nazi Germany and Fascist Italy. In 1974, he received the Nobel Prize in Economics for his penetrating analysis of the interdependence of economic, social, and institutional phenomena. Both George Orwell and Margaret Thatcher believed that *The Road to Serfdom* should be compulsory reading, the latter at one point in a Cabinet meeting pounding the table while holding up a copy and proclaiming, "This is what we believe!" A critical assessment of the man and his work can be found in Andrew Gamble, *Hayek: The Iron Cage of Liberty* (2013).

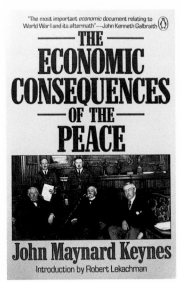

Keynes, John Maynard, *The Economic Consequences of the Peace* (1919; Skyhorse, intro. Paul Volcker, 2007). Keynes was a member of the British delegation at the Paris Peace Conference, which negotiated the treaties after World War I. In this clear-sighted analysis, he warns that the draconian terms imposed on Germany would destroy world peace and prosperity. His prediction was proved true by the rise of Nazism little over a decade later. Keynes's *General Theory of Employment, Interest, and Money* (1936), his magnum opus, challenged long-held assumptions of classical economics, which, he argued, applied only under particular conditions. The work shaped the modern study of macroeconomics. The standard biography is by Robert Skidelsky, published in three volumes but condensed into one: *John Maynard Keynes, 1883–1946* (2004).

Malthus, Thomas Robert, *An Essay on the Principle of Population* (1798; Cambridge, 1992). Malthus's thought has often been reduced to caricature, but in fact he caught the seemingly intractable tension between population growth and the food supply. At the time, speculation on the subject was controversial—and even sensational when linked with prostitution, contraception, and sexual diseases as ways to keep population in check. (War and famine were also effective in this regard.) He was farsighted regarding Europe's expansion into other parts of the world, projecting four possible outcomes for indigenous peoples: assimilation with Europeans; voluntary mass migration; forced exile; and extermination. Alison Bashford and Joyce

E. Chaplin, T*he New Worlds of Thomas Robert Malthus* (2016), makes clear that Malthus deserves fresh thought in a global context.

Piketty, Thomas, *The Economics of Inequality* (1997; Harvard, 2015). In this controversial book, Piketty draws on the patterns of economic development in Europe and the United States to explain the historical context of inequality. He shows how unions have limited inequality in France, which helps explain broader differences between the economies of the United States and Europe. The heart of the controversy concerns the redistribution of income: some believe that it would lead to catastrophe, and others, like Piketty, claim that redistribution is needed for social justice and can be achieved without inflicting widespread damage. Piketty's most recent book, *Capital in the Twenty-first Century* (2014), uses two centuries of data to show how ever-rising levels of economic inequality—currently, in Paul Krugman's words, "back to 'Great Gatsby' levels"—threaten democracy.

Ricardo, David, *Principles of Political Economy and Taxation* (1817; Dover, 2004). During his life, Ricardo stood second only to Adam Smith as an economist. He was more zealous and uncompromising than Smith in advocating both free trade, which would make Britain the "happiest country in the world," and market capitalism with minimal government interference. He advanced the proposition of "comparative advantage," by which a country could benefit from trade despite having a disadvantage in the production of commodities. Ricardo's influence continued into the twentieth century, though he did not lack critics, including Joseph Schumpeter, who denounced the "Ricardian vice" of applying simple economic models to complex questions. Terry Peach, *Interpreting Ricardo* (1993), explicates the economist's thought by looking closely at his writings and taking account of his objectives.

Schumacher, E. F., *Small Is Beautiful* (1973; Harper, 2010). Schumacher was an economist who protested against ever-larger corporations and globalization. A polemic against industry's brutality and the despoiling of the environment, the book puts forward practical solutions such as farmers' markets and local cafes: people matter. The spiritual dimension of the book is informed by Buddhism and, especially, the teachings of Gandhi. The book claims that industrial and commercial behemoths can be foiled by buying locally and being on guard against the depletion of resources. In 2012, Schumacher's daughter-in-law, who cofounded several organizations linked with his work, produced *Small Is Beautiful in the 21st Century*, which carries forward Schumacher's ideas in the fields of ethics, ecology, and the environment. "Small is Beautiful" remains an undiminished rallying call.

Schumpeter, Joseph A., *Capitalism, Socialism, and Democracy* (1942; Routledge, 2006). Schumpeter's hero is the entrepreneur. He deals with recurrent market challenges through innovative reinvestment, a process Schumpeter calls *creative destruction*. Perhaps surprisingly, then, Schumpeter predicts that capitalism will inevitably be succeeded by socialism as intellectual elites in advanced democracies advocate for increasing restrictions on business. He could not have foreseen the disruptive economic forces unleashed by the digital revolution. In *"Imperialism" and "Social Classes"* (1951), a study of empire, Schumpeter emphasizes the irrational element in motivation: expansion for the sake of expansion, war for the sake of war. Thomas K. McCraw's *Prophet of Innovation: Joseph Schumpeter and Creative Destruction* (2007) depicts the eventful life of the economist, who constantly struggled to escape the shadow of his rival John Maynard Keynes.

Sen, Amartya, *Poverty and Famines: An Essay on Entitlement and Deprivation* (1981; Oxford, 1983). As a nine-year-old, Sen witnessed the Bengal famine of 1943, the focus of the book. Three million people perished. There was an adequate food supply, but landless laborers and low-skilled urban workers did not have the means to buy food. British military requirements in the war took precedence. Consequently, on a massive scale, there was panic buying, hoarding, and price gouging. The complex concentration on a single crisis reveals Sen's use of economics, sociology, and political theory to conceptualize poverty. His research has shown that nearly all famines of the twentieth and twenty-first centuries were man-made—not due to shortages of food. For this work, he was awarded the Nobel Prize in Economics in 1998.

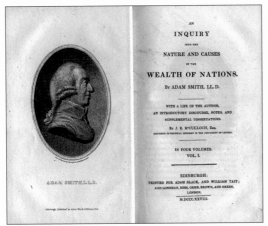

Smith, Adam, *The Wealth of Nations* (1776; Hackett, abridged, 1993). The fundamental work on the free market holds that an unobservable market force—the "invisible hand"—brings about equilibrium in the market between demand and supply. Self-interest, expressed through the workings of capitalism, is the engine of a productive society. And although it is money that makes modern economies run smoothly, Smith worried that people would become driven to acquire money itself, rather than put it to good use. Donald Winch, *Adam Smith's Politics* (2010), is a clear, and concise account that brings together the strands of Smith's thought as he himself viewed them at the time. It comments also on Smith's other major work, *The Theory of Moral Sentiments* (1759).

Tawney, R. H., *Religion and the Rise of Capitalism* (1926; Verso, 2015). The economic historian's best-known work traces the ravenous and predatory ascendancy of capitalism from medieval times, assessing the tension between religion and economic activity. Arguing that the Protestant Reformation led to the elevation of the pursuit of wealth over Christian morality, the book calls for social equality in the context of distrust of the state and the need to uphold ethical standards. The historian A. L. Rowse believed that "Tawney exercised the widest influence of any historian of his time." For a good biography of Tawney, see Lawrence Goldman, *The Life of R. H. Tawney: Socialism and History* (2014).

Psychology
Adorno, Theodor, Else Frenkel-Brunswik, Daniel Levinson, and Nevitt Sanford, *The Authoritarian Personality* (1950; Norton, 1993). A philosopher and sociologist—as well as a classically

trained pianist—Adorno was known for his critique of fascism and his philosophy of aesthetics. The argument of *Authoritarian Personality* is best expressed in his own words: "Psychological dispositions do not actually cause fascism; rather, fascism defines a psychological area which can be successfully exploited by the forces which promote it for entirely non-psychological reasons of self-interest." In the 1960s, Adorno publicly protested the war in Vietnam, which, he said, proved the continued existence of the "world of torture that had begun in Auschwitz." For an explication of Adorno's major ideas, see Martin Jay, *Adorno* (1984).

Erikson, Erik, *Young Man Luther: A Study in Psychoanalysis and History* (1958; Norton, 1993). A developmental psychologist and a psychiatrist, Erikson aimed to make the heroic Luther and his rebellion against the church comprehensible by studying Luther's identity crisis—Erikson originated the concept. As a corollary, the shattering schism brought on by the Reformation signified a comparable identity crisis for the church. In *Gandhi's Truth: On the Origins of Militant Nonviolence* (1969), Erikson attempts to understand the psychological reasons for Gandhi's rebellion and his success in mobilizing the Indian people both spiritually and politically.

Frankl, Viktor, *Man's Search for Meaning* (1946; Beacon, trans. Ilse Lasch, 1959). Frankl, a Jewish Austrian psychiatrist, was interned in four Nazi concentration camps: Theresienstadt, Auschwitz, Kaufering, and Türkheim. By closely observing his own reactions and those of other prisoners to conditions in the camps and to life outside after their release, he developed a theory of psychology that puts the quest for meaning—rather than the search for pleasure, as Freud believed—at the center of human existence. Those who fared best held on to hope and an experience of love: "A man who has nothing left in this world still may know bliss, be it only for a brief moment, in the contemplation of his beloved." He concluded that life is always meaningful, even in suffering.

Freud, Sigmund, *New Introductory Lectures on Psycho-Analysis* (1933; Norton, trans. James Strachey, intro. Peter Gay, 1990). A clear and readable summary of Freud's mature theory of dreams, anxiety, and personality dynamics. Whether or not one finds Freud's ideas psychologically plausible, they have unquestionably had a profound influence on our general culture. The introduction by Gay provides historical and biographical perspectives for Freud's work. Freud deals with wish fulfillment and the unconscious in *The Interpretation of Dreams* (1899), which distinguishes between the manifest (overt) and latent (hidden) content of dreams. The book takes dream symbolism seriously, treating it often as a form of self-censorship of disturbing dream content.

Fromm, Erich, *Escape from Freedom* (1941; Routledge, 2001). A German American psychoanalyst and social philosopher, Fromm delved deeply into the problems presented by the increased freedom millions of people experienced in the twentieth century. In *Escape from Freedom*, his seminal work, he argues that the experience of radical freedom can lead to feelings of hopelessness, which people try to alleviate by turning to conformity, authoritarianism, or destructiveness—as in Nazism, for example. Authenticity—the discovery of one's moral compass and individuality—is the antidote. In the 1960s Fromm's work acquired a nearly cultlike following in the counterculture as a justification for radical nonconformity. Fromm's most popular book, *The Art of Loving* (1956), offers a concept of love contrary to notions of romance or sentimentality.

Hoffer, Eric, *The True Believer: Thoughts on the Nature of Mass Movements* (1951; Harper, 2010). Hoffer was a migrant worker in California who felt at one with the Okies as well as drifters in the slums of Los Angeles. Although lacking a formal education, he borrowed books from public libraries and read obsessively. After the attack on Pearl Harbor, he worked on the waterfront and became known as the "Longshoreman Philosopher." *The True Believer* has penetrating insights into human nature and fanaticism, both religious and political. People join mass movements when they feel their lives are worthless; they become attracted by the promise of radical change. Such was Hoffer's aphoristic style and intuitive understanding that he caught the attention of Presidents Eisenhower and Johnson and received the Presidential Medal of Honor in 1983.

Jung, C. G., *Psychology of the Unconscious: A Study of the Transformations and Symbolism of the Libido* (1912; Princeton, trans. Beatrice Hinkle, 2001). Jung believed that the aim of psychotherapy was to help people come to grips with basic emotions such as fear and anxiety. In this book, he conceives of libido as psychic rather than sexual energy, marking a break with Freudian orthodoxy. Via libido, each person undertakes a heroic journey out of the unconscious, for self-definition, and then back into it, for renewal. In consciousness, this struggle takes symbolic form, often mythological in character. Jung's self-analysis can be found in *Memories, Dreams, Reflections* (1962), written at the end of his life. The historian Peter Gay commented, "It is more revealing than the author meant it to be."

Madariaga, Salvador de, *Englishmen, Frenchmen, Spaniards: An Essay in Comparative Psychology* (1928, preface by Alfred Zimmern; Hill and Wang, 2nd ed., 1969). Educated in France and Spain and fluent in English, Madariaga was a League of Nations official who watched the English and French sort out their differences on disarmament in Geneva. With broad cultural and intellectual knowledge as well as acute observation and intuition, he describes the English as *people of action*, the French as *people of thought*, and the Spanish as *people of passion*. In *The League of Nations and the Rule of Law* (1936), Alfred Zimmern proposes that the witty differences described by Madariaga collectively reveal a concern for idealism and power.

Rieff, Philip, *Freud: The Mind of the Moralist* (1959; Chicago, 3rd ed., 1979). Rieff was a sociologist and cultural critic who was once married to the writer Susan Sontag—she is frequently described by critics as the silent coauthor of the book, though Rieff in the acknowledgments thanks "Susan Rieff" merely for her assistance. Rieff sees Freud as a melancholy realist, a thinker in the line of Montaigne, Burton, and Hobbes, and sets the ethical assumptions of his "compulsive morality" in the intellectual and cultural circumstances of his time. The book argues that Freud's overall belief was that people should bear up and make the best of life, even in dismal conditions. He attempted to ease suffering through therapy and at least sometimes helped the anxious and insecure accept their unhappy fates.

Sociology

Comte, Auguste, *Auguste Comte and Positivism: The Essential Writings* (1819–54; Routledge, ed. Gertrud Lenzer, 1998). Comte set out to discover a set of ideas that might help correct the excesses of the French Revolution. He believed that there were scientific—quantifiable, correctable—principles of human society. This sociological theory became known as positivism, and Comte is credited as its founder. Comte was also a philosopher of science, a calendar reformer, and a proponent of the "religion of humanity." He maintained a close friendship with John Stuart Mill, who approved of Comte's positivism but not his secular religious ideas. Ironically, Comte came to doubt whether positivism would help regenerate, or indeed have any bearing on, human society.

Dahrendorf, Ralf, *LSE: A History of the London School of Economics and Political Science, 1895–1995* (Oxford, 1995). Dahrendorf was a German sociologist who in 1995 became director of the LSE for a decade. His institutional history traces its founding by the socialist and economist Sidney Webb in 1895 to its development into an academic body rivaling and in some ways surpassing Oxford and Cambridge. It is rich in personality, for example, William Beveridge, the school's director (1919–37), who defined its purpose as "a study of man in society" and persuaded the Rockefeller Foundation to support a quarter of its expenditure. Dahrendorf's volume is equally important as a history of the social sciences.

Durkheim, Émile, *On Suicide* (1897; Penguin, trans. Robin Buss, intro. Richard Sennett, 2007). Durkheim, a late nineteenth-century French sociologist, is often regarded as one of the founders of the discipline. He argues that there are four main kinds of suicide, which is usually an act of despair: *egotistical* suicide, which reflects a sense of not belonging, meaninglessness, and depression; *altruistic* suicide, as in a soldier's willingness to risk his life for his country or comrades; *anomic* or *breakdown* or *uprooted* suicide, as in a response to financial collapse; and *fatalistic* suicide, as when a prisoner gives in to hopelessness in the face of abuse and brutality. A book as relevant now as when it was written.

Foucault, Michel, *Discipline and Punish: The Birth of the Prison* (1975; Pantheon, trans. Alan Sheridan, 1977). Foucault examines torture and execution in eighteenth-century France, arguing that they must be seen in the context of social and political control. In the nineteenth century, such control expanded, in "gentler" form, in schools, factories, and hospitals in order to create a "docile" public. Social scientists and, especially, historians have challenged his evidence and his interpretations, but Foucault presents a sophisticated sociological argument of overall control by the police and other arms of government. Social and political elites manipulate public opinion and persecute outsider groups such as homosexuals and the mentally ill. Foucault's exploration of the themes of sex and violence help explain the book's passion and radical appeal.

Glazer, Nathan, and Daniel P. Moynihan, *Beyond the Melting Pot: The Negroes, Puerto Ricans, Jews, Italians, and Irish of New York City* (1963; 2nd ed., MIT Press, 1970). The Anglo-Jewish writer Israel Zangwill coined the term "melting pot" in 1908 to describe American society. A half century later, Glazer and Moynihan argued that the "melting pot" is a false conception. In New York City, the children of Irish, Italian, and Jewish immigrants had persistent identities, as did middle-class blacks and the economically depressed Puerto Ricans. Glazer and Moynihan concluded that complete assimilation simply does not happen. Discriminated against economically and socially, ethnic groups advanced the status and fortune of their own members, which in turn fostered ethnic loyalty and economic pride.

Manent, Pierre, *The City of Man* (1994; Princeton, trans. Marc A. LePain, 1998). Manent is a witty disciple of Raymond Aron with a reputation as a Voltaire in public and intellectual affairs. It is Augustine, however, who hovers over *The City of Man*, a thoroughgoing assault on the failures of modernity. Manent leaves no doubt of the outcome of a contest between the City of God and the City of Man. Western society has descended into rootlessness and multiculturalism, and has even lost the sense of what it means to be human. Manent traces a decline in human agency and a gradual divorce from the religious traditions that previously anchored society in the struggle against impersonal forces. Despite this bleak analysis, Manent has robust hope for the future.

Marcuse, Herbert, *One-Dimensional Man: Studies in the Ideology of Advanced Industrial Society* (1964; 2nd ed., Beacon, 1991). Marcuse inspired radical and political activists in the 1960s and 1970s, becoming known as the "father of the New Left in the United States." He argued that democratic societies can impose "totalitarian" control and that capitalism alienates and dehumanizes the working class, "who find their soul in their automobile, hi-fi set, split-level home, kitchen equipment"—consumerism as a form of social manipulation. His critical account of the "one-dimensional" obsession with material objects advanced the earlier arguments of David Riesman in *The Lonely Crowd* (1950).

Mills, C. Wright, *The Power Elite* (1956; Oxford, afterword by Alan Wolfe, 2000). Mills identifies three main sources of power in the United States—large corporations, the federal government, and the military—and traces the movement of leaders (many of them educated at Ivy League schools, whereas Mills attended the University of Texas) and influence from one to the other. These enormous bureaucracies and their activities become largely self-perpetuating. Mills's *White Collar: The American Middle Classes* (1951) looks at the class of workers who keep the institutions of the power elite functioning.

Moore, Barrington, Jr., *Social Origins of Dictatorship and Democracy: Lord and Peasant in the Making of the Modern World* (1966; Beacon, 1993). Moore's aim is to explain the paths that lead from agrarian societies to modern industrial ones. The principal cases are Germany and Japan, which exemplify the *capitalist reactionary route*; Russia and China, the *communist route*; and England, France, and the United States, the *capitalist democratic route*. The conditions for the development of modern democracies can be boiled down to, in Moore's phrase, "no bourgeois, no democracy." Moore's work is a bold and rewarding inquiry of vast magnitude. His overarching question cuts through the complexity of the subject: which historical circumstances favor, and which inhibit, the making of modern societies that are decent and worth living in?

Parkinson, C. Northcote, *Parkinson's Law: Or the Pursuit of Progress* (1955; Penguin, 1986). The law states, "Work expands to fill the time available for its completion." Parkinson, an historian who taught in Malaya, intended his observation as wry criticism of bureaucracy. He later devised a second, corollary law, "Expenditure rises to meet income," a jibe at government functionaries who would expand their ranks indefinitely as long as taxes could be raised. A related observation was put forward by Laurence J. Peter in *The Peter Principle: Why Things Always Go Wrong* (1969; Harper, 2010), namely, that people rise to the level of their incompetence—for example, an excellent military officer is promoted to a senior position in the executive branch and turns out to be a disaster.

Parsons, Talcott, *The Structure of Social Action* (1937; Free Press, 1967). Parsons was severely criticized in his own time for his ponderous and excessively abstract style, but there can be no doubt that he was one of the great social scientists of the twentieth century. *Social Action* is his most famous work. Often described as a "charter for sociology," it was written at Harvard in the 1930s. Synthesizing works by Max Weber and Emile Durkheim, among others, his social action theory attacked the behaviorists, who, in his view, reduced human life to biological and material forces. Parsons believed that culture was an independent variable that must be part of a systematic theory of social institutions. Uta Gerhardt, *Talcott Parsons: An Intellectual Biography* (2002), is a useful guide to his thought.

Reed, John Shelton, *The Enduring South: Subcultural Persistence in Mass Society* (1972; North Carolina, 1986). Reed, a sociologist, is an authority on the American South who has been described as the "H. L. Mencken of Dixie." Challenging conventional views of a South homogenized by strip malls, chain restaurants, glass-towered cities, and decreasing racial tension, he argues that southerners are America's only genuine ethnic group, bound together, as always, by culture as much as geography. Foodways, religion, music, and speech contribute to this distinctiveness. Though the image of the South is no longer a "whiskey soaked and hell bound" landscape of Jim Crow and Bull Connor, it is still indisputably a place unto itself, apart from the rest of the country.

Riesman, David, Nathan Glazer, and Reuel Denney, *The Lonely Crowd: A Study of the Changing American Character* (1950; Yale, abridged and rev. ed., 2001). The classic analysis of the movement in American society from strict adherence to traditional roles and ideals to the ascendance of individual, "inner-directed" motives as guides for living. This change was accompanied by an intense awareness of how one's peers lived and how best to emulate them—which, somewhat paradoxically, led to a reduction in personal autonomy. Daniel Bell's *The End of Ideology: On the Exhaustion of Political Ideas in the Fifties* (1960; rev. ed., 2000) tracks the collapse of grand humanistic political philosophies and the rise of narrow, technocratic regimes; the revised edition includes an essay on global politics after the fall of communism.

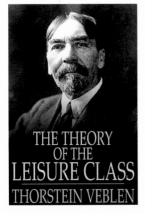

Veblen, Thorstein, *Theory of the Leisure Class* (1899; Oxford World's Classics, 2009). Veblen, a sociologist and economist, scathingly denounced America's affluent society in the Gilded Age of the late nineteenth century. John Kenneth Galbraith once described him as not only a leading economist but also a witty, incisive critic of capitalism. To describe the behavior of wealthy Americans, Veblen coined the terms "conspicuous consumption" and "conspicuous leisure." These are strategies that the upper classes use to compete for prestige, and according to Veblen, they not only add nothing productive to the economy, but also are un-American, in that they run contrary to the country's creed of individualism. In fact, he saw them as holdovers from Europe's barbarian and aristocratic past. Such activities are irrational and often fail to bring happiness.

Wallerstein, Immanuel, *The Uncertainties of Knowledge* (2004; Temple, 2004). Widely regarded as having rejuvenated the discipline of historical sociology, Wallerstein believes that academic fields such as anthropology, economics, and political science are circumscribed by "culture-bound" values. *Uncertainties* pursues that concept and gives insight into the work of a prodigious scholar who brings humility as well as erudition to the search for an understanding of ongoing transformations of human society. In other works, especially *The Decline of American Power* (2003), he argues that the dominance of the United States in world affairs has faded since the war in Vietnam and that the American response to terrorist attacks will diminish it further. In the view of the historian William H. McNeill, Wallerstein may well prove to be "a visionary prophet."

Weber, Max, *The Protestant Ethic and the Spirit of Capitalism* (1905; Dover, trans. Talcott Parsons, intro. R. H. Tawney, 2003). Weber, one of the founders of sociology, held that capitalistic drive and devotion to one's craft were inherent in Protestant, particularly Calvinist, religious values. Success in business was a cherished sign of God's favor, yet Weber also explained capitalism as a rational pursuit of economic gain. Paradoxically,

according to Weber, the triumph of capitalism contributed to the "disenchantment" of the world, including a widespread loss of religious belief. His phrase "the spirit of capitalism" refers to a set of values, the spirit of hard work and progress. The life of the sociologist is told in Joachim Radkau, *Max Weber: A Biography* (2009).

Williams, Raymond, *Keywords: A Vocabulary of Culture and Society* (1976; Oxford, new ed., 2015). Pursuing the theme of culture and society, Williams helped lay the foundation of cultural studies in the 1950s and remained central to the field up to the time of his death in 1988. He objected to academic departmentalization and elucidated the interconnection between education, institutions, and ideas, not only in lectures in Cambridge but also in weekly columns in the *Guardian*. *Keywords* examines concepts embodied in words such as *anarchism, bourgeois, culture, hegemony,* and *sex*. He was also influential beyond academia, known for his steadfast purpose, integrity, and generosity of spirit. In *Culture and Society, 1780–1850* (1958), Williams surveys English literature since the time of Edmund Burke to examine how economic life affects imagination.

Politics

Anderson, Benedict, *Imagined Communities: Reflections on the Origin and Spread of Nationalism* (1983; Verso, 2006). Anderson traces the idea of the nation-state to the French Revolution in 1789 and later developments in the West. A nation is "imagined" when a people regard themselves as a community, usually one sharing a common language and cultural traditions, and eventually limit their borders and possess sovereignty. For example, League of Nations delegates from the former Austro-Hungarian, German, Ottoman, and Russian Empires presented themselves as national representatives rather than imperial ones. Ideas about the nation-state were transmitted to Asia and Africa through colonization. Nationalism has thus shaped the modern world. Anderson's *Java in a Time of Revolution: Occupation and Resistance, 1944–1946* (1972) is one of his distinguished works on Indonesia.

Angell, Norman, *The Great Illusion: A Study of the Relation of Military Power to National Advantage* (1909). Angell believed it erroneous to think that war and conquest would lead to security and prosperity. In later editions of *The Great Illusion,* he pursed the theme of collective defense while always maintaining the proposition that war was futile. He was awarded the Nobel Peace Prize in 1933. He thought that Britain, France, and the eastern European countries could bind themselves together to prevent military aggression by Hitler. *The Great Illusion* sold over a million copies and was translated into twenty-five languages. J. D. B. Miller's *Norman Angell and the Futility of War: Peace and the Public Mind* (1990) is a perceptive and searching work by one of Australia's leading scholars.

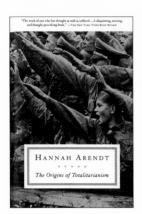

Arendt, Hannah, *The Origins of Totalitarianism* (1951; Houghton Mifflin Harcourt, 1973). The power of Arendt's concept is that totalitarianism exerts control over entire societies, holding them in fear of arbitrary arrest, exile, torture, and murder. She argues that state power in Germany and the Soviet Union derived from imperialism. Her book can be read as a classic of the Cold War inquiring into the origins and nature of Hitler's anti-Semitism and Stalin's ongoing oppression; but in retrospect, the Nazi and Soviet regimes were less totalitarian than authoritarian, rackety as well as oppressive. Arendt's *Eichmann in Jerusalem* (1963) deals with the trial of the captured Nazi war criminal, in which she coined the phrase the "banality of evil." Elisabeth Young-Bruehl's *Why Arendt Matters* (2009) concisely explicates Arendt's principal ideas.

Bagehot, Walter, *The English Constitution* (1867; Oxford, 2001). Bagehot, a journalist with an independent and analytical mind, inquired into the underlying realities of English society. The dignified aspect dealt mainly with the monarchy and its function of keeping the public focused on ceremonial functions. The other part was the efficient, which enabled the House of Commons to appoint a Cabinet to rule without excessive interference from an uneducated public. Bagehot's celebrated work laid the basis for comparisons between parliamentary and presidential types of government. Another of his enduring legacies is the weekly newsmagazine *The Economist,* which he edited for the last seventeen years of his life, 1860–77. Ferdinand Mount's *The British Constitution Now: Recovery or Decline?* (1992) offers an updated look at the points raised by Bagehot.

Bodin, Jean, *On Sovereignty* (excerpted from *The Six Books of the Republic,* 1576; Cambridge, 1992). Bodin represents a landmark in the concept of sovereignty. Writing against the background of religious conflict in sixteenth-century France, he holds that the power of the king is supreme: "The sovereign state is only accountable to God." The state does not depend for its validity on the consent of its subjects; its power is absolute. The concept of absolutism was debated in England as well as France, but the evolution of French thought after Bodin helps explain political life in the era between Louis XIV in the seventeenth century and the French Revolution at the end of the eighteenth. Bodin believed that only passive resistance to authority was justified.

Brown, Archie, *The Myth of the Strong Leader: Political Leadership in the Modern Age* (2014; Vintage, 2015). Brown is well known as an authority on Russia, the author of books on perestroika and the role of Mikhail Gorbachev in the transformation of the Soviet system and the ending of the Cold War. In *The Myth of the Strong Leader,* he combines conceptual analysis with telling descriptions of a diverse range of leaders: Stalin, Hitler, Roosevelt, Churchill, Mao, Castro, LBJ, and Mandela. The book reaches a crescendo in relating the critical interaction between Mikhail Gorbachev and Margaret Thatcher. It is a lucid guide to distinctive kinds of political leadership and provides insight into sources of military and economic power.

Bull, Hedley, *The Anarchical Society: A Study of Order in International Politics* (1977; 3rd ed., Columbia, 1995). The book reflects the author's personality: a dedication to intellectual combat and an aversion to the "scientific" study of international relations. He argues that the system of sovereign states, though without central authority, forms a society with common characteristics based on self-interest. Individual states collectively share a common concern in preventing unrestricted violence and promoting their own survival. Hedley Bull and Adam Watson, eds., *The Expansion of International Society* (1985), explains how non-European states may or may not make the transition from a system based on European hegemony to become members of a worldwide international society.

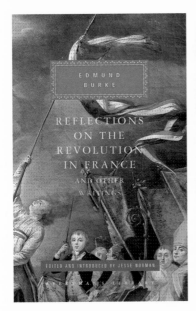 

Burke, Edmund, *Reflections on the Revolution in France* (1790; Hackett, intro. J. G. A. Pocock, 1987). The revolution released in Burke's writings and speeches a cascade of thoughts about possible radical change in England. He attacked the Jacobin doctrine of equality and human rights by defending monarchy, property, and heredity succession. His views became even stronger after the revolution, in his view, began devouring its own children. Conor Cruise O'Brien's *The Great Melody: A Thematic Biography of Edmund Burke* (1992) is an idiosyncratic but masterly study. O'Brien argues that Burke grasped the strength of the colonists' case in America, the cause of the Indians of Bengal, and the injustice and corruption in Ireland—all in relation to the cold-blooded and cruel revolution in France.

Carr, E. H., *The Twenty Years' Crisis, 1919–1939* (1938; Harper, 1964). Carr was a Foreign Office official, a writer of leading articles for *The Times* of London, an historian of the Soviet Union, and a theorist of international relations. He published *The Twenty Years' Crisis* shortly before the outbreak of World War II, sharply criticizing the peace settlement from two decades previously, which stirred up false hopes by creating the League of Nations. He argues that the realities of international affairs are based on military and economic strength and not necessarily on rational ideas. In a sense, Carr's book began the debate on the origins of World War II. For the life of the historian, see Jonathan Haslam, *The Vices of Integrity: E. H. Carr, 1892–1982* (1999).

Chomsky, Noam, *Hegemony or Survival: America's Quest for Global Dominance* (2003; Penguin, 2004). Chomsky, a major figure in cognitive science and linguistics, is also a prolific critic of American foreign policy. His theme is American hypocrisy, racism, exploitation, and cynical manipulation of public opinion. Especially since the end of World War II, the United States has supported regimes responsible for human rights abuses, including ethnic cleansing and genocide. In Chomsky's view, the fundamental aim was "to further U.S. capitalism" and allow a wealthy elite to thrive at the expense of the majority, with little or no interest in the welfare of the people directly affected. After the book's publication, the *New York Times* proclaimed Chomsky to be "the most widely read voice on foreign policy on the planet."

Cicero, Marcus Tullius, *Cicero: Selected Political Speeches* (1st century BC; Penguin, ed. and trans. Michael Grant, 1977). The translator, Michael Grant, was one of the preeminent classicists of the mid-twentieth century. He portrays the eccentricity of Cicero as well as the standards of liberty and justice that he upheld while rejecting the demagoguery rampant during the late Roman Republic. The selections make clear the influence of Cicero's speeches and writings on ethics, politics, and oratory, even letter writing. He remains a major influence on political thinkers and writers to the present, not least because he rejects the idea of determinative fate and espouses free will. The speeches reach a climax in a defense of liberty that ultimately cost him his life.

Commager, Henry Steele, *The American Mind: An Interpretation of American Thought and Character since the 1880s* (1950; Yale, 1959). Commager, who taught at Columbia and Amherst, was a leading American historian for more than fifty years. *The American Mind*, a work of intellectual history, traces the evolution of liberalism in American political thought; it embodies Commager's belief in the principles of the U.S. Constitution and his faith in a strong, just American government. His writing is lucid and pointed, presenting robust views entirely without jargon. Commager was a vigorous opponent of McCarthyism, and during the Vietnam War, which he opposed, he upheld the right of free speech. He believed that the idealism of the 1960s represented a rebirth of American values, not a denial or repudiation of them.

Evola, Julius, *Revolt against the Modern World* (1934; Inner Traditions, trans. Guido Stucco, 1995). Evola wrote during the era of Fascism in Italy. Inspired by the French writer René Guénon, he

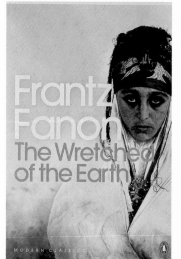

believed that the West had fallen into an age of decadence, claiming that "no idea is as absurd as the idea of progress." He held that Italian Fascism should be more radical, and Nazism less tied to the middle class. He wrote of "inferior non-European races" and argued that both Italy and Germany should revitalize the Aryan race. Despite the disaster of World War I, he believed, as did Ernst Jünger in Germany, that war could be spiritually fulfilling.

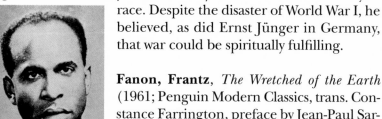

Fanon, Frantz, *The Wretched of the Earth* (1961; Penguin Modern Classics, trans. Constance Farrington, preface by Jean-Paul Sartre, 2001). A physician and psychiatrist from Martinique, Fanon supported the Algerian war of independence. Inspired by the poet and activist Aimé Césaire, he pursued similar ideas of cultural identity and negritude. His work defended the Algerians' right to use violence, arguing that those fighting in anticolonial movements should not be bound by principles of the colonizers. Violence was the only language the French understood. His views about violence were shaped by treating French soldiers compelled to torture Algerians. Fanon's background makes his views on violence relevant to sociology and anthropology as well as psychology. The Caribbean Philosophical Association offers the Frantz Fanon Prize for work that furthers the liberation of mankind.

Fukuyama, Francis, *The End of History and the Last Man* (1992; Free Press, 2006). At the end of the Cold War, Fukuyama pursued the concept of the "end of history," arguing that traditional power politics would continue indefinitely but without any further major changes in society or systems of governance. More substantial than many of his critics granted, his ideas embraced a line of thought extending to Thomas More's *Utopia*. The political philosopher Perry Anderson was among Fukuyama's fiercest critics, pointing out that capitalist democracies were still riven by poverty and racial tension, and that ethnic loyalties and religious fundamentalism agitated huge populations. Fukuyama later expounded on the danger of radical Islam and warned that America's "political rot" might cause a breakdown "as big as the Soviet collapse."

Gellner, Ernest, *Nations and Nationalism* (1983; Cornell, 2009). Taking a multicultural perspective, Gellner argues that European nationalism developed during the transition from agrarian to industrial society. In an emerging nation-state, one or more ethnic groups share a bureaucracy, an educational system, sometimes but not always a common language and faith, and, above all, a sense of collective identity. A state is a political entity with a high degree of sovereignty, but a nation need not be a fully sovereign state, and many aren't. A leading theorist of nationalism, Gellner was a colorful personality—according to his entry in the *Oxford Dictionary of National Biography*, "brilliant, forceful, irreverent, mischievous, sometimes perverse, with a biting wit and love of irony."

Gramsci, Antonio, *Selections from the Prison Notebooks* (International Publishers, trans. Quintin Hoare and Geoffrey Nowell Smith, 1971). Gramsci, a founding member of the Italian Communist Party, was imprisoned by Mussolini in 1926. He died a little over a decade later, out of prison but a broken man with a hunched back and rotten teeth. His intricate notebooks, sometimes obscure because of prison censorship, range over the French and Russian revolutions, Italian nationalism, and above all the original concept of *cultural hegemony*—the way in which capitalist states use cultural institutions to maintain power. The *Prison Notebooks* are not an easy read but essential for understanding Gramsci's significant contribution to political thought; not least, they enabled Italian historians to write more realistically about their recent past.

Greenfeld, Liah, *Nationalism: Five Roads to Modernity* (1992; Harvard, 1993). Explicating concepts such as identity and modernity, this sociological history traces the rise of nationalism in England, France, Russia, Germany, and the United States. At a basic level, its purpose is "to understand the world in which we live." It argues that there is an interplay between culture and individual psychology, and between a common language and ethnic heritage. In distinct ways, the five cases reveal that nationalism is the necessary condition for modernity. Avoiding sociological jargon and keeping an eye out for historical detail, the author attempts to bid farewell to previous studies by reversing the view that nationalism is a form of atavism and demonstrating how social change captures its essence.

Habermas, Jürgen, *The Lure of Technocracy* (2013; Polity, trans. Ciaran Cronin, 2015). Sociologist, philosopher, and historian, Habermas is perhaps best described as a leading intellectual. His major works span such concepts as modernity and civil society, the Enlightenment as an "unfinished project," and the French Revolution as having been caused by the collapse of "representational" culture. On the subject of the Third Reich, he argues that Nazi rule and the Holocaust belong in the mainstream of German history. In the *Lure of Technocracy*, he puts forward arguments in favor of the European Union by drawing on European history and philosophy, legal scholarship, and social science theory.

Halévy, Élie, *The Era of Tyrannies: Essays on Socialism and War* (1938; Penguin, trans. R. K. Webb, with a note by Fritz Stern, 1967). Halévy was a brilliant French historian and political philosopher, often compared with his German counterpart Max Weber. His great work is the six-volume *History of the English People in the Nineteenth Century* (1913–46), the theme of which is the avoidance of social violence by restricting the power of the state. In *The Era of Tyrannies*, he envisages a new age of state socialism and national control of citizens, beginning in August 1914. As an historian with prophetic insight, he believed that World War I would lead to the regimentation of society and predicted that it would last twenty-five years, interrupted only by a false peace.

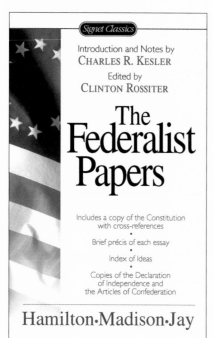

Hamilton, Alexander, James Madison, and John Jay, *The Federalist Papers* (1787; Signet Classics, ed. Clinton Rossiter, intro. Charles Kesler, 2003). Hamilton and Madison disagreed about politics, but they united under the name "Publius" to write a series of essays in support of ratification of the U.S. Constitution. They believed that destructive self-interest, which they saw as inherent in democracy, could be mitigated by balancing power among the three branches of government. A sense of the overall argument can be found in numbers 1 (statement of intent), 10 (the separation of powers), 14 (republican government as appropriate for the country), 39 (republican principles), 51 (checks and balances), 70 (the presidency), and 78 (federal judiciary). Ron Chernow's *Alexander Hamilton* (2004) is a large, engrossing biography of its subject.

Hartz, Louis, *The Liberal Tradition in America: An Interpretation of American Political Thought since the Revolution* (1955; Harcourt Brace, 1991). In riveting lectures at Harvard in the 1940s and 1950s, Hartz argued that there was a consensus on American values and that the lack of a feudal past explained the exceptionalism of the United States. But the consensus had begun to crack well before he wrote his book. Racial tensions and the inequities facing women were only two examples of deep-seated conflict. One reason the consensus theory lasted as long as it did was the need for unity during World War II. Hartz's book deserves its place as a classic because of its unswerving belief that the United States is a free and open society.

Hobbes, Thomas, *Leviathan*, rev. ed. (1651; Broadview, ed. A. P. Martinch and Brian Battiste, 2011). In Hobbes's famous formulation, life in the state of nature would be "solitary, poor, nasty, brutish, and short." People therefore cede to the government, through a social contract, as much power as it needs to ensure the peace and safety of the commonwealth. In the course of Hobbes's argument, he discusses human nature, the forms of a commonwealth (monarchy, aristocracy, democracy), and the role of religion in government. Written in the aftermath of the English Civil War, *Leviathan* is a trenchant philosophical defense of absolutism. For the definitive version of Hobbes's masterpiece, see the three-volume Oxford edition (2012), edited by Noel Malcolm. Richard Tuck's *Hobbes: A Very Short Introduction* (1989) provides a concise summary of the ideas of a prolific, multifarious author.

Hofstadter, Richard, *The American Political Tradition and The Men Who Made It* (1948; Vintage, 1989). A levelheaded, balanced, yet witty analysis of American politics using vignettes of American presidents and statesmen. Hofstadter presents his subjects as paradoxes: for example, Jefferson is the "Aristocrat as Democrat," and Franklin Delano Roosevelt, the "Patrician as Opportunist." Hofstadter endorses pragmatism and compromise over strong ideological commitment and describes his own work as "literary anthropology." Hofstadter's *The Paranoid Style in American Politics* (1964) traces the history of conspiracy theories in American political thought as "movements of suspicious discontent." In most of Hofstadter's work there is a sense of humor and a feel for the comic. The distinguished historian John Higham judged that Hofstadter possessed "the finest and also the most humane historical intelligence of our generation."

Huntington, Samuel P., *The Clash of Civilizations and the Remaking of World Order* (1996; Simon & Schuster, 2011). Huntington argues that with the end of the Cold War, a new division sprang up between the West and other parts of the world. Despite American hopes, it was naïve to believe that human rights and democracy would flourish worldwide, in part because of divergent religious and cultural traditions. He identifies nine major cultures, or "civilizations": Western, Eastern, Eastern Orthodox, Latin American, Islamic, Japanese, Chinese, Hindu, and African.

The most threatening to the West is resurgent, expansionist Islam. Huntington's thesis has caused considerable controversy. Noam Chomsky, for example, believes that it merely provides a new justification for American intervention throughout the world.

Joll, James, *The Anarchists* (1964; 2nd ed., Methuen, 1979). An historian of ideas, Joll explains the beginning of European anarchism as extending to the antiauthoritarian attitude of early Christian heretics. Anarchists embrace a faith in the goodness of man; freed from the control of the state, they would reorganize society into decentralized and voluntary communities, through revolution if necessary. Joll discusses such anarchists as England's William Godwin, France's Pierre-Joseph Proudhon, and Russia's Peter Kropotkin. The book reaches a high point with a perceptive analysis of the moral basis for anarchists' participation in Spanish Civil War and the student movements of the late 1960s. Joll's *Origins of the First World War* (1984; 3rd ed., 2007, revised by Gordon Martel) looks closely at the interplay between individuals and larger forces in the buildup to the catastrophe of August 1914.

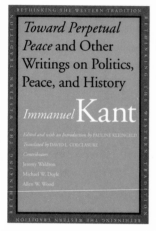

Kant, Immanuel, *"Toward Perpetual Peace,"* and *Other Writings on Politics, Peace, and History* (1795; Yale, trans. David L. Colclasure, ed. Pauline Kleingeld, 2006). Given the tension between the "moral imperative" of peace and the reality of the "state of war" among nations, Kant is not at all sanguine about the prospect of lasting peace. Nevertheless, he argues powerfully that it can be secured through universal democracy and a "league of nations." Michael Howard, in *The Invention of Peace: Reflections on War and International Order* (2001), argues that only after the massive slaughter of two world wars did Kant's idea of peace become the declared aim of civilized states.

Key, V. O., Jr., *Southern Politics in State and Nation* (1949; Tennessee, 1984). Key received his B.A. from the University of Texas in 1929 and eventually became a renowned scholar at Harvard and president of the American Political Science Association in 1958. Drawing on more than 500 interviews, he argued against the common view that "Southern backwardness" could be attributed to "poor whites." On the contrary, he demonstrated that a relatively small group of "Southern Bourbons" manipulated working-class whites to preserve the prevailing economic and social order. Key became widely known for his empirical study of American elections and voting behavior—and his conclusion that "voters are not fools." He is widely regarded as the leading student of American politics of his generation.

Kirk, Russell, *The Conservative Mind: From Burke to Santayana* (1951; later editions bore the subtitle *From Burke to Eliot*; Gateway, 2001). Kirk was an academic and everyday maverick, declining to drive and calling cars "mechanical Jacobins." He left his faculty position at Michigan State University, referring to it as "Cow College." At his home in Mecosta, Michigan, he gave shelter to refugees and hoboes while developing his political philosophy in a syndicated column. He was an early contributor to the *National Review*. His originality in *The Conservative Mind* consists of a "canon" of respect for divine intent, social order, and private property. The book is idiosyncratic and elitist, but Kirk had considerable influence as an *éminence grise* in defining the conservative heritage and strengthening its tradition in America.

Kolakowski, Leszek, *Main Currents of Marxism: The Founders—The Golden Age—The Breakdown* (1976; Eng. trans., P. S. Falla, 1978; Norton, 2008). A preeminent political philosopher and historian of ideas, Kolakowski lost his job at Warsaw University in 1968 when he concluded that the cruelty of Stalinist Russia was the logical consequence of Marxism. Two years later he became a Senior Research Fellow at All Souls College, Oxford. Moving from skeptical belief to vitriolic apostasy, Kolakowski concedes Marx's originality but subjects his writings and concepts to acute, often witty analysis, especially in relation to Marx's claim of having discovered a science of human history. His conclusion: most of it is simply "nonsense." Kolakowski's equal interest in religion is explored in *Is God Happy?* (2012).

Kristol, Irving, *Neo-Conservatism: The Autobiography of an Idea* (1995; Dee, 1900). Kristol, often referred to as the godfather of neoconservatism, was skeptical and pragmatic: "Will it work?" he often asked. Neoconservatism is a political movement that originated among disenchanted Democrats in the 1960s, particularly those associated with the journal *Commentary*. Neoconservatives generally favor socially conservative domestic policies and a strongly activist foreign policy, as in the Iraq War; many of them trace their ideas to the political philosophy of Leo Strauss. Kristol cofounded the journal *Encounter* in 1953. When later asked whether he knew the CIA had subsidized it, he stated that he did not disapprove. In his own view, one of his most useful functions as a neoconservative writer was simply to demonstrate the absurdity of what he called "liberal legislation."

Lincoln, Abraham, *Selected Speeches and Writings* (1832–65; Vintage / Library of America, ed. Don E. Fehrenbacher, intro. Gore Vidal, 1992). Lincoln's eloquent prose, steeped in classical and biblical rhythms and allusions, gave voice to a vision that continues to shape political debate in this country. Included here, along with many letters and other speeches, are the "House Divided" speech, the First and Second Inaugurals, the Emancipation Proclamation, and the Gettysburg Address. Of the hundreds of biographies of Lincoln, James B. McPherson, the distinguished historian of the Civil War, recommends David Herbert Donald's *Lincoln* (1995) as the best single-volume life. Donald demystifies Lincoln and tells the story of his life unsentimentally, presenting events and decisions as Lincoln saw them.

Lippmann, Walter, *Public Opinion* (1922; Free Press, foreword by Ronald Steel, 1997). Lippmann was probably the most influential political writer in twentieth-century America. His syndicated column, "Today and Tomorrow," ran in over 200 newspapers for thirty-six years, conveying his ideas simply and directly, and winning pubic trust because of his fair-mindedness. In *Public Opinion*, he introduced the recurrent theme of American politicians' incapacity to understand complex public issues. The theme is a critical assessment of irrational and self-serving motives in government. Lippmann introduced the concept of "manufacturing consent," which had a substantial influence on later works of social psychology and the study of propaganda. He wrote that the "governing class" had to face the dangers of "polluted information," or what later became known as "fake news."

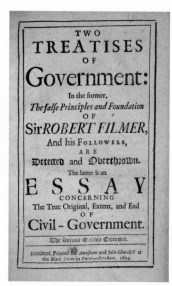

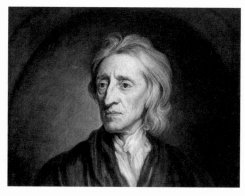

Locke, John, *Second Treatise of Government* in *Two Treatises of Government* (1689; Cambridge, ed. Peter Laslett, 1988). The first great defense of self-rule by a people. Locke believed that people were always governed by law; but that relying on natural law was inefficient and subject to human prejudices. As a solution, Locke recommended limited government that would protect "life, liberty, and property." Further, law was the safeguard of freedom: "The end of law is, not to abolish or restrain, but to preserve and enlarge freedom." In *A Letter Concerning Toleration* (1689), Locke issues a plea for religious tolerance based on the idea that the proper role of government is to ensure external things such as security and the general welfare; it should not be involved in the care of souls.

Machiavelli, Niccolò, *The Prince* (1513; Chicago, trans. Harvey Mansfield, 1998). In this short, revolutionary work, Machiavelli attacks all previous moral and political thought, both Christian and classical, for its lack of realism. The author famously asks whether it is better for a leader to be feared than loved. (Feared, as it turns out.) Another of Machiavelli's unflinching maxims notes, "Men should either be caressed or eliminated, because they avenge themselves for slight offenses but cannot do so for grave ones." The book's bracing insights have had a profound effect on subsequent political thought and the modern world. For an explication of both *The Prince* and Machiavelli's *Discourses on Livy*, see Philip Bobbitt, *The Garments of Court and Palace: Machiavelli and the World That He Made* (2013).

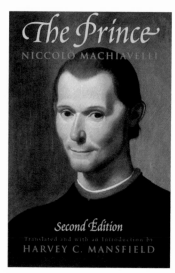

Mao Tse-tung, *Quotations from Chairman Mao Tse-tung* (1964–76). Bound in distinctive vinyl, the "Little Red Book"—it measures four by six inches—contains 267 aphorisms, including the famous adages "A revolution is not a dinner party" and "Political power grows out of the barrel of a gun." During the Cultural Revolution (1966–76), every Chinese citizen had to carry a copy, thus contributing to the cult of devotional allegiance to Mao. It was originally used as an ideological field manual for soldiers in the People's Liberation Army; it had a waterproof cover and fit in the breast pocket of an army uniform. Mao himself liked its resemblance to a book of quotations by Confucius. Some 6.5 *billion* copies have been distributed worldwide by the Chinese government.

Marx, Karl, and Friedrich Engels, *The Communist Manifesto* (1848; Verso, intro. Eric Hobsbawm, 2008). From its famous opening—"A spectre is haunting Europe, the spectre of communism"—to its ringing conclusion urging workers of the world to unite, this brief interpretation of history and economics lays out a case for the inevitability of global socialism in the form of communism. It influenced successive generations of revolutionary leaders, including Lenin, Stalin, Mao, Ho Chi Minh, and Fidel Castro. The biography of Marx by Gareth Stedman Jones, *Karl Marx: Greatness and Illusion* (2016), aims to separate the actual or "real" man from the "mythical" Marx and the Marxist movement he inspired. Marx as constructed in the twentieth century bore only an incidental resemblance to the Marx who lived in the nineteenth.

Montesquieu, Charles-Louis de Secondat, baron de La Brède et de, *The Spirit of the Laws* (1748; Cambridge, trans. Anne M. Cohler, Basia C. Miller, and Harold S. Stone, 1989). A political philosopher of the Enlightenment, Montesquieu believed that despotism could be prevented by a system of government in which different parts exercised judicial, legislative, and executive power, all bound by the rule of law. The idea of the clear and balanced separation of powers had a critical impact on the framers of the U.S. Constitution. The book met with a hostile reception in France, and the Catholic Church banned it and entered it on the *List of Prohibited Books*. For Montesquieu's life and thought, see Robert Shackleton, *Montesquieu: A Critical Biography* (1961), based on family papers and archives.

Oakeshott, Michael, *What Is History? and Other Essays* (Imprint Academic, ed. Luke O'Sullivan, 2004). Oakeshott was a British political philosopher whose views were so conservative that they seemed to critics to border on the anarchic. In his own words, he believed that historical and philosophical inquiry should be protected from popular trends and "relevance." He was concerned with evidence, not with the "lessons of history." The aim of historical inquiry was to be restricted to the recording of historical events. What was identified as an event depended on *evidence*, which he examined relentlessly, especially in political philosophy and the concept of the state. The political philosopher Kenneth Minogue wrote that Oakeshott's knowledge of the modern state was "the most profound of anyone in his generation."

Popper, Karl, *The Open Society and Its Enemies* (1945; Princeton, intro. Alan Ryan, 1994). A philosopher of science, Popper argues that scientific methods should be applied to politics. Believing that psychoanalytic theories had more in common with primitive myths than with genuine science, he denounces, not without a little intellectual arrogance, Plato, Hegel, and Marx for their totalitarian tendencies. Above all, he upholds the desirability of liberal democracy (the open society of the title) and the principle of "negative utilitarianism," the thought that suffering should be reduced as much as possible rather than happiness maximized. Popper's *The Poverty of Historicism* (1957) attacks the belief that the future of human beings can be predicted. Historicism, he argued, leads to fascism and communism.

Rahe, Paul A., *Republics Ancient and Modern: Classical Republicanism and the American Revolution* (North Carolina, 1992; 3 pb. vols., 1994). In this massive work, Rahe asks to what extent the Americans were inspired by philosophical thought from ancient Greece to the seventeenth century, especially the political theories of John Locke. Most politicians at the time of the American Revolution did not read philosophical works; but popular and political journalism produced a distinct trail from the thought of Locke to the ideas embraced by the founders of the American republic—specifically, Locke's principle that to be legitimate, government must rest on the consent of the governed. The weight of the volume reflects Rahe's expertise as a classical philologist, historian, and scholar of political theory.

Rawls, John, *A Theory of Justice* (1971; Harvard, rev. ed., 1999). Rawls taught at Harvard for forty years, each semester elaborating and perfecting his theory of "justice as fairness." Working in the social contract tradition running from Hobbes and Locke to Rousseau, and also drawing on the thought of Hume and Kant, he assesses in an American context basic questions of how best to reconcile freedom and equality. Rawls explicitly countered utilitarian ideas of justice; in his own words: "Each person possesses an inviolability founded on justice that even the welfare of society as a whole cannot override." In Rawls's conception, the fairest rules for establishing justice would be formulated behind a "veil of ignorance," meaning that the rule makers would know nothing about their own or others' personal attributes.

Skinner, Quentin, *The Foundations of Modern Political Thought*, vol. 1, *The Renaissance* (1978; Cambridge, 1998). The theme is political thought in the West from the late thirteenth through the early sixteenth century. (The second volume covers Luther, Calvin, and other leaders of the Reformation.) Skinner deals especially with ideas about the nature of the state, including princely government, and debates about political liberty in the Italian city-republics, Florence in particular. He covers the development of the major isms of the time—scholasticism, humanism, republicanism—placing them firmly in their historical context. The principal theorists discussed are Dante, Machiavelli, Erasmus, and Thomas More. The account ends with an analysis of More's *Utopia* as a humanist criticism of humanism.

Strauss, Leo, *What Is Political Philosophy? and Other Studies* (1959; Chicago, 1988). Strauss taught at the University of Chicago, where he acquired an intellectual following, including the critic Susan Sontag and Paul Wolfowitz, a former deputy secretary of defense. He advocated a close reading of political texts, believing that the great works of political philosophy transcend culture and have timeless value. Strauss had little faith in modern democracy, believing instead in an intellectual and political aristocracy. He is often regarded as the godfather of American neoconservatism. His enduring intellectual significance may be his belief in the need for a broad classical understanding of contemporary society acquired through the study of "great books." In *Natural Right and History* (1965; Chicago, 1999), Strauss deals with right and wrong in ethics and politics.

Talmon, J. L., *The Origins of Totalitarian Democracy* (1952; Praeger, 1960). Talmon's essential idea is that totalitarian democracy gives rise to a dictatorship based on mass enthusiasm, which is irrational and dangerous when expressing messianic expectations. A system of government might be lawfully elected but offer its citizens little or no participation in its decision-making processes. Talmon criticizes the work of Jean-Jacques Rousseau, whose ideas influenced the French Revolution. For Talmon, the French Revolution was refracted through the lens provided by the Russian Revolution and its aftermath, with the result that Robespierre became a Stalin, and Rousseau an ideologist of the gulag. Talmon was Professor of Modern History at the Hebrew University, and his historical ideas on totalitarianism were reflected in his opposition to Israeli settlements in the occupied territories.

Wight, Martin, *International Theory: The Three Traditions* (1990; Holmes and Maier, 1994). Wight's scholarly strength lay in his historical study of sovereign states and the ways in which they protected their security and attempted to achieve their aims through alliances, intervention, war, and—the vital part of his general argument—the manipulation of the balance of power. *International Theory*, a posthumously published collection of lectures, examines the categories of realism, rationalism, and revolution, which he identifies respectively as Machiavellian, Grotian, and Kantian. In his university teaching at the London School of Economics, Wight urged students to study not only history but also languages and literature, not least the classics. In *Power Politics* (1946), his classic work, he explains that "every dominant power aspires to become a universal empire."

Witte, John, Jr., and Joel A. Nichols, *Religion and the American Constitutional Experiment* (2000; 4th ed., Oxford, 2016). In this survey of religious freedom in America, the authors analyze historic principles and early Supreme Court cases to determine the original intent of the First Amendment, which guarantees the free exercise of religion. They explain how religious principles were central to the creation of the United States, and how they remain basic to many Americans' self-identity. They broaden the scope by comparing Supreme Court cases on religious freedom with those of the European Court of Human Rights. By presenting an historical perspective on religious liberty and church-state relations, the book provides a valuable background for understanding current debates about religion in American public life.

Wittfogel, Karl A., *Oriental Despotism: A Comparative Study of Total Power* (1957; Vintage, 1981). Wittfogel was a German Sinologist and playwright as well as a Marxist and active communist. His fame rests mainly on his study of the control of water resources in China and Russia. Building on Marx's idea of an "Asiatic" way of pre-capitalist development, he studied the bureaucratic systems needed to build and maintain large-scale networks of canals and irrigation projects. In China and Russia, the state relied on forced labor on a massive scale, which led to the "bureaucratic despotism" of a powerful and wealthy elite. Wittfogel's faith in the Soviet Union was destroyed by the Nazi-Soviet pact of 1939. He immigrated to the United States, eventually teaching Chinese history at the University of Washington.

Racial, Ethnic, and Gender Studies

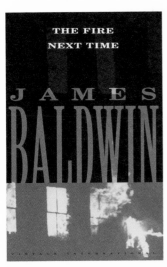

Baldwin, James, *The Fire Next Time* (1963; Vintage, 1992). Two essays by an unflinching observer of race relations in the United States in the mid-20th century: a letter to Baldwin's fifteen-year-old nephew, setting out an intellectual and cultural map of the adult world he is about to enter, and "Down at the Cross," an acute analysis of the effects of racism on whites and blacks that manages to resist despair. The book's title comes from a Negro spiritual: "God gave Noah the rainbow sign / No more water, the fire next time." Ta-Nehisi Coates's *Between the World and Me* (2015) is modeled explicitly on "My Dungeon Shook," a pitiless examination of the ways in which progress in racial matters has lagged in the half century since Baldwin wrote.

Beauvoir, Simone de, *The Second Sex* (1949; Vintage, trans. Constance Borde and Sheila Malovany-Chevallier, 2011). An existentialist philosopher closely associated with Jean-Paul Sartre, Beauvoir was among the first of the post–World War II feminists to put forward persuasive reasons for women's equality and economic independence—women in France had gained the right to vote only in 1945. She argued especially against male stereotypes of innate female inferiority, writing, "One is not born, but rather becomes, a woman." *The Second Sex* was a precursor of the more sexually charged works on women's liberation published in the 1960s and 1970s. For Beauvoir's long, complicated relationship with Sartre, see Hazel Rowley, *Tête-à-Tête: Simone de Beauvoir and Jean-Paul Sartre* (2005).

Cornell, Stephen, *Return of the Native: American Indian Political Resurgence* (1988; Oxford, 1990). From the sixteenth century, Indians sustained tribal structures and identities by playing off competing European powers and, subsequently, different branches of the U.S. government, including the army. American expansion in the West brought about the loss of land, a decline in economic independence, and sometimes the disintegration of social cohesion. Yet Indian tribes maintained degrees of autonomy. Cornell traces the re-emergence in the twentieth century of Indian identity, "ethnic renewal," and, since the 1960s, political activism—"from power to powerlessness and back to power again." Gord Hill's *500 Years of Indigenous Resistance* (2010) is a slim volume that covers European-Indian encounters in North and South America over the course of several centuries.

Davis, Angela, *Angela Davis: An Autobiography* (1974; International Publishers, 2013). A political activist and feminist scholar, Angela Davis was a radical, countercultural activist in the 1960s. She grew up in Birmingham, Alabama, where she witnessed the bombing of middle-class black homes. Inspired especially by the ideas of Herbert Marcuse, who helped her develop a coherent political philosophy, she became a member of the Communist Party USA and a supporter of the Black Panther movement. In 1970 she was charged with involvement in the armed takeover of a California courtroom in which four people were killed. She praised Cuba ("a racism-free country"), opposed male chauvinism, and referred to the U.S. penal system as the "prison-industrial complex."

Davis, David Brion, *The Problem of Slavery in the Age of Revolution, 1770–1823* (1975; Oxford, 1999). *The Problem of Slavery* is a landmark study for its examination of controversies surrounding slavery in the intellectual currents of the time—for example, attitudes toward social order and the authority of law and religion. What were the consequences of the French Revolution for the institution of slavery? Did the evangelical churches in the American South, like the Society of Friends in England, preach antislavery as a tenet of the Christian faith? Part of the complicated answer is that slaves were considered domesticated savages who would, if given the chance, revert to murder and mayhem. Such examples, which are integrated into a general argument, make this a wide-ranging and invaluable book.

Du Bois, W. E. B., *The Souls of Black Folk* (1903; Yale, 2015). The work in which Du Bois famously declared that "the problem of the Twentieth Century is the problem of the color-line" is a pioneering sociology of African Americans. *Souls* covers politics, education, religion, and labor during the forty years immediately following emancipation. It provides a look from within the

"Veil," as Du Bois termed the physical and psychological boundary between white and black Americans. It deals also with "double consciousness," the idea that blacks are forced to see themselves through the eyes of whites as well as through their own eyes. His life and thought are covered in Kwame Anthony Appiah, *Lines of Descent: W. E. B. Du Bois and the Emergence of Identity* (2014).

Franklin, John Hope, *From Slavery to Freedom: A History of African Americans* (1947; 9th ed., with Evelyn Higginbotham, McGraw-Hill, 2010). In 1947, Franklin published this meticulously written, subtly subversive book. It tells the story of black America as part of the larger history of the United States. It has sold over three million copies and changed the way in which the black experience in America is studied and taught. *Mirror to America: The Autobiography of John Hope Franklin* (2005), an account of growing up in the era of segregation, has occasional bitter passages, such as one in which his family was packed into a hot, blacks-only railroad car while the lounge car in front held only four or five white men—all German prisoners of war.

Friedan, Betty, *The Feminine Mystique* (1963; Norton, 2013). Friedan came from a privileged background—she graduated from Smith College in 1942—that nonetheless included radical politics and labor journalism. Trained in psychology, she conducted surveys and interviews of women across the United States who seemed to have everything: marriage, material comfort, and children. And yet they were miserable. Friedan called this "the problem that has no name." By publicizing the problem and treating it sympathetically, she helped launch the second wave of feminism, which dealt with concerns beyond property rights and suffrage. Above all, Friedan sensed the crisis in women's identity. The book, a runaway best seller, made her a key figure in the women's liberation movement.

Greer, Germaine, *The Female Eunuch* (1970; Harper, 2008). In a male-dominated society, women are devitalized and turned into eunuchs. Published nearly fifty years ago, the book resembles a time capsule containing Greer's voice as heard in the women's movement of the 1960s. Aiming at liberation rather than equality, she hoped to do for women what was done for onetime colonized nations. She has a sense of humor and uses coarse language entertainingly, for example, "I'm fucked if I'll work my tits off for a bunch of dickheads." One reader belonging to the "Greer cult" remarks, "Greer remains germane." She took inspiration from Simone de Beauvoir's *The Second Sex*, but her goal reflected her Australian origin: "Freedom to run, shout, talk loudly and sit with your knees apart."

Myrdal, Gunnar, *An American Dilemma: The Negro Problem and Modern Democracy*, 2 vols. (1944; vol. 1, Routledge, 1995). Myrdal, a Swedish Nobel laureate in economics, wrote one of the most influential books on racial issues in the United States, composed during World War II and taking the view that democracy would triumph over racism. Notably, Ralph Bunche was Myrdal's chief researcher. The theme is the moral contradiction between the nation's allegiance to its highest ideals and its awareness of the realities of racial discrimination. At the center of Myrdal's work is the concept of the American Creed, a combination of individualism, civil liberties, and equality of opportunity. The work was so influential that it was cited in the landmark Supreme Court decision *Brown v. Board of Education* (1954).

Pankhurst, Sylvia, *The Suffragette Movement: An Intimate Account of Persons and Ideals* (1931; Chatto & Windus, 1984). In a family committed to women's suffrage, Sylvia Pankhurst became more revolutionary than her mother, Emmeline, or her sister Christabel, who are heroes of women's emancipation. Sylvia was imprisoned eight times before 1918 for militantly protesting against the war as well as the subjection of women. In 1920 she traveled to Russia, meeting Lenin, and then returned to help found the British Communist Party. Shortly thereafter she was expelled for voicing fiercely independent views on women's rights and sexual freedom. In the 1930s she took up antifascist causes such as opposition to the Italian invasion of Ethiopia. For an account of the remarkable Pankhurst clan, see Hugh Pugh, *The Pankhursts: The History of One Radical Family* (2002).

Ruiz, Vicki L., *From Out of the Shadows: Mexican Women in Twentieth-Century America* (1998; Oxford, 2008). In the decades during and after the Mexican Revolution, over one million Mexican men and women—amounting to one-tenth of Mexico's population—migrated to join the hundreds of thousands living in the southern border states, from Texas to California. Whether in mining towns, boxcar settlements, migrant worker camps, or urban ghettos, the women worked for minimal wages, nourished their families, and sustained contact with distant family members while coping with the tensions of their children adopting American ways. For a thorough, readable survey of the largest U.S. ethnic minority, see Zaragosa Vargas, *Crucible of Struggle: A History of Mexican Americans from the Colonial Period to the Present Era* (2nd. ed., 2016).

Takaki, Ronald, *Strangers from a Different Shore: A History of Asian Americans* (1989; Little, Brown, 1998). Focusing mainly on East Asian immigrants, Takaki writes of the Chinese who laid the tracks for the transcontinental railroad, the Japanese Americans held behind barbed-wire fences in internment camps during World War II, and Korean Americans working in hot kitchens and laundries. "Chinatowns," to many Americans, meant brothels and ghettos, and "Little Tokyos," the concentrated communities of Japanese. Takaki's parents worked in the sugarcane fields in Hawaii, and his wife's family referred to him as a "Jap." He writes in a spirit of reconciliation, yet with the aim of giving voice to "invisible Americans."

Tannenbaum, Frank, *Slave and Citizen: The Negro in the Americas* (1947; Beacon, 1992). Shortly after World War II, Tannenbaum studied slave history and race relations in Brazil, including the topic of the slave as property, with no rights to the products of his own labor, or to marriage and children. He concluded that sex between blacks and their Portuguese masters blurred the color line. On the basis of his research on the Caribbean, Mexico, and Latin America more generally, he inquired into the reasons for the sharp distinction in the United States between whites and blacks. *Slave and Citizen* became a source of inspiration for later scholars of race relations in the Americas.

Wollstonecraft, Mary, *A Vindication of the Rights of Woman* (1792; Penguin Classics, 2004). The foundation of feminist political theory and philosophy, Wollstonecraft's polemic offers a stinging rebuke to the belief that women should be kept passive and credulous, and trained primarily to please men. She argues that women are not naturally inferior to men, but appear to be so only because they lack education. She imagines a social order founded on reason in which both men and women are treated as rational beings. Her arguments in favor of equality of opportunity, especially in education, continue to resonate today. *The Subjection of Women* (1869), by John Stuart Mill, an early proponent in Parliament of women's suffrage, continues the argument for equality of the sexes.

Science

Bronowski, Jacob, *The Ascent of Man* (1973; Penguin, foreword by Richard Dawkins, 2002). *The Ascent of Man* originated as a thirteen-part BBC television series. In the accompanying book, clearly written for the general reader, Bronowski charts the development of human civilization through the lens of scientific progress. He traces the history of discovery from its earliest days to the present, with stops along the way at agriculture, the wheel, geometry, alchemy, genetics, and the theory of relativity. He places his discussion in a social context of discovery, thus elucidating how man can control nature. Bronowski was a mathematician, biologist, and historian of science. The title of the book, an allusion to Darwin's *The Descent of Man*, conveys his belief that human progress is ongoing.

Carson, Rachel, *Silent Spring* (1962; Mariner, 2002). Carson was a marine biologist whose research demonstrated damage to the environment caused by DDT spraying. Her book met with fierce opposition from the chemical companies, especially DuPont and Monsanto, but it had an unprecedented public influence and gave critical help to the fledgling environmental movement. Justice William O. Douglas supported her at the time, and Vice President Al Gore wrote an introduction to a later edition. A fair-minded assessment of Carson's influence on the larger environmental movement is found in Robert Gottlieb, *Forcing the Spring: The Transformation of the American Environmental Movement* (1993).

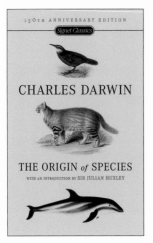

Darwin, Charles, *On the Origin of Species* (1859; Signet Classics, intro. Julian Huxley, 2003). Darwin presents the theory of evolution by natural selection, along with an abundance of evidence for the theory. He describes, but could not at the time explain, the biological mechanism at work, and stresses the essential role of geology in species formation. One of the most influential scientific works of all time, *Origin* shows that design in nature need not imply the existence of an intelligent designer. Darwin's *Voyage of HMS Beagle* (1839; rev. ed., 1845) is a detailed account of the five-year

(1831–36) circumnavigation of the globe during which Darwin gathered the observations—in particular, of finches in the Galápagos Islands—that proved pivotal for the theory developed in *On the Origin of Species*.

Dawkins, Richard, *The Selfish Gene* (1976; Oxford, 4th. ed., 2016). Dawkins explains biological evolution as a gene-centered process, rather than one driven by individual fitness or group selection. Genes are not literally selfish, as the author makes clear, but their effects can be described as if they were. To help account for higher levels of organization, Dawkins coined the term "meme" to designate human artifacts and practices (such as religions and ideologies) that drive cultural evolution somewhat in the way that genes drive biological evolution. Edward O. Wilson's *On Human Nature* (1978) is a biological explanation for human behavior that treats as critical the co-evolution of genes and culture across the millennia, combining findings from evolutionary biology, neuroscience, and the social sciences.

Einstein, Albert, *Relativity: The Special and the General Theory* (1916; Penguin, trans. Robert W. Lawson, 2006). Einstein's stated aim was to provide a clear explanation of his theory of relativity for readers "not conversant with the mathematical apparatus of theoretical physics." Besides covering special relativity (which reconciles discrepancies between Newton's laws of motion and Maxwell's laws of electromagnetism) and general relativity (a comprehensive theory of gravitation), the book includes a section titled "Considerations on the Universe as a Whole." Einstein's thoughts on a range of topics—nuclear war, religion, human rights, government, economics, and Nazi Germany as well as physics—can be found in the essays, most of them very short, in *Ideas and Opinions* (1954).

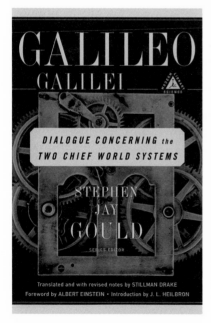

Galileo, *Dialogue Concerning the Two Chief World Systems: Ptolemaic and Copernican* (1632; Modern Library, trans. Stillman Drake, foreword by Albert Einstein, 2001). For upholding the Copernican system over the Ptolemaic in this work, Galileo was tried for heresy by the Inquisition. The *Dialogue* undermined official Church dogma. Galileo was found guilty and forced to recant. The Church banned the work until 1835, and only in 1992 acknowledged Galileo to be correct. In *The Starry Messenger* (*Sidereus Nuncius*, 1610), Galileo became the first to report observations made with a telescope, including the moons of Jupiter (which proved that not all heavenly bodies revolved around Earth), the pitted surface of Earth's moon, and the huge number of stars, most invisible to the naked eye, that make up the Milky Way.

Gardner, Martin, *The Night Is Large: Collected Essays, 1938–1995* (1996; St. Martin's, 1997). The author of more than fifty books, Gardner is best known for writing the "Mathematical Games" column in *Scientific American* for twenty-five years. This volume collects forty-seven essays on topics in physical science, social science, pseudoscience, and mathematics, but also in the arts, philosophy, and religion. Whether discussing quantum mechanics, the nature of time, the Klingon language, or Joyce's *Ulysses*, Gardner writes clearly, often humorously, and always with the intent of reaching the general reader. In furtherance of his campaign for sound reasoning, he debunks ludicrous claims of baseless certainty, whether made by enthusiasts of the paranormal or supply-side economists.

Gould, Stephen Jay, *Wonderful Life: The Burgess Shale and the Nature of History* (1989; Norton, 1990). The Burgess Shale is a Canadian site full of fossils dating from around 500 million years ago. Gould contends that organisms preserved there, almost none of which have modern descendants, became extinct for reasons other than a lack of biological fitness. He explains this by the notion of contingency, namely, that traits allowing a species to survive an extinction event—a large meteor strike, for example—have little relation to their fitness in the pre-extinction environment. According to Gould, if it were possible to "rewind the tape" of evolution, contingency implies that there is no guarantee that human intelligence would necessarily arise again.

Haldane, J. B. S, *On Being the Right Size, and Other Essays* (c. 1926–49; Oxford, ed. John Maynard Smith, 1985). Besides being a brilliant geneticist, Haldane was a communist, a humanist, an atheist, and a student of the classics. He left Britain in 1956 in protest against the country's role in the Suez crisis and became a citizen of India. This collection of his writings includes the delightful title essay ("For every type of animal there is a most convenient size"), along with ruminations on the origin of life, on ways life on earth might end, and on cats. The Nobel laureate Sir Peter Medawar called Haldane "the cleverest man I ever knew" and said that he wrote "in a style as distinctive as Ernest Hemingway's."

Hofstadter, Douglas, *Gödel, Escher, Bach: An Eternal Golden Braid* (1979; Basic, 1999). The subject of this unique book is summed up in its second subtitle: a metaphorical fugue on minds and machines in the spirit of Lewis Carroll. Its three guiding spirits are Kurt Gödel, the Austrian logician and mathematician who formulated the famous "incompleteness" theorems regarding mathematical systems; M. C. Escher, the Dutch artist who drew seemingly impossible, paradoxical scenes; and Johann Sebastian Bach, the greatest composer of the German baroque. Hofstadter shows how formal rules and self-reference—concepts critical to the work of the three titular geniuses—can give rise to meaning, perhaps even in a system as complex as human cognition. The book's multi-stranded organization is as ingenious as its contents.

Humboldt, Alexander von, *Cosmos: A Sketch of the Physical Description of the Universe*, vol. 1 (1845; Johns Hopkins, trans. E. C. Otté, 1997). Humboldt was one of the great scientists of the nineteenth century, an explorer of Latin America as well as a naturalist, botanist, and geographer. In the early nineteenth century, he traveled extensively in New Spain (Mexico) and also in the United States, at one time visiting Thomas Jefferson. In *Cosmos*, he helped popularize science. The book gives a generally comprehensible account of the structure of the universe as it was then known. Its aim is to assess the influence of science on nature and religion. At the same time, Humboldt conveys a scientist's enjoyment of his discoveries. Charles Darwin refers to Humboldt frequently in his *Voyage of the Beagle*.

Kuhn, Thomas, *The Structure of Scientific Revolutions* (1962; Chicago, 2012). In this conceptually engaging book, Kuhn holds that scientific progress is marked not by steady advance but by a "series of peaceful interludes punctuated by intellectually violent revolutions." One theoretical world can replace another by a "paradigm shift," in which social and psychological propositions often play a critical part. Some scientists disagree with the concept of paradigm shift, but most nevertheless believe that *Structure* has had a wider influence than any other book on the history of science.

Lorenz, Konrad, *On Aggression* (1963; Harcourt Brace, trans. Marjorie Kerr Wilson, 1966). Lorenz, an ethologist, shared the Nobel Prize in Physiology in 1973. The basic concept of this book is best expressed in own words: "The subject of this book is *aggression*, that is to say the fighting instinct in beast and man which is directed *against* members of the same species." Aggressive tendencies, especially when used to secure scarce resources, are an essential part of the life-preserving process. He emphasizes animals whose behavioral patterns are most analogous to man's, for example, rats and geese. In addition, Lorenz came to share Freud's view of the constant, causeless buildup of aggression in humans. Steven Pinker's *The Blank Slate: The Modern Denial of Human Nature* (2002) challenges Lorenz's assumptions.

Mayr, Ernst, *The Growth of Biological Thought: Diversity, Evolution, and Inheritance* (1982; Harvard, 1985). A monumental history of 2,400 years of biological science, with special emphasis on taxonomy, evolution, and genetics. The author demonstrates that biologists' philosophical and cultural assumptions both guided and limited their investigations. Jacques Monod, *Chance and Necessity: An Essay on the Natural Philosophy of Modern Biology* (1970; Eng. trans., 1971), a provocative work by a Nobel Prize–winning biochemist, argues for the role of pure chance in the development of natural processes, including the molecular operations that undergird genetics and, hence, life.

Nasr, Hossein, *Science and Civilization in Islam* (1968; Kazi, 2007). Nasr is a leading authority on Islam, and this is one of the few books dealing with Islamic science as it is understood by Muslims. Topics range from mathematics and medicine to theology and alchemy in relation to Islamic concepts of religion and culture. He argues that the world is not a phenomenon of the individual psyche but of the Universal, or World, Soul, in which the human soul must participate. This interpretation takes account of mystical traditions as well as the rational basis of Islamic science and the way in which it most directly affected the West. Nasr's *Islam: Religion, History, and Civilization* (2001) is a sound and reliable basic work.

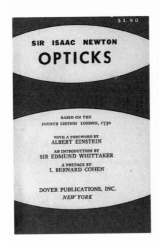 

Newton, Isaac, *Opticks* (1704; Dover, 1952). One of the great works of science: an analysis of the fundamental nature of light by its separation into a spectrum of its component colors. It supplanted ancient Greek or Roman methods of deductive reasoning from first principles with mathematical reasoning. Although the English is dated and sometimes complex, it is still easily understood. In *Newton* (2003), the science writer James Gleick provides a succinct, compelling account of the life of the man who identified such concepts as mass, gravity, and velocity, and gave them names. The reclusive, irascible Newton—professor of mathematics at Cambridge, Member of Parliament, astronomer royal, master of the Royal Mint, and president of the Royal Society—comes alive in this biography.

Polanyi, Karl, *Personal Knowledge: Towards a Post-Critical Philosophy* (1958; Chicago, 1974). Polanyi, a physical chemist and philosopher, stresses the importance of scientists' personal involvement in the production and validation of their discoveries. Commitment and a passion for discovery are indispensable for knowing a subject. Polanyi's view is a direct challenge to the ideal of scientific endeavors as detached and impersonal. Victor F. Weisskopf's *Knowledge and Wonder: The Natural World as Man Knows It* (2nd ed., 1979) provides a lucid introduction to the natural sciences, starting with elementary physical concepts (force, light) and working up to human evolution, as well as promoting a sense of the world's dazzling complexity.

Porter, Roy, *The Greatest Benefit to Mankind: A Medical History of Humanity* (1997; Norton, 1999). With an ebullient, sometimes ironic style, Porter traces the history of medicine from antiquity and in different cultures, including the Chinese. He includes passages on such problems as trying to cure George III, who may have suffered from porphyria, while more broadly helping the general reader understand basic problems in the evolution of "medicine from below," in other words, from the perspective of those subjected to primitive "cures" through the ages as well as those benefiting from the miracles of modern medicine.

Sacks, Oliver, *The Man Who Mistook His Wife for a Hat, and Other Clinical Tales* (1985; Touchstone, 1998). This collection of twenty-four neurological case studies, written in clear, vivid prose, catalogues bizarre, extraordinary effects resulting from brain injuries and deficits. In the title essay, the patient's eyesight is fine, but damage to his brain has left him unable to recognize what he sees. "The Twins" tells of a pair of autistic savants who cannot multiply numbers but make a game of computing prime numbers up to twenty digits long. The subject of "The Dog beneath the Skin," a medical student who develops a prodigiously enhanced sense of smell after a night of extensive drug taking, was later revealed to be Sacks himself.

Watson, James D., *The Double Helix: A Personal Account of the Discovery of the Structure of DNA* (1968; Touchstone, 2001). When first published, *The Double Helix* soared to the top of best-seller lists, recognized as one of the important books of the century. It provides Watson's firsthand account of how he and Francis Crick worked out the shape of the DNA molecule, a radical breakthrough in fundamental genetics. The book is controversial because it neglects the contribution to the discovery made independently by the chemist Rosalind Franklin, who first established DNA's double helix structure. Franklin's story is told in Brenda Maddox, *Rosalind Franklin: The Dark Lady of DNA* (2003).

Weinberg, Steven, *To Explain the World* (Harper, 2015). In a narrative ranging from antiquity to the present, Weinberg argues that scientists have by no means fully comprehended the phenomena they study, even when the mysteries they solved were fundamental—among others, the rise and fall of tides and the movement of planets. The book relates the clashes between science and other systems of thought and belief such as philosophy and religion. The explanation of scientific methods includes an examination of the goals of science as well as the techniques of discovery. The book is of especial interest because it is based on Weinberg's teaching experience.

Whitehead, Alfred North, *Science and the Modern World* (1925; Free Press, 1997). Whitehead, a mathematician with a strong background in physics, was a teacher and collaborator of Bertrand Russell. In this work, intended for a general readership, the author criticizes scientific materialism, including the concept of matter, which he claims is an abstraction mistakenly treated as a real entity. As an alternative, Whitehead proposed a holism of sorts: what is most real are events and the relationships between them. Another seminal work in the philosophy of science, Karl Popper's *The Logic of Scientific Discovery* (1959), turns the traditional idea of verification on its head; in the author's revolutionary formulation, falsifiability becomes the test of scientific validity, including the determination whether something falls within the province of scientific investigation.

Art, Architecture, Music, Film

Abraham, Gerald, *The Concise Oxford History of Music* (1979; Oxford, 1980). The warhorse of guides to music, this singular book is informative and authoritative about musicians and music of all periods and styles. Abraham was a musicologist who had a gift of bringing music alive to readers as well as listeners with perceptive vignettes of composers and their works. The book is strongest on music before the 20th century, and is useful above all for Mozart, Beethoven, Brahms, and Tchaikovsky. Not only readable but also simply a book enjoyable to dip into—many readers refer to it as a music bible.

Clark, Kenneth, *The Nude: A Study in Ideal Art* (1956; Penguin, 1993). Clark makes clear to the general reader that to be naked is simply to be without clothes, whereas the nude is a form of art and an expression of Western civilization. A humanist connoisseur of ancient sculpture, he traces the way the nude has been viewed throughout Western history, a judgment that has swung between the extremes of laudatory praise and moral guilt. One critic catches a significant intellectual connection by commenting that *The Nude* is as packed with meaning "as you might expect to find in the writing of Reinhold Niebuhr." Clark's *Leonardo da Vinci* (1939; rev. ed., 1988) is an insightful, engagingly written account of the artist's development, written with an encyclopedic knowledge of its subject.

Copland, Aaron, *What to Listen for in Music* (1939; Signet, 2011). The composer of such classic American musical works as the ballets *Appalachian Spring* and *Billy the Kid*, the soundtrack to *The Red Pony*, and *Fanfare for the Common Man*, here presents a guide to listening to music from a composer's point of view. His analysis takes in traditional forms (sonatas, fugues), contemporary genres (jazz, film music), and opera. Examples are drawn from composers ranging from Monteverdi to Stravinsky. In the end, Copland tries to help listeners answer the question, are you hearing everything that is going on? If not, he is there to help.

Frank, Robert, *The Americans* (1958; Steidl, intro. Jack Kerouac, 2008). Frank was a Swiss photographer who came to New York in 1947. With the assistance of a Guggenheim fellowship, he crisscrossed America in the mid-1950s, taking some 28,000 pictures, of which 83 appear in the book. They catch the racism of segregated trolleys, a culture of consumption, the glamorous rich in shiny sedans, and an ever-present sense of loneliness, even spiritual emptiness. His trips resembled the travels of Jack Kerouac, who saw similarities between his impressions and

Frank's, as well as the irony of an acute portrayal of America coming through the eyes and lens of a foreigner—a sort of Tocqueville of photography. *Looking In: Robert Frank's "The Americans"* (2009, ed. Sarah Greenough) is an expanded edition of the original.

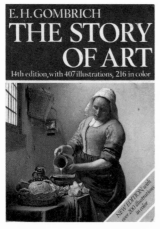

Gombrich, E. H., *The Story of Art* (1950; Phaidon, 16th rev. ed., 1995). Probably the best-known and most respected book on art ever written, translated into over thirty languages and selling over two million copies in the author's lifetime. Half the book is devoted to color reproductions of paintings, drawings, and sculptures. The first line has become famous: "There really is no such thing as Art. There are only Artists." Gombrich was a humanist with wide-ranging knowledge of such fields as psychology and biology. He was instrumental in the publication of *The Open Society and Its Enemies* by Karl Popper, a fellow Austrian.

Le Corbusier, *Towards a New Architecture* (1923; 13th ed., trans. Frederick Etchells, 1931; Dover, 1986). Charles-Edouard Jenneret, a Swiss-born architect known professionally as Le Corbusier, wrote this manifesto as an attack on art deco and other architectural styles that did not fundamentally comport with the industrial age. The seven essays discuss not only building forms but also ocean liners, airplanes, and automobiles. There is a section on ancient Rome, and one on houses constructed of prefabricated parts. The use of reinforced concrete, one of Le Corbusier's favored materials, is examined at length. The book is strident and insistent in tone, aphoristic in style, famously pronouncing that "a house is a machine for living in." The most influential work on architecture published in the twentieth century.

Panofsky, Erwin, *Perspective as Symbolic Form* (1927; Zone, trans. Christopher Wood, 1991). How can a three-dimensional world be realistically portrayed on a two-dimensional surface? Every culture with a history a pictorial representation has had to confront the problem. Byzantine and medieval art ignored it, concentrating instead on sacred images important for their own sake. The development of single-point perspective in fifteenth-century Italy, primarily by the artist-architects Brunelleschi and Alberti, offered a solution that has remained the standard in Western art. This "mathematization" of the visual plane is the subject of Panofsky's short, seminal work. In detail, and with a formidable stockpile of erudition, the author covers optics, theology, and art history, arguing that a culture's treatment of perspective offers a key to understanding its cognitive, psychological, and technical practices.

Ruskin, John, *Modern Painters* (5 vols., 1843-60; abridged edn., Knopf, 1988). Ruskin was concerned above all to uphold the reputation of J. M. W. Turner, whose paintings, he believed, provided profound insight into nature. In volume 3, Ruskin coined the term "pathetic fallacy" for the ascribing of human emotions to nature (weeping clouds, smiling flowers, etc.). In addition to art criticism, Ruskin wrote on history, political economy, and social reform. Although a self-described "violent old Tory," he devoted himself to improving the condition of the poor. His political ideas, which included abandoning capitalism and creating cooperative societies, influenced such diverse figures as the political economist John A. Hobson and Mohandas Gandhi. Tim Hilton provides a magisterial life of the author in *John Ruskin* (2 vols., 1985, 2000).

Solomon, Maynard, *Mozart: A Life* (1995; Harper Perennial, 2005). By the time of his death, at age thirty-five, Wolfgang Amadeus Mozart had composed more than 600 works—including more than 20 operas—many of them staples of the classical repertoire. While it is impossible to capture fully the nature of such a prolific genius, Maynard Solomon's fine biography grapples with the problem, paying particular attention to Mozart's tempestuous relations with his father. A less formal, more novelistic life of the composer—the first one written in English—was published by Marcia Davenport in 1932; an unfiltered sense of Mozart's personality comes through in the collection of his correspondence published as *A Life in Letters* (Penguin, trans. Stewart Spencer, 2007).

Truffaut, François, *Hitchcock: A Definitive Study of Alfred Hitchcock* (1966; Simon and Schuster, rev. ed., 2008). Hitchcock usually guarded his thoughts and only rarely disclosed his recollections of movies or anything else. Yet the French film director François Truffaut got him to open up and reveal himself as he had never done before and never did again. The two directors spent a week in 1962 at Universal Studios talking about Hitchcock's movies, each in succession, including, for example, Hitchcock's impressions of the classic *Rear Window.* "I was feeling very creative at the time, the batteries were well charged." After Hitchcock's death, Truffaut updated the book with a new preface and final chapter on Hitchcock's films. It reveals Hitchcock's insight into filmmaking and his peculiar, slightly askew sense of humor.

Vasari, Giorgio, *The Lives of the Artists* (1550; Oxford World's Classics, trans. Julia Conaway Bonadella and Peter Bonadella, 1991). Vasari was a Renaissance painter and architect, a student of Andrea del Sarto and a contemporary of Michelangelo. But his fame rests on the enormous collection of short biographies of Italian (particularly Florentine) painters, sculptors, and architects from the twelfth to the sixteenth centuries, starting with Cimabue and ending with himself. Gossipy, opinionated, and not always factually accurate, they nonetheless remain the principal starting point for art history of the period that runs from Giotto to Raphael to Titian. His accounts of the artists he knew personally are invaluable. Not least among his contributions: he was the first to use the word *Renaissance* in print.

Miscellaneous

Addiction

Alcoholics Anonymous (1939; Alcoholics Anonymous, 4th ed., 2001). The foundational text of AA (often called the Big Book) was composed by "Bill W." (William G. Wilson) and "Dr. Bob" (Robert Holbrook Smith). Their deliberate anonymity reflected the stigma of degeneracy and moral weakness associated with alcoholism, which lasted far beyond the time of the book's original publication. The core of the book is the twelve steps, along with a strong spiritual emphasis. Yet atheists and agnostics also benefit from the fundamental solution of abstinence: an alcoholic can never return to drinking, however moderate; once an alcoholic, always an alcoholic. The twenty-five millionth copy of the book was printed in 2005; the thirty millionth, in 2010. For sheer benevolent influence, *Alcoholic Anonymous* is virtually in a class of its own.

Gill, A. A., *Pour Me: A Life* (2015; Blue Rider, 2016). A journalist known for his sharp wit, honesty and, as one critic put it, flamethrowing reviews, Gill writes as an alcoholic who stopped drinking at age twenty-nine. The book, written thirty years later, offers no self-help lessons (though the author's initials, A. A., seem to carry symbolic significance). He tells the story of his life as a failed artist (he studied at the Slade School of Fine Art), porn seller, and cook. He describes frankly and flamboyantly the reality of intense alcoholic craving. Though he disclaims redemption, the book will not fail to give hope to "those who still stagger." In 2014 he won an Amnesty International Award for writing about refugees in the Congo, Jordan, and Lampedusa.

Cooking and Food

David, Elizabeth, *A Book of Mediterranean Food* (1950; NYRB, 2002). World War II–era food rationing in Britain continued into 1954. During this period of austerity, Elizabeth David published a cookbook that arrived like a burst of light in the arctic darkness. *Mediterranean Food* draws on David's experiences in wartime Alexandria, where she worked for the Ministry of Information. Her writing is full of sharp observations: "Foreigners in the Middle East are often heard to complain that they are being served with camel instead of beef. If they had ever eaten camel meat they would soon know the difference." The recipes, with measurements often less than precise, are creative in the best sense: they insist that cooks use their own imagination and ingenuity to discover how a recipe works best.

Fisher, M. F. K., *How to Cook a Wolf* (1942; North Point Press, 1988). How to cook proper meals when the wolf is at the door and there is barely enough money for food? Mary Frances Kennedy Fisher in 1942 wrote a cookbook providing a guide to healthy meals on a wartime budget. She had an eye for simple but wholesome food, and her recipes are as ingenious and healthy now as they were during World War II. She recommends keeping in the icebox an old gin bottle to be filled from time to time with vegetable juices, fruit juices, and canned juices, calling the concoction a "bracing tonic." For an account of cooking and eating in less straitened times, see Fisher's *Gastronomical Me* (1943), a food memoir with recipes from her time in Dijon and other parts of France.

Liebling, A. J., *Between Meals: An Appetite for Paris* (1962; North Point 2004). Liebling, a staff writer at the *New Yorker* for almost thirty years, went to Paris in 1926 ostensibly to study medieval French literature at the Sorbonne. Instead, he spent almost all his time—and money—exploring the hundreds of excellent restaurants and bistros in the city. He lovingly describes epic, eleven-course dinners, and lunches only slightly less lavish. Concerns about cholesterol levels or the state of one's liver are humorously dismissed. Best of all, he is at pains to prove that eating well need not be expensive. Besides food, Liebling wrote about sports, and *The Sweet Science* (1956), a collection of his pieces about boxing, was named by *Sports Illustrated* the best sports book of the twentieth century.

Toklas, Alice B., *The Alice B. Toklas Cook Book* (1954; Harper, 2010). Toklas's cookbook is full of personal recollections as well as recipes for the dishes she served to the stream of visitors who dropped in on Gertrude Stein and her in Paris from around 1910 through the 1940s. It includes piquant observations on the French, noting that they "do not eat of the innumerable kinds of pickles." Many of the dishes are elaborate; one calls for injecting a leg of lamb with orange juice twice a day for a week as it marinates. The most famous (or notorious) recipe is for Brion Gysin's Haschich Fudge, which Toklas calls "the food of Paradise." She comments that it is "easy to whip up on a rainy day."

Crime

Capote, Truman, *In Cold Blood* (1966; Vintage, 1994). Capote traveled to Holcomb, Kansas, to write an account of the murder of four members of a farm family in 1959. He was accompanied by his childhood friend, the novelist Harper Lee, who helped him interview investigators, witnesses, and others involved in the case. His 8,000 pages of detailed notes included the recipe for cherry pie made by one of the victims. He talked to the killers at length, and eventually described their execution by hanging. During the six years Capote spent writing the book, he created a new literary form by adapting techniques of fiction to factually accurate reporting. The book became an immediate success and acquired a reputation as one of the greatest true-crime books ever written.

Malcolm, Janet, *The Journalist and the Murderer* (1990; Vintage, 1990). In this slim but substantial volume, Malcolm explores the question, how much should a journalist be allowed to deceive a person he or she is writing about? The journalist Joe McGinniss interviewed Jeffrey MacDonald, in prison for murdering his wife and children, over the course of several years. MacDonald had strong reasons to believe, from McGinniss's sympathetic and supportive attitude, that the resulting book would amount to an exoneration. Instead, McGinniss's *Fatal Vision* (1983) portrayed MacDonald as a psychopathic monster. Malcolm dissects McGinniss's motives, which seemed more concerned with telling a good story than with exploring questionable aspects of the case. Malcolm's book ignited a firestorm in journalistic circles, with its implication that all journalist-subject encounters are based on deceit and double-dealing.

Trillin, Calvin, *Killings* (1984; rev. ed., Random House, 2018). Trillin, a longtime reporter for the *New Yorker*, chronicles twenty-two cases of violent death, mostly in small-town America. Trillin is not interested in the ways of killing (guns, mostly) but the whys: what would lead a man to murder his wife, or a woman to kill her child? Many of the stories are heartbreaking because the motives are utterly ordinary: insurance money, feuds, bigotry. Not ordinary are the responses of communities to murders committed in their midst, and Trillin's understated reportage captures their disturbing absurdity. He covers the trials, too, fascinated by judges, juries, prosecutors, defense attorneys, and even court reporters, all playing their roles in what can seem more like a scripted drama than a matter of life and death.

Education

Bloom, Allan, *The Closing of the American Mind: How Higher Education Has Failed Democracy and Impoverished the Souls of Today's Students* (1987; Simon & Schuster, foreword by Saul Bellow, 2012). Bloom laments the decline of the humanities and the plight of higher education in American universities, especially the devaluation of the "great books" of Western thought. The failure to maintain standards of critical reading has been particularly damaging. He alienated many readers by broadening his criticism to include rock music, sexual promiscuity, binge drinking, drugs, Black Power, divorce, and feminism. Nevertheless the book remains an important guide to significant reading. In retrospect, Bloom underestimated the intellectual curiosity of students, who, with encouragement, are as willing as ever to read broadly.

Dewey, John, *Experience and Education* (1938; Free Press, 1997). Dewey was a philosopher, psychologist, and public intellectual, but his influence in education will probably have the most enduring legacy. He argued that effective instruction should promote purposeful learning and allow students to connect with their interests and previous experiences. He believed that classroom teachers had a responsibility to shape character as well as develop skills in analysis and writing. Expertise was required, also: "A teacher ought to have an unusual love and aptitude in some one subject: history, mathematics, literature, science, a fine art, whatever." In *The Forgotten Conditions of Teaching and Learning* (1991), Jacques Barzun deals with cultural aspects of teaching, educational practices, and curricula. He gives F grades to multiple-choice tests and "counterfeit" social studies courses.

Montessori, Maria, *The Discovery of the Child* (1909; Ballantine, 1986). Montessori's philosophy of education is to allow children to develop at their own pace and discover "spontaneous self-discipline." In the classroom, children practice everyday activities such as hand washing, songs, and rhythmic movement. With the aim of developing individual abilities to deal with abstract concepts, they are encouraged to come and go in a classroom with different areas and lessons at different levels. Her methods proved controversial in the United States, especially to John Dewey, who believed that classroom education required more structure. It was not until after World War II that her educational ideas inspired the Montessori schools, which have spread throughout the country. The educator's life is told in Rita Kramer, *Maria Montessori: A Biography* (1976).

Strunk, William, Jr., and E. B. White, *The Elements of Style* (1959; Penguin, 4th ed., 2007). A venerable writing guide—Strunk's original version was published in 1920—full of fundamental advice on such aspects of good prose style as omitting needless words and using the active voice. The book includes a section on commonly misused words and expressions, and one on basic principles of composition. Too often, usage guides can seem like long lists of things not to do and rules to be followed, but Strunk and White are always encouraging, and they remind beginning writers of an important truth: "The whole duty of a writer is to please and satisfy himself, and the true writer always plays to an audience of one."

Law
Bingham, Tom, *Rule of Law* (2010; Penguin, 2011). This book was written by a disciplined legal mind but it is not a law book. It explains to a general readership, and especially to students, what the rule of law means and how it is important as the foundation of a fair and just society. What are the best examples of the rule of law since 1200? With a jaunty style, he deals with the Magna Carta and such milestones as the writ of habeas corpus, the U.S. Bill of Rights, and the abolition of slavery. He argues the illegality of the Iraq War while discussing the strains imposed on the rule of law by the danger of international terrorism. This is a clear, brilliant, and useful book.

Hart, H. L. A., *The Concept of Law* (1961; 3rd ed., Oxford, 2012). Hart was a legal philosopher whose work included political and sociological assessments as well as legal theory. He argues generally that use of the abstract word "law" reflects distinctive features of primary and secondary legal rules. Primary rules govern conduct, such as those that define criminal activity, and secondary rules govern procedural methods. Among other topics, the book addresses the relation between law and morality. With Tony Honoré, he later wrote another work of fundamental significance, *Causation in the Law* (1983). In the 1960s, Hart criticized legislation decriminalizing homosexuality, asserting that it did not go far enough. He is generally regarded as one of the foremost legal philosophers of the twentieth century.

Marshall, John, *Writings* (1779–1835; Library of America, 2008). Chief justice of the U.S. Supreme Court from 1801 to 1835, Marshall almost singlehandedly made the court a coequal partner of Congress and the presidency. This collection of 200 documents—letters, speeches, essays, and judicial decisions—runs from his time as an officer in the Continental Army through his last days. Especially recommended are the landmark decisions that form the bedrock of American jurisprudence: *Marbury v. Madison* (1803), *Fletcher v. Peck* (1810), *Dartmouth College v.*

Woodward (1819), *McCullough v. Maryland* (1819) and *Gibbons v. Ogden* (1824). Thirty of Marshall's letters to his beloved wife, "Polly," are reprinted, along with an excerpt from Marshall's *Life of George Washington* (rev. ed., 1832).

Linguistics
Culler, Jonathan, *Ferdinand de Saussure* (1976; Penguin Modern Masters, 1977). Saussure was the Swiss philosopher and linguist who laid the basis for twentieth-century linguistics in his *Course in General Linguistics* (posthumous, 1916), which cut across academic boundaries and influenced a range of disciplines, including anthropology, psychology, and philosophy. The full sweep of his work can be grasped in Culler's short monograph, which is also a clear assessment of Saussure's basic argument that language is a social phenomenon that changes over time. Saussure makes the distinction between the speech of the individual and the system underlying individual languages—a proposition critical to structural linguistics, a concept well explained by Culler.

Travel
Bryson, Bill, *The Lost Continent: Travels in Small-Town America* (1989; Harper Perennial, 2001). Bill Bryson comes from Des Moines—"someone had to." After ten years abroad, he returned for his father's funeral and decided to explore America in search of a storybook small town. He describes the gas stations, seedy motels, and countless hamburger joints encountered while traveling 13,978 miles in thirty-eight states. He found his native land blighted by pollution and "cheap little houses." He tried to avoid tourist destinations and kept loneliness at bay by reading the *New York Times*. The quintessential small town proved elusive. Having become a stranger in his own country, he was able to view it critically—in his own phrase, as a prodigal son—yet possessing, the reader discovers, a kind heart.

Fermor, Patrick Leigh, *A Time of Gifts: On Foot to Constantinople* (1977; NYRB, intro. Jan Morris, 2005). In 1933 at age eighteen, Fermor set out to walk from Holland to Turkey. He took with him the *Oxford Book of English Verse* and Horace's *Odes*. The travelogue, based on his diaries, was published four decades later. With an adventurous spirit and romantic rapture, he describes paintings, sculptures, and churches as well as his daily struggles with food, clothing, and lodging. His account of the journey is continued in *Between the Woods and the Water* (1986) and *The Broken Road* (2015). During World War II, he became famous as the British officer who kidnapped a German general in Crete, recounted in Fermor's *Abducting a General* (2015).

Kinglake, A. W., *Eothen: Traces of Travel Brought Home from the East* (1844; Oxford, intro. Jan Morris, 1991). In 1834, twenty-five-year-old Alexander Kinglake set out on a tour of the Near East: Turkey, Syria, the Holy Land, and Egypt. His friends and family assumed he would not return, since in the European imagination, those regions were marked mainly by barbarity and the plague. (And in fact, the plague breaks out while he is in Cairo.) His traveling companions likewise have doubts, one of them being "not frightened exactly, but sternly prepared for death, or the Koran, or even for plural wives." Kinglake looked at everything (Constantinople, Lady Hester Stanhope, the Sphinx) with clear-eyed curiosity and wrote, with concision and grace, about all he had seen.

O'Hanlon, Redmond, *Into the Heart of Borneo* (1987; Penguin, 2005). In 1983, O'Hanlon was the natural history editor of the *Times Literary Supplement;* his friend James Fenton, a celebrated poet. They traveled to Borneo to try to spot the fabled Bornean rhinoceros. On their trek, they encountered vipers, cholera, ticks, malaria, rabies, and crocodiles. They survived on jungle-worm gruel. Fenton was nearly swept away in a whirlpool. No one had attempted an expedition to the island since 1926, so O'Hanlon and Fenton's insights on culture and nature are scientifically and historically useful as well as incomparably entertaining. When later asked by O'Hanlon to join him on another expedition, Fenton replied, "Redmond, I wouldn't even go as far as High Wycombe with you."

Theroux, Paul, *The Great Railway Bazaar: By Train through Asia* (1975; Penguin, 2008). In Theroux's most famous travel book, he spends four months in 1973 on a journey across Europe via the Orient Express to the Khyber Pass and on to points in India and Southeast Asia. His return takes him 6,000 miles from Japan to Moscow on the Trans-Siberian Railway. The theme is discovery shadowed by danger. Theroux writes with wry humor, and his style is authoritative and confident, yet he is also condescending and petty, constantly complaining in disgust about his fellow travelers. One critic writes: "Set in 1973, the colonial hangover comes along as an undertone for the entire journey." Yet the *Great Railway Bazaar* is a classic work in the post-1945 travelogue genre.

Titles Sorted by Category

Authors of 150 highly recommended titles are in boldface.

History

United States

Allison, *Destined for War: Can America and China Escape Thucydides's Trap?*

Bailyn, *Ideological Origins of the American Revolution*

Beard and Beard, *The Rise of American Civilization*

Boorstin, *The Americans: The National Experience*

Bowen, *Miracle at Philadelphia*

Branch, *Parting the Waters: America in the King Years, 1954–63*

Brown, *Bury My Heart at Wounded Knee*

DeVoto, ed., *The Journals of Lewis and Clark*

Evans, *The American Century*

Genovese, *Roll, Jordan, Roll: The World the Slaves Made*

Gordon-Reed, *The Hemingses of Monticello*

Grant, *Personal Memoirs*

Halberstam, *The Making of a Quagmire*

Higham, *Strangers in the Land: Patterns of American Nativism, 1860–1925*

Howe, *What Has God Wrought: The Transformation of America, 1815–1848*

Jefferson, *The Life and Selected Writings of Thomas Jefferson*

Limerick, *The Legacy of Conquest: The Unbroken Past of the American West*

Miller, *The New England Mind: The Seventeenth Century*

Morgan, *The Puritan Dilemma*

Noll, *America's God: From Jonathan Edwards to Abraham Lincoln*

Osborn, *The Wild Frontier*

Rhodes, *The Making of the Atomic Bomb*

Ricks, *Fiasco*

Schlesinger, *The Age of Roosevelt: The Crisis of the Old Order*

Sheehan, *A Bright Shining Lie*

Sledge, *With the Old Breed*

Stampp, *The Peculiar Institution*

Tansill, *Back Door to War: The Roosevelt Foreign Policy*

Tocqueville, *Democracy in America*

Turner, "The Significance of the Frontier in American History"

Webb, *The Great Plains*

Woodward, *The Strange Career of Jim Crow*

Zinn, *A People's History of the United States*

Britain

Arnstein, *The Bradlaugh Case: Atheism, Sex, and Politics among the Late Victorians*

Bede, *Ecclesiastical History of the English People*

Carlyle, *On Heroes, Hero-Worship, and the Heroic in History*

Colley, *Britons: Forging the Nation, 1707–1837*

Dangerfield, *The Strange Death of Liberal England*

Gallagher, *The Decline, Revival, and Fall of the British Empire*

Hammond, *Gladstone and the Irish Nation*

Hill, *The World Turned Upside Down: Radical Ideas during the English Revolution*

Hobson, *Imperialism*

Howard, *The Continental Commitment: The Dilemma of British Defence Policy in the Era of the Two World Wars*

Hyde, *The History of the Rebellion*

Kedourie, *The Chatham House Version*

Langford, *A Polite and Commercial People: England, 1727–1783*

Macaulay, *The History of England*

Maitland, *Domesday Book and Beyond*

Marcus, *The Other Victorians: A Study of Sexuality and Pornography in Mid-Nineteenth-Century England*

Mattingly, *The Defeat of the Spanish Armada*

McFarlane, *The Nobility of Later Medieval England*

Namier, *The Structure of Politics at the Accession of George III*

O'Shaughnessy, *The Men Who Lost America*

Perham, *The Colonial Reckoning*

Robinson and Gallagher, *Africa and the Victorians*

Seeley, *The Expansion of England*

Thomas, *Religion and the Decline of Magic*

Thompson, *The Making of the English Working Class*

Thornton, *The Imperial Idea and Its Enemies: A Study in British Power*

Trevelyan, *The English Revolution, 1688–1689*

Woodham-Smith, *The Reason Why*

Young, *Victorian England: Portrait of an Age*

World History

Belloc, *The Crusades*

McNeill, *The Rise of the West*

Phillips, *The Fourth Crusade and the Sack of Constantinople*

Spengler, *The Decline of the West*

Toynbee, *A Study of History*

Vico, *New Science*

Europe

Barzun, *From Dawn to Decadence, 1500 to the Present*

Braudel, *The Mediterranean and the Mediterranean World*

Cohn, *The Pursuit of the Millennium: Revolutionary Millenarians and Mystical Anarchists of the Middle Ages*

Dawidowicz, *The War against the Jews*

Elliott, *Empires of the Atlantic World*

Guizot, *The History of Civilization in Europe*

Huizinga, *The Autumn of the Middle Ages*

Kershaw, *To Hell and Back*

MacCulloch, *The Reformation*

Pirenne, *Mohammed and Charlemagne*

Southern, *The Making of the Middle Ages*

Wedgwood, *The Thirty Years War*

Yates, *The Rosicrucian Enlightenment*

France

Bloch, *The Historian's Craft* and *Strange Defeat*
Cobb, *Reactions to the French Revolution*
Darnton, *The Great Cat Massacre*
Furet, *Interpreting the French Revolution*
Herold, *Bonaparte in Egypt*
Horne, *A Savage War of Peace: Algeria, 1954–1962*
Lefebvre, *The Coming of the French Revolution*
May, *Strange Victory: Hitler's Conquest of France*
Staël, *Considerations on the Principal Events of the French Revolution*
Tillion, *Algeria: The Realities*
Zeldin, *France, 1848–1945*

Germany and Austria-Hungary

Browning, *The Origins of the Final Solution*
Buller, *Darkness over Germany*
Evans, *Death in Hamburg: Society and Politics in the Cholera Years*
Fischer, *Germany's Aims in the First World War*
Macartney, *The Habsburg Empire, 1790–1918*
Nolte, *Three Faces of Fascism*
Sheehan, *German History, 1770–1866*
Stern, *Blood and Iron*
Stoye, *The Siege of Vienna*
Taylor, *The Origins of the Second World War*
Trevor-Roper, *The Last Days of Hitler*

Greece

Clogg, *A Concise History of Greece*
Woodhouse, *The Struggle for Greece, 1941–1949*

Ireland

Fitzpatrick, *Politics and Irish Life, 1913–21*
Foster, *Vivid Faces: The Revolutionary Generation in Ireland, 1890–1923*
Kee, *The Green Flag: A History of Irish Nationalism*
Townshend, *Easter 1916*

Italy

Burckhardt, *The Civilization of the Renaissance in Italy*
Holmes, *Florence, Rome, and the Origins of the Renaissance*
Mack Smith, *Cavour and Garibaldi 1860*
Norwich, *A History of Venice*

Low Countries

Humes, *Belgium: Long United, Long Divided*
Israel, *The Dutch Republic*
Kossmann, *The Low Countries, 1780–1940*

Poland

Davies, *God's Playground: A History of Poland*

Portugal

Boxer, *The Portuguese Seaborne Empire, 1415–1825*
Disney, *A History of Portugal and the Portuguese Empire*

Romania

Hitchins, *Rumania, 1866–1947*

Russia

Conquest, *The Great Terror*
Pipes, *Russia under the Old Regime*
Reed, *Ten Days That Shook the World*
Wilson, *To the Finland Station*

Spain

Brenan, *The Spanish Labyrinth*
Carr, *Spain, 1808–1938*
Thomas, *The Spanish Civil War*

Turkey

Lewis, *The Emergence of Modern Turkey*
Reynolds, *Shattering Empires: The Clash and Collapse of the Ottoman and Russian Empires, 1908–1918*
Rogan, *The Fall of the Ottomans: The Great War in the Middle East, 1914–1920*
Stone, *Turkey: A Short History*
Zürcher, *Turkey: A Modern History*

Yugoslavia

Deakin, *The Embattled Mountain*
West, *Black Lamb and Grey Falcon*

Africa

Buell, *The Native Problem in Africa*
Gluckman, *Custom and Conflict in Africa*
Iliffe, *Africans: The History of a Continent*
Lugard, *The Dual Mandate in British Tropical Africa*
Mazrui, *Nkrumah's Legacy*
Moorehead, *The White Nile*
Oliver and Fage, *A Short History of Africa*
Ranger, *Revolt in Southern Rhodesia, 1896–97*
Rodney, *How Europe Underdeveloped Africa*

Middle East

Amanat, *Iran: A Modern History*
Antonius, *The Arab Awakening*
Batatu, *The Old Social Classes and the Revolutionary Movements of Iraq*
Blunt, *Secret History of the English Occupation of Egypt*
Heikal, *Cutting the Lion's Tale: Suez through Egyptian Eyes*
Herzl, *The Jewish State*
Hourani, *A History of the Arab Peoples*
Ibn Battutah, *The Travels of Ibn Battutah*
Ibn Khaldun, *Muqaddimah*
Khalidi, *From Haven to Conquest: Readings in Zionism and the Palestine Problem*
Kyle, *Suez*
Nasser, *Philosophy of the Revolution*
Seale, *The Struggle for Arab Independence*
Shlaim, *The Iron Wall: Israel and the Arab World*

China

Bickers, *Out of China: How the Chinese Ended the Era of Western Domination*
Fairbank, *The United States and China*
Isaacs, *The Tragedy of the Chinese Revolution*

Peyrefitte, *The Immobile Empire*
Polo, *The Travels*
Schiffrin, *Sun Yat-sen and the Origins of the Chinese Revolution*
Snow, *Red Star over China*
Spence, *The Search for Modern China*
Wright, *The Last Stand of Chinese Conservatism*

India

Bayly, *Empire and Information: Intelligence Gathering and Social Communication in India, 1780–1870*
Copland, *The Princes of India in the Endgame of Empire*
Guha, *India after Gandhi*
Hardy, *The Muslims of British India*
Hibbert, *The Great Mutiny: India, 1857*
Marston, *The Indian Army and the End of the Raj*
Nehru, *The Discovery of India*
Thapar, *A History of India*

Japan

Bix, *Hirohito and the Making of Modern Japan*
Dower, *Embracing Defeat: Japan in the Wake of World War II*
Hall, *Government and Local Power in Japan, 500–1700*
Hersey, *Hiroshima*
Jansen, *The Making of Modern Japan*
Nish, *Alliance in Decline*
Reischauer, *Japan*
Sansom, *The Western World and Japan*

Pakistan

Hamid, *Disastrous Twilight: A Personal Record of the Partition of India*
Jalal, *The Sole Spokesman: Jinnah, the Muslim League, and the Demand for Pakistan*

Southeast Asia

Bayly and Harper, *Forgotten Armies: Britain's Asian Empire and the War with Japan*
Benda, *The Crescent and the Rising Sun: Indonesian Islam under the Japanese Occupation, 1942–1945*
Fall, *Hell in a Very Small Place: The Siege of Dien Bien Phu*
Friend, *Indonesian Destinies*
Furnivall, *Colonial Policy and Practice*
Harper, *The End of Empire and the Making of Malaya*
Kahin, *Nationalism and Revolution in Indonesia*
Slim, *Defeat into Victory: Battling Japan in Burma and India, 1942–1945*

Ancient World

Dodds, *The Greeks and the Irrational*
Gibbon, *Decline and Fall of the Roman Empire*
Herodotus, *The History*
Livy, *The Early History of Rome*
Mommsen, *The History of Rome*
Syme, *The Roman Revolution*
Tacitus, *The Annals of Imperial Rome*
Thucydides, *History of the Peloponnesian War*

Antarctica and the Arctic

Alexander, *The Endurance: Shackleton's Legendary Antarctic Expedition*
Peary, *The North Pole*
Solomon, *The Coldest March: Scott's Fatal Antarctic Expedition*

Australia, New Zealand, Oceania

Clark, *A History of Australia*
Hancock, *Australia*
Hughes, *The Fatal Shore*
Reeves, *The Long White Cloud: Ao-tea-roa*
Sinclair, *The Origins of the Maori Wars*

Canada

Bothwell, *The Penguin History of Canada*
Brebner, *North Atlantic Triangle*
Granatstein, *How Britain's Economic, Political, and Military Weakness Forced Canada into the Arms of the United States*
Martin, *The Durham Report and British Policy*
Winks, *The Blacks in Canada*

Mexico, Latin America, South America, the Caribbean

Bethell, *A Cultural History of Latin America*
Brown, *Cuba's Revolutionary World*
Crow, *The Epic of Latin America*
Freyre, *Brazil: An Interpretation*
Galeano, *Open Veins of Latin America*
James, *The Black Jacobins*
Pares, *War and Trade in the West Indies, 1739–1763*
Paz, *The Labyrinth of Solitude*
Prescott, *History of the Conquest of Mexico*
Williams, *Capitalism and Slavery*

Military History

Clausewitz, *On War*
Grotius, *The Rights of War and Peace*
Keegan, *The Face of Battle: A Study of Agincourt, Waterloo, and the Somme*
Tuchman, *The Guns of August*
U.S. Army / Marine Corps Counterinsurgency Field Manual, The
Walzer, *Just and Unjust Wars*

Naval History

Mahan, *The Influence of Sea Power upon History*
Marder, *From the Dreadnought to Scapa Flow*, vol. 1
Massie, *Dreadnought*
Roskill, *Naval Policy between the Wars*

Historiography, Intellectual History, the History of Ideas

Annan, *Our Age*
Aron, *The Opium of the Intellectuals*
Benda, *The Treason of the Intellectuals*
Berlin, *The Hedgehog and the Fox*
Butterfield, *The Whig Interpretation of History*
Collingwood, *The Idea of History*
Crossman, *The God That Failed*
Hobsbawm and Ranger, *The Invention of Tradition*
Ortega y Gasset, *Revolt of the Masses*
Ranke, *The Theory and Practice of History*
Snow, *The Two Cultures*

Energy History

Tarbell, *The History the of Standard Oil Company*
Yergin, *The Prize*

Autobiographies, Biographies, Memoirs

Britain

Bate, *John Keats*
Beaglehole, *The Life of Captain James Cook*
Besant, *Annie Besant: An Autobiography*
Blake, *Disraeli*
Blunden, *Undertones of War*
Boswell, *The Life of Samuel Johnson*
Bourke, *Empire and Revolution: The Political Life of Edmund Burke*
Brittain, *Testament of Youth*
Cecil, *A Great Experiment: An Autobiography*
Churchill, *My Early Life*
Corbett, *Man-Eaters of Kumaon*
Gosse, *Father and Son*
Graves, *Good-Bye to All That*
Greenblatt, *Will in The World: How Shakespeare Became Shakespeare*
Hardy, *A Mathematician's Apology*
Harris, *William Beveridge*
Holmes, *Shelley: The Pursuit*
Jenkins, *Gladstone*
Lawrence, *The Seven Pillars of Wisdom*
Lee, *Virginia Woolf*
Medawar, *Memoir of a Thinking Radish*
Newman, *Apologia pro Vita Sua*
Pepys, *Diary*
Pritchett, *A Cab at the Door* and *Midnight Oil*
Reynolds, *In Command of History: Churchill Fighting and Writing the Second World War*
Spear, *Master of Bengal: Clive and His India*
Strachey, *Eminent Victorians*
Wavell, *The Viceroy's Journal*
Webb, Beatrice, *My Apprenticeship*
Woolf, *The Journey Not the Arrival Matters*
Ziegler, *Mountbatten*

United States

Acheson, *Present at the Creation*
Adams, *The Education of Henry Adams*
Berg, *Max Perkins: Editor of Genius*
Berkman, *Prison Memoirs of an Anarchist*
Blum, *The Republican Roosevelt*
Buchwald, *I'll Always Have Paris: A Memoir*
Chambers, *Witness*
Dana, *Two Years before the Mast*
Douglass, *Narrative of the Life of Frederick Douglass*
Eastman, *Love and Revolution: My Journey through an Epoch*
Franklin, *Autobiography*
Goldman, *Living My Life*
Greenstein, *The Hidden-Hand Presidency: Eisenhower as Leader*
Hook, *Out of Step: An Unquiet Life in the 20th Century*
Kennan, *The Kennan Diaries*
Malcolm X, *The Autobiography of Malcolm X*
Morris, *The Rise of Theodore Roosevelt*
Obama, *Dreams from My Father*
Sanger, *The Autobiography of Margaret Sanger*
Steel, *Walter Lippmann and the American Century*
Stein, *The Autobiography of Alice B. Toklas*
Thoreau, *Walden*
Urquhart, *Ralph Bunche*
Utley, *Geronimo*
Washington, *Up From Slavery*
Williams, *Huey Long*

Africa

Hancock, *Smuts: The Sanguine Years*
Huxley, *The Flame Trees of Thika*
Mandela, *Long Walk to Freedom*
Soyinka, *The Man Died: Prison Notes*

Ancient World

Plutarch, *Parallel Lives*

Canada

English, *Just Watch Me: The Life of Pierre Elliott Trudeau, 1968–2000*
Levine, *King: William Lyon Mackenzie King*
Pearson, *Words and Occasions*

China

Chang, *Wild Swans*
Pakula, *The Last Empress: Madame Chiang Kai-shek and the Birth of Modern China*

France

Chateaubriand, *Memoirs from Beyond the Grave, 1768–1800*
de Gaulle, *War Memoirs*
Geyl, *Napoleon: For and Against*
Jackson, *A Certain Idea of France: The Life of Charles de Gaulle*
Lacouture, *De Gaulle: The Rebel, 1890–1944*
Mitford, *The Sun King: Louis XIV at Versailles*
Reiss, *The Black Count* [Thomas-Alexandre Dumas]

Germany and Austria

Blanning, *Frederick the Great: King of Prussia*
Fest, *Hitler*
Hitler, *Mein Kampf*
Jünger, *Storm of Steel*
Ritter, *Frederick the Great*
Safranski, *Martin Heidegger: Between Good and Evil*
Speer, *Inside the Third Reich*
Steinberg, *Bismarck: A Life*
Zweig, *The World of Yesterday*

India

Chaudhuri, *The Autobiography of an Unknown Indian*
Gandhi, *The Story of My Experiments with Truth*
Gopal, *Jawarhalal Nehru*

Israel

Oz, *A Tale of Love and Darkness*
Teveth, *The Burning Ground: A Biography of David Ben-Gurion*
Weizmann, *Trial and Error: The Autobiography of Chaim Weizmann*

Italy

Cellini, *Autobiography*
Levi, *If This Is a Man*

Jamaica

Hall, *Familiar Stranger*

Latin America and South America

Arana, *Bolívar: American Liberator*
Katz, *The Life and Times of Pancho Villa*
Womack, *Zapata and the Mexican Revolution*

Middle East

Burton, *Personal Narrative of a Pilgrimage to El-Madinah and Meccah*
Musaddiq, *Musaddiq's Memoirs*
Nafisi, *Reading Lolita in Tehran*

Russia

Herzen, *My Past and Thoughts*
Kotkin, *Stalin: Waiting for Hitler, 1929–1941*
Kropotkin, *Memoirs of a Revolutionist*
Taubman, *Khrushchev: The Man and His Era*

Spain

Fernández-Armesto, *Columbus*
Morison, *Admiral of the Ocean Sea* [Columbus]
Payne and Palacios, *Franco*

Sweden

Urquhart, *Hammarskjold*

Vietnam

Brocheux, *Ho Chi Minh: A Biography*
MacDonald, *Giap: The Victor in Vietnam*

Literature

Key: (d): drama; (e): essays; (n): novel; (p): poetry; (s): stories

Britain

17th century and earlier
Aubrey, *Brief Lives* (e)
Bacon, *Essays* (e)
Beowulf (p)
Browne, *Religio Medici* and *Urne-Buriall*
Bunyan, *The Pilgrim's Progress* (n)
Burton, *The Anatomy of Melancholy*
Chaucer, *The Canterbury Tales* (p)
Donne, *The Complete Poetry and Selected Prose*
Dryden, *The Major Works* (d, p)
Ford, *'Tis Pity She's a Whore, and Other Plays* (d)
Jonson, *Volpone* (p)
Langland, *Piers the Ploughman* (p)
Milton, *Paradise Lost* (p)
More, *Utopia* (n)
Shakespeare, *Works* (d), esp. *A Midsummer Night's Dream, Hamlet, King Lear, Macbeth, The Tempest, Twelfth Night*
Spenser, *The Faerie Queene* (p)

18th century
Blake, *The Marriage of Heaven and Hell* (p)
Burns, *Selected Poems* (p)
Defoe, *Robinson Crusoe* (n)
Fielding, *The History of Tom Jones* (n)
Jones, *Selected Poetical and Prose Works* (p, e)
Pope, *The Major Works* (p)
Richardson, *Clarissa* (n)
Stanhope, *Lord Chesterfield's Letters*
Sterne, *Tristram Shandy* (n)
Swift, *Gulliver's Travels* (n)

19th century
Arnold, *Culture and Anarchy* (e)
Austen, *Pride and Prejudice* (n)
Brontë, C., *Jane Eyre* (n)
Brontë, E., *Wuthering Heights* (n)
Browning, E. B., *Aurora Leigh, and Other Poems* (p)
Browning, R., *The Major Works* (p)
Bulwer-Lytton, *Last Days of Pompeii* (n)
Byron, *The Major Works* (p)
Carroll, *Alice's Adventures in Wonderland* (n)
Coleridge, *Selected Poetry* (p)
Collins, *The Moonstone* (n)
Conrad, *Heart of Darkness* (n)
De Quincey, *Confessions of an English Opium-Eater* (e)
Dickens, *Great Expectations* (n)
Doyle, *The Complete Sherlock Holmes* (n, s)
Eliot, *Middlemarch* (n)
Gaskell, *Cranford* (n)
Gissing, *New Grub Street* (n)
Hardy, *Far from the Madding Crowd* (n)
Housman, *A Shropshire Lad, and Other Poems* (p)

Jerome, *Three Men in a Boat* (n)
Keats, *Selected Poetry* (p)
Kingsley, *Westward Ho!* (n)
Lamb and Lamb, *Tales from Shakespeare* (s)
Lear, *The Owl and the Pussy-Cat* (p)
Scott, *Ivanhoe* (n)
Shelley, M., *Frankenstein* (n)
Shelley, P. B., *The Major Works* (p)
Stevenson, *The Strange Case of Dr. Jekyll and Mr. Hyde* (n)
Stoker, *Dracula* (n)
Tennyson, *The Major Works* (p)
Thackeray, *Vanity Fair* (n)
Trollope, *The Way We Live Now* (n)
Wells, *The Time Machine* (n)
Wilde, *The Importance of Being Earnest* (d)
Wordsworth, *The Prelude* (p)

20th century
Amis, *Lucky Jim* (n)
Auden, *The Shield of Achilles* (p)
Ballard, *Empire of the Sun* (n)
Bennett, *The Old Wives' Tale* (n)
Betjeman, *The Best of Betjeman* (p)
Bradbury, *The History Man* (n)
Buchan, *The Thirty-Nine Steps* (n)
Burgess, *A Clockwork Orange* (n)
Butler, *The Way of All Flesh* (n)
Cary, *Mister Johnson* (n)
Chesterton, *The Man Who Was Thursday* (n)
Childers, *Riddle of the Sands* (n)
Christie, *Murder on the Orient Express* (n)
Dahl, *Charlie and the Chocolate Factory* (n)
du Maurier, *Rebecca* (n)
Durrell, *The Alexandria Quartet* (n)
Eliot, *The Waste Land* (p)
Farrell, *The Singapore Grip* (n)
Ford, *Parade's End* (n)
Forester, *Lieutenant Hornblower* and *Flying Colours* (n)
Forster, *A Passage to India* (n)
Galsworthy, *The Forsyte Saga* (n)
Golding, *Lord of the Flies* (n)
Grahame, *The Wind in the Willows* (n)
Green, *Loving* (n)
Greene, *The Heart of the Matter* (n)
Hughes, *Collected Poems* (p)
Huxley, *Brave New World* (n)
Isherwood and Auden, *The Ascent of F6* (d)
Ishiguro, *The Remains of the Day* (n)
Kipling, *Kim* (n)
Koestler, *Darkness at Noon* (n)
Larkin, *Collected Poems* (p)
Lawrence, *Lady Chatterley's Lover* (n)
Le Carré, *The Spy Who Came in from the Cold* (n)
Lessing, *The Golden Notebook* (n)
Lively, *Moon Tiger* (n)
Lodge, *Changing Places* (n)

Lowry, *Under the Volcano* (n)
Mackenzie, *Whisky Galore* (n)
MacNeice, *Collected Poems* (p)
Manning, *The Levant Trilogy* (n)
Mansfield, *Selected Stories* (s)
Mantel, *Wolf Hall* (n)
Masters, *Bhowani Junction* (n)
Maugham, *The Razor's Edge* (n)
Milne, *Winnie-the-Pooh* and *The House at Pooh Corner* (n)
Murdoch, *Under the Net* (n)
Naipaul, *A Bend in the River* (n)
Opie and Opie, *The Oxford Book of Nursery Rhymes* (p)
Orwell, *1984* (n)
Osborne, *Look Back in Anger* (d)
Owen, *The War Poems* (p)
Potter, *The Tailor of Gloucester* (n)
Powell, *A Question of Upbringing* (n)
Priestley, *The Good Companions* (n)
Ransome, *Swallows and Amazons* (n)
Ricks, *The Oxford Book of English Verse* (p)
Sassoon, *Memoirs of a Fox-Hunting Man* (n)
Scott, *The Raj Quartet* (n)
Sebald, *Austerlitz* (n)
Shaw, *Pygmalion* (d)
Spark, *The Prime of Miss Jean Brodie* (n)
Thompson, *Lark Rise to Candleford* (n)
Waugh, *Brideshead Revisited* (n)
Wodehouse, *Right Ho, Jeeves* (n)
Woolf, *Mrs. Dalloway* (n)

United States
19th century
Alcott, *Little Women* (n)
Cooper, *The Last of the Mohicans* (n)
Crane, *The Red Badge of Courage* (n)
Dickinson, *Selected Poems* (p)
Emerson, *Nature, and Selected Essays* (e)
Harris, *Uncle Remus: His Songs and Sayings* (s)
Hawthorne, *The Scarlet Letter* (n)
Irving, *The Legend of Sleepy Hollow, and Other Stories* (s)
James, *The Portrait of a Lady* (n)
Longfellow, *Selected Poems* (p)
Melville, *Moby-Dick* (n)
Poe, *Complete Stories and Poems* (s, p)
Stowe, *Uncle Tom's Cabin* (n)
Twain, *The Adventures of Huckleberry Finn* (n)
Whitman, *Leaves of Grass* (p)

20th century
Anderson, *Winesburg, Ohio* (s)
Bellow, *Herzog* (n)
Berryman, *77 Dream Songs* (p)
Bishop, *The Complete Poems, 1927–1979* (p)
Bowles, *The Sheltering Sky* (n)
Burroughs, E. R., *Tarzan of the Apes* (n)
Burroughs, W., *Naked Lunch* (n)

Cather, *My Ántonia* (n)
Chandler, *The Big Sleep* (n)
Cummings, *e. e. cummings: Complete Poems, 1904–1962* (p)
DeLillo, *White Noise* (n)
Dick, *Do Androids Dream of Electric Sheep?* (n)
Didion, *Slouching towards Bethlehem* (e)
Dos Passos, *USA* (n)
Dreiser, *Sister Carrie* (n)
Ellison, *Invisible Man* (n)
Faulkner, *Light in August* (n)
Fitzgerald, *The Great Gatsby* (n)
Frost, *The Poetry of Robert Frost* (p)
Gaddis, *The Recognitions* (n)
Ginsberg, *Howl, Kaddish, and Other Poems* (p)
Hammett, *The Maltese Falcon* (n)
Heinlein, *Stranger in a Strange Land* (n)
Heller, *Catch-22* (n)
Hemingway, *The Sun Also Rises* (n)
Herbert, *Dune* (n)
Hughes, *The Collected Poems* (p)
Hurston, *Their Eyes Were Watching God* (n)
Jarrell, *The Woman at the Washington Zoo* (p)
Kerouac, *On the Road* (n)
Kingsolver, *The Poisonwood Bible* (n)
Lee, *To Kill a Mockingbird* (n)
Lehman, ed., *The Oxford Book of American Poetry* (p)
Leonard, *52 Pickup* (n)
Lewis, *Babbitt* (n)
London, *The Call of the Wild* and *White Fang* (n)
Lovecraft, *The Call of Cthulhu, and Other Weird Stories* (s)
Lowell, *For the Union Dead* (p)
Macdonald, *The Galton Case* (n)
Mailer, *Armies of the Night* (e)
McCarthy, C., *Blood Meridian* (n)
McCarthy, M., *The Group* (n)
McCullers, *The Heart Is a Lonely Hunter* (n)
Mencken, *The Vintage Mencken* (e)
Millay, *The Selected Poetry* (p)
Miller, A., *Death of a Salesman* (d)
Miller, H., *Tropic of Cancer* (n)
Morrison, *Song of Solomon* (n)
Nabokov, *Lolita* (n)
O'Connor, Flannery, *The Complete Stories* (s)
O'Neill, *Long Day's Journey into Night* (d)
Pirsig, *Zen and the Art of Motorcycle Maintenance* (n)
Plath, *The Bell Jar* (n)
Porter, *Ship of Fools* (n)
Pound, *Selected Poems* (p)
Pynchon, *Gravity's Rainbow* (n)
Rand, *The Fountainhead* (n)
Roth, *American Pastoral* (n)
Salinger, *The Catcher in the Rye* (n)
Sinclair, *The Jungle* (n)
Singer, *A Crown of Feathers, and Other Stories* (s)
Sontag, *Against Interpretation* (e)

Steinbeck, *The Grapes of Wrath* (n)
Stevens, *Collected Poems* (p)
Styron, *The Confessions of Nat Turner* (n)
Traven, *The Treasure of the Sierra Madre* (n)
Vidal, *United States: Essays* (e)
Vonnegut, *Cat's Cradle* (n)
Wharton, *The Age of Innocence* (n)
White, *Charlotte's Web* (n)
Wilder, *The Bridge of San Luis Rey* (n)
Williams, T., *A Streetcar Named Desire* (d)
Williams, W.C., *Selected Poems* (p)
Wister, *The Virginian* (n)
Wolfe, Thomas, *Look Homeward, Angel* (n)
Wolfe, Tom, *The Bonfire of the Vanities* (n)
Wouk, *The Caine Mutiny* (n)

Central and Eastern Europe

Eliade, *Bengal Nights* (n)
Hašek, *The Good Soldier Švejk* (n)
Hrabal, *Closely Watched Trains* (n)
Kafka, *The Trial* (n)
Krúdy, *The Adventures of Sinbad* (s)
Lem, *Solaris* (n)
Milosz, *Selected and Last Poems, 1931–2004* (p)
Szabó, *The Door* (n)
Szymborska, *View with a Grain of Sand: Selected Poems* (p)
Vazov, *Under the Yoke* (n)

France

Balzac, *The Human Comedy: Selected Stories* (s)
Baudelaire, *Selected Poems* (p)
Camus, *The Stranger* (n)
Corneille, *Le Cid* (d)
Diderot, *The Nun* (n)
d'Ormesson, *The Glory of the Empire* (n)
Dumas, *The Count of Monte Cristo* (n)
Feydeau, *A Flea in Her Ear* (d)
Flaubert, *Madame Bovary* (n)
France, *The Revolt of the Angels* (n)
Gide, *The Counterfeiters* (n)
Hugo, *The Hunchback of Notre-Dame* (n)
La Fayette, *La Princesse de Clèves* (n)
Malraux, *Man's Fate* (n)
Maupassant, *Selected Works* (s)
Molière, *The Misanthrope* and *Tartuffe* (d)
Montaigne, *Essays* (e)
Proust, *Swann's Way* (n)
Rabelais, *Gargantua and Pantagruel* (n)
Racine, *Phèdre* (d)
Sartre, *Nausea* (n)
Song of Roland, The (p)
Stendhal, *The Red and the Black* (n)
Verne, *Around the World in Eighty Days* (n)
Voltaire, *Candide* (n)
Zola, *The Dreyfus Affair* (e)

Germany and Austria

Brecht, *The Threepenny Opera* (d)
Fontane, *Effie Briest* (n)
Goethe, *Faust* (p)
Grass, *The Tin Drum* (n)
Grimm and Grimm, *The Original Folk and Fairy Tales of the Brothers Grimm* (s)
Hesse, *Siddhartha* (n)
Kleist, *The Marquise of O, and Other Stories* (s)
Mann, *Death in Venice* (n)
Musil, *The Man without Qualities* (n)
Remarque, *All Quiet on the Western Front* (n)
Roth, *The Radetzky March* (n)
Schiller, *The Robbers* and *Wallenstein* (d)
Schnitzler, *The Road into the Open* (n)
Werfel, *The Forty Days of Musa Dagh* (n)

Ireland

Beckett, *Waiting for Godot* (d)
Donleavy, *The Ginger Man* (n)
Heaney, Seamus, *Death of a Naturalist* (p)
Joyce, *Dubliners* (s)
O'Brien, E., *The Country Girls* (n)
O'Brien, F., *The Third Policeman* (n)
Trevor, *The News from Ireland, and Other Stories* (s)
Yeats, *Collected Poetry* (p)

Italy

Ariosto, *Orlando Furioso* (p)
Boccaccio, *Tales from the Decameron* (s)
Calvino, *If on a winter's night a traveler* (n)
Dante, *Inferno* (p)
Eco, *The Name of the Rose* (n)
Lampedusa, *The Leopard* (n)
Manzoni, *The Betrothed* (n)
Sciascia, *The Day of the Owl* (n)
Silone, *Bread and Wine* (n)

Low Countries

Couperus, *Eline Vere* (n)
Maeterlinck, *The Life of the Bee* (e)
Multatuli, *Max Havelaar: Or the Coffee Auctions of the Dutch Trading Company* (n)
Simenon, *Maigret and Monsieur Charles* (n)

Portugal

Lobo Antunes, *The Inquisitor's Manual* (n)
Saramago, *The Gospel according to Jesus Christ* (n)

Russia

Babel, *Red Cavalry, and Other Stories* (s)
Brodsky, *To Urania: Selected Poems* (p)
Bulgakov, *The Master and Margarita* (n)
Chekhov, *The Cherry Orchard* (d)
Dostoyevsky, *The Brothers Karamazov* (n)
Gogol, *Dead Souls* (n)
Goncharov, *Oblomov* (n)
Gorky, *The Collected Short Stories* (s)

Grossman, *Life and Fate* (n)
Pasternak, *Doctor Zhivago* (n)
Pushkin, *Eugene Onegin* (n)
Serge, *Midnight in the Century* (n)
Solzhenitsyn, *One Day in the Life of Ivan Denisovich* (n)
Tolstoy, *War and Peace* (n)
Turgenev, *Fathers and Sons* (n)
Yevtushenko, *The Collected Poems, 1952–1990* (p)

Scandinavia and Finland

Andersen, *Fairy Tales* (s)
Dinesen, *Seven Gothic Tales* (s)
Ibsen, *A Doll's House* (d)
Laxness, *The Atom Station* (n)
Strindberg, *Plays: The Father, Miss Julie,* and *The Ghost Sonata* (d)
Undset, *Kristin Lavransdatter* (n)
Waltari, *The Egyptian*

Spain

Alas y Ureña, *The Regent's Wife* (n)
Cervantes, *Don Quixote* (n)
Delibes, *The Heretic* (n)
Galdós, *Fortunata and Jacinta* (n)
Goytisolo, Juan, *Count Julian* (n)
Life of Lazarillo de Tormes, The (n)

Africa

Achebe, *Things Fall Apart* (n)
Coetzee, *Waiting for the Barbarians* (n)
Gordimer, *July's People* (n)
Ngũgĩ wa Thiong'o, *The River Between* (n)
Paton, *Cry, the Beloved Country* (n)
Schreiner, *The Story of an African Farm* (n)

Asia

China
Cao, *The Story of the Stone* (n)
Du Fu, *Selected Poems* (p)
Hua, *To Live* (n)
Wu, *Journey to the West* (n)

India
Anand, *Untouchable* (n)
Mistry, *A Fine Balance* (n)
Roy, *The God of Small Things* (n)
Rushdie, *Midnight's Children* (n)
Singh, *Train to Pakistan* (n)
Tagore, *Selected Poems* (p)

Indonesia
Toer, *This Earth of Mankind* (n)

Japan
Kawabata, *The Master of Go* (n)
Mishima, *The Temple of the Golden Pavilion* (n)
Murasaki, *The Tale of the Genji* (n)
Ōe, *A Personal Matter* (n)

Sōseki, *Kokoro* (n)
Tanizaki, *The Key* (n)

Middle East

Arabian Nights, The (s)
FitzGerald, *Rubáiyát of Omar Khayyám* (p)
Grossman, *A Horse Walks into a Bar* (n)
Idris, *The Essential Yusuf Idris* (s)
Iqbal, *Poems from Iqbal* (p)
Johnson-Davies, ed., *The Anchor Book of Modern Arabic Fiction* (s)
Kemal, *Memed, My Hawk* (n)
Khoury, *Broken Mirrors: Sinalcol* (n)
Mahfouz, *The Cairo Trilogy* (n)
Pamuk, *My Name Is Red* (n)
Rumi, *Rumi: Swallowing the Sun* (p)
Saadawi, *Frankenstein in Baghdad* (n)
Salih, Tayeb, *Season of Migration to the North* (n)
Shalev, *Blue Mountain* (n)
Tamer, *Tigers on the Tenth Day, and Other Stories* (s)

Ancient World

Aeschylus, *Agamemnon* (d)
Aristophanes, *The Complete Plays* (d)
Epic of Gilgamesh, The (p)
Euripides, *Medea* (d)
Homer, *Odyssey* (p)
Horace, *The Odes* (p)
Ovid, *The Erotic Poems* (p)
Pliny the Younger, *Fifty Letters*
Sophocles, *Antigone* (d)
Virgil, *The Aeneid* (p)
Xenophon, *The Education of Cyrus* (n)

Australia and New Zealand

Cook, *Wake in Fright* (n)
Mulgan, *Man Alone*
Shute, *On the Beach* (n)
White, *Voss* (n)

Canada

Atwood, *The Handmaid's Tale* (n)
Davies, *The Cornish Trilogy* (n)
Gallant, *Paris Stories* (s)
Munro, *A Wilderness Station: Selected Stories* (s)
Ondaatje, *The English Patient* (n)

Caribbean

Carpentier, *The Kingdom of This World* (n)
Césaire, *The Collected Poetry* (p)
Guillén, *Cuba Libre* (p)
Rhys, *Wide Sargasso Sea* (n)
Walcott, *Dream on Monkey Mountain, and Other Plays* (d)

Latin America and South America

Asturias, *Mulata* (n)
Borges, *Ficciones* (s)
Cortázar, *Hopscotch* (n)

Fuentes, *The Old Gringo* (n)
García Márquez, *One Hundred Years of Solitude* (n)
Güiraldes, *Don Segundo Sombra* (n)
Guzmán, *The Eagle and the Serpent* (n)
Harris, *Palace of the Peacock* (n)
Machado de Assis, *Dom Casmurro* (n)
Mutis, *The Adventures and Misadventures of Maqroll* (n)
Neruda, *100 Love Sonnets* (p)
Puig, *Eternal Curse on the Reader of These Pages* (n)
Rulfo, *The Burning Plain, and Other Stories* (s)
Vargas Llosa, *Aunt Julia and the Scriptwriter* (n)

Literary Criticism

Auerbach, *Mimesis*
Bloom, *The Visionary Company: A Reading of English Romantic Poetry*
Empson, *Seven Types of Ambiguity*
Epstein and Moser, *Literary Genius: 25 Classic Writers Who Define English and American Literature*
Fussell, *The Great War and Modern Memory*
Leavis, *The Great Tradition*
Said, *Orientalism*
Shattuck, *Forbidden Knowledge: From Prometheus to Pornography*
Steiner, *The Death of Tragedy*
Trilling, *The Liberal Imagination*

Philosophy and Religion

Philosophy

Ancient and Medieval
Aristotle, *Nicomachean Ethics*
Confucius, *Analects*
Cartledge, *Democritus*
Epicurus, *The Epicurus Reader*
Lucretius, *De Rerum Natura*
Maimonides, *Eight Chapters on Ethics*
Marcus Aurelius, *Meditations*
Mo Zi, *The Book of Master Mo*
Plato, *Dialogues*, esp. *Apology, Euthyphro, Phaedo. Republic, Symposium*
Sun Tzu, *The Art of War*

Modern
Austin, *Philosophical Papers*
Ayer, *Language, Truth, and Logic*
Bentham and Mill, *Utilitarianism, and Other Essays*
Cassirer, *An Essay on Man*
Descartes, *Meditations on First Philosophy*
Erasmus, *Praise of Folly*
Guénon, *The Crisis of the Modern World*
Herder, *J. G. Herder on Social and Political Culture*
Hume, *An Enquiry Concerning Human Understanding*
James, *The Varieties of Religious Experience*
Mill, *On Liberty*
Moore, *Principia Ethica*
Niebuhr, *Moral Man and Immoral Society*
Nietzsche, *Beyond Good and Evil*

Pascal, *Pensées*
Rousseau, *The Social Contract*
Russell, B., *The Problems of Philosophy*
Ryle, *The Concept of Mind*
Santayana, *The Life of Reason*
Schopenhauer, *The Essential Schopenhauer*
Spinoza, *Ethics*
Weil, Simone, *The Need for Roots*
Wittgenstein, *Philosophical Investigations*

Religion

Augustine, *Confessions*
Bhagavad Gita
Bible, King James Version and *New Oxford Annotated*
Blavatsky, *The Secret Doctrine*
Bonhoeffer, *Letters and Papers from Prison*
Book of Common Prayer
Buber, *I and Thou*
Buddhist Scriptures
Calvin, *Institutes of the Christian Religion*
Gauchet, *Disenchantment of the World: A Political History of Religion*
Ignatius of Loyola, *Personal Writings*
John of the Cross, *Dark Night of the Soul*
Kierkegaard, *Fear and Trembling*
Küng, *On Being a Christian*
Laozi, *Daodejing*
Lewis, *The Screwtape Letters*
Mather, *On Witchcraft*
Müller, *Introduction to the Science of Religion*
Nasr, *The Shia Revival*
Paine, *The Age of Reason*
Qur'an
Schama, *The Story of the Jews: Belonging, 1492–1900*
Teresa of Avila, *The Life of Saint Teresa of Avila*
Thomas à Kempis, *The Imitation of Christ*
Thomas Aquinas, *Selected Writings*
Tillich, *The Courage to Be*
Wesley, *John Wesley*

Anthropology, Economics, Psychology, Sociology

Anthropology

Benedict, *Patterns of Culture*
Boas, *Anthropology and Modern Life*
Evans-Pritchard, *Witchcraft, Oracles, and Magic among the Azande*
Firth, *Elements of Social Organization*
Frazer, *The Golden Bough*
Geertz, *The Interpretation of Cultures*
Kenyatta, *Facing Mount Kenya*
Lévi-Strauss, *Tristes Tropiques*
Malinowski, *Sex and Repression in Savage Society*
Mead, *Coming of Age in Samoa*

Taussig, *Shamanism, Colonialism, and the Wild Man*
Tilak, *The Arctic Home in the Vedas*

Economics

Frank, *Capitalism and Underdevelopment in Latin America*
Friedman, *Capitalism and Freedom*
Galbraith, *The Affluent Society*
George, *Progress and Poverty*
Hayek, *The Road to Serfdom*
Keynes, *The Economic Consequences of the Peace*
Malthus, *An Essay on the Principle of Population*
Piketty, *The Economics of Inequality*
Ricardo, *Principles of Political Economy and Taxation*
Schumacher, *Small Is Beautiful*
Schumpeter, *Capitalism, Socialism, and Democracy*
Sen, *Poverty and Famines*
Smith, *The Wealth of Nations*
Tawney, *Religion and the Rise of Capitalism*

Psychology

Adorno et al., *The Authoritarian Personality*
Erikson, *Young Man Luther*
Frankl, *Man's Search for Meaning*
Freud, *New Introductory Lectures on Psycho-Analysis*
Fromm, *Escape from Freedom*
Hoffer, *The True Believer*
Jung, *Psychology of the Unconscious*
Madariaga, *Englishmen, Frenchmen, Spaniards: An Essay in Comparative Psychology*
Rieff, *Freud: The Mind of the Moralist*

Sociology

Comte, *Auguste Comte and Positivism: The Essential Writings*
Dahrendorf, *LSE*
Durkheim, *On Suicide*
Foucault, *Discipline and Punish*
Glazer and Moynihan, *Beyond the Melting Pot*
Manent, *The City of Man*
Marcuse, *One-Dimensional Man*
Mills, *The Power Elite*
Moore, *Social Origins of Dictatorship and Democracy*
Parkinson, *Parkinson's Law*
Parsons, *The Structure of Social Action*
Reed, *The Enduring South*
Riesman, Glazer, and Denney, *The Lonely Crowd*
Veblen, *Theory of the Leisure Class*
Wallerstein, *The Uncertainties of Knowledge*
Weber, *The Protestant Ethic and the Spirit of Capitalism*
Williams, *Keywords: A Vocabulary of Culture and Society*

Politics

Anderson, *Imagined Communities*
Angell, *The Great Illusion*
Arendt, *The Origins of Totalitarianism*
Bagehot, *The English Constitution*

Bodin, *On Sovereignty*

Brown, *The Myth of the Strong Leader: Political Leadership in the Modern Age*

Bull, *The Anarchical Society*

Burke, *Reflections on the Revolution in France*

Carr, *The Twenty Years' Crisis, 1919–1939*

Chomsky, *Hegemony or Survival: America's Quest for Global Dominance*

Cicero, *Selected Political Speeches*

Commager, *The American Mind*

Evola, *Revolt against the Modern World*

Fanon, *The Wretched of the Earth*

Fukuyama, *The End of History and the Last Man*

Gellner, *Nations and Nationalism*

Gramsci, *Selections from the Prison Notebooks*

Greenfeld, *Nationalism: Five Roads to Modernity*

Habermas, *The Lure of Technocracy*

Halévy, *The Era of Tyrannies: Essays on Socialism and War*

Hamilton, Madison, and Jay, *The Federalist Papers*

Hartz, *The Liberal Tradition in America*

Hobbes, *Leviathan*

Hofstadter, *The American Political Tradition and the Men Who Made It*

Huntington, *The Clash of Civilizations and the Remaking of World Order*

Joll, *The Anarchists*

Kant, *Toward Perpetual Peace*

Key, *Southern Politics in State and Nation*

Kirk, *The Conservative Mind*

Kolakowski, *Main Currents of Marxism*

Kristol, *Neo-Conservatism: The Autobiography of an Idea*

Lincoln, *Selected Speeches and Writings*

Lippmann, *Public Opinion*

Locke, *Second Treatise of Government*

Machiavelli, *The Prince*

Mao, *Quotations from Chairman Mao Tse-tung*

Marx and Engels, *The Communist Manifesto*

Montesquieu, *The Spirit of the Laws*

Oakeshott, *What Is History? and Other Essays*

Popper, *The Open Society and Its Enemies*

Rahe, *Republics Ancient and Modern*

Rawls, *A Theory of Justice*

Skinner, *The Foundations of Modern Political Thought*

Strauss, *What Is Political Philosophy?*

Talmon, *The Origins of Totalitarian Democracy*

Wight, *International Theory*

Witte and Nichols, *Religion and the American Constitutional Experiment*

Wittfogel, *Oriental Despotism*

Racial, Ethnic, and Gender Studies

Baldwin, *The Fire Next Time*

Beauvoir, *The Second Sex*

Cornell, *Return of the Native: American Indian Political Resurgence*

Davis, A., *Angela Davis: An Autobiography*

Davis, D., *The Problem of Slavery in the Age of Revolution, 1770–1823*

Du Bois, *The Souls of Black Folk*

Franklin, *From Slavery to Freedom*

Friedan, *The Feminine Mystique*

Greer, *The Female Eunuch*

Myrdal, *An American Dilemma: The Negro Problem and Modern Democracy*

Pankhurst, *The Suffragette Movement*

Ruiz, *From Out of the Shadows: Mexican Women in Twentieth-Century America*

Takaki, *Strangers from a Different Shore: A History of Asian Americans*

Tannenbaum, *Slave and Citizen*

Wollstonecraft, *A Vindication of the Rights of Women*

Science

Bronowski, *The Ascent of Man*

Carson, *Silent Spring*

Darwin, *On the Origin of Species*

Dawkins, *The Selfish Gene*

Einstein, *Relativity*

Galileo, *Dialogue Concerning the Two Chief World Systems*

Gardner, *The Night Is Large: Collected Essays*

Gould, *Wonderful Life: The Burgess Shale and the Nature of History*

Haldane, *On Being the Right Size, and Other Essays*

Hofstadter, *Gödel, Escher, Bach: An Eternal Golden Braid*

Humboldt, *Cosmos: A Sketch of the Physical Description of the Universe*

Kuhn, *The Structure of Scientific Revolutions*

Lorenz, *On Aggression*

Mayr, *The Growth of Biological Thought*

Nasr, *Science and Civilization in Islam*

Newton, *Opticks*

Polanyi, *Personal Knowledge*

Porter, *The Greatest Benefit to Mankind: A Medical History of Humanity*

Sacks, *The Man Who Mistook His Wife for a Hat*

Watson, *The Double Helix*

Weinberg, *To Explain the World*

Whitehead, *Science and the Modern World*

Art, Architecture, Music, and Film

Abraham, *The Concise Oxford History of Music*

Clark, *The Nude*

Copland, *What to Listen for in Music*

Frank, *The Americans*

Gombrich, *The Story of Art*

Le Corbusier, *Towards a New Architecture*

Ruskin, *Modern Painters*

Solomon, *Mozart: A Life*

Truffaut, *Hitchcock: A Definitive Study of Alfred Hitchcock*

Vasari, *The Lives of the Artists*

Miscellaneous

Addiction

Alcoholics Anonymous
Gill, *Pour Me: A Life*

Cooking and Food

David, *A Book of Mediterranean Food*
Fisher, *How to Cook a Wolf*
Liebling, *Between Meals: An Appetite for Paris*
Toklas, *The Alice B. Toklas Cook Book*

Crime

Capote, *In Cold Blood*
Malcolm, *The Journalist and the Murderer*
Trillin, *Killings*

Education

Bloom, *The Closing of the American Mind*
Dewey, *Experience and Education*
Montessori, *The Discovery of the Child*
Strunk and White, *The Elements of Style*

Law

Bingham, *Rule of Law*
Hart, *The Concept of Law*
Marshall, *Writings*

Linguistics

Culler, *Ferdinand de Saussure*

Travel

Bryson, *The Lost Continent: Travels in Small-Town America*
Fermor, *A Time of Gifts: On Foot to Constantinople*
Kinglake, *Eothen: Traces of Travel Brought Home from the East*
O'Hanlon, *Into the Heart of Borneo*
Theroux, *The Great Railway Bazaar: By Train through Asia*

Titles Sorted by Region

Authors of 150 highly recommended titles are in boldface.

United States and Canada

Acheson, *Present at the Creation*
Adams, *The Education of Henry Adams*
Alcott, *Little Women*
Allison, *Destined for War: Can America and China Escape Thucydides's Trap?*
Anderson, *Winesburg, Ohio*
Atwood, *The Handmaid's Tale*

Bailyn, *Ideological Origins of the American Revolution*
Baldwin, *The Fire Next Time*
Beard and Beard, *The Rise of American Civilization*
Bellow, *Herzog*
Benedict, *Patterns of Culture*
Berg, *Max Perkins: Editor of Genius*
Berkman, *Prison Memoirs of an Anarchist*
Berryman, *77 Dream Songs*
Bishop, *The Complete Poems, 1927–1979*
Bloom, *The Closing of the American Mind*
Blum, *The Republican Roosevelt*
Boorstin, *The Americans: The National Experience*
Bothwell, *The Penguin History of Canada*
Bowen, *Miracle at Philadelphia*
Bowles, *The Sheltering Sky*
Branch, *Parting the Waters: America in the King Years, 1954–63*
Brebner, *North Atlantic Triangle*
Brown, *Bury My Heart at Wounded Knee*
Bryson, *The Lost Continent: Travels in Small-Town America*
Buchwald, *I'll Always Have Paris: A Memoir*
Burroughs, E. R., *Tarzan of the Apes*
Burroughs, W., *Naked Lunch*

Capote, *In Cold Blood*
Carson, *Silent Spring*
Cather, *My Ántonia*
Chambers, *Witness*
Chandler, *The Big Sleep*
Chomsky, *Hegemony or Survival: America's Quest for Global Dominance*
Commager, *The American Mind*
Cooper, *The Last of the Mohicans*
Cornell, *Return of the Native: American Indian Political Resurgence*
Crane, *The Red Badge of Courage*
Cummings, *e. e. cummings: Complete Poems, 1904–1962*

Dana, *Two Years before the Mast*
Davies, *The Cornish Trilogy*
Davis, A., *Angela Davis: An Autobiography*
Davis, D., *The Problem of Slavery in the Age of Revolution, 1770–1823*
DeLillo, *White Noise*

DeVoto, ed., *The Journals of Lewis and Clark*
Dick, *Do Androids Dream of Electric Sheep?*
Dickinson, *Selected Poems*
Didion, *Slouching towards Bethlehem*
Dos Passos, *USA*
Douglass, *Narrative of the Life of Frederick Douglass*
Dreiser, *Sister Carrie*
Du Bois, *The Souls of Black Folk*

Eastman, *Love and Revolution: My Journey through an Epoch*
Ellison, *Invisible Man*
Emerson, *Nature, and Selected Essays*
English, *Just Watch Me: The Life of Pierre Elliott Trudeau, 1968–2000*
Evans, *The American Century*

Faulkner, *Light in August*
Fitzgerald, *The Great Gatsby*
Frank, *The Americans*
Franklin, B., *Autobiography*
Franklin, J. H., *From Slavery to Freedom*
Friedan, *The Feminine Mystique*
Frost, *The Poetry of Robert Frost*

Gaddis, *The Recognitions*
Galbraith, *The Affluent Society*
Gallant, *Paris Stories*
Genovese, *Roll, Jordan, Roll: The World the Slaves Made*
Ginsberg, *Howl, Kaddish, and Other Poems*
Glazer and Moynihan, *Beyond the Melting Pot*
Goldman, *Living My Life*
Gordon-Reed, *The Hemingses of Monticello*
Granatstein, *How Britain's Economic, Political, and Military Weakness Forced Canada into the Arms of the United States*
Grant, *Personal Memoirs*
Greenstein, *The Hidden-Hand Presidency: Eisenhower as Leader*

Halberstam, *The Making of a Quagmire*
Hamilton, Madison, and Jay, *The Federalist Papers*
Hammett, *The Maltese Falcon*
Harris, *Uncle Remus: His Songs and Sayings*
Hartz, *The Liberal Tradition in America*
Hawthorne, *The Scarlet Letter*
Heinlein, *Stranger in a Strange Land*
Heller, *Catch-22*
Hemingway, *The Sun Also Rises*
Herbert, *Dune*
Higham, *Strangers in the Land: Patterns of American Nativism, 1860–1925*
Hofstadter, *The American Political Tradition*
Hook, *Out of Step: An Unquiet Life in the 20th Century*

Howe, *What Has God Wrought: The Transformation of America, 1815–1848*
Hughes, *The Collected Poems*
Hurston, *Their Eyes Were Watching God*

Irving, *The Legend of Sleepy Hollow, and Other Stories*

James, H., *The Portrait of a Lady*
James, W., *The Varieties of Religious Experience*
Jarrell, *The Woman at the Washington Zoo*
Jefferson, *The Life and Selected Writings of Thomas Jefferson*

Kennan, *The Kennan Diaries*
Kerouac, *On the Road*
Key, *Southern Politics in State and Nation*
Kristol, *Neo-Conservatism: The Autobiography of an Idea*

Lee, *To Kill a Mockingbird*
Lehman, ed., *The Oxford Book of American Poetry*
Leonard, *52 Pickup*
Levine, *King: William Lyon Mackenzie King*
Lewis, *Babbitt*
Limerick, *The Legacy of Conquest: The Unbroken Past of the American West*
Lincoln, *Selected Speeches and Writings*
Lippmann, *Public Opinion*
London, *The Call of the Wild* and *White Fang*
Longfellow, *Selected Poems*
Lovecraft, *The Call of Cthulhu, and Other Weird Stories*
Lowell, *For the Union Dead*

Macdonald, *The Galton Case*
Mailer, *Armies of the Night*
Malcolm, *The Journalist and the Murderer*
Malcolm X, *The Autobiography of Malcolm X*
Marcuse, *One-Dimensional Man*
Marshall, *Writings*
Martin, *The Durham Report and British Policy*
McCarthy, C., *Blood Meridian*
McCarthy, M., *The Group*
McCullers, *The Heart Is a Lonely Hunter*
Melville, *Moby-Dick*
Mencken, *The Vintage Mencken*
Millay, *The Selected Poetry*
Miller, A., *Death of a Salesman*
Miller, H., *Tropic of Cancer*
Miller, P., *The New England Mind: The Seventeenth Century*
Mills, *The Power Elite*
Morgan, *The Puritan Dilemma*
Morris, *The Rise of Theodore Roosevelt*
Morrison, *Song of Solomon*
Munro, Alice, *A Wilderness Station: Selected Stories*
Myrdal, *An American Dilemma: The Negro Problem and Modern Democracy*

Nabokov, *Lolita*

Niebuhr, *Moral Man and Immoral Society*
Noll, *America's God: From Jonathan Edwards to Abraham Lincoln*

Obama, *Dreams from My Father*
O'Connor, Flannery, *The Complete Stories*
Ondaatje, *The English Patient*
O'Neill, *Long Day's Journey into Night*
Osborn, *The Wild Frontier*

Paine, *The Age of Reason*
Pearson, *Words and Occasions*
Pirsig, *Zen and the Art of Motorcycle Maintenance*
Plath, *The Bell Jar*
Poe, *Complete Stories and Poems*
Porter, *Ship of Fools*
Pound, *Selected Poems*
Pynchon, *Gravity's Rainbow*

Rand, *The Fountainhead*
Reed, *The Enduring South*
Rhodes, *The Making of the Atomic Bomb*
Ricks, *Fiasco*
Riesman, Glazer, and Denney, *The Lonely Crowd*
Roth, *American Pastoral*
Ruiz, *From Out of the Shadows: Mexican Women in Twentieth-Century America*

Sacks, *The Man Who Mistook His Wife for a Hat*
Salinger, *The Catcher in the Rye*
Sanger, *The Autobiography of Margaret Sanger*
Schlesinger, *The Age of Roosevelt: The Crisis of the Old Order*
Sheehan, *A Bright Shining Lie*
Sinclair, *The Jungle*
Singer, *A Crown of Feathers, and Other Stories*
Sledge, *With the Old Breed*
Sontag, *Against Interpretation*
Stampp, *The Peculiar Institution*
Steel, *Walter Lippmann and the American Century*
Stein, *The Autobiography of Alice B. Toklas*
Steinbeck, *The Grapes of Wrath*
Stevens, *Collected Poems*
Stowe, *Uncle Tom's Cabin*
Styron, *The Confessions of Nat Turner*

Takaki, *Strangers from a Different Shore: A History of Asian Americans*
Tansill, *Back Door to War: The Roosevelt Foreign Policy*
Tarbell, *The History the of Standard Oil Company*
Thoreau, *"Walden" and "Civil Disobedience"*
Tocqueville, Democracy *in America*
Traven, *The Treasure of the Sierra Madre*
Trillin, *Killings*
Trilling, *The Liberal Imagination*
Turner, "The Significance of the Frontier in American History"
Twain, *The Adventures of Huckleberry Finn*

Urquhart, *Ralph Bunche*
U.S. Army / Marine Corps Counterinsurgency Field Manual, The
Utley, *Geronimo*

Veblen, *Theory of the Leisure Class*
Vidal, *United States: Essays*
Vonnegut, *Cat's Cradle*

Washington, B., *Up From Slavery*
Webb, *The Great Plains*
Wharton, *The Age of Innocence*
White, E. B., *Charlotte's Web*
Whitman, *Leaves of Grass*
Wilder, *The Bridge of San Luis Rey*
Williams, T., *A Streetcar Named Desire*
Williams, T. H., *Huey Long*
Williams, W. C., *Selected Poems*
Winks, *The Blacks in Canada*
Wister, *The Virginian*
Witte and Nichols, *Religion and the American Constitutional Experiment*
Wolfe, Tom, *The Bonfire of the Vanities*
Wolfe, Thomas, *Look Homeward, Angel*
Woodward, *The Strange Career of Jim Crow*
Wouk, *The Caine Mutiny*

Zinn, *A People's History of the United States*

Latin America, the Caribbean, South America

Arana, *Bolívar: American Liberator*
Asturias, *Mulata*

Bethell, *A Cultural History of Latin America*
Borges, *Ficciones*
Brown, *Cuba's Revolutionary World*

Carpentier, *The Kingdom of This World*
Césaire, *The Collected Poetry*
Cortázar, *Hopscotch*
Crow, *The Epic of Latin America*

Frank, *Capitalism and Underdevelopment in Latin America*
Freyre, *Brazil: An Interpretation*
Fuentes, *The Old Gringo*

Galeano, *Open Veins of Latin America*
García Márquez, *One Hundred Years of Solitude*
Guillén, *Cuba Libre*
Güiraldes, *Don Segundo Sombra*
Guzmán, *The Eagle and the Serpent*

Hall, *Familiar Stranger*
Harris, *Palace of the Peacock*

James, *The Black Jacobins*

Katz, *The Life and Times of Pancho Villa*

Lévi-Strauss, *Tristes Tropiques*
Lowry, *Under the Volcano*

Machado de Assis, *Dom Casmurro*
Mutis, *The Adventures and Misadventures of Maqroll*

Neruda, *100 Love Sonnets*

Pares, *War and Trade in the West Indies, 1739–1763*
Paz, *The Labyrinth of Solitude*
Prescott, *History of the Conquest of Mexico*
Puig, *Eternal Curse on the Reader of These Pages*

Rhys, *Wide Sargasso Sea*
Rulfo, *The Burning Plain, and Other Stories*

Tannenbaum, *Slave and Citizen*
Taussig, *Shamanism, Colonialism, and the Wild Man: A Study in Terror and Healing*

Vargas Llosa, *Aunt Julia and the Scriptwriter*

Walcott, *Dream on Monkey Mountain, and Other Plays*
Williams, *Capitalism and Slavery*
Womack, *Zapata and the Mexican Revolution*

Britain

Amis, *Lucky Jim*
Annan, *Our Age*
Arnold, *Culture and Anarchy*
Arnstein, *The Bradlaugh Case: Atheism, Sex, and Politics among the Late Victorians*
Aubrey, *Brief Lives*
Auden, *The Shield of Achilles*
Austen, *Pride and Prejudice*

Bacon, *Essays*
Bagehot, *The English Constitution*
Ballard, *Empire of the Sun*
Bate, *John Keats*
Beaglehole, *The Life of Captain James Cook*
Bede, *Ecclesiastical History of the English People*
Bennett, *The Old Wives' Tale*
Beowulf (trans. Heaney)
Besant, *Annie Besant: An Autobiography*
Betjeman, *The Best of Betjeman*
Blake, R., *Disraeli*
Blake, W., *The Marriage of Heaven and Hell*
Bloom, *The Visionary Company: A Reading of English Romantic Poetry*
Blunden, *Undertones of War*

Book of Common Prayer
Boswell, *The Life of Samuel Johnson*
Bourke, *Empire and Revolution: The Political Life of Edmund Burke*
Bradbury, *The History Man*
Brittain, *Testament of Youth*
Brontë, C., *Jane Eyre*
Brontë, E., *Wuthering Heights*
Browne, *Religio Medici* and *Urne-Buriall*
Browning, E. B., *Aurora Leigh, and Other Poems*
Browning, R., *The Major Works*
Buchan, *The Thirty-Nine Steps*
Bulwer-Lytton, *Last Days of Pompeii*
Bunyan, *The Pilgrim's Progress*
Burgess, *A Clockwork Orange*
Burke, *Reflections on the Revolution in France*
Burns, *Selected Poems*
Burton, *The Anatomy of Melancholy*
Butler, *The Way of All Flesh*
Butterfield, *The Whig Interpretation of History*
Byron, *The Major Works*

Carlyle, *On Heroes, Hero-Worship, and the Heroic in History*
Carroll, *Alice's Adventures in Wonderland*
Cecil, *A Great Experiment: An Autobiography*
Chaucer, *The Canterbury Tales*
Chesterton, *The Man Who Was Thursday*
Childers, *Riddle of the Sands*
Christie, *Murder on the Orient Express*
Churchill, *My Early Life*
Coleridge, *Selected Poetry*
Colley, *Britons: Forging the Nation, 1707–1837*
Collins, *The Moonstone*
Corbett, *Man-Eaters of Kumaon*

Dahl, *Charlie and the Chocolate Factory*
Dahrendorf, *LSE*
Dangerfield, *The Strange Death of Liberal England*
Defoe, *Robinson Crusoe*
De Quincey, *Confessions of an English Opium-Eater*
Dickens, *Great Expectations*
Donne, *The Complete Poetry and Selected Prose*
Doyle, *The Complete Sherlock Holmes*
Dryden, *The Major Works*
du Maurier, Daphne, *Rebecca*
Durrell, *The Alexandria Quartet*

Eliot, G., *Middlemarch*
Eliot, T.S., *The Waste Land*
Epstein and Moser, *Literary Genius: 25 Classic Writers Who Define English and American Literature*

Fielding, *The History of Tom Jones*
Ford, F. M., *Parade's End*
Ford, J., *'Tis Pity She's a Whore, and Other Plays*
Forester, *Lieutenant Hornblower* and *Flying Colours*

Fussell, *The Great War and Modern Memory*

Gallagher, *The Decline, Revival, and Fall of the British Empire*
Galsworthy, *The Forsyte Saga*
Gaskell, *Cranford*
Gill, *Pour Me: A Life*
Gissing, *New Grub Street*
Golding, *Lord of the Flies*
Gosse, *Father and Son*
Grahame, *The Wind in the Willows*
Graves, *Good-Bye to All That*
Green, *Loving*
Greenblatt, *Will in The World: How Shakespeare Became Shakespeare*
Greene, *The Heart of the Matter*

Hammond, *Gladstone and the Irish Nation*
Hardy, G. H., *A Mathematician's Apology*
Hardy, T., *Far from the Madding Crowd*
Harris, *William Beveridge: A Biography*
Hill, *The World Turned Upside Down: Radical Ideas during the English Revolution*
Hobbes, *Leviathan*
Hobson, *Imperialism*
Holmes, *Shelley: The Pursuit*
Housman, *A Shopshire Lad, and Other Poems*
Howard, *The Continental Commitment: The Dilemma of British Defence Policy in the Era of the Two World Wars*
Hughes, Ted, *Collected Poems*
Hume, *An Enquiry Concerning Human Understanding*
Huxley, *Brave New World*
Hyde, *The History of the Rebellion*

Isherwood and Auden, *The Ascent of F6*
Ishiguro, *The Remains of the Day*

Jenkins, *Gladstone*
Jerome, *Three Men in a Boat*
Jones, *Selected Poetical and Prose Works*
Jonson, *Volpone*

Keats, *Selected Poetry*
Kedourie, *The Chatham House Version*
Kingsley, *Westward Ho!*

Lamb and Lamb, *Tales from Shakespeare*
Langford, *A Polite and Commercial People: England, 1727–1783*
Langland, *Piers the Ploughman*
Larkin, *Collected Poems*
Lawrence, D. H., *Lady Chatterley's Lover*
Lawrence, T. E., *The Seven Pillars of Wisdom*
Lear, *The Owl and the Pussy-Cat*
Leavis, *The Great Tradition*
Le Carré, *The Spy Who Came in from the Cold*
Lee, *Virginia Woolf*
Lessing, *The Golden Notebook*

Lewis, *The Screwtape Letters*
Lively, *Moon Tiger*
Locke, *Second Treatise of Government*
Lodge, *Changing Places*

Macaulay, *The History of England*
Mackenzie, *Whisky Galore*
MacNeice, *Collected Poems*
Mahan, *The Influence of Sea Power upon History*
Maitland, *Domesday Book and Beyond*
Manning, *The Levant Trilogy*
Mansfield, *Selected Stories*
Mantel, *Wolf Hall*
Marcus, *The Other Victorians: A Study of Sexuality and Pornography in Mid-Nineteenth-Century England*
Marder, *From the Dreadnought to Scapa Flow*, vol. 1
Massie, *Dreadnought*
Mattingly, *The Defeat of the Spanish Armada*
Maugham, *The Razor's Edge*
McFarlane, *The Nobility of Later Medieval England*
Medawar, *Memoir of a Thinking Radish*
Mill, *On Liberty*
Milne, *Winnie-the-Pooh* and *The House at Pooh Corner*
Milton, *Paradise Lost*
More, *Utopia*
Murdoch, *Under the Net*

Namier, *The Structure of Politics at the Accession of George III*
Newman, *Apologia pro Vita Sua*

Opie and Opie, *The Oxford Book of Nursery Rhymes*
Orwell, *1984*
Osborne, *Look Back in Anger*
O'Shaughnessy, *The Men Who Lost America*
Owen, *The War Poems*

Pepys, *Diary*
Perham, *The Colonial Reckoning*
Pope, *The Major Works*
Potter, *The Tailor of Gloucester*
Powell, *A Question of Upbringing*
Priestley, *The Good Companions*
Pritchett, *A Cab at the Door* and *Midnight Oil*

Ransome, *Swallows and Amazons*
Reynolds, *In Command of History: Churchill Fighting and Writing the Second World War*
Richardson, *Clarissa*
Ricks, *The Oxford Book of English Verse*
Robinson and Gallagher, *Africa and the Victorians*
Roskill, *Naval Policy between the Wars*
Russell, *The Problems of Philosophy*

Sassoon, *Memoirs of a Fox-Hunting Man*
Scott, *Ivanhoe*
Sebald, *Austerlitz*

Seeley, *The Expansion of England*
Shakespeare, *Works*, esp. *A Midsummer Night's Dream, Hamlet, King Lear, Macbeth, The Tempest, Twelfth Night*
Shaw, *Pygmalion*
Shelley, M., *Frankenstein*
Shelley, P. B., *The Major Works*
Smith, *The Wealth of Nations*
Snow, *The Two Cultures*
Spark, *The Prime of Miss Jean Brodie*
Spear, *Master of Bengal: Clive and His India*
Spenser, *The Faerie Queene*
Stanhope, *Lord Chesterfield's Letters*
Sterne, *Tristram Shandy*
Stevenson, *The Strange Case of Dr. Jekyll and Mr. Hyde*
Stoker, *Dracula*
Strachey, *Eminent Victorians*
Swift, *Gulliver's Travels*

Tennyson, *The Major Works*
Thackeray, *Vanity Fair*
Thomas, *Religion and the Decline of Magic*
Thompson, E. P., *The Making of the English Working Class*
Thompson, F., *Lark Rise to Candleford*
Thornton, *The Imperial Idea and Its Enemies*
Trevelyan, *The English Revolution, 1688–1689*
Trollope, *The Way We Live Now*
Truffaut, *Hitchcock: A Definitive Study of Alfred Hitchcock*

Waugh, *Brideshead Revisited*
Wavell, *The Viceroy's Journal*
Webb, Beatrice, *My Apprenticeship*
Wells, *The Time Machine*
Wesley, *John Wesley* [ed. Outler]
Wilde, *The Importance of Being Earnest*
Wodehouse, P. G., *Right Ho, Jeeves*
Wollstonecraft, *A Vindication of the Rights of Women*
Woodham-Smith, *The Reason Why*
Woolf, L., *The Journey Not the Arrival Matters*
Woolf, V., *Mrs. Dalloway*
Wordsworth, *The Prelude*

Young, *Victorian England: Portrait of an Age*

Ziegler, *Mountbatten*

Europe

Abraham, *The Concise Oxford History of Music*
Aeschylus, *Agamemnon*
Alas y Ureña, *The Regent's Wife*
Andersen, *Fairy Tales*
Angell, *The Great Illusion*
Arendt, *The Origins of Totalitarianism*
Ariosto, *Orlando Furioso*
Aristophanes, *The Complete Plays*
Aristotle, *Nicomachean Ethics*
Aron, *The Opium of the Intellectuals*

Auerbach, *Mimesis*
Augustine, *Confessions*

Babel, *Red Cavalry, and Other Stories*
Balzac, *The Human Comedy: Selected Stories*
Barzun, *From Dawn to Decadence, 1500 to the Present*
Baudelaire, *Selected Poems*
Beauvoir, *The Second Sex*
Beckett, *Waiting for Godot*
Belloc, *The Crusades*
Benda, *The Treason of the Intellectuals*
Berlin, *The Hedgehog and the Fox*
Blanning, *Frederick the Great: King of Prussia*
Bloch, *Strange Defeat*
Boccaccio, *Tales from the Decameron*
Boxer, *The Portuguese Seaborne Empire, 1415–1825*
Braudel, *The Mediterranean and the Mediterranean World*
Brecht, *The Threepenny Opera*
Brenan, *The Spanish Labyrinth*
Brodsky, *To Urania: Selected Poems*
Browning, *The Origins of the Final Solution*
Bulgakov, *The Master and Margarita*
Buller, *Darkness over Germany*
Burckhardt, *The Civilization of the Renaissance in Italy*

Calvino, *If on a winter's night a traveler*
Camus, *The Stranger*
Carr, *Spain, 1808–1938*
Cartledge, *Democritus*
Cellini, *Autobiography*
Cervantes, *Don Quixote*
Chateaubriand, *Memoirs from Beyond the Grave, 1768–1800*
Chekhov, *The Cherry Orchard*
Cicero, *Selected Political Speeches*
Clark, *The Nude*
Clausewitz, *On War*
Clogg, *A Concise History of Greece*
Cobb, *Reactions to the French Revolution*
Cohn, *The Pursuit of the Millennium: Revolutionary Millenarians and Mystical Anarchists of the Middle Ages*
Conquest, *The Great Terror*
Corneille, *Le Cid*
Couperus, *Eline Vere*
Crossman, *The God That Failed*

Dante, *Inferno*
Darnton, *The Great Cat Massacre*
David, *A Book of Mediterranean Food*
Davies, *God's Playground: A History of Poland*
Dawidowicz, *The War against the Jews*
Deakin, *The Embattled Mountain*
de Gaulle, *War Memoirs*
Delibes, *The Heretic*
Descartes, *Meditations on First Philosophy*
Diderot, *The Nun*
Dinesen, *Seven Gothic Tales*

Disney, A *History of Portugal and the Portuguese Empire*
Dodds, *The Greeks and the Irrational*
Donleavy, *The Ginger Man*
d'Ormesson, *The Glory of the Empire*
Dostoyevsky, *The Brothers Karamazov*
Dumas, *The Count of Monte Cristo*

Eco, *The Name of the Rose*
Eliade, *Bengal Nights*
Elliott, *Empires of the Atlantic World*
Epicurus, *The Epicurus Reader*
Erasmus, *Praise of Folly*
Erikson, *Young Man Luther*
Euripides, *Medea*
Evans, *Death in Hamburg: Society and Politics in the Cholera Years*

Fermor, *A Time of Gifts: On Foot to Constantinople*
Fernández-Armesto, *Columbus*
Fest, *Hitler*
Feydeau, *A Flea in Her Ear*
Fischer, *Germany's Aims in the First World War*
Fitzpatrick, *Politics and Irish Life, 1913–21*
Flaubert, *Madame Bovary*
Fontane, *Effie Briest*
Foster, *Vivid Faces: The Revolutionary Generation in Ireland, 1890–1923*
Foucault, *Discipline and Punish*
France, *The Revolt of the Angels*
Frankl, *Man's Search for Meaning*
Freud, *New Introductory Lectures on Psycho-Analysis*
Furet, *Interpreting the French Revolution*

Galdós, *Fortunata and Jacinta*
Geyl, *Napoleon: For and Against*
Gibbon, *Decline and Fall of the Roman Empire*
Gide, *The Counterfeiters*
Goethe, *Faust*
Gogol, *Dead Souls*
Gombrich, *The Story of Art*
Goncharov, *Oblomov*
Gorky, *The Collected Short Stories*
Goytisolo, *Count Julian*
Gramsci, *Selections from the Prison Notebooks*
Grass, *The Tin Drum*
Grimm and Grimm, *The Original Folk and Fairy Tales of the Brothers Grimm*
Grossman, Vasily, *Life and Fate*
Grotius, *The Rights of War and Peace*
Guizot, *The History of Civilization in Europe*

Habermas, *The Lure of Technocracy*
Hašek, *The Good Soldier Švejk*
Heaney, *Death of a Naturalist*
Herder, *J. G. Herder on Social and Political Culture*
Herodotus, *The History*
Herzen, *My Past and Thoughts*

Hesse, *Siddhartha*
Hitchins, *Rumania, 1866–1947*
Hitler, *Mein Kampf*
Hobsbawm and Ranger, *The Invention of Tradition*
Holmes, *Florence, Rome, and the Origins of the Renaissance*
Homer, *Odyssey*
Horace, *The Odes*
Horne, *A Savage War of Peace: Algeria, 1954–1962*
Hrabal, *Closely Watched Trains*
Hugo, *The Hunchback of Notre-Dame*
Huizinga, *The Autumn of the Middle Ages*
Humes, *Belgium: Long United, Long Divided*

Ibsen, *A Doll's House*
Israel, *The Dutch Republic*

Jackson, *A Certain Idea of France: The Life of Charles de Gaulle*
Joll, *The Anarchists*
Joyce, *Dubliners*
Jung, *Psychology of the Unconscious*
Jünger, *Storm of Steel*

Kafka, *The Trial*
Kant, "Toward Perpetual Peace"
Kee, *The Green Flag: A History of Irish Nationalism*
Keegan, *The Face of Battle: A Study of Agincourt, Waterloo, and the Somme*
Kershaw, *To Hell and Back*
Keynes, *The Economic Consequences of the Peace*
Kierkegaard, *Fear and Trembling*
Kleist, *The Marquise of O, and Other Stories*
Koestler, *Darkness at Noon*
Kolakowski, *Main Currents of Marxism*
Kossmann, *The Low Countries, 1780–1940*
Kotkin, *Stalin: Waiting for Hitler, 1929–1941*
Kropotkin, *Memoirs of a Revolutionist*
Krúdy, *The Adventures of Sinbad*

Lacouture, *De Gaulle: The Rebel, 1890–1944*
La Fayette, *La Princesse de Clèves*
Lampedusa, *The Leopard*
Laxness, *The Atom Station*
Lefebvre, *The Coming of the French Revolution*
Lem, *Solaris*
Levi, *If This Is a Man*
Lewis, *The Emergence of Modern Turkey*
Liebling, *Between Meals: An Appetite for Paris*
Life of Lazarillo de Tormes, The
Livy, *The Early History of Rome*
Lobo Antunes, *The Inquisitor's Manual*

Macartney, *The Habsburg Empire, 1790–1918*
MacCulloch, *The Reformation*
Machiavelli, *The Prince*
Mack Smith, *Cavour and Garibaldi 1860*
Madariaga, *Englishmen, Frenchmen, Spaniards*

Maeterlinck, *The Life of the Bee*
Maimonides, *Eight Chapters on Ethics*
Malraux, *Man's Fate*
Mann, *Death in Venice*
Manzoni, *The Betrothed*
Marcus Aurelius, *Meditations*
Marx and Engels, *The Communist Manifesto*
Maupassant, *Selected Works*
May, *Strange Victory: Hitler's Conquest of France*
McNeill, *The Rise of the West*
Milosz, *Selected and Last Poems, 1931–2004*
Mitford, *The Sun King: Louis XIV at Versailles*
Molière, *The Misanthrope* and *Tartuffe*
Mommsen, *The History of Rome*
Montaigne, *Essays*
Morison, *Admiral of the Ocean Sea* [Columbus]
Multatuli, *Max Havelaar: Or the Coffee Auctions of the Dutch Trading Company*
Musil, *The Man without Qualities*

Nietzsche, *Beyond Good and Evil*
Nolte, *Three Faces of Fascism*
Norwich, *A History of Venice*
O'Brien, E., *The Country Girls*
O'Brien, F., *The Third Policeman*
Ortega y Gasset, *Revolt of the Masses*
Ovid, *The Erotic Poems*

Pascal, *Pensées*
Pasternak, *Doctor Zhivago*
Payne and Palacios, *Franco*
Phillips, *The Fourth Crusade and the Sack of Constantinople*
Pipes, *Russia under the Old Regime*
Pirenne, *Mohammed and Charlemagne*
Plato, *Dialogues*, esp. *Apology, Euthyphro, Phaedo, Republic, Symposium*
Pliny the Younger, *Fifty Letters of Pliny*
Plutarch, *Parallel Lives*
Popper, *The Open Society and Its Enemies*
Proust, *Swann's Way*
Pushkin, *Eugene Onegin*

Rabelais, *Gargantua and Pantagruel*
Racine, *Phèdre*
Ranke, *The Theory and Practice of History*
Reed, *Ten Days That Shook the World*
Reiss, *The Black Count* [Thomas-Alexandre Dumas]
Remarque, *All Quiet on the Western Front*
Reynolds, *Shattering Empires: The Clash and Collapse of the Ottoman and Russian Empires, 1908–1918*
Rieff, *Freud: The Mind of the Moralist*
Ritter, *Frederick the Great*
Rogan, *The Fall of the Ottomans: The Great War in the Middle East, 1914–1920*
Roth, *The Radetzky March*
Rousseau, *The Social Contract*

Safranski, *Martin Heidegger: Between Good and Evil*
Saramago, *The Gospel according to Jesus Christ*
Sartre, *Nausea*
Schama, *The Story of the Jews: Belonging, 1492–1900*
Schiller, *The Robbers* and *Wallenstein*
Schnitzler, *The Road into the Open*
Sciascia, *The Day of the Owl*
Serge, *Midnight in the Century*
Sheehan, *German History, 1770–1866*
Silone, *Bread and Wine*
Simenon, *Maigret and Monsieur Charles*
Solomon, *Mozart: A Life*
Solzhenitsyn, *One Day in the Life of Ivan Denisovich*
Song of Roland, The
Sophocles, *Antigone*
Southern, *The Making of the Middle Ages*
Speer, *Inside the Third Reich*
Spinoza, *Ethics*
Staël, *Considerations on the Principal Events of the French Revolution*
Steinberg, *Bismarck: A Life*
Stendhal, *The Red and the Black*
Stern, *Blood and Iron*
Stone, *Turkey: A Short History*
Stoye, *The Siege of Vienna*
Strauss, *What Is Political Philosophy?*
Strindberg, *Plays: The Father, Miss Julie, and The Ghost Sonata*
Syme, *The Roman Revolution*
Szabó, *The Door*
Szymborska, *View with a Grain of Sand: Selected Poems*

Tacitus, *The Annals of Imperial Rome*
Taubman, *Khrushchev: The Man and His Era*
Taylor, *The Origins of the Second World War*
Thomas, *The Spanish Civil War*
Thucydides, *History of the Peloponnesian War*
Tillion, *Algeria: The Realities*
Tolstoy, *War and Peace*
Townshend, *Easter 1916: The Irish Rebellion*
Trevor, *The News from Ireland, and Other Stories*
Trevor-Roper, *The Last Days of Hitler*
Tuchman, *The Guns of August*
Turgenev, *Fathers and Sons*

Undset, *Kristin Lavransdatter*
Urquhart, *Hammarskjold*

Vasari, *The Lives of the Artists*
Vazov, *Under the Yoke*
Verne, *Around the World in Eighty Days*
Virgil, *The Aeneid*
Voltaire, *Candide*

Waltari, *The Egyptian*
Weber, *The Protestant Ethic and the Spirit of Capitalism*
Wedgwood, *The Thirty Years War*

Werfel, *The Forty Days of Musa Dagh*
West, *Black Lamb and Grey Falcon*
Wilson, *To the Finland Station*
Woodhouse, *The Struggle for Greece, 1941–1949*

Yates, *The Rosicrucian Enlightenment*
Yeats, *Collected Poetry*
Yevtushenko, *The Collected Poems, 1952–1990*

Zeldin, *France, 1848–1945*
Zola, *The Dreyfus Affair*
Zürcher, *Turkey: A Modern History*
Zweig, *The World of Yesterday*

Africa, Antarctica, the Arctic, Asia, Oceania

Achebe, *Things Fall Apart*
Alexander, *The Endurance: Shackleton's Legendary Antarctic Expedition*
Amanat, *Iran: A Modern History*
Anand, *Untouchable*
Antonius, *The Arab Awakening*
Arabian Nights, The

Batatu, *The Old Social Classes and the Revolutionary Movements of Iraq*
Bayly, *Empire and Information: Intelligence Gathering and Social Communication in India, 1780–1870*
Bayly and Harper, *Forgotten Armies: Britain's Asian Empire and the War with Japan*
Benda, *The Crescent and the Rising Sun: Indonesian Islam under the Japanese Occupation, 1942–1945*
Bhagavad Gita
Bickers, *Out of China: How the Chinese Ended the Era of Western Domination*
Bix, *Hirohito and the Making of Modern Japan*
Blunt, *Secret History of the English Occupation of Egypt*
Brocheux, *Ho Chi Minh: A Biography*
Buell, *The Native Problem in Africa*
Burton, *Personal Narrative of a Pilgrimage to El-Madinah and Meccah*

Cao, *The Story of the Stone*
Cary, *Mister Johnson*
Chang, *Wild Swans*
Chaudhuri, *The Autobiography of an Unknown Indian*
Clark, *A History of Australia*
Coetzee, *Waiting for the Barbarians*
Confucius, *Analects*
Conrad, *Heart of Darkness*
Cook, *Wake in Fright*
Copland, *The Princes of India in the Endgame of Empire*

Dower, *Embracing Defeat: Japan in the Wake of World War II*
Du Fu, *Selected Poems*

Salih, *Season of Migration to the North*
Sansom, *The Western World and Japan*
Schiffrin, *Sun Yat-sen and the Origins of the Chinese Revolution*
Schreiner, *The Story of an African Farm*
Scott, *The Raj Quartet*
Seale, *The Struggle for Arab Independence*
Shalev, *Blue Mountain*
Shlaim, *The Iron Wall: Israel and the Arab World*
Shute, *On the Beach*
Sinclair, *The Origins of the Maori Wars*
Singh, *Train to Pakistan*
Slim, *Defeat into Victory: Battling Japan in Burma and India, 1942–1945*
Snow, *Red Star over China*
Solomon, *The Coldest March: Scott's Fatal Antarctic Expedition*
Sōseki, *Kokoro*
Soyinka, *The Man Died: Prison Notes*
Spence, *The Search for Modern China*
Sun Tzu, *The Art of War*

Tagore, *Selected Poems*
Tamer, *Tigers on the Tenth Day, and Other Stories*
Tanizaki, *The Key*
Teveth, *The Burning Ground: A Biography of David Ben-Gurion*
Thapar, *A History of India*
Theroux, *The Great Railway Bazaar: By Train through Asia*
Tilak, *The Arctic Home in the Vedas*
Toer, *This Earth of Mankind*

Weizmann, *Trial and Error: The Autobiography of Chaim Weizmann*
White, *Voss*
Wittfogel, *Oriental Despotism*
Wright, *The Last Stand of Chinese Conservatism*
Wu, *Journey to the West*

Xenophon, *The Education of Cyrus*

Universal Topics

Adorno et al., *The Authoritarian Personality*
Alcoholics Anonymous
Anderson, *Imagined Communities*
Austin, *Philosophical Papers*
Ayer, *Language, Truth, and Logic*

Bentham and Mill, *Utilitarianism, and Other Essays*
Bible, King James Version and *New Oxford Annotated*
Bingham, *Rule of Law*
Blavatsky, *The Secret Doctrine*
Bloch, *The Historian's Craft*
Boas, *Anthropology and Modern Life*
Bodin, *On Sovereignty*
Bonhoeffer, *Letters and Papers from Prison*
Bronowski, *The Ascent of Man*
Brown, *The Myth of the Strong Leader: Political Leadership in the Modern Age*

Buber, *I and Thou*
Buddhist Scriptures
Bull, *The Anarchical Society*

Calvin, *Institutes of the Christian Religion*
Carr, *The Twenty Years' Crisis, 1919–1939*
Cassirer, *An Essay on Man*
Collingwood, *The Idea of History*
Comte, *Auguste Comte and Positivism: The Essential Writings*
Copland, *What to Listen for in Music*
Culler, *Ferdinand de Saussure*

Darwin, *On the Origin of Species*
Dawkins, *The Selfish Gene*
Dewey, *Experience and Education*
Durkheim, *On Suicide*

Einstein, *Relativity*
Empson, *Seven Types of Ambiguity*
Evola, *Revolt against the Modern World*

Firth, *Elements of Social Organization*
Fisher, *How to Cook a Wolf*
Frazer, *The Golden Bough*
Friedman, *Capitalism and Freedom*
Fromm, *Escape from Freedom*
Fukuyama, *The End of History and the Last Man*

Galileo, *Dialogue Concerning the Two Chief World Systems*
Gardner, *The Night Is Large: Collected Essays*
Gauchet, *Disenchantment of the World: A Political History of Religion*
Gellner, *Nations and Nationalism*
George, *Progress and Poverty*
Gould, *Wonderful Life: The Burgess Shale and the Nature of History*
Greenfeld, *Nationalism: Five Roads to Modernity*
Guénon, *The Crisis of the Modern World*

Haldane, *On Being the Right Size, and Other Essays*
Halévy, *The Era of Tyrannies: Essays on Socialism and War*
Hart, *The Concept of Law*
Hayek, *The Road to Serfdom*
Hoffer, *The True Believer*
Hofstadter, *Gödel, Escher, Bach: An Eternal Golden Braid*
Humboldt, *Cosmos: A Sketch of the Physical Description of the Universe*
Huntington, *The Clash of Civilizations and the Remaking of World Order*

Ignatius of Loyola, *Personal Writings*

John of the Cross, *Dark Night of the Soul*

Kirk, *The Conservative Mind*
Kuhn, *The Structure of Scientific Revolutions*
Küng, *On Being a Christian*

Laozi, *Daodejing*
Le Corbusier, *Towards a New Architecture*
Lorenz, *On Aggression*
Lucretius, *De Rerum Natura*

Malthus, *An Essay on the Principle of Population*
Manent, *The City of Man*
Mao, *Quotations from Chairman Mao Tse-tung*
Mather, *On Witchcraft*
Mayr, *The Growth of Biological Thought*
Montesquieu, *The Spirit of the Laws*
Montessori, *The Discovery of the Child*
Moore, G. E., *Principia Ethica*
Moore, B., *Social Origins of Dictatorship and Democracy*
Müller, *Introduction to the Science of Religion*

Nasr, H., *Science and Civilization in Islam*
Nasr, V., *The Shia Revival*
Newton, *Opticks*

Oakeshott, *What Is History? and Other Essays*

Pankhurst, S., *The Suffragette Movement*
Parkinson, *Parkinson's Law*
Parsons, *The Structure of Social Action*
Piketty, *The Economics of Inequality*
Polanyi, *Personal Knowledge*
Porter, *The Greatest Benefit to Mankind: A Medical History of Humanity*

Qur'an

Rahe, *Republics Ancient and Modern*
Rawls, *A Theory of Justice*
Ricardo, *Principles of Political Economy and Taxation*
Ruskin, *Modern Painters*
Ryle, *The Concept of Mind*

Santayana, *The Life of Reason*
Schopenhauer, *The Essential Schopenhauer*
Schumacher, *Small Is Beautiful*
Schumpeter, *Capitalism, Socialism, and Democracy*
Sen, *Poverty and Famines*
Shattuck, *Forbidden Knowledge: From Prometheus to Pornography*
Skinner, *The Foundations of Modern Political Thought*
Spengler, *The Decline of the West*
Steiner, *The Death of Tragedy*
Strunk and White, *The Elements of Style*

Talmon, *The Origins of Totalitarian Democracy*
Tawney, *Religion and the Rise of Capitalism*
Teresa of Avila, *The Life of Saint Teresa of Avila*
Thomas à Kempis, *The Imitation of Christ*
Thomas Aquinas, *Selected Writings*
Tillich, *The Courage to Be*
Toklas, *The Alice B. Toklas Cook Book*
Toynbee, *A Study of History*

Vico, *New Science*

Wallerstein, *The Uncertainties of Knowledge*
Walzer, *Just and Unjust Wars*
Watson, *The Double Helix*
Weil, *The Need for Roots*
Weinberg, *To Explain the World*
Whitehead, *Science and the Modern World*
Wight, *International Theory*
Williams, *Keywords: A Vocabulary of Culture and Society*
Wittgenstein, *Philosophical Investigations*

Yergin, *The Prize*

Author Illustrations

Index of Authors

Authors and titles of 150 highly recommended books are in boldface.

Index of Titles
Titles and authors of 150 highly recommended books are in boldface.